Sympathy for the Cyberbully

COMMUNICATION LAW

Susan J. Drucker
General Editor

Vol. 6

The Communication Law series is part of the Peter Lang Media and Communication list.
Every volume is peer reviewed and meets
the highest quality standards for content and production.

PETER LANG
New York • Bern • Frankfurt • Berlin
Brussels • Vienna • Oxford • Warsaw

Arthur S. Hayes

Sympathy for the Cyberbully

How the Crusade to Censor Hostile and Offensive Online Speech Abuses Freedom of Expression

PETER LANG
New York • Bern • Frankfurt • Berlin
Brussels • Vienna • Oxford • Warsaw

Library of Congress Cataloging-in-Publication Data

Names: Hayes, Arthur S., author.
Title: Sympathy for the cyberbully: how the crusade to censor hostile and offensive online speech abuses freedom of expression / Arthur S. Hayes.
Description: New York: Peter Lang Publishing, 2017.
Communication law; vol. 6 | ISSN 2153-1390
Includes bibliographical references and index.
Identifiers: LCCN 2016059650 (print) | LCCN 2017004328 (ebook)
ISBN 978-1-4331-3212-4 (hardcover: alk. paper)
ISBN 978-1-4331-3211-7 (paperback: alk. paper) | ISBN 978-1-4539-1725-1 (ebook pdf)
ISBN 978-1-4331-4152-2 (epub) | ISBN 978-1-4331-4153-9 (mobi)
Subjects: LCSH: Bullying—United States. | Bullying—Canada.
Cyberbullying—United States. | Cyberbullying—Canada. | Civil rights—United States.
Civil rights—Canada. | Freedom of speech—United States.
Freedom of speech—Canada. | United States. Constitution. 1st Amendment.
Classification: LCC BF637.B85 H357 2017 (print) | LCC BF637.B85 (ebook)
DDC 302.34/30973—dc23
LC record available at https://lccn.loc.gov/2016059650
DOI 10.3726/978-1-4539-1725-1

Bibliographic information published by **Die Deutsche Nationalbibliothek**.
Die Deutsche Nationalbibliothek lists this publication in the "Deutsche Nationalbibliografie"; detailed bibliographic data are available on the Internet at http://dnb.d-nb.de/.

29 Broadway, 18th floor, New York, NY 10006
www.peterlang.com

CONTENTS

PREFACE

Sympathy for the Cyberbully: How the Crusade to Censor Hostile and Offensive Online Speech Abuses Freedom of Expression offers a defense for online acid-tongued disparagers and youthful and adult sexters who have been victims of cyberbullying laws. Not all anti-cyberbullying laws. Just the ones that do not conform to well-settled free speech and due process principles, which is to say the vast majority of such statutes, as well the attempts by public school administrators to rein in off-campus student cyberspace speech.

In the first decade of the 21st century, sincere concerns about the harmful effects of cyberbullying degenerated into moral panic, as this text documents. The most troubling aspect of the panic has been an ensuing spate of censorship—the creation of laws authorizing police to arrest, judges to issue restraining orders to censor online speech and juries to convict teens and adults for engaging in online expression that would have been constitutionally protected had it been communicated offline. Even among legislators, as the accounts provided here show, clarity, nuance and reflection mattered little when the panic set in.

Apologists argue that legislators had the best intentions when they enacted laws criminalizing disparaging and abusive cyberspeech. They wanted only to protect individuals from embarrassment, emotional distress and exploitation by criminalizing cyberharassment, online impersonation, cyberstalking, youthful sexting and non-consensual sharing of sexually explicit photos, commonly called revenge porn.

A skeptic, however, would be remiss if he failed to note that many law makers were motivated by expediency and ignorance, if not timidity, when confronted with the hot-button issue of cyberbullying. Few elected officials wished to be seen as insensitive to the demands of outraged parents, mortified divorcees and ex-girl friends and their fellow anti-cyberbullying crusaders. In contrast, it's quite easy to ignore the rights of a foul-mouthed teen, a mischievous lawyer pulling a prank on a politician with an online impersonation or a jilted lover posting nude photographs of a former intimate partner, all widely perceived as egregious violations of social norms.

Meanwhile, the U.S. Supreme Court has offered no comprehensive approach to determining the limits imposed on public schools to regulate off-campus cyberspeech. In its absence, school administrators, often aided by recently enacted laws, have expanded their censuring authority at the expense of student free speech rights.

Much of the impetus for the scramble in recent years to censor cyberbullying stems from the spate of youthful suicide-related cyberbullying incidents that drew worldwide media coverage. Though the 13-year-old Megan Meier's suicide in October 2006 was not the first reported incident of suicide attributed to online harassment, it quickly became the most inflammatory case of online bullying. Meier, of Dardenne Prairie, Missouri, hanged herself. Her suicide was attributed to a cruel hoax that a mother of a friend of hers, Lori Drew, had perpetrated via the social networking site, MySpace. Drew soon became, as one Australian newspaper put it, "America's most reviled mother."[1]

The shock and outrage felt by many about Drew's behavior was compounded by a sense of powerlessness—prosecutors could not turn to a statute that specifically banned Drew's expressive conduct because no such laws existed. In response, Missouri enacted the Megan Meier Law in 2008, though a proposed federal version, the Megan Meier Cyberbullying Prevention Act, failed.

Soon after, other state lawmakers enlisted in the crusade to wipeout what many saw as an epidemic of unacceptable online speech that caused emotional and psychological problems such as anxiety, depression, annoyance, anger, embarrassment, low self-esteem and suicidal ideation; in short, online speech that offended, criticized others, or made them feel bad about themselves. In Canada, similar youthful suicides involving Amanda Todd and Rehtaeh Parsons, spurred the passage of the Nova Scotia's Cyber-safety Act and C-13, the Protecting Canadians from Online Crime Act). Such legislators, however, conveniently ignored the undisputed fact that the alleged causal link between cyberbullying and suicide has no scientific support and that cyberbullying-linked suicides are multi-causal. In the incidents involving Todd and Parsons, for example, offline bullying played as prominent a role as online bullying.

The legislators, here and in Canada, which has similar constitutional protections for free speech, also ignored the wise counsel of civil libertarian lawyers. In the U.S., just about every time lawmakers proposed cyberbullying legislation, civil libertarians—the ACLU and the Electronic Frontier Foundation (EFF), for the most part—reminded them about the gravity of more than 50 years of First Amendment precedents protecting harsh and offensive expression.

Be careful how you draft these laws, they advised lawmakers. You must define cyberbullying—an extremely elastic concept as used by sociologists, psychologists and lay people—narrowly. Otherwise, they warned, the statutes will be highly vulnerable to constitutional challenges of overbreadth and vagueness. A statute is unconstitutional overbroad when it deters individuals from exercising their legitimate rights. A statute is unconstitutionally vague when a person of ordinary intelligence cannot determine the kind of conduct the law forbids. (Cyberbullying harassment statutes are also subject to strict scrutiny analysis.)

They also reminded legislators that the U.S. Constitution imposes strict limits on legislative authority to devise new types of constitutionally unprotected speech. Anti-cyberbullying laws, which are content-based restrictions on expression, can only criminalize speech that falls within the established proscribed categories—true threats, fighting words, incitement, speech integral to criminal conduct, intentional infliction of emotional distress, obscenity and fraud—unless there is a long tradition of regulating the speech. At the risk of stating the obvious, there is no long tradition of regulating hostile, offensive or abusive cyberspeech.

Public school students have free speech rights, too, First Amendment lawyers reminded school administrators and legislators. Generally, schools can only sanction students for lewd or obscene content and speech advocating illegal drug use, and speech that causes or threatens to cause substantial disruption to the school environment, or infringes on the rights of others.

Free-speech advocates, however, were widely ignored. Generally, lawmakers defended their actions arguing that the cost to society's well being was too great to conform to free speech precedents, that the effects of cyberspeech were more pernicious than offline speech, or that the new cyberbullying statutes were constitutionally sound despite their obvious flaws, well obvious at least to a free-speech advocate.

By early 2014, almost every state had enacted laws criminalizing online hostile expression. Some states amended their offline criminal harassment and stalking laws to cover online speech. Others crafted new laws aimed solely at online speech. States also passed laws and imposed policies authorizing public schools to discipline cyberbullies.

By 2011, however, a countertrend emerged. Accused and convicted cyberbullies fought back. And by 2016, several convicted cyberbullies prevailed on appeal as judges struck down cyberbullying state statutes for the very reasons civil libertarians had cited early on—the statutes were unconstitutional vague or overbroad, or both. During those five years, courts here and in Canada, struck down 15 cyberbullying statutes.

Grounded in moral panic, framing, First Amendment free speech and criminal law analysis, *Sympathy for the Cyberbully* tells the stories of the accused and convicted cyberbullies who successfully challenged the constitutionality of the new breed of censorship.

Chapter 1, "Anti-Cyberbullying Laws: A Sober Analysis through the Moral Panic Theory Lens," reviews framing studies of news coverage of cyberbullying incidents and applies moral panic theory analysis to media coverage of cyberbullying, with an emphasis on the plight of middle-school students Katelyn Roman and Guadalupe Shaw, of Polk County, Florida.

In Fall 2013, Roman and Shaw were the victims of an overzealous and moralizing sheriff who arrested them on stalking charges with the implication that their online taunts drove another girl to commit suicide. The news media mostly aided and abetted the sheriff's crusade to brand the girls as remorseless cyberbullies. It turned out, however, the sheriff's arrests fell apart once the local prosecutor examined the case.

Communication studies framing analysis identifies how the media structure meaning by their editorial choices—how they characterize political, economic and social controversies and their actors, and which assertions they accept uncritically, such as the myth that a causal connection exists between cyberbullying and suicide. Moral panic theorists argue that periodically society—aided by media coverage and moral crusaders—overreacts to cultural or technological change by branding groups, individuals and cultural trends as existential threats to social stability. Over the years, these social deviants have included witches, horror comic books, rock and roll music, urban youth of color and the widespread belief in the 1990s that pedophiles lurked everywhere.

In such an environment of fear, moral crusaders and lawmakers typically turn to tough criminal punishment as the only solution to combat an imagined or exaggerated threat when civil sanctions, further discussion, investigation, education or no collective public response at all would suffice. This first systematic moral panic analysis of the cyberbullying phenomenon helps to explain the public's misconceptions about the constitutional validity of censoring cyberbullying and why so many lawmakers have endorsed poorly written and constitutionally flawed statutes to combat the supposed menace.

To provide readers with a basic understanding of the constitutional foibles of censuring cyberbullying, Chapter 2, "Cyberbullying and Free Speech," identifies the current state of First Amendment free speech doctrines and criminal due process principles that limit government authority to censure or regulate abusive, offensive and dangerous speech, the categories of state cyberbullying statutes and tracks recent rulings in which courts have struck down cyberbullying laws or stayed the hands of disapproving school administrators.

Chief among the outlawed forms of abusive cyberspeech is cyberharassment and the related cyberstalking. Almost every state has chosen to codify cyberbullying as illegal electronic harassment, for example. Yet, cyberharassment statutes have been the first to fall because of their unclear or misapplied criminal intent requirements, the failure by legislators to limit the statutes' scope to traditional categories of constitutionally unprotected speech, such as true threats, and their misapplication to speech posted for the world to see but never sent to the target's email, social media page, twitter account or smartphone by the alleged cyberbully. UCLA law professor and blogger Eugene Volokh has characterized this distinction as "one-to-one speech vs. one-to-many speech."[2] Volokh argues that traditionally "one-to-one" speech—offline unwanted communications sent to a specific individual—has not been protected under the First Amendment. In contrast, unwanted speech about a person sent to willing listeners has traditionally been protected. Yet, many recently enacted cyberharassment statutes target online one-to-many speech, which he argues is unconstitutional except for when speech falls within the traditional categories of unprotected speech.

As Chapter 3, "The Unnecessary and Unjust Creation of Virtual Juvenile Delinquents," documents, teens living in North Carolina and a New York county who engaged in merely talking smack, thrash, harshly teasing others or spreading rumors online risked criminal prosecution under cyberbullying laws adopted in 2009 and 2010, respectively.

At first, several accused high school students in both states capitulated and plea-bargained. Because they risked being branded a criminal, a mark that might haunt them in their efforts to attend college or find jobs, avoiding trial was a safe and reasonable tactic.

Richard Bishop, of North Carolina, and Marquan Mackey-Meggs of New York, however did not play it safe, and the First Amendment free speech protections have been bolstered as a result.

The Albany County of New York statute predicated criminal culpability on intent to harass, annoy, threaten, abuse, taunt, intimidate, torment, humiliate, or otherwise inflict significant emotional harm on another person. The North Carolina statute required a finding of intent to intimidate or torment a minor. The highest courts in each state, however, found the statutes unconstitutional mostly because the intent standards were poorly defined and allowed prosecutors to target constitutionally protected speech. One lesson to be drawn from the two rulings is that a cyberharassment statute banning speech that merely annoys, pesters, intimidates, torments or alarms is unlikely to survive constitutional scrutiny.

Chapter 4, "Enclaves of Totalitarianism," explores the legality of state anti-bullying school statutes that implicate cyberspeech by examining New Jersey's Anti-Bullying Bill of Rights Act. The New Jersey law is widely considered the toughest and most comprehensive anti-bullying statute directed at schools in the nation. But prolific tweeter and high school student Bethany Koval's successful online protest against attempts by school administrators to punish her exposed the flaws in the language and enforcement of the statute.

Like many states, the New Jersey law muddies the distinctions between terms such as bullying, harassment and intimidation, allowing schools to sanction students for online speech that includes constitutionally protected unintended verbal slights and emotionally charged political statements. The statute, however, has survived challenges at the state administrative law level. The only challenged raising federal constitutional due process concerns was settled out of court. This chapter, focusing on Koval's out-of-court triumph, argues that the New Jersey statute and similar state laws are highly unlikely to survive First Amendment overbreadth and vagueness challenges.

Chapter 5, "Censorship Redux: The 21st Century Attack on the First Amendment Right of Public Criticism by the Use of Cyberharassment,

Cyberstalking and Online Impersonation Laws," addresses what is perhaps the most disturbing aspect of the anti-cyberbullying crusade—the abuse of cyber-harassment, cyberstalking and criminal impersonation laws to make criminals out of adults who mock, parody, scorn and vilify private and public figures engaged in matters of public concern. A citizen's right to disparage individuals involved in public controversy lies at the heart of First Amendment free speech protections. The U.S. Supreme Court affirmed that principle in its landmark ruling, *New York Times v. Sullivan* (1964), when it noted that the U.S. has "a profound national commitment to the principle that debate on public issues should be uninhibited, robust, and wide-open, and that it may well include vehement, caustic, and sometimes unpleasantly sharp attacks on government and public officials."[3] Yet, between 2011 and 2016, eight accused or convicted adult cyberbullies had to seek reaffirmation from judges that the profound national commitment to protect the right to criticize extended to cyber space. Chapter 5 tells their stories.

Chapter 6, "Image Control: Who Loses When Teen Sexting and Revenge Porn Are Criminalized?" delves into the use of the Internet to exchange or distribute private sexually explicit photographs. Teens who engage in the consensual sharing of sexually explicit photos of themselves online are probably the most sympathetic type of cyberbully. Conversely, adults who post sexually explicit photos of other adults without consent are widely considered reprehensible. Nevertheless, the censoring of both types of sexting is likely to continue to inflict injustices.

The cases of high school students Cormega Copening and Brianna Denson, both of Fayetteville, N.C., are offered in this chapter as an example of one type of injustice created by the criminalizing of consensual teen sexting. Under North Carolina law, Copening, 17, and Denson, 16, had the right to engage in sexual relations in the real world—the age of consent is sixteen in North Carolina—but not in the virtual version. Thus, when their private sexting photos wound up in the hands of law enforcement, they were charged with sexual exploitation of a minor under a state law targeting individuals who sexually exploit and abuse children and with creating child pornography. The indictment was recognized as a travesty of justice worldwide, but the local prosecutors did not back down. Instead, the teens reached a plea bargain for misdemeanor charges.

The problem with banning nonconsensual adult sexting, or revenge porn, is mostly in the wording of the statutes, Chapter 6 argues. One faction promoting the adoption of such laws argues that statutes must require prosecutors to prove that a defendant intended to cause harm, including emotional and reputational harm or financial loss, by knowing disclosure. A statute that fails to require intent to harm is unlikely to meet constitutional due process standards, argues a minority of feminist lawyers promoting revenge porn laws.

In contrast, the most ardent and influential promoters of such bans, led by law professor Mary Anne Franks and the Cyber Civil Rights Initiative (CCRI), insist that statutes require only that the accused knew that publication required consent, or acted recklessly or negligently in publishing the photos without consent. An intent to harm requirement, Franks contends, is little more than a loophole that would allow defendants motivated by desires to entertain, make money, or achieve notoriety slip through. But the CCRI's preferred statute puts unwitting third parties at risk, who, for example, may see a nude photo online and share it with others without knowledge of its origins.

By late 2016, the revenge porn law advocates had suffered judicial setbacks in Arizona and Vermont and a veto of a bill by Rhode Island Governor Gina Raimondo. Accordingly, this book argues that a constitutionally sound revenge porn statute must include an intent to cause serious emotional distress or harm requirement, link disclosure to a breach of reasonable expectation of privacy, provide a public interest and newsworthiness exemption, explicitly shield third parties like websites from culpability unless they extort victims for financial gain and ban only images that would be considered obscene under the three-prong *Miller v. California* obscenity test.[4]

Nevertheless, as this book went to press, none of the 34 state revenge porn statutes or the proposed Federal Intimate Privacy Protection Act conformed to this standard.

Lastly, Chapter 7, "The Short Life and Quick Death of the First Cyberbullying Law in Canada (August 6, 2013–December 10, 2015)," profiles the Nova Scotia's Cyber-safety Act, the first cyberbullying statute in Canada. Cyberbullying, and efforts to ban it, is a near global phenomenon. U.S. and Canadian free speech law, however, are related and outliers even among Western democracies.

U.S. and Canada share a free expression tradition dating back to the mid-1600s, have single document written constitutions, share similar free speech and due process doctrines and Canadian courts are not averse to citing U.S. precedents. Thus, the demise of the Cyber-safety Act—the Supreme of Court of the Nova Scotia province struck it down in December 2015 as irrational, arbitrary, vague, overbroad and an infringement on fundamental rights under the Canadian Charter—underscores the threat that cyberbullying legislation, passed in the frenzy of a moral panic, poses to the liberal free speech tradition.

Based on the analysis presented in *Sympathy for the Cyberbully*, this author offers the following suppositions:

- Legislators who have passed poorly drafted cyberharassment or cyberstalking statutes have engaged in headstrong acts of reckless disregard or inexcusable ignorance of firmly established free speech precedents and constitutional principles. Thus, this first generation of cyberbullying defendants has been victimized.
- Cyberharassment and cyberstalking statutes have been misused to censor political and social commentary as this book documents. Thus, they strike at the core of our free speech protections because they authorize government to ban speech that makes government officials and other individuals merely uncomfortable.
- It is impossible to draft a constitutionally valid cyberharassment or cyber-stalking statute by criminalizing the types of expression that most lawmakers and anti-cyberbullying advocates classify as cyberbullying, which is to say lewd, derogatory, alarming or annoying comments.
- Public schools should have no authority to punish students for their off-campus, cyberspeech regardless of whether the expression leads to substantial disruption in schools or interferes with the rights of other students.
- It is unjust to prosecute teens for engaging in the consensual sharing of self-produced sexually provocative or explicit images, most commonly known as sexting, because such minors lack the intent to cause harm to themselves or others.
- So-called revenge porn laws are unconstitutional because they ban the distribution of indecent or sexually explicit content by adults, expressive activity that is constitutionally protected until it has been adjudged obscene.

I harbor no illusions about the appeal of my arguments. I have taken on a tough sell. Some are plainly unreceptive to the notion that a cyberbully might be a victim. As one anonymous scholarly reviewer said when he or she rejected my book proposal, “I can’t work up much sympathy for anyone abusing another one for whatever reason.”

Yet, under our death penalty laws, for example, convicted murderers are allowed to present a case before a jury or file a clemency petition arguing that they are not death-worthy because they were victimized during their youth. If jurors or clemency boards can muster sympathy for a convicted murder, is it too much to ask for sympathy for a cyberbully?

To those whose knowledge of cyberbullying is drawn from tabloid news headlines, daytime infotainment television reports and chatter, socially conscious melodramatic made-for-teen movies, anti-cyberbullying web sites or word-of-mouth, at first blush my argument might seem farfetched. I submit, however, that you have been misinformed about online free speech rights and the dangers of cyberbullying. Thus, this book's arguments and supporting evidence should prove revelatory.

If you are a cyberbullying victim or know someone who has been one, you are probably inclined to reject this book outright. But I ask for your indulgence. My argument against imposing criminal penalties and school sanctions on those who use the Internet to abuse, offend and annoy is not intended to discount your distress. Instead, I ask you to weigh the possibility that counseling, education and civil penalties might be alternatives preferable to the current course of action that infringes on the constitutional rights of online speakers.

Finally, I hope that the message of *Sympathy for the Cyberbully* reaches local, state and federal lawmakers confronted with the decision to approve a cyberbullying ordinance or statute. I like to think that the book provides a sober retort to the emotionally charged pleas to devise a feel-good, quick criminal law fix to a complex social phenomenon.

Notes

1. "How Lori Drew Became America's Most Reviled Mother," *The Age.com*, December 1, 2007, http://www.theage.com.au/news/web/americas-most-reviled-mother/2007/11/30/1196394672124.html (accessed December 30, 2016).
2. Eugene Volokh, "One-to-One Speech vs. One-to-Many Speech, Criminal Harassment Laws, and 'Cyberstalking,' " *Northwestern University Law Review* 107 (2013): 731, 767–68, http://scholarlycommons.law.northwestern.edu/nulr/vol107/iss2/9 (accessed December 30, 2016).
3. New York Times v. Sullivan, 376 U.S. 254, 271 (1964).
4. Miller v. California, 413 U.S. 15 (1973).

ACKNOWLEDGMENT

It is likely that this text would have never seen the light of day or have been published at a much later date but for the foresight of Mary Savigar, my former editor who has since left Peter Lang. I am also grateful to Martin B. Marqulies, Professor Emeritus of Law, Quinnipiac University School of Law, for his help in preparing this text. Margulies, who taught me criminal law, defended two accused Connecticut cyberbullies in *Doninger v. Niehoff* and *State v. Michael Adams*, discussed in this book.

· 1 ·

ANTI-CYBERBULLYING LAWS

A Sober Analysis through the Moral Panic Theory Lens

> Societies appear to be subject, every now and then, to periods of moral panic. A condition, episode, person or group of persons emerges to become defined as a threat to societal values and interests; its nature is presented in a stylized and stereotypical fashion by the mass media; the moral barricades are manned by editors, bishops, politicians and other right-thinking people; socially accredited experts pronounce their diagnoses and solutions; ways of coping are evolved or (more often) resorted to; the condition then disappears, submerges or deteriorates and becomes more visible. Sometimes the object of the panic is quite novel and at other times it is something which has been in existence long enough, but suddenly appears in the limelight. Sometimes the panic passes over and is forgotten, except in folklore and collective memory; at other times it has more serious and long-lasting repercussions and might produce such changes … in legal and social policy or even in the way the society conceives itself.[1]

Polk County sits in the middle of Florida, east of Tampa, southwest of Orlando. It's probably best known for its theme parks, Cypress Gardens, which closed in 2009, and Legoland, built on the same spot. In mid-October 2013, however, the county became big news. That's when local and national television journalists turned their attention to Polk County Sheriff Grady Judd, giving him the kind of coverage No. 1 G-Man and publicity hound J. Edgar Hoover would have envied, and the story went viral, too.[2] For about six weeks, Polk County was the epicenter of a moral panic outbreak over cyberbullying.

First, on Tuesday, October 15, Judd, dressed in military green and gold, and flanked by flags, held a press conference carried by local and national media.[3] The following day, NBC's Today Show host Matt Lauer interviewed him.[4] Judd was talking about cyberbullying and cyberbullicide, or suicide attributable to bullying. He spoke with the righteous indignation and bulldog-like steeliness of the original G-Man crowing over an arrest of a Public Enemy One. But in these times, news media become spellbound when a minor-league sheriff claims to have snared two remorseless criminals whose online words supposedly helped to push a teenage girl to jump to her death. It didn't seem to matter that the alleged criminals were middle-school students. Or, perhaps, their youth made all the difference to the media; made the story a titillating cautionary narrative about the evils of soulless children driven astray by social media?

At the press conference, Judd announced that he was charging Katelyn Roman, 12, and Guadalupe Shaw, 14, with third-degree felony aggravated stalking in connection with the death of Rebecca Sedwick, 12, of Lakeland, Fla. The previous month, Sedwick committed suicide by jumping from a cement factory tower.[5] Judd, who "has long approached crime fighting as a moral quest, a clear-cut fight between good and evil, with no-nonsense punishments for offenders,"[6] expressed no qualms about revealing the juveniles' names and showing their mug shots. "We have these wonderful photographs of our two new felons," Judd said."[7] The girls faced the possibility of five-year prison sentences under the state's anti-cyberbullying law.[8]

The Florida sheriff said his office arrested the girls earlier than it had initially planned after Shaw, said, "Yes ik [I know] I bullied Rebecca nd she killed her self but IDGAF [I don't give a (expletive)]," on her Facebook, a post that ended with a heart symbol.[9] The girls were "remorseless and 'cold,'" Judd said.[10] "We were going to arrest them anyway, but we were trying to put the entire case together, and as you know, we're having trouble getting information from (social media site) Ask.fm because they're offshore, so it was taking some time," Judd said. "But when we saw that cavalier attitude, when we saw that despite Rebecca dying, jumping to her death, being bullied by this girl and another girl, and she's back on Facebook, she can be taunting or bullying another child. We're not going to accept that."[11]

This is the era of the cyberbullicide scourge; a time when many believe words kill and the weapons are digital. "Sedwick's suicide is another somber reminder of the dangers of cyberbullying by peers who may be technologically literate but oblivious to the consequences of using *a keyboard as a weapon*," [italics added] opined the *Tampa Bay Times* editorial board.[12]

A small minority of observers, however, counseled caution. Tampa defense attorney Jeff Brown accused Judd of grandstanding, being too quick to charge the girls and indiscreet for publicly identifying the minors.

"Let's let the system play out," Brown said on the day of the press conference. "There may be an appropriate time to make them the example of what went on. But now is not the time. Now is the time to find out what went on, and let the professionals, not Sheriff Judd, look into this."[13]

Thirty-five days later, after the "professionals," the Polk County prosecutors, analyzed thousands of Facebook messages, no case was brought against the two girls.[14] Yet, the bulk of the news coverage that followed barely reflected exoneration. For instance, there was little reflection about the sheriff's rush to judgment and grandstanding. There was little news coverage given to the voices calling for moderation.

And, typical of most coverage of bullying-related suicide cases, news media ignored or marginalized evidence of traditional bullying, while magnifying the impact of online speech.[15] (According to the 2012 study, "Cyberbullying and Suicide: A Retrospective Analysis of 41 Cases," "78 percent of adolescents who committed suicide were bullied both at school and online, while 17 percent were targeted online only.")[16]

Opinion writers continued the call for cyberbullying bans. News reports gave two days of coverage to Sedwick's mother, Tricia Norman. She said the dismissal signaled that bullying is acceptable, as she announced a crusade against cyberbullying flanked by her lawyers and former Florida Gov. Charlie Crist.[17] Her campaign includes a long-shot wrongful death action[18] against the girls and the passage of "Rebecca's Law," which would punish underage bullies with juvenile detention.[19]

Meanwhile, the girls became online targets of vitriol largely thanks to Sheriff Judd's moral crusade. "You guys are a disgrace in the human race," one commenter wrote on Katelyn Roman's Instagram page. "You guys deserve no happiness."[20]

Were they not cyberbullied, too? Judd made no condemnation of those individuals; he did not threaten them with cyberbullying charges.

About six months later, a police report revealed that Sedwick's suicide apparently was linked to offline-domestic turmoil and a breakup with an Internet boyfriend, among other traumas, that had little if anything to do with online harassment.[21] Yet, Roman and Shaw agreed to undergo counseling to get the charges dropped.[22] (In a similar widely covered alleged bullicide case in the United Kingdom, officials later reported that there was strong evidence that the alleged victim, Hannah Smith, 14, had posted the messages to herself.)[23]

So, Katelyn Roman and Guadalupe Shaw were victims of an overzealous and moralizing police officer. Add their parents to the list of victims, because Judd announced that he was considering charging them with contributing to the delinquency of minors on ABC-TV's "Good Morning America," though it never came to fruition.[24] But more to the point, Roman, Shaw and their parents were victims of an outbreak of moral panic.

Moral Panic Theory

British sociologist and criminologist Stanley Cohen, whose opening paragraph to his groundbreaking study *Folk Devils and Moral Panics* leads this chapter, coined the term "moral panic," now a well-established social deviance theory. Cohen argued that moral panics are characterized by "drama, emergency and crisis; exaggeration; cherished values threatened; an object of concern, anxiety and hostility; evil forces or people to be identified and stopped; the eventual sense of the episodic and transitory …"[25]

Moral panic characterizes the overreaction by news media, opinion makers and advocates to abrupt changes in the status quo. As sociologists Richard C. Fuller and Richard R. Myers argued more than 70 years ago, sometimes societies decide that social problems require only private solutions, while other times, such as when moral panic erupts, segments of society seek government-imposed remedies for new and unsettling social disruptions. "*Social problems are what people think they are* [emphasis added] and if conditions are not defined as social problems by the people involved in them, they are not problems to those people, although they may be problems to outsiders or to scientists, e.g., the condition of poor southern sharecroppers is a social problem to the braintrusters of the New Deal but not to many southern landowners."[26] Thus, moral panics are socially constructed problems that call for public solutions.

As the title of Cohen's work implies, moral panics require "folk devils,"—the demonized deviants, the "visible reminders of what we should not be,"[27] or, as sociologists Eric Goode and Nachman Ben-Yehuda later described them, "the agents responsible for the threat … stereotyped and classified as deviants."[28] "Moral panics then," sociologist Chas Critcher says, "are a reaction to changes: bad things are happening which didn't use to."[29]

In his seminal work, Cohen analyzed how the British press covered brawls between the Mods and Rockers youth subcultures that took place in British seaside resort towns in 1964. Mods and Rockers were young adults who took on different styles of dress, attitudes and vehicles, signifying their class differences in a very class-conscious Britain. Mods tended to be middle-class, and "adopted what was briefly called the 'Italianate' style of dressing, drifted into the world of Expresso bars and were drawn musically to rhythm and blues."[30] They drove scooters. The Beatles and Rolling Stones of the 1960s British Invasion adopted many of the Mods clothing fashions. In contrast, Rockers drove motorcycles and wore leather jackets. They had the "rebel without a cause" juvenile delinquent look of the 1950s and a reputation of being loutish and scruffy.[31]

The news media painted the clashes between the two youth groups as gang fights. The Mods and Rockers, however, were not criminal gangs, but youth sub-culture groups. But as Cohen noted by conducting a qualitative content analysis of news reports, editorials and community leaders quotes, Mods and Rockers were labeled hooligans, thugs, wild ones, human wolves, misfits and morons.[32] The groups were a threat to "'all the conventions and values of life.' As the *Birmingham Post* (19 May 1964) put it, drawing on [Winston] Churchill's 'we will fight them [Nazi Germany] on the beaches' speech: the external enemies of 1940 had been replaced on our shores in 1964 by internal enemies who 'bring about disintegration of a nation's character.'"[33]

Such rhetoric was hyperbolic and absurd, but it reflected mainstream British society's failure to understand the youth movement phenomenon beyond its limited, reflexive and highly judgmental moral filter. In reality, they were never the deviants and threats the press made them out to be. As Cohen observed, by 1972 "these groups have all but disappeared from the public consciousness, remaining only in the collective memory of as folk devils of the past."[34] In a 2014 retrospective, the British Broadcasting Corporation (BBC) noted:

> Fifty years ago this month, on the Whitsun weekend of the 16–18 May 1964, the youth of Britain went mad. If you believed the newspapers, that is, who went with screaming headlines like "Battle of Brighton", and "Wild Ones 'Beat Up' Margate." Editorials fulminated with predictions of national collapse, referring to the youths as "those vermin" and "mutated locusts wreaking untold havoc on the land."[35]

In *Media and Crime*, British criminologist Yvonne Jewkes reexamined the moral panic concept 40 years after its introduction by Cohen.[36] Jewkes's revised moral panic thesis has five defining features, two of which are particularly relevant to understanding the roots of the illogical and exaggerated fear of cyberbullying: "… Moral panics occur during periods of rapid social change, and can be said to locate and crystallize social anxieties about risk. It is usually *young people who are targeted* [emphasis added], as they are a metaphor for the future and their behavior is regarded as a barometer with which to test the health or sickness of a society."[37]

Moral Panic in the Age of the Social Media

The period of rapid social change that spawned the cyberbullying moral panic is, of course, the second phase of the World Wide Web, or Web 2.0, that developed in the wake of the "bursting of the dot-com bubble in the autumn of 2001."[38] Web 2.0's development is characterized by increased user interactivity—one-to-one and one-to-many communication—facilitated by social media, video sharing sites and smart phones. Teens are near habitual users of smart phones and social media.[39] It is not surprising then that about an average of 25% of teenagers have reported being cyberbullied in reports covering 2004–2015.[40] Though the bulk of the panic over cyberbullying concerns teens, "13% of social media-using adults 18 and older reported that someone had been mean or cruel to them on a social network in the last 12 months" in 2011, for example.[41] Nevertheless, alarm over teenage cyberbullying is mostly what fuels the panic that drives parents, anti-cyberbullying advocacy groups, educators and legislators to call for cyberbullying bans.

The hallmarks of a moral panic—the expression of outrage at unacceptable behavior that supposedly threatens the public good, and the overreaction—the nationwide public pillorying and branding of young girls—barely teenagers—and adults as social deviants by the news media and others and charging them with crimes disproportionate to their alleged misconduct—crystallized in Sheriff Judd's failed campaign against Roman and Shaw and their parents. All the usual suspects appeared in the Polk County moral panic drama,

> the media, which publishes or broadcasts stories about a supposed threat; the public at large, the members of which feel, verbialize, or act upon their concern; representatives of the law, including politicians, lawmakers, and police, who propose, enact and enforce legislation; and social movement activists, who organize, recruit, proselytize, assemble, demonstrate, and lobby on behalf of their cause against the putative threat.[42]

This chapter argues that legitimate concerns about the harmful effects of cyberbullying degenerated into a moral panic late in the first decade of the 21st century soon after news and entertainment media, moral entrepreneurs[43] and claimsmakers[44] erroneously identified hostile online expression as a cause of teenage suicide and labeled cyberbullying teens as deviants and threats to the moral order. As sociologists Eric Goode and Nachman Ben-Yehuda observed, "The mass media are both an independent manifestation of moral panics as well as a causal agent in firing up the other manifestations of moral panics, specifically public concern, political and legislative activity, and social movement activism."[45]

Communication scholar and moral panic analyst Chas Critcher notes that the effects of moral panics "may involve minor adjustments of law enforcement, entirely new laws or new types of law which breach long-standing constitutional principles."[46] Accordingly, this chapter argues that the most troubling effect of the cyberbullying moral panic has been a spate of legislation enacted here and in Canada, which breach long-standing constitutional principles.

There is a legal maxim that says, "Hard cases, it has frequently been observed, are apt to introduce bad law."[47] Likewise, moral panics are apt to introduce bad law, and that is the argument made here. In the climate of a moral panic, claimsmakers, moral entrepreneurs and the media, acting on highly selective evidence, atypical, high profile incidents and moral indignation, respond with outrage to a new and complex social phenomenon, particularly, as Cohen and others have documented, when it concerns youth subcultures. In turn, opportunistic and well-intended politicians forgo reasoned assessments of threats, and, instead, hastily draft laws mirroring the skewed views and evidence presented by the press, claimsmakers and moral entrepreneurs.

Such a process has played out in many of the states here and nations abroad since mid-2008, producing the new breed of laws specifically targeting online embarrassing and hostile speech. To a large degree, the cyberbullying moral panic climate explains why many legislators have passed laws marred with glaring constitutional defects. Arguably, under calmer circumstances, reasonable legislators would have written cyberbullying laws to conform to longstanding constitutional protections or simply not have passed such laws. For example, federal legislators in the U.S. did not succumb to the irrationality of the cyberbullying moral panic. A proposed "Megan Meier Cyberbullying Prevention Act," a cyberharassment law, died in a House committee in 2009.[48]

Unfortunately, the demise of the federal proposal became the exception. Though cyberbullying laws did not exist in early 2008, by mid-2014, almost every state had enacted laws criminalizing online hostile expression whether it was labeled cyberstalking, cyberharassment, cyberbullying, sexting or revenge porn.[49] Some of the recently enact cyberharassment laws have been misused to stifle political commentary; they criminalize speech that has previously been protected under the First Amendment. Some sexting laws targeting minors and the application of child pornography laws to prosecute teenage sexters are excessive and counterproductive because they are unnecessarily brand minors as criminal deviants when education and counseling can prove more effective. Many of the so-called revenge porn criminal statutes are either unnecessary because current civil remedies are available, or excessive, because, among other defects, they criminalize pornography and other forms of speech that are protected from censorship under the First Amendment. In constitutional terms, many of these new laws are overbroad, they ban protected and unprotected speech, or they are unconstitutionally too vague for the average individual to understand which speech is protected and which is not.

Too often unheeded, civil libertarians have made such arguments to legislators in just about every state since 2008. By early 2016, civil libertarians gained some vindication as courts had struck down or blocked the enforcement of cyberbullying laws in Missouri, New York, Rhode Island, Arizona, Georgia and in the Canadian province of Nova Scotia. But there is little talk about the victims of those unconstitutional laws. Thus, a view through the lens of moral panic analysis illuminates why many branded as cyberbullies and subjected to criminal or civil sanctions warrant further consideration—if not sympathy—as underserving scapegoats of a moral panic.

Studies on Cyberbullying as a Moral Panic: A Literature Review

"[M]oral panic analysis has been designed to test whether an issue is being distorted and exaggerated, prompting massive overreaction"[50] and, typically, scholars employ qualitative or quantitative content analysis to determine the nature and extend of media's framing of coverage, or Eric Goode and Nachman Ben-Yehuda's five-component analytical framework, or both, to determine whether concern over a social controversy has been distorted. News outlets frame their coverage; they select "aspects of a perceived reality and make them more salient … in such a way as to promote a particular definition, causal interpretation, moral evaluation, and/or treatment."[51]

Building on Cohen's seminal study, Goode and Ben-Yehuda require a finding of five crucial elements to properly characterize the overreaction of the news media, claims makers, moral entrepreneurs and legislators as a moral panic: concern, hostility, consensus, disproportionality and volatility.[52] In this chapter, framing and moral panic analysis are applied to the Polk County, Fl., alleged cyberbullycide incident and cyberbullying news reports in the U.S. in general. Additionally, the findings of three studies are referenced to support the argument that the response to cyberbullying is a moral panic and a great deal of the legislative responses to criminalize it or expand public school authority to sanction are unreasonable or unnecessary. Those studies are: "Cyberbullying: The Social Construction of a Moral Panic";[53] "Framing 'Cyberbullying': Competing Frame Coverage of Rehtaeh Parsons' Death";[54] and "The Incessant Image: How Dominant News Coverage Shaped Canadian Cyberbullying Law."[55]

Political and social commentators, writing for the popular press and websites, have not been shy about labeling the campaign to punish cyberbullies a moral panic. In 2010, a writer/editor for @YouthRadio, noting how the media was framing the suicide of Massachusetts teenager Phoebe Prince, said,

> If you look at the moral panic that the mainstream media seems to be manufacturing about its number one competitor—social media—in the past few weeks, you'd think pulling the plug on the Internet is our only solution. The tragic suicide of Phoebe Prince is being used as an example of how social media services are a corrosive force in our society—even when the facts may not quite back that up.[56]

Techdirt blog editor Mike Masnick noted in 2010 that despite a decrease in actual rates of cyberbullying, legislators were passing more laws to criminalize hostile online speech:

> If you hadn't noticed, there's been a growing moral panic around the concept of 'cyberbullying,' with various states passing laws against it and Congress even considering it as well. And, of course, if you read stories in the news these days, you might think that cyberbullying is happening everywhere and that *It Must Be Stopped* at all costs *To Protect the Children.*[57]

Gavin Titley, a lecturer in media studies at the National University of Ireland, said Irish politicians were exploiting a moral panic concerning social media to distract attention from other issues.

> Recent reporting of suicides, a corrosive debate on abortion rights and transparent attempts to stifle political criticism have been fused into a full-throated moral panic over social media. Coming from a political class still convinced that LOL promises them lots of love, the wheels are likely to fall off this bandwagon long before it trundles from tawdry to totalitarian. But as deliberate exercises in displacement, moral panics illustrate something of the dominant political culture, and this opportunistic trolling is no exception.[58]

Journalism teachers, press critics, scholars and at least one prominent American journalist former New York Times executive editor Bill Keller have argued that news media have played a significant role in manufacturing the cyberbullying moral panic. In *Sexting and Cyberbullying*, McGill University leadership and policy expert Shaheen Shariff tied the Canadian news media's repeated airing of the suicide of Amanda Todd, 15, to a moral panic. "It increased the pressure on politicians to come down hard on cyberbullying no matter how young the perpetrators," Shariff said. "Despite the fact that Amanda's main perpetrator was a 35-year-old male pedophile, the primary dialogue around the case was about cyberbullying by her peers."[59]

In a March 11, 2013 panel discussion sponsored by South by Southwest, "Digital Drama: Growing Up in the Age of Facebook," Keller, Danah Boyd, a Principal Researcher at Microsoft Research, a Visiting Researcher at New York University, and a research affiliate at Harvard's Berkman Center for Internet and Society; and Emily Bazelon, the author of *Sticks and Stones*, a book about bullying, talked about the news media coverage of cyberbullying.[60]

Keller said the news media had painted the complex social and technological phenomenon in Manichean terms: "I should feel obliged to leap up to the defense of media, but actually I don't," Keller said. "The fundamental problems are not created by the digital age; they're inherent in what we do. There is a tendency in media to oversimplify. Stories require protagonists and antagonists, and victims and villains, and we sometimes strain to supply them."[61]

Writing soon after the arrest of Roman and Shaw, Kellie McBride, a media ethicist on the St. Petersburg, Fl., -based Poynter Institute faculty, debunked the link between bullying and suicide—"There is no scientific evidence that bullying causes suicide. None at all"—while noting that, "One reason these stories gain such traction is they are easy to sensationalize and they tap into a common narrative that children today are spinning out of control as a result of technology and popular culture."[62] McBride identified the following common mistakes journalists making reporting on suicides linked to cyberbullying:

> Perpetuating falsehoods through hyperbole or by confusing anecdotes with facts, such as stating that cyber-bullying is on the rise or is an epidemic. Implying that suicide is caused by a single factor, like a romantic breakup, a bad test score or being bullied. Suggesting, or allowing others to suggest, that bullying is criminal behavior. Allowing sources to reach beyond their anecdotal experience; parents, teachers and school administrators are rarely qualified to describe research or trends. Equating all teenage aggression as bullying, when in fact there is a specific definition that involves sustained behavior and a power imbalance. Describing an act of suicide in vivid detail

> so that it creates a contagion effect among vulnerable populations. Glorifying a suicide victim in saintly or heroic terms, which could also contribute to the spread of suicides. Forgetting to link to local and national resources about suicide and bullying, including warning signs and strategies for intervention.[63]

Information technology executive and researcher Jonathan Bishop argued that a moral panic has stigmatized internet trolling in his scholarly article, "Representations of 'Trolls' in Mass Media Communication: A Review of Media-Texts and Moral Panics Relating to 'Internet Trolling.'"[64] In a scholarly journal article discussing the lack of consensus among experts about the definition of online harassment, Criminologists Carla Cesaroni, Steven Downing and Shahid Avi suggest that "current concerns around cyberbullying might in fact amount to a moral panic. Certainly the way in which the interest around cyberbullying has manifested itself appears to fulfill some of the classic signs of a panic as described by Cohen, including the role of "experts" in solving what is perceived to be a new social problem."[65]

A handful of scholars have conducted framing analysis of media coverage of cyberbullying in attempt to determine the media's role in fueling the cyberbullying moral panic. A team of communication studies scholars and psychologists conducted a content analysis exploring how 43 newspapers in Australia, Belgium, Greece, Italy, Lithuania, Poland, Slovenia and the United Kingdom framed their coverage of cyberbullying in "a first large-scale content analysis designed to explore the amount and nature of the coverage on cyberbullying in 43 national, daily newspapers in eight countries (Austriala, Belgium, Greece, Italy, Lithuania, Poland, Slovenia and the United Kingdom)" published between January 2004 and December 2011.[66] The scholars found "only a few indications of moral panic framing ... related to the negativity aspect of reported cases in the articles where cyberbullying was the main topic, and where a less reassuring and neutral tone is used in the articles on cyberbullying in the popular press.[67] The study, however, did not apply Goode & Ben-Yehuda's moral panic analysis. Nevertheless, the scholars acknowledged that an

> increased attention and alarming tone [of the press coverage] may lead to a moral panic. This is especially important in the context of scientific studies suggesting that cyberbullying is an overestimated phenomenon. Inducing fear might lead to a call for repressive measures focusing on criminalizing cyberbullying and cyberbullies (e.g. by adopting new laws), or a call for restrictive and controlling measures from parents and schools (e.g. limiting youngsters' time spent online), while a more educational, nuanced and trusting approach would probably be better-suited.[68]

University of Calgary doctoral student J. Mylynn Felt conducted two systematic studies of news media coverage of cyberbullying controversies in Canada spurred the passage of two highly controversial criminal statutes: Nova Scotia's Cyber-safety Act (2013) and the federal *Protecting Canadians from Online Crime Act*," or Bill C-13 (2014). In "Framing 'Cyberbullying': Competing Frame Coverage of Rehtaeh Parsons' Death," Felt analyzed news, feature and opinion articles from the Canadian newspapers *Toronto Star* and The *Globe and Mail* about Parsons between the days she died on April 7, 2013 and the day Nova Scotia proposed the Cyber-safety Act on April 25, 2013.[69] Parsons, a target of alleged sexual assault, malicious sexting and months of slut shaming, died after attempting suicide.[70] The hastily written Cyber-safety Act, the first Canadian law targeting cyberbullying, went into effect in the province of Nova Scotia in August 2013.[71] The Cyber-safety Act allowed alleged cyberbullying victims to apply for court-order protection and to sue for civil damages, and, empowered courts to hold parents responsible for the children's online misconduct under some circumstances.[72] The Nova Scotia Supreme Court struck down the Act as unconstitutional in December 2015. (See Chapter Seven.)

Felt did not attempt to determine whether the news media's coverage of the Parsons tragedy stirred up a moral panic. She limited her study to framing analysis, concluding that news journalists, in contrast to opinion and feature writers, depicted "cyberbullying as a villain deserving blame for Parsons' death," and acted as "agenda setters framing cyberbullying as a social problem requiring updated legislation."[73]

In "The Incessant Image: How Dominant News Coverage Shaped Canadian Cyberbullying Law," another framing analysis, Felt linked news media characterization of the deaths of four teens identified as victims of cyberbullying and traditional bullying—Parsons, Todd, and 15-year-olds Jamie Hubley and Todd Loik—directly to the language of Bill C-13, though she never used the term "moral panic." (Canada's Bill C-13, essentially a combination of a revenge porn, anti-sexting and surveillance laws, authorizes government to order online intermediaries and others to track and preserve data of alleged revenge porn purveyors, and under certain circumstances, hand over such information without requiring a warrant.)[74] "Analysis shows that the mediated public discourse of cyberbullying as a social problem closely aligns with the image of cyberbullying as defined in the Protecting Canadians from Online Crime Act."[75]

> Overall, the dominant frame in mainstream news coverage of the death of these teens focuses on cyberbullying as a social problem in need of reform. Such a frame clusters disparate cases into a recognizable pattern, minimizing attention to unique

> circumstances and emphasizing common characteristics in the name of advancing a social cause. Though this frame is effective for socially constructing a recognizable problem, this treatment oversimplifies individual cases and strips these teens of personhood as they become little more than victims for a cause. Another problem with the frame of cyberbullying as a social problem is that characterizing the problem according to the most intense circumstances omits discussion addressing the most common forms. These consequences are reflected in the legislation that emerges as a direct result.[76]

As noted earlier, a moral panic is a socially constructed problem. The Canadian media could have branded incidents of, say, school-related verbal online harassment as a condition that deviated from the social norm and required legislative remedies. But they did not. Rather, Felt says, that by focusing on the high profile bullicide cases of Parsons and Todd, that involved nonconsensual distribution of images of teenage girls involved in sex or posing partially nude, news media and the public identified an atypical type of online expression as a social problem and a threat to fundamental societal values. In turn, C-13 codifies the socially constructed conception of cyberbullying as only nonconsensual distribution of intimate images.

> Bill C-13, the *Protecting Canadians from Online Crime Act*, reflects a uniquely Canadian construction of cyberbullying as a social problem. Although the legislation does not specifically make use of the term "cyberbullying," the Honourable Steven Blaney, Minister of Public Safety and Emergency Preparedness, and the Honourable Peter MacKay, Minister of Justice and Attorney General of Canada, connect the term to Bill C-13 … Bill C-13 is clearly written in the image of cyberbullying as portrayed through the high profile deaths of teens such as Parsons and Todd, given that the emphasis is on distributed photos more than written or verbal harassment.[77]

Consequently, Felt contends, C-13 missed the mark and overreached. Like the public discourse that it echoed, the statute oversimplifies the complex phenomenon of cyberbullying and diverse types of cyberbullying cases, it erroneously makes a causal connection between suicide and hostile speech, and fails to address the fact that the roles of cyberbullying victim and bully often overlap.[78] In other words, offline bulling is more common than cyberbullying and the link between suicide and cyberbullying is not causal.

> While Bill C-13 may fill a legal gap, it should not be seen as the solution to cyberbullying. It is time to broaden the public discourse beyond what some term bullicide, to include a more comprehensive approach. Social change is unlikely until we reconstruct the Canadian definition of cyberbullying to reflect a more complicated issue, one deeply imbedded in teen culture.[79]

Sociologist Linda M. Waldron analyzed 477 articles from national and local news publications in the U.S. and applied content analysis and the Goode and Ben-Yehuda criteria in an effort to determine the news media's role in constructing cyberbullying as a moral panic.[80] Waldron said the Goode and Ben-Yehuda model suggests that,

> Although the media has certainly influenced the level or degree of concern over this issue, given the rise of new media technology and existing concern over bullying in general … the moral panic over cyberbullying likely predated the increase in media coverage on this issue (i.e., the media did not necessarily create the moral panic). *That being said, the media does participate in fueling the moral panic by framing this issue in very particular ways, which in essence contributes to the construction of it as a moral panic* [emphasis added].[81]

Like Felt, Waldron voiced concern that anti-cyberbullying rhetoric has spurred simplistic, overreaching and misdirected government-created solutions, though Felt did not apply moral panic analysis.

> If the problem involves everyone, it almost becomes too large to effectively deal with. On the other hand, if the problem is only caused by a few "folk devils" then punishing these individuals creates the sense that we are "solving" the problem, even if we are not. If we do not fully understand the causes or extent of the problem, it makes it equally difficult to provide thoughtful solutions. This is perhaps why educators and legislators have created sweeping and vague policies about cyberbullying, but it is unclear how these policies will be enacted to create change in the day-to-day lives of children.[82]

Content Analysis: Concern, Hostility, Consensus, Disproportionality and Volatility

The conclusions that Waldron and Felt have drawn are shared by this author and supported by the findings below, the result of an application of Goode and Ben-Yehuda's framework and google searches of the terms "cyberbullying," "cyberbullying laws," "revenge porn" and "teenage sexting" conducted September 29, 2015. As noted above, according to Goode and Ben-Yehuda, concern, hostility, consensus, disproportionality and volatility are the conditions that determine whether a moral panic truly exists. Goode and Ben-Yehuda also subscribe to the theory that moral panics are created by one of three status groups or a combination of the three: the general public, the grassroots model; those who dominate the media, legislatures and laws enforcement, the elite-engineered model; or by the moral crusaders, the interest group model.

Though Waldron argues that the construction of cyberbullying as a moral panic tends to fall under a "'grassroots model' for moral panics,"[83] the results of the "consensus" analysis here points to the interest group model, which argues "that moral panics originate neither from the top nor from the bottom, but somewhere in society's middle rungs—professional associations, the police, the media, religious groups, educational organizations, middle-level associations, organizations, groups, institutions, sectors, and categories of every description."[84] In the cyberbullying context those middle-rung parties are people such as Sheriff Judd, grieving parents such as Tricia Norman, who is fighting for the passage of a "Rebecca's Law"[85] and anti-cyberbullying advocacy groups. It would appear that grass roots and middle-level groups are stoking the panic.

The google search results in this study identify news articles on cyberbullying and legal controversies and reveal how news media have highlighted, or framed, certain aspects of the cyberbullying legal issue while downplaying, distorting or ignoring other aspects. For instance, cyberbullying was characterized as causing suicide in the majority of the news articles though scientific studies reject such causality.[86] Because a high Google PageRank suggests that results are "pages that are well cited from many places around the web [and] are worth looking at,"[87] the results of the word search of "cyberbullying laws" suggest that the public has been poorly informed about the highly questionable constitutionality of many cyberbullying laws.

Concern

Goode and Ben-Yehuda defined "concern" as "a heighten level of *concern* over the behavior of a certain group or category and the consequences that that behavior presumably causes for the rest of society. This concern should be manifested or measurable in concrete ways, through, for example, public opinion pools, public commentary in the form of media attention, proposed legislation, social movement activity, and so on."[88]

Though adults have been charged with criminal offenses stemming from antagonistic online speech, cyberbullying involving minors linked to teenage suicides and school-related cyberbullying incidents—have drawn the most attention, indignation and angst from parents, activists and legislators and sensationalized coverage from the news and entertainment media.

Headline-making teenage "bullicide" tragedies like the Sedwick story have framed the cyberbullying threat narrative from as early as 2004.

- A target of offline and online harassment, Ryan Halligan, 13, of Vermont committed suicide and the state enacted a Bullying Prevention Policy Law in May 2004.[89]
- Megan Meier, 13, committed suicide in October 2006, leading to the passage of Missouri's Megan Meier Law in 2008[90] and the proposed but failed federal Megan Meier Cyberbullying Prevention Act.[91]
- Jessica Logan, 18, committed suicide in 2008. As a result, Ohio enacted the Jessica Logan Act requiring schools to prohibit cyberbullying.[92]
- The suicide of 18-year-old Rutgers University student Tyler Clementi in 2010 inspired the Tyler Clementi Higher Education Anti-Harassment Act requiring colleges and universities receiving federal student aid funding to enact an anti-harassment policy.[93]
- The suicide of Canadian Amanda Todd, 15, in 2012, which spurred the enactment of Canada's C-13.[94]
- The suicide of Rehtaeh Parsons, 17, in 2013, which sparked public outrage and a hastily enacted Cyber-safety Act in Nova Scotia, Canada.[95]
- Phoebe Prince, 15, took her own life in 2010, which spurred Massachusetts to pass a law making anti-bullying curriculum mandatory for every student in every grade, K–12, in both public and private schools.[96]

The prominence teen suicide has played in the social construction of cyberbullying as a moral panic is suggested by a google search of "cyberbullying." The second result, for instance, http://www.meganmeierfoundation.org/resourcecenter.html, displayed a banner toward the bottom of the page that read: "The National Suicide Prevention Lifeline 1-800-273-TALK (8255)." The third result produced http://americanspcc.org/bullying/statistics-and-information/?gclid=CK_88MqshMoCFcGRHwode0kHew, which displayed a link "About Teen Suicide & Depression.

The 10th result, a wikipedia entry, "Cyberbullying," mentions "suicide" 27 times: "Awareness has also risen, due in part to high-profile cases like the suicide of Tyler Clementi." "Children have killed each other and committed suicide after having been involved in a cyberbullying incident." "The suicide of Megan Meier is a recent example that led to the conviction of the adult perpetrator of the attacks." "These would include the suicide of Ryan Halligan and the suicide of Megan Meier, the latter of which resulted in United States v. Lori Drew."

According to a *New York Times* report, "Online Bullies Pull Schools into the Fray," the 13th result, "Often, school district discipline codes say little about educators' authority over student cellphones, home computers and off-campus speech. Reluctant to assert an authority they are not sure they have, educators can appear indifferent to parents frantic with worry, alarmed by recent adolescent suicides linked to bullying."[97]

In contrast, news media coverage of exoneration of cyberbullies and judicial setbacks of anti-cyberbullying laws has been restrained, a Google search of "cyberbullying" suggests. Consider that between 2012 and mid-2015, there were six rulings in the U.S. in which courts struck down a cyberharassment or cyberstalking law in whole or in part, or limited a cyberbullying law's application: *State v. Vaugh*, 366 S.W.3d 513 at 519 (Mo. banc 2012); *People v. Golb, 23 N.Y.3d 455, 467 (2014)*; *State v. Leidecker*, P3/11-2685 (R.I. July 30, 2014); *People v. Marquan*, 24 NY 3d 1 (2014); *Chan v. Ellis*, S14A1652 (Ga. Supreme Ct., 2015); and *Minnesota v. Timothy Robert Turner*, A14-1408 (Minn. Ct. App. 2015). Similarly, a federal judge imposed a permanent injunction upon Arizona's revenge porn law in *Antigone Books v. Brnovi*ch, 2:14-cv-02100 (2015). All of these are highly significant and newsworthy rulings, led by *Marquan*, the first case in which a state's highest court struck down an entire anticyberbullying law on First Amendment grounds.

Yet, no reference to those rulings, or, for that matter, the exoneration of cyberbullying defendants—adults or minors—appears within the first 17 pages of hits from a google search of "cyberbullying." For example, the aforementioned Wikipedia entry makes no mention of such rulings nor does it discuss First Amendment concerns raised by the new laws. Instead, the first 160 or more hits identify websites and reports mostly focusing on cyberbullying as a problem of great social concern: StopBullying.gov, Cyberbullyhelp.com, "How Schools Should Handle Cyberbully?" "Confronting My Cyberbully: 13 Years Later" and "Stalker in the Attic: The Cyberbully Who Spies on 12-Year-Old Girls in Their Home." Not until the 18th page of hits did a *Slate.com* story discussing *People v. Marquan*, the New York Supreme Court's July 2014 ruling striking down Albany County, N.Y.'s cyberbullying statute as unconstitutional, appear.[98] (See Chapters Two and Three)

A narrower search using the phrase "cyberbullying laws" produced websites and articles that identified laws that criminalized or regulated cyberbullying framed mostly as trend pieces in the first five pages of results, though the *Slate* article, "The Legal Difficulties of Fighting Cyberbullying," which referenced the *Marquan* ruling and took a critical approach, appeared in the first page of results. On the fifth page, a *Wall Street Journal* article, discussing the possible implications of a ruling on the *Marquan* case, appeared.[99] On that same page of results, an *American Bar Association Journal* article, "NY High Court Says Anti-Cyberbullying Law Won't Pass First Amendment Muster" appeared discussing *Marquan*.[100] Similarly, 10 pages of hits from a search of "cyberharassment" yielded not one report on *Golb*, a ruling in which New York's highest court struck down the state's cyberharassment statute as unconstitutional. In contrast, a search of "Cyberbullying First Amendment" yielded reports of courts striking down anti-cyberbullying laws within the first page of results. These results suggest that the general reader would be unlikely to be exposed to news reports in which sources question the constitutionality of cyberbullying laws or reports on rulings that support the civil libertarian argument against such laws.

Though a search for "revenge porn" identified an opinion piece entitled, "Revenge Porn is Bad. Criminalizing It Is Worse,"[101] by the 9th hit, no mention of the significant July 2015 ruling by a federal judge imposing a permanent injunction on Arizona's revenge porn statute could be identified until the 7th page of results. There an Associated Press news report, published on the *Arizona Capitol Times* website, reported "State to Pay Fees, Costs for Challenge to Revenge Porn Law."[102] (See Chapter Six.)

In contrast, google search returns of "teenage sexting" apparently reflect society's mixed view on imposing harsh criminal penalties, or any at all, on teenagers who share nude images of themselves. As noted in "Cyberbullying and Free Speech," "by early 2015, seventeen states had sexting statutes on their books, many of which shielded consensual youthful sharers of sexting from child pornography prosecution.[103] Accordingly, the first 23 results identified stories and columns warning of the potential psychological, social and physical damages of teen sexting or reports of sexting arrests. But among those 23 results were a *Washington Post* column, "Stop Demonizing Teen Sexting. In Most Cases, it is Completely Harmless," and an Associated Press piece, published by the *Christian Science Monitor*, discussing the prosecution of two Fayetteville, N.C., sexting teens who were charged with being child porn victims and distributors, "When does Teen Sexting Become Child Porn?" (See Chapter Six.)

In a moral panic, concern and fear are "seen by those who feel them to be a reasonable response to what is regarded as a very real and palpable threat," Goode and Ben-Yehuda argue.[104] By that measure, Sheriff Judd's actions and rhetoric, and much of the news media's early coverage of the arrests of minors

Roman and Shaw are evidence of "concern" as defined by Goode and Ben-Yehuda. Case in point is the October 16, 2013 *NBC Today Show* host Matt Lauer's interview of Judd, focusing on a sheriff "who has now taken a very strong stand (against teenage cyberbullies)," said Lauer at the opening of the segment.[105] Next, a voice of a woman reporter announced that after a month-long investigation of Sedwick's suicide, Judd said, "enough was enough."[106] The off-screen reporter's statements of the case were interspersed with video and audio footage of Judd at a press conference announcing the arrests of Roman and Shaw. (Though Judd held up photos of the two girls, NBC blanked out their images.)

Next, video and audio footage of Sedwick's mother, Tricia Norman at a press conference was shown, followed by an interview with her. All the reporting focused on the tragedy of Sedwick, while the accused were given no voice—neither the girls, their parents, their legal representatives nor any legal or criminal expert appeared to present the girls' side of the arrests.

After about two minutes, Lauer returned to the screen. In the nearly three-minute interview that ensued, Lauer did not ask Judd whether the charges were excessive, or whether he could have recommended noncriminal penalties for the minors instead, nor did he question the sheriff about the propriety of identifying the minor suspects or cast any doubt on Judd's decision to arrest the girls. Instead, he allowed Judd to tar the girls and their parents. "I can tell you the parents are in total denial … It's kinda like the apple doesn't fall far from the tree. That's what we have here."[107]

Surprisingly, Lauer also never questioned the motive of the sheriff who is well known and criticized by some in Florida as a man who "envisions himself as not just a local enforcer of laws but a more universal arbiter of morals."[108] Apparently, Lauer assumed the young girls were guilty as charged. Otherwise, he would have operated as a fair and objective reporter by asking tougher questions or aired a response from the accused or their representatives. Lauer's sign-off to the interview was perhaps most telling. It showed that he had bought into the moral panic, and suggests that many of his viewers should do the same. Lauer: "[The threat of cyberbully by minors] has clearly struck an emotional chord with you and I think it will with a lot of parents."[109]

Opinion polls have measured the public's heightened concern over cyberbullying. According to the results of a poll conducted by Ipsos Global Public Affairs for Reuters News in 2012, 77% of global citizens (18,687 adults) said, "cyberbullying is a fundamentally different type of bullying that needs special attention from parents and schools, in addition to existing efforts to address bullying in general."[110] In Canada, results of an online survey of 1,006 representative Canadian adults conducted in 2012 revealed 90% would make it a crime to use electronic means to "coerce, intimidate, harass or cause other substantial emotional distress."[111]

Finally, alone, the number of interest groups devoted to eradicating cyberbullying may constitute sufficient evidence of a finding of a heightened level of concern: the Cyberbullying Research Center, Stomp Out Bullying, End to Cyberbullying, the Megan Meier Foundation, Delete Cyberbullying, The Cybersmile Foundation, NoBully.com, Stop Bullying Now.gov, the Cyber Civil Rights Initiative, and End Revenge Porn, to name a handful. Certainly, large numbers of individuals—parents of teenagers, teenagers, themselves, and single and divorced women—are also unsettled by online abusive words and images, as the findings of the Canadian poll suggest.

In the U.S., a Pew Study found that 40% of Internet users experienced online harassment.[112] Their unpleasant online experiences, however, did not necessarily lead to calls for new laws. "Sixty per cent said they had ignored" the online harassment and others confronted the cyberbully online, unfriended, blocked them or reported them to online intermediaries.[113] There is no denying that the public's uneasiness and fears about online harassment exist, yet many of the interest groups in the study provided, as Goode and Ben-Yehuda have said, the "appropriate triggering device and a vehicle to express [themselves] in a moral panic."[114]

Hostility

Goode and Ben-Yehuda's second criterion requires a finding of "an enemy … a clearly identifiable group or segment of the society must be seen as *responsible* for the threat."[115] In a phrase, the enemy is a "folk devil." Sociologists have identified moral panic folk devils as witches, welfare state mothers, recreational drug users, pornographers, child molesters, cyber-predators, illegal aliens, and, of course, young people who deviated from social norms.[116] Hostility towards cyberbullies as deviates is displayed in the depiction of them as far more dangerous than traditional bullies, society's praise of celebrities who stand up to them, and the widely accepted belief that online shaming—even shaming political figures and other public figures—is a form of deviant cyberbullying.[117]

There are many, notably psychologists, who subscribe to the claim asserted by Elizabeth Carll in her talk, "Electronic Harassment and Cyberstalking:

Intervention, Prevention and Public Policy," delivered before the American Psychological Association's 119th Annual Convention in 2011, that cyberbullying victims experience higher levels of stress and trauma than their offline counterparts. "It is my observation that the symptoms related to cyberstalking and e-harassment may be more intense than in-person harassment, as the impact is more devastating due to the 24/7 nature of online communication, inability to escape to a safe place, and global access of the information," Carll said.[118] Carll's assertions, disputed by other experts,[119] is nevertheless repeated in the popular press and cited in government documents such Canada's Department of Justice's "A Handbook for Police and Crown Prosecutors on Criminal Harassment."[120] Such highly debatable assertions promoted hostility toward cyberbullies as a new and more threatening species of bully and, thus, a justification for new criminal laws.

> One of the biggest distinguishing factors in determining whether malicious use of technology consists of criminal harassment in bullying-type cases will be whether the online conduct is merely annoying, or whether it causes the target to fear for his or her physical or psychological safety. In fact, recent research has shown that online harassment and bullying result in higher levels of trauma and stress for the victim than more traditional forms of stalking ... The sense of humiliation they experience is often increased due to the public nature of the bullying or harassment. This type of harm was recently recognized by the Supreme Court of Canada in the civil case of *AB v Bragg Communications*, 2012 SCC 46.[121]

As discussed in "Cyberbullying and Free Speech," the term cyberbullying encompasses a wide range of expressive conduct from constitutionally protected parody, taunting, minors ridiculing other minors, flaming, caustic and robust criticism of elected officials, political candidates and celebrities to constitutionally unprotected stalking, speech integral to criminality, harassment, true threats and false defamation. Because the term encompasses a wide variety of speech—legal, illegal and ethical and unethical—tagging someone as a "cyberbully" unfairly stigmatizes. Once the label is affixed, nuance is lost.

Many in the news media and the public incorrectly assume that the accused cyberbully intended to harm absent a legitimate motive, that all types of cyberbullying inflict serious harm, and that all mean and cruel online speech is illegal, or valueless, solely because it can be emotionally disturbing. Accordingly, it is easy for many to conclude that cyberbully should be criminalized, particularly when minors are involved. NBC's Lauer's woeful and unnecessarily deferential questioning of Sheriff Judd—aimed more at producing an emotional impact from viewers than producing an accurate and fair report—is indicative of the hostility the term "cyberbully," particularly teenage cyberbully, engenders among an audience such as *NBC's Today Show's* mainstream coffee-and-cereal audience.

Judging from the interview of Judd, accused cyberbullies are perceived as moral degenerates, who do not deserve fair treatment from the news media. It is as though an indictment of cyberbullying is something akin to an arrest for suspicion of child molesting. The accused is guilty as charged, and even after exoneration the suspicion still lingers. In *Moral Panic: Changing Concepts of the Child Molester in Modern America*, Historian Philip Jenkins observed, "During the twentieth century … such dangerous outsiders [predators, psychopaths and pedophiles] have attracted a vastly disproportionate share of official attention, precisely because they represent the easiest targets for anyone wishing, however sincerely, to protect children."[122] The same can be said of the cyberbully accused of attacking minors.

Contempt for cyberbullies is so strong that one needs only to claim one self a victim of hostile online speech to gain sympathy. At least that is what appears to be the strategy and effect of Monica Lewinsky's "I-was-the-world's-first-cyberbullying-victim campaign" kicked off in 2014, 19 years after she became notorious worldwide as former President Clinton's White House intern lover.[123] Lewinsky defines cyberbullying as public speech that shames. "Public shaming as a blood sport has to stop," says Lewinsky said. "I was Patient Zero of losing a personal reputation on a global scale almost instantaneously."[124]

Though her plea for compassion from online snarkers has ethical merit, there is a significant difference between speech that publicly shames an innocent teenage girl who has no public profile and ridiculing Lewinsky, who as a woman of majority age, 22, engaged in an adulterous affair with the President of U.S. Under the First Amendment, public speech about public figures enjoys a great deal of protection because the U.S. Supreme Court has recognized society's interest in public free-wheeling discussion of public people who affect and shape public matters and policies. Consistent with that societal interest, state laws provide for civil remedies—not criminal punishment—for verbal abuse that falsely defames an individual's reputation or amounts to the intentional infliction of serious mental or emotional distress.[125]

Additionally, shaming, in and of itself, is not actionable as an intentional infliction of emotion distress action because scholars and courts agree that liability under the tort "does not extend to mere insults, indignities, threats, annoyances, petty oppressions, or other trivialities."[126] Moreover, under the First Amendment a public figure such as Lewinsky cannot recover damages for intentional emotional distress.[127] Under defamation law, a public figure such as Lewinsky would have to show that shaming was false and made with reckless regard for the truth.[128] Accordingly, Lewinsky has no credible intentional infliction of emotional harm or defamation case. Nevertheless, Lewinsky's plea resonates with many largely because of the ambiguity of the term cyberbullying and because few can muster sympathy for cyberbullies.

Branding cyberbullies as social deviants also has allowed cyberbully disparagers to be treated as avenging heroes as seen in the coverage of former Philadelphia Phillies baseball star Curt Schilling's tracking down of two young men who posted lewd comments about his daughter[129] and actress and University of Kentucky basketball fan Ashley Judd telling off fans of opposing teams and threatening lawsuits, none of which materialized.[130]

Consensus

"Third, there must be a certain minimal measure of agreement in society as a whole or in designated segments of the society that the threat is real, serious and caused by the wrongdoing of group members and their behavior."[131] As we have seen certain segments of society—some news media, psychologists, sociologists, pundits, many parents, legislators, here and abroad, and, of course, anti-cyberbullying crusaders believe that cyberbullies pose a serious threat to society that requires intervention by school authorities and the criminal justice system.

Criminologists Sameer Hindaju and Justin W. Patchin, heads of the Cyberbullying Research Center who have surveyed nearly 15,000 teenage students about cyberbullying, are widely recognized experts on cyberbullying. In one of their reports, the criminologists identified some of cyberbullying's harms:

> There are many detrimental outcomes associated with cyberbullying ... First, many targets of cyberbullying report feeling depressed, sad, angry, and frustrated ... cyberbullying youth also report having suicidal thoughts, and there have been a number of examples in the United States where youth who were victimized enduing up taking their own lives ... We also need to get everyone involved—youth, parents, educators, counselors, law enforcement, social media companies, and the community at large.[132]

From Child psychologist Dr. Vicki Panaccione, who writes a blog for the Better Parenting Institute: "The effects of cyberbullying are devastating and ruining lives. Lately in the news there have been reports of suicides due to cyberbullying by kids as young as 12!"[133]

Though the New York Court of Appeals struck down a county cyberbullying law in 2014 in *People v. Marquan*, it nevertheless acknowledged the threat of cyberbullying by quoting Pepperdine Law professor Naomi Goodno, who proposed "a comprehensive model cyberbullying policy for primary and secondary public schools that meets educational goals and considers constitutional challenges."[134]

> The advent of the Internet with "twenty-four hour connectivity and social networking" means that "[b]ullying that begins in school follows students home every day" and "bullying through the use of technology can begin away from school property" … Unlike traditional bullying, victims of cyberbullying can be "relentlessly and anonymously attack[ed] twenty-four hours a day for the whole world to witness. There is simply no escape."[135]

One news headline suggested that many Brits saw cyberbullying as a growing threat in 2011. "Cyberbullying is a New Threat to Children," proclaimed a June 2011 trend piece published in *The Telegraph*.[136] CBS television news' take on the Sedwick suicide treated it as a cautionary tale: "12-Year-Old's Suicide Spotlights Cyber-Bullying Threat."[137]

The Cyber Civil Rights Project, which seeks to make revenge porn illegal, plays the suicide card.

> With the click of a mouse, a bitter ex or mischievous hacker can upload compromising photos or videos of a victim to public websites without the consent of the pictured individual. These sexually explicit images quickly make their way to the attention of the victim's family members, friends, co-workers, classmates, colleagues, and employers. Victims are routinely threatened, stalked, and tormented. They have difficulty finding work and often get fired from or are forced to leave their current jobs or schools because of the severity of the harassment. *Some victims of nonconsensual pornography have even committed suicide* [emphasis added].[138]

Disproportionality

> Fourth, there is the implicit assumption in the use of the term moral panic that the concern is out of proportion to the nature of the threat, that it is, in fact, considerably greater than that which a sober empirical evaluation could support … if the figures that are cited to measure the scope of the problem are grossly exaggerated, we may say that the criterion of disproportionality has been meet.[139]

Several experts argue that prevailing claims about cyberbullying have been exaggerated. They say that it is not as prevalent and dangerous as portrayed in the media and by anti-bullying advocates, nor are such claims sufficiently supported by empirical scientific evidence.

Dan Olweus, psychologist and world-renown expert on bullying, was one of the first to debunk the conventional wisdom about cyberbullying as a threat. Olweus's study included the questioning of 450,000 U.S. students and 9,000 Norwegian students from 2007 to 2010 about their experiences with traditional verbally and cyberbullying.[140] He scrutinized three claims: (1) cyberbullying is a very frequent phenomenon among youth (2) the frequency or prevalence of cyberbullying has increased dramatically and (3) cyberbully has created new bullying perpetrators and victims.

> The general picture created in the media—and often also by researchers and authors of books on cyberbullying—is that cyberbullying is very frequent, that it has increased dramatically over time and that this new form of bullying has created many new victims and bullies in addition to the victims and bullies involved in "traditional" bullying. In addition, it is often argued or implied that cyberbullying is very difficult for adults to discover and counteract, creating a feeling of powerlessness in adults and maybe students as well.[141]

According to the findings of Olweus's questionnaires, traditional verbal bullying occurred far more frequently than cyberbullying in the U.S. and Norway—"cyberbullying is actually a quite low-prevalence phenomenon, representing only some 25 to 35% of the level of traditional bullying by direct verbal means."[142] With regard to the second claim, his findings showed cyberbullying did not increase from 2007 to 2010. "This is true of both cyber-bullying and cyberbulling others—as well as of being bullied and bullying others by direct verbal means."[143] As for the third claim, the findings of the study suggested that access to social media has created few new perpetrators and victims. "In these analyses, there was only a small percentage, about 10%, of the participants, who had only been cyberbullied or had only cyber-bullied others."[144]

Olweus says that some forms of cyberbullying should still be taken seriously. Nevertheless, it is necessary to have a realistic picture of its impact and prevalence because,

> a distorted portrayal of reality will probably generate a lot of unnecessary anxiety and tension among parents and maybe teachers and students. It may also create feelings of powerlessness and helplessness in the face of the presumably "huge" and ubiquitous cyberbullying problem. Second, such a picture is likely to result in an unfortunate shift in the focus of anti-bullying work if digital bullying is seen as the key bullying problem in the schools. This would probably also result in funnelling a lot of resources in a "wrong" direction while traditional bullying—which is clearly the most prevalent and most serious problem—would be correspondingly downgraded.[145]

In 2010, technology journalist Larry Magid, citing several statistical studies, concluded: "There is no question that there is a problem and I certainly don't want to sugarcoat it, but it's also important to look at it from the positive side as well. It's worth pointing out that about 80 percent of teens say they have not been cyberbullied while 90 percent of teens say they haven't cyberbullied other teens."[146]

Criminologist Justin Patchin of the Cyberbullying Research Center agreed with Magid. "He is right that the public can sometimes view a particular problem as epidemic in nature simply from one or two high profile incidents (for example, the school shootings of the late 1990s, or more recently the panic over online sexual predators). And many in the media often fan the flames."[147]

Stopbullying.gov, a federal government website managed by the U.S. Department of Health & Human Services, listed common errors of media coverage of cyberbullying: overstating the problem; stating or implying that bullying caused a suicide; oversimplifying issues related to a bullying incident; using under-qualified sources; blaming/criminalizing those who bully; and sensationalizing. It notes that "bullying is not an epidemic" and cyberbullying "is less prevalent than other forms of bullying."[148]

Findings of a poll conducted by the Pew Research Center released in 2015, call into question the conventional belief that most parents are in a near cataleptic state over fears about their children's online activities. "Just 12% of parents say they have ever felt uncomfortable about something a spouse, family member, or friend posted about their child on social media."[149] Another Pew Research Center poll found that, "Overall, 69% of social media-using teens think that peers are mostly kind to each other on social network sites. Another 20% say that peers are mostly unkind, while 11% volunteered that 'it depends.' Some 15% of teen social media users have experienced such harassment themselves in the past 12 months, while 85% of them have not."[150]

Volatility

Goode and Ben-Yehuda have said, "moral panics are volatile: They erupt fairly suddenly … and, nearly as suddenly, they subside … and are relatively short-lived."[151]

But Goode and Ben-Yehuda also acknowledge that panics can endure, erupting from time to time. "In fact, moral panics that are sustained over long periods of time are almost certainly conceptual groupings of a series of more or less discrete, more or less localized, more or less short-term panics. Likewise, describing a concern as volatile does not mean that moral panics do not, or cannot, leave a cultural and institutional legacy."[152]

For example, the black mugger panic, identified in the influential moral panic analysis, *Policing the Crisis: Mugging, the State and Law and Order*, started in the late 1960s in the United States and in 1972–1973 in Great Britain.[153] The afterwords section of the 2013 edition of *Policing the Crisis* argues that the stereotype of the black mugger as a folk devil has lasted over 40 years in England, and has morphed. "Arguably, the contemporary 'folk devil' … is no longer black, but has widened to include all disaffected youth: the 'underclass,' 'chavs,' 'hoodies,' and post 9/11 terrorists."[154]

The same thing can be said of the U.S. version of the phenomenon. In the U.S., the panic endured for more than 20 years. The Republican Presidential Candidate G.W. Bush tapped into the irrational fear of the violent black street criminal in his 1988 Willie Horton ad campaign and beyond.[155] The moral panic resurfaced again during the nationwide debate over racial profiling and stand-your-ground laws that erupted during the pretrial phase and trial exoneration of George Zimmerman for the shooting death of black teen Trayvon Martin.[156] It suggests that the black mugger as a folk devil persists in the U.S. in the second decade of the 21st century.

Critcher also identifies the pattern as serial:

> Serial moral panics start and end more than once. Child abuse, drugs and crime all seem to have serial status in many developed societies across the world. All it takes is a new kind of abuse, type of drug or form of violent crime, as symbolized by a key event, claimed by a law enforcement agency or revealed by a commissioned report. The cycle is played out all over again until there is introduced a new law, reform of an existing one or change in the activities of enforcement agencies. Then the topic is dropped—until the next time.[157]

Arguably, teenager Meier's suicide in October 2006 marks the start of the transnational cyberbullying panic, and over the years it has taken on different forms—fear of anonymous manipulative, hostile, profane, sexually explicit and insulting expression by adults and teens, including the most recent phenomenon dubbed revenge porn. Given the decades-old duration of the black mugging panic, which has re-erupted, triggered by cynical politicians, economic down turns or newsmaking white vs. black deadly street confrontations, the cyberbullying panic may persist for decades. As Goode and Ben-Yehuda noted, "elements of panics may be established at one point in time that remain in place and help stimulate incipient concerns later on, at the appropriate time."[158]

Conclusion

Since 2008, legislators have enacted laws to censor cyberbullying that too many civil libertarians raised obvious and substantial free speech concerns because the terms of the statutes were out of step with decades of well-settled First Amendment principles. It has been long settled under the First Amendment that candidates for political office are fair game for parody, satire and other forms of harsh criticism. Therefore, one would not anticipate that a labor leader's impersonation of a voter and a political candidate in email conversations between a political candidate and the fake personas would constitute illegal speech. Yet, a Rhode Island prosecutor won a conviction against the labor leader, which, not surprisingly, was overturned as unconstitutional.[159] (See "Cyberbullying and Free Speech," and "Censorship Redux: The 21st Century Attack on the First Amendment Right of Public Criticism by the Use of Cyberharassment, Cyberstalking and Online Impersonation Laws.")

Other recent court rulings striking down cyberbullying laws and overturning verdicts examined in this text attests to the threat the new breed of censorship poses to the right to criticize and offend without fear of imprisonment. Beyond criminal sanctions, the regulation of public school student off-campus, online speech based on brick-and-mortar era precedents and new laws passed mandating schools to punish such speech are troubling to free speech advocates, too. As examined in Chapters Two and Four, many school districts are interpreting precedents broadly, sometimes unconstitutionally so, to police off-campus speech.

Though there are many explanations for why law makers draft new constitutionally defective cyberbullying laws or why prosecutors and judges incorrectly apply old laws, moral panic theory offers a credible motive for why these errors have been repeated in state after state, and Canada. Here, based on the findings of published studies and the application of the Goode-Ben Yehuda analysis to media accounts, it is argued that a cyberbullying moral panic does exist and has directly led to the enactment of constitutionally dubious statutes and ones that courts have struck down as unconstitutional.

Admittedly, the scope of this content analysis examining whether the backlash against cyberbullying meets the Goode-Ben-Yehuda criteria of concern, hostility, consensus, disproportionality and volatility is narrow. But combined with the findings of previous studies, it is reasonable to conclude that a cyberbullying moral panic exists. The findings of previous studies and the original analysis offered here also suggest that the media and professional and grassroots organizations have stoked the panic.

Ultimately, moral panic-generated legislation and prosecutions, because they are spawned from righteous indignation and misunderstanding and are poorly drafted, often miss their intended targets. Such is the case with the cyberbullying moral panic-fueled arrests and prosecutions. Katelyn Roman and Guadalupe Shaw never said anything that merited being treated as accused felons, but they are likely to suffer for their insensitive words and the ensuing publicity for years to come; at least that is what Michelle Gill, Katelyn's mother, fears.

"She's just a kid," Gill said about Katelyn in a magazine interview in April 2014. "This will follow her for her entire life—when she applies to college, when she looks for jobs."[160]

Notes

1. Stanley Cohen, *Folk Devils and Moral Panics* (London: Routledge, 2004), 1.
2. Christopher Lydon, "J. Edgar Hoover Made the F.B.I. Formidable with Politics, Publicity and Results," *New York Times*, May 3, 1972, https://www.nytimes.com/learning/general/onthisday/bday/0101.html (accessed August 17, 2016).
3. Anna Werner, "Fla. Sheriff on Why He Charged Dead 12-Year-Olds' Alleged Bullies," *CBS Evening News*, October 15, 2013, 8:14 PM, http://www.cbsnews.com/news/fla-sheriff-on-why-he-charged-dead-12-year-olds-alleged-bullies/ (accessed August 17, 2016).
4. Scott Stump, "Fed Up Sheriff: Alleged Teen Bully 'Did Something Despicable,'" *Today News*, October 16, 2013, at 9:53, http://www.today.com/news/fe d-sheriff-alleged-teen-bully-did-something-despicable-8C11401636 (accessed August 17, 2016).
5. Tamara Lush, "Florida Bullying Case Raises Questions for Parents," *Associated Press*, October 16, 2013, 8:45 PM EDT, http://www.bigstory.ap.org/article/2-charged-fla-after-bullied-girls-suicide (accessed August 17, 2016).
6. Lizette Alvarez, "Charges Dropped in Cyberbullying Death, but Sheriff isn't Backing Down," *New York Times*, November 21, 2014, http://www.nytimes.com/2013/11/22/us/charges-dropped-against-florida-girls-accused-in-cyberbullying-death.html?pagewanted=all&_r=0
7. Inside Edition, "Accused Teen Bullies Identities Revealed at Press Conference," October 16, 2013, 10:44 AM EDT, http://www.insideedition.com/headlines/7183-accused-teen-bullies-identities-revealed-at-press-conference (accessed August 17, 2016).
8. Assault; Battery; Culpable Negligence, Florida Statutes Chapter 784.048 (2010), http://www.leg.state.fl.us/Statutes/index.cfm?App_mode=Display_Statute&URL=0700-0799/0784/Sections/0784.048.html (accessed August 17, 2016).
9. Arelis Hernández and Jerriann Sullivan, "Cyberbullying-suicide Suspect: Yes, I Bullied Girl Who Killed Herself," *Orlando Sentinel*, October 15, 2013, http://articles.orlandosentinel.com/2013-10-15/news/os-rebecca-sedwick-cyber-bully-arrests-20131015_1_rebecca-ann-sedwick-12-year-old-girl-saying-rebecca (accessed August 17, 2016).

10. Amanda Paulson, "Rebecca Sedwick Suicide: Parents to Blame for their Bullying Children?" *Christian Science Monitor*, October 16, 2013, http://www.csmonitor.com/USA/2013/1016/Rebecca-Sedwick-suicide-Parents-to-blame-for-their-bullying-children-video (accessed July 19, 2016).
11. Stump, "Fed Up Sheriff: Alleged Teen Bully 'Did Something Despicable.'"
12. "Editorial: Terrible Toll of Cyberbullying," *Tampa Bay Times*, October 15, 2013 6:08pm, http://www.tampabay.com/opinion/editorials/editorial-terrible-toll-of-cyberbullying/2147409 (accessed July 19, 2016).
13. "Analysis: Critics say Polk Sheriff Grady Judd is Overstepping his Bounds," *Fox 13/WTVT-TV*, October 16, 2013, 6:25 PM EDT, http://www.myfoxtampabay.com/story/23711135/2013/10/16/analysis-polk-sheriff-grady-judd-is-overstepping-his-bounds (accessed July 19, 2016).
14. Alvarez, "Charges Dropped in Cyberbullying Death, but Sheriff isn't Backing Down."
15. Mallary Jean Tenore, "Why Journalists Have Trouble with Bullying," *Poynter.org* (blog), March 12, 2013, 8:36 AM, http://www.poynter.org/news/mediawire/206723/why-journalists-have-trouble-with-bullying/ (accessed July 19, 2016); Kelly McBride, "Bullying is Not on the Rise and It Does Not Lead to Suicide," *Poynter.org* (blog), November 25, 2014, 8:08 AM, http://www.poynter.org/news/mediawire/227095/bullying-is-not-on-the-rise-and-it-does-not-lead-to-suicide/ (accessed July 19, 2016).
16. The American Academy of Pediatrics (Press Release), "Cyberbullying Only Rarely the Sole Factor Identified in Teen Suicides," October 20, 2012, http://www.aap.org/en-us/about-the-aap/aap-press-room/Pages/Cyberbullying-Only-Rarely-the-Sole-Factor-Identified-in-Teen-Suicides.aspx (accessed July 19, 2016).
17. Fabien Tepper, "Rebbeca Sedwick Suicide: Mother Vows 'Crusade' for Tougher Bullying Laws," *The Christian Science Monitor*, November 25, 2013, http://www.csmonitor.com/USA/USA-Update/2013/1125/Rebecca-Sedwick-suicide-Mother-vows-to-crusade-for-tougher-bullying-laws-video (accessed July 19, 2016).
18. CNN Staff, "Mother of Florida Girl Who Committed Suicide Plans to Sue," *CNN.Com*, November 26, 2013, 9:19 AM ET, http://www.cnn.com/2013/11/25/justice/rebecca-sedwick-bullying-death/index.html (accessed August 18, 2016).
19. Tepper, "Rebbeca Sedwick Suicide: Mother Vows "Crusade" for Tougher Bullying Laws."
20. Abagail Pesta, "Who are You Calling a Bully," *Cosmopolitan*, April 8, 2014, 9:15 AM, http://www.cosmopolitan.com/lifestyle/advice/a6303/twelve-year-old-bully (accessed July 29, 2016); Emily Bazelon, "The Sheriff Overstepped," *Slate.com*, April 10, 2014, 6:23 PM, http://www.slate.com/articles/news_and_politics/doublex/2014/04/rebecca_sedwick_suicide_sheriff_grady_judd_never_should_have_arrested_katelyn.html (accessed July 29, 2016).
21. Associated Press, *Bullying May Not Have Caused Girl's Suicide, Report Shows*, April 7, 2014, http://www.tampabay.com/news/nation/bullying-may-not-have-caused-girls-suicide-report-shows/2173979 (accessed July 29, 2016).
22. Christian Dem, "FL Girls Who Helped Bully Classmate to Death Agree to Counseling in Return for Charges Being Dropped," *Daily Kos.com*, November, 21, 2013, 3:04 PM PST, http://www.dailykos.com/story/2013/11/21/1257393/-FL-girls-who-helped-bully-classmate-to-death-agree-to-counseling-in-return-for-charges-being-dropped# (accessed July 29, 2016).

23. Caroline Davies, "Hannah Smith Wrote 'Vile' Posts to Herself Before Suicide, Say Police," *The Guardian*, May 4, 2014 17.40 EDT, http://www.theguardian.com/uk-news/2014/may/06/hannah-smith-suicide-teenager-cyber-bullying-inquests (accessed July 29, 2016).
24. Matt Gutman, "Sheriff Would Arrest Cyberbully Suspect's Parents If He Could," *ABC News*, October 17, 2013, http://abcnews.go.com/US/rebecca-sedwick-suicide-sheriff-arrest-cyberbully-suspects-parents/story?id=20594342 (accessed July 29, 2016).
25. Cohen, *Folk Devils and Moral Panics*, xxvii.
26. Richard C. Fuller and Richard R. Myers, "The Natural History of a Social Problem," *American Sociological Review* 6 (June 1941): 320–28, 320.
27. Cohen, *Folk Devils and Moral Panics*, 2.
28. Eric Goode and Nachman Ben-Yehuda, "Moral Panics: Culture, Politics, and Social Construction," *Annual Review of Sociology* 20 (1994): 149.
29. Chas Critcher, ed., *Critical Readings: Moral Panics and the Media* (Maidenhead: Open University Press, 2006), 9.
30. Cohen, *Folk Devils and Moral Panics*, 155.
31. Ibid., 156, 155.
32. Ibid., 40, 41.
33. Ibid., 38.
34. Ibid., 2.
35. Jon Savage, "Mods v. Rockers: Two Tribes go to War," *British Broadcasting Corporation*, October 21, 2014, http://www.bbc.com/culture/story/20140515-when-two-tribes-went-to-war (accessed August 18, 2016).
36. Yvonne Jewkes, *Media and Crime* (London: Sage, 2011).
37. Ibid., 77.
38. Tim O' Reilly, "What Is Web 2.0: Design Patterns and Business Models for the Next Generation of Software," *Communications & Strategies* 65 (March 2007): 17–37, https://mpra.ub.uni-muenchen.de/4578/1/MPRA_paper_4578.pdf (accessed December 28, 2015).
39. Amanda Lenhart, *Teens, Social Media & Technology Overview 2015* (Washington, D.C.: Pew Research Center, April 9, 2015), http://www.pewinternet.org/2015/04/09/teens-social-media-technology-2015/ (accessed December 28, 2015).
40. Justin w. Patchin, "Cyberbullying Facts Summarizing What is Known," Cyberbullying Research Center, 2015, http://cyberbullying.org/facts/ (accessed December 28, 2015).
41. Maeve Duggan et al., "Teens, Kindness and Cruelty on Social Network Sites," *Pew Research Center: Internet, Science & Technology*, November 9, 2011, http://www.pew-internet.org/2011/11/09/teens-kindness-and-cruelty-on-social-network-sites/ (accessed December 28, 2015).
42. Eric Goode and Nachman Ben-Yehuda, "Grounding and Defending the Sociology of Moral Panic," in *Moral Panic and the Politics of Anxiety*, ed. Sean P. Hier (London: Routledge, 2011), 21.
43. Howard Beck, *Outsiders: Studies in the Sociology of Deviance* (New York: Free Press, 1997), 147–63.
44. Joel Best, "Social Problems," *Oxford Bibliographies*, August 31, 2015, http://www.oxford-bibliographies.com/view/document/obo-9780199756384/obo-9780199756384-0052.xml (accessed December 29, 2015).

45. Eric Goode and Nachman Ben-Yehuda, *Moral Panics: The Social Construction of Deviance* (Malden: Wiley-Blackwell, 2009), 90.
46. Critcher, *Critical Readings: Moral Panics and the Media*, 9.
47. *Winterbottom v Wright* (1842) 10 M. & W. 109.
48. Megan Meier Cyberbullying Prevention Act of 2009, H.R.1966, 111th Cong. (2009–2010), http://thomas.loc.gov/cgi-bin/query/z?c111:H.R.1966 (accessed December 29, 2015).
49. Ashley Hauck, "Cyberbullying Laws by State," *Crime Wire*, July 1, 2014, http://www.instantcheckmate.com/crimewire/cyberbullying-laws-by-state (accessed December 29, 2015).
50. Chas Critcher, "Moral Panic Analysis: Past, Present and Future," *Sociology Compass* 4 (July 2008): 1127–44, 1141, http://www.penelopeironstone.com/Critcher.pdf (accessed December 29, 2015).
51. R. M. Entman, "Framing: Toward Clarification of a Fractured Paradigm," *Journal of Communication* 43 (1993): 51–58, 52.
52. Goode and Ben-Yehuda, "Moral Panics: Culture, Politics, and Social Construction," 156–59.
53. Linda M. Waldron, "Cyberbullying: The Social Construction of a Moral Panic," in *Communication and Information Technologies Annual*, ed. Laura Robinson, Shelia R. Cotton, and Jeremy Schulz (Bingley: Emerald Group Publishing Limited, 2014), 197–230.
54. Mylynn Felt, "Framing 'Cyberbullying': Competing Frame Coverage of Rehtaeh Parsons' Death," in *TEM 2014 Proceedings of the Technology and Emerging Media Track—Annual Conference of the Canadian Communication Association*, ed. A. Buckland and C. Caron (Ottawa), May 28–30, 2012), 4, http://www.tem.fl.ulaval.ca/webroot/wp-content/PDF/Saint-Catharines_2014/FELT-TEM2014.pdf (accessed December 29, 2015).
55. MyLynn Felt, "The Incessant Image: How Dominant News Coverage Shaped Canadian Cyberbullying Law," *University of New Brunswick Law Journal* 66 (2015): 137–60, http://www.academia.edu/14853196/THE_INCESSANT_IMAGE_HOW_DOMINANT_NEWS_COVERAGE (accessed December 29, 2015).
56. Noah Nelson, "Cyberbullying: Problem or Panic?" *Huffington Post*, May 25, 2011, 4:00 PM EDT, http://www.huffingtonpost.com/youth-radio-youth-media-international/cyberbullying-problem-or_b_522078.html (accessed December 29, 2015).
57. Mike Masnick, "As Cyberbullying Moral Panic Heats Up, Actual Rates of Cyberbullying Decreasing," *TechDirt*, April 9, 2010, 12:15 PM, https://www.techdirt.com/articles/20100408/0218098933.shtml (accessed December 29, 2015).
58. Gavin Titley, "The Moral Panic over Social Media in Ireland is a Convenient Distraction," *The Guardian*, January 7, 2013, 10:30 EST, http://www.theguardian.com/commentisfree/2013/jan/07/moral-panic-social-media-ireland (accessed December 29, 2015).
59. Shaheen Shariff, *Sexting and Cyberbullying* (New York: Cambridge University Press, 2015), 40.
60. Mallary Jean Tenore, "Why Journalists have Trouble with Bullying," *Poynter.org* (blog), March 12, 2013, 8:36 AM, http://www.poynter.org/news/mediawire/206723/why-journalists-have-trouble-with-bullying/ (accessed January 5, 2016).
61. Ibid.
62. Kelly McBride, "Bullying Is Not on the Rise and It Does Not Lead to Suicide," *Poynter.org* (blog), updated November 25, 2014, 8:09 AM, http://www.poynter.org/news/

mediawire/227095/bullying-is-not-on-the-rise-and-it-does-not-lead-to-suicide/ (accessed January 5, 2016).

63. Ibid.
64. Jonathan Bishop, "Representations of 'Trolls' in Mass Media Communication: A Review of Media-Texts and Moral Panics Relating to 'Internet Trolling,'" *International Journal of Web Based Communities* 10 (2014): 7–24, http://www.scribd.com/doc/190884079/Representations-of-trolls-in-mass-media-communication-A-review-of-media-texts-and-moral-panics-relating-to-internet-trolling (accessed December 29, 2015).
65. Carla Cesaroni, Steven Downing, and Shahid Avi, "Bullying Enters the 21st Century? Turning a Critical Eye to Cyber-bullying Research," *Youth Justice* 12 (2012): 199–211, 200.
66. Heidi Vandebosch et al., "The Role of the Media. Coping and Guidelines," in *Cyberbullying Through the New Media: Findings from an International Network*, ed. Peter K. Smith and Georges Steffgen (London: Psychology Press, 2013), 100.
67. Ibid., 115.
68. Ibid., 114–15.
69. Felt, "Framing 'Cyberbullying': Competing Frame Coverage of Rehtaeh Parsons' Death," 4.
70. Emily Bazelon, "Sex Scourge," *Slate*, April 10, 2013, 6:43 PM, http://www.slate.com/articles/double_x/doublex/2013/04/rehtaeh_parsons_rape_case_why_do_these_keep_happening.single.html (accessed December 29, 2015).
71. *Cyber-safety Act*, S.N.S. 2013, c. 2, s. 3(1), http://www.canlii.org/en/ns/laws/stat/sns-2013-c-2/latest/sns-2013-c-2.html (accessed December 29, 2015).
72. Ibid.
73. Felt, "Framing 'Cyberbullying': Competing Frame Coverage of Rehtaeh Parsons' Death," 2.
74. Parliament of Canada, "Protecting Canadians from Online Crime Act," December 9, 2014, http://www.parl.gc.ca/HousePublications/Publication.aspx?Language=E&Mode=1&DocId=6830553&File=27#1 (accessed December 30, 2015).
75. Felt, "The Incessant Image: How Dominant News Coverage Shaped Canadian Cyberbullying Law," 137.
76. Ibid., 151–52.
77. Ibid., 147.
78. Ibid., 152.
79. Ibid., 159.
80. Waldron, "Cyberbullying: The Social Construction of a Moral Panic," 205.
81. Ibid., 207.
82. Ibid., 225.
83. Ibid., 207.
84. Goode and Ben-Yehuda, "Moral Panics: Culture, Politics, and Social Construction," 160.
85. Julia Dahl, "'Rebecca's Law' Aims to Punish Bullying in Fla.," *CBS News*, January 17, 2014, 3:56 PM, http://www.cbsnews.com/news/rebeccas-law-aims-to-punish-bullying-in-florida/ (accessed December 30, 2015).
86. Sameer Hinduja and Justin Patchin, "Bullying, Cyberbullying and Suicide," *Archives of Suicide Research* 14 (2010): 206.

87. Sergey Brin and Lawrence Page, "The Anatomy of a Large-Scale Hypertextual Web Search Engine," Computer Science Department, Stanford University, http://infolab.stanford.edu/~backrub/google.html (accessed December 30, 2015).
88. Eric Goode and Nachman Ben-Yehuda, "Moral Panics: An Introduction," in *Critical Readings: Moral Panics and the Media*, (Maidenhead: Open University Press, 2006), ed. Chas Critcher, 51.
89. 16 V.S.A. § 570. Harassment, hazing and bullying prevention policies, http://www.wvwvermont.org/cgi-bin/vt_legis/fullsection.cfm?form_access_date=20151106&Title=16&Chapter=009&Section=00570 (accessed December 30, 2015).
90. Richard Koman, "Megan's Law: Mo. Prosecutors Using New Cyberbullying Laws," *Zdnet.com*, December 21, 2008, http://www.zdnet.com/article/megans-law-mo-prosecutors-using-new-cyberbullying-laws/ (accessed December 30, 2015).
91. H.R.1966—Megan Meier Cyberbullying Prevention Act, 111th Congress (2009–2010).
92. Richard Wilson, "New State Law Gives School Districts Reach to Punish Cyberbullying," *The Springfield News-Sun*, February 14, 2012, 10:42 AM, http://www.springfieldnewssun.com/news/news/local/new-state-law-gives-school-districts-reach-to-pu-1/nMyqm/ (accessed December 30, 2015).
93. Tyler Clementi Higher Education Anti-Harassment Act of 2011, S. 540, 112th Congress (2011), https://www.congress.gov/bill/112th-congress/senate-bill/540/text/is (accessed December 30, 2015).
94. Andre Mayer, "New Cyberbullying Law has 'Larger Agenda,' Expands Police Powers," *CBC News*, November 22, 2013, 9:51 AM ET, http://www.cbc.ca/news/canada/new-cyberbullying-law-has-larger-agenda-expands-police-powers-1.2434797 (accessed December 30, 2015).
95. "The Top Six Unforgettable Cyberbulling Cases Ever," September 10, 2015, *NoBullying.com*, http://nobullying.com/six-unforgettable-cyber-bullying-cases/ (accessed December 30, 2015).
96. Ann Curry, "Bullied Girl's Suicide has Ongoing Impact," *NBC News*, December 28, 2011, 5:50 PM, http://usnews.nbcnews.com/_news/2011/12/28/9781587-bullied-girls-suicide-has-ongoing-impact?lite (accessed December 30, 2015).
97. Jan Hoffman, "Online Bullies Pull Schools into the Fray," *New York Times*, June 27, 2010, http://www.nytimes.com/2010/06/28/style/28bully.html (accessed December 30, 2015).
98. Mark Joseph Stern, "The Legal Difficulties of Fighting Cyberbullying," *Slate*, July 9, 2014, 9:59 AM, http://www.slate.com/blogs/outward/2014/07/09/are_cyberbullying_laws_unconstitutional.html (accessed December 31, 2015).
99. Joe Palazzolla, "Cyberbullying Law Challenged in Court," *Wall Street Journal*, June 4, 2014, 7:45 PM ET, http://www.wsj.com/articles/cyberbullying-law-challenged-in-court-1401925445 (accessed December 30, 2015).
100. David L. Hudson Jr., "NY High Court Says Anti-Cyberbullying Law Won't Pass First Amendment Muster," *American Bar Association Journal*, November 1, 2014, 5:20 AM CDT, http://www.abajournal.com/magazine/article/bully_fighting_new_yorks_high_court_says_anti_cyberbullying_law_wont_pass_f (accessed December 31, 2015).
101. Sarah Jeong, "Revenge Porn Is Bad. Criminalizing It Is Worse," *Wired.com*, October 28, 2013, 9:30 AM, http://www.wired.com/2013/10/why-criminalizing-revenge-porn-is-a-bad-idea/ (accessed December 30, 2015).

102. Associated Press, "State to Pay Fees, Costs for Challenge to Revenge Porn Law," *Arizona Capitol Times*, August 4, 2015, 6:42 AM, http://azcapitoltimes.com/news/2015/08/04/state-to-pay-fees-costs-for-challenge-to-revenge-porn-law/#ixzz3mbV8Xnsk (accessed December 31, 2015).
103. Sameer Hinduja and Justin Patchin, "State Sexting Laws," Cyberbullying Research Center, 2015, http://www.cyberbullying.us/state-sexting-laws.pdf (accessed December 31, 2015).
104. Goode and Ben-Yehuda, "Moral Panics: An Introduction," 51.
105. "Breaking Point: Fed Up Sheriff Speaks Out on Bullying Arrests," *NBC Today*, October 16, 2013, http://www.today.com/video/sheriff-we-wont-tolerate-cyberbullying-54498371841 (accessed December 31, 2015).
106. Ibid.
107. Ibid.
108. Michael Kruse, "Polk Sheriff Grady Judd Makes His Name on Moral Outrage," *Tampa Bay Times*, February 4, 2011, 12:24 PM, http://www.tampabay.com/news/publicsafety/polk-sheriff-grady-judd-makes-his-name-on-moral-outrage/1149570 (accessed December 31, 2015).
109. *NBC Today*, "Breaking Point: Fed Up Sheriff Speaks Out on Bullying Arrests."
110. Ipsos Global Public Affairs, "One in Ten (12%) Parents Online, Around the World Say Their Child Has Been Cyberbullied, 26% Say They Know of a Child Who Has Experienced Same in Their Community," January 9, 2012, http://www.ipsos-na.com/news-polls/pressrelease.aspx?id=5462 (accessed January 5, 2016).
111. "Many Canadians Believe Bullying Should Be Considered a Crime," *Angus Reid Public Opinion*, February 29, 2012, http://angusreidglobal.com/wp-content/uploads/2012/02/2012.02.29_Bullying_CAN.pdf (accessed January 5, 2016).
112. Stuart Dredge, "Online Harassment Experienced by 40% of US Internet Users, Study Says," *The Guardian*, October 22, 2014, 10:04 EDT, http://www.theguardian.com/technology/2014/oct/22/young-women-harassment-online-pew-games (accessed January 5, 2016).
113. Ibid.
114. Goode and Ben-Yehuda, "Moral Panics: Culture, Politics, and Social Construction," 167.
115. Goode and Ben-Yehuda, "Moral Panics: An Introduction," 52.
116. Mary deYoung, "Folk Devils Reconsidered," in *Moral Panic and the Politics of Anxiety*, ed. Sean P. Hier (London: Routledge, 2011), 118–20.
117. Lindsay Hoffman, "Public Shamming on the Internet," *The Blog*, http://www.huffington-post.com/lindsay-hoffman/public-shaming-on-the-internet_b_6849036.html (accessed January 6, 2016).
118. American Psychological Association (Press Release), "Dealing with Cyberworld's Dark Side," August 6, 2011, http://www.apa.org/news/press/releases/2011/08/cyberworld.aspx (accessed January 6, 2016).
119. Fabio Sticca and Sonja Perrin, "Is Cyberbullying Worse Than Traditional Bullying? Examining the Differential Roles of Medium, Publicity, and Anonymity for the Perceived Severity of Bullying," *Journal of Youth and Adolescence* 42 (2013): 739–50.
120. Government of Canada Department of Justice, *A Handbook for Police and Crown Prosecutors on Criminal Harassment*, July 1, 2015, http://www.justice.gc.ca/eng/rp-pr/cj-jp/fv-vf/har/part1.html (accessed January 6, 2016).
121. Ibid.

122. Philip Jenkins, *Moral Panic: Changing Concepts of the Child Molester in Modern America* (New Haven: Yale University Press, 1998), 238.
123. Dan Merica, "Lewinsky Makes Emotional Plea to End Cyberbullying," *CNN*, October 21, 2014, Updated 12:19 ET PM, http://www.cnn.com/2014/10/20/politics/lewinsky-cyber-bullying/index.html (accessed January 6, 2016).
124. Monica Lewinsky, "The Price of Shame," *TED*, March 2015, https://www.ted.com/talks/monica_lewinsky_the_price_of_shame?language=en (accessed January 6, 2015).
125. Leslie Yalof Garfield, "The Case for a Criminal Law Theory of Intentional Infliction of Emotional Distress," *American University Law Brief* 5 (2009): 33–50, http://digital-commons.wcl.american.edu/cgi/viewcontent.cgi?article=1069&context=clb (accessed January 6, 2016).
126. John Kircher, "The Four Faces of Tort Law: Liability for Emotional Harm," *Marquette Law Review* 90 (2007): 800.
127. Hustler Magazine v. Falwell, 485 U.S. 770 (1984).
128. New York Times v. Sullivan, 376 U.S. 254 (1964).
129. Phyliss Stark, "Curt Schilling Gets Revenge on Cyber Bullies Harassing his Daughter," *Scripps Media*, March 3, 2015, http://www.scrippsmedia.com/now-trending/Curt-Schilling-gets-revenge-on-cyber-bullies-harassing-his-teen-daughter-294878531.html (accessed January 7, 2016).
130. David Just, "Video: Ashley Judd Says She's Pressing Charges after Twitter Threats," *Chicago Sun-Times*, March 17, 2015, 12:44 PM, http://chicago.suntimes.com/basket-ball/7/71/447881/video-ashley-judd-says-shes-pressing-charges-twitter-threats (accessed January 7, 2015).
131. Goode and Ben-Yehuda, "Moral Panics: Culture, Politics, and Social Construction," 157.
132. Sameer Hindaju and Justin W. Patch, "Cyberbullying: Identification, Prevention, and Response," Cyberbullying Research Center, http://www.wcs.edu/gms1/wp-content/uploads/sites/87/2014/05/Cyberbullying_Identification_Prevention_Response_Fact_Sheet.pdf (accessed January 7, 2016).
133. Vicki Panaccione, "The Effects of Cyberbullying—A Real Threat to Your Children," *Better Parent Institute*, November 12, 2010, http://www.betterparentinginstitute.com/Better-Parenting/parenting-child-raising-skills/cyberbullying-a-real-threat-to-your-kids (accessed January 7, 2016).
134. Naomi Harlin Goodno, "How Public Schools Can Constitutionally Halt Cyberbullying," *Wake Forest Law Review* 46 (2011): 641.
135. Marquan, 24 N.Y. 3d at 5.
136. Angela Pertusini, "Cyberbullying is a New Threat to Children," *The Telegraph*, June 23, 2011, 4 PM, BST, http://www.telegraph.co.uk/education/educationadvice/8593880/Cyberbullying-is-a-new-threat-for-children.html (accessed January 7, 2016).
137. Don Dahler, "12-Year-Old's Suicide Spotlights Cyber-Bullying Threat," *CBSnews.com*, September 14, 2014 PM, http://www.cbsnews.com/news/12-year-olds-suicide-spotlights-cyber-bullying-threat/ (accessed January 8, 2016).
138. Civil Rights Legal Project, "What is Revenge Porn," https://www.cyberrightsproject.com (accessed January 8, 2016).
139. Goode and Ben-Yehuda, "Moral Panics: Culture, Politics, and Social Construction," 158.

140. Dan Olweus, "Invited Expert Discussion Paper. Cyberbullying: An Overrated Phenomenon?," *European Journal of Developmental Psychology* 9 (2012): 520–38, 522, http://blogs.edweek.org/edweek/inside-school-research/Cyberbullying,%20Olweus.pdf (accessed January 8, 2016).
141. Ibid., 521.
142. Ibid., 528.
143. Ibid., 526.
144. Ibid., 529.
145. Ibid., 538.
146. Larry Magid, "Let's Not Create a Cyberbullying Panic," *C/Net*, April 7, 2010, http://www.cnet.com/news/lets-not-create-a-cyberbullying-panic (accessed January 8, 2016).
147. Justin W. Patchin, "Cyberbullying Moral Panic?," Cyberbullying Research Center, April 8, 2010, http://cyberbullying.org/cyberbullying-panic (accessed January 8, 2016).
148. Stopbullying.gov, "What to Avoid," http://www.stopbullying.gov/news/media/avoid/index.html (accessed January 8, 2016).
149. Maeve Duggan et al., "Concerns about Children, Social Media and Technology Use," *Pew Research Center: Internet, Science and Tech*, July 16, 2015, http://www.pewinternet.org/2015/07/16/concerns-about-children-social-media-and-technology-use (accessed January 8, 2016).
150. Amanda Lenhart et al., "Teens, Kindness and Cruelty on Social Media Sites," *Pew Research Center Internet Science & Technology*, November 9, 201, http://www.pewinternet.org/2011/11/09/teens-kindness-and-cruelty-on-social-network-sites (accessed January 9, 2016).
151. Goode and Ben-Yehuda, "Moral Panics: Culture, Politics, and Social Construction," 158.
152. Ibid., 159.
153. Stuart Hall et al., *Policing the Crisis: Mugging, the State and Law and Order* (London: MacMillan, 2013).
154. Ibid., 392.
155. Roger Simon, "How a Murderer and Rapist Became the Bush Campaign's Most Valuable Player," *The Baltimore Sun*, November 11, 1930, http://articles.baltimoresun.com/1990-11-11/features/1990315149_1_willie-horton-fournier-michael-dukakis (accessed January 8, 2016).
156. CNN Library, "Trayvon Martin Shooting Facts," *CNN.com*, February 11, 2015, 2:38 PM ET, http://www.cnn.com/2013/06/05/us/trayvon-martin-shooting-fast-facts/index.html (accessed January 9, 2016).
157. Critcher, *Critical Readings: Moral Panics and the Media*, 12.
158. Goode and Ben-Yehuda, "Moral Panics: Culture, Politics, and Social Construction," 159.
159. State v. Leidecker, P3/11-2685 (R.I. July 30, 2014), http://www.washingtonpost.com/news/volokh-conspiracy/wp-content/uploads/sites/14/2014/10/Leidecker.pdf (accessed September 7, 2016).
160. Abigail Pesta, "Who Are You Calling a Bully," *Cosmopolitan*, April 8, 2014, http://www.cosmopolitan.com/lifestyle/advice/a6303/twelve-year-old-bully/ (accessed August 16, 2016).

· 2 ·

CYBERBULLYING AND FREE SPEECH

Here is one set of rap lyrics Anthony Douglas "Tone-Dougie" Elonis posted on his Facebook page about his estranged wife that made him the subject of a U.S. Supreme Court ruling.

> Did you know that it's illegal for me to say I want to kill my wife?
> It's illegal.
> It's indirect criminal contempt.
> It's one of the only sentences that I'm not allowed to say.
> Now it was okay for me to say it right then because I was just telling you that it's illegal for me to say I want to kill my wife.
> I'm not actually saying it.
> I'm just letting you know that it's illegal for me to say that.
> It's kind of like a public service.
> I'm letting you know so that you don't accidently go out and say something like that
> Um, what's interesting is that it's very illegal to say I really, really think someone out there should kill my wife.
> That's illegal.
> Very, very illegal.
> But not illegal to say with a mortar launcher.
> Because that's its own sentence.
> It's an incomplete sentence but it may have nothing to do with the sentence before that. So that's perfectly fine.

> Perfectly legal.
>
> I also found out that it's incredibly illegal, extremely illegal, to go on Facebook and say something like the best place to fire a mortar launcher at her house would be from the cornfield behind it because of easy access to a getaway road and you'd have a clear line of sight through the sun room.
>
> Insanely illegal.
>
> Ridiculously, wrecklessly, insanely illegal.
>
> Yet even more illegal to show an illustrated diagram.
>
> Insanely illegal.
>
> Ridiculously, horribly felonious.
>
> Cause they will come to my house in the middle of the night and they will lock me up.
>
> Extremely against the law.
>
> Uh, one thing that is technically legal to say is that we have a group that meets Fridays at my parent's house and the password is sic simper tyrannis.[1]

Police arrested Elonis, a former amusement park worker from Pennsylvania's Lehigh Valley,[2] in December 2010 and indicted him on 15 counts of threatening to injure someone under 18 U.S.C. § 875(c).[3] If it is valid to define cyberbullying as expansively as "bullying that takes place using electronic technology,"[4] then Elonis engaged in it. There is, however, no such thing as a federal cyberbullying statute. (There is a federal cyberstalking statute, which is discussed later in this chapter.) Instead, Elonis was charged with making an illegal threat under federal law, and the Constitution does not protect true threats.

> "True threats" encompass those statements where the speaker means to communicate a serious expression of an intent to commit an act of unlawful violence to a particular individual or group of individuals. The speaker need not actually intend to carry out the threat. Rather, a prohibition on true threats "protect[s] individuals from the fear of violence" and "from the disruption that fear engenders," in addition to protecting people "from the possibility that the threatened violence will occur."[5]

Elonis, however, said he meant no harm. His postings were "therapeutic" and "cathartic," a way for him to overcome the pain caused by separating from his wife, and, he also argued, that posting lyrics similar to Eminen's raps about wanting to kill his ex-wife were artistic expression protected under the First Amendment-protected.[6]

It was a losing defense at the trial level. So, when Elonis's appeal of his conviction reached the Supreme Court, some saw the case as a possible turning point in the fight against hostile online speech because "the court hasn't yet looked at the question of true threats through the lens of modern technology."[7]

The Court, however, did not deliver the watershed ruling some had anticipated. The scope of its review was narrow—"The question is whether the statute also requires that the defendant be aware of the threatening nature of the communication, and—if not—whether the First Amendment requires such a showing."[8] The majority of the Court reversed his conviction, ruling that it was essential that the jury have found that Elonis had intended to intimidate, not merely that a reasonable person would foresee that his lyrics would be interpreted by recipients as a serious expression of an intention to inflict bodily injury or take the life of an individual.[9]

The ruling was a victory for free speech, and a setback to anti-cyberbullying advocates. Had the Court upheld Elonis's conviction, the fate of cyberbullies and entertainers who appear to threaten others by using hyperbole, double entendre and artistic language would have been largely left up to what juries reasonably believed was threating language. In its aftermath, some anti-cyberbullying activists, such as criminologist Justin W. Patchin, lamented, "Unfortunately we aren't any closer to understanding the point at which online speech crosses the line to become a crime. Am I now free to post comments of a threatening nature so long as I include the caveat that I do not intend them as a threat? What if I include 'JK' or a smiley-faced emoji?"[10]

The short answer to Patchin's question is no. Such signals would not provide immunity from conviction because a prosecutor's duty is to show guilt beyond a reasonable doubt. As Eugene Volokh, a UCLA School of Law professor and publisher of the blog, "The Volokh Conspiracy," explained,

> Usually, if someone says something that a reasonable person would perceive as threatening, the speaker would likely also know that the target would perceive it as threatening … I expect a jury would conclude—even beyond a reasonable doubt—that Elonis did indeed know that his wife would perceive the speech as threatening (even if he didn't have the purpose of threatening her, but was just trying to work out his frustrations in artistic expression, which seems to be his theory). To be sure, in some situations there might be a plausible case that there was just an unfortunate misunderstanding, or a joke gone wrong. The defendant might plausibly argue that he was just goofing around, and didn't know anyone would take the statement seriously, or that he meant one thing and didn't know the subject of the statement would understand it as meaning another.[11]

On remand, the U.S. Court of Appeals for the Third Circuit reinstated Elonis's conviction, ruling that the flawed jury instructions amounted to harmless error because the record contained "overwhelming evidence demonstrating beyond a reasonable doubt that Elonis knew the threatening nature of his communications."[12] The Third Circuit, however, did not address which mens rea standard—specific intent, recklessness or negligence—was required under 18 U.S.C. § 875(c). Still, *Elonis* has the potential to upend cyberbullying statutes and convictions that only take into account a jury's objective view of a speaker's statements intent to intimidate. That is precisely the rationale an Illinois appeals panel in *People v. Relerford* (2016) applied when it struck down provisions of a state stalking and cyberstalking statute.[13]

The First Amendment Makes Criminalizing Cyberbullying Complicated and Nuanced

Banning cyberbullying is a complicated and nuanced undertaking. Yet, as the multitude of poorly drafted cyberbullying statutes passed by state lawmakers since 2008 attests, many think otherwise. These lawmakers, however, have ignored or glossed over the limits imposed on government by at least 60 years of First Amendment precedents. Thus, this chapter's purpose is to identity the types of statutes targeting hostile online expression, or cyberbullying, and the relevant free expression doctrines and recent rulings in which courts have struck down laws that specifically criminalize cyberbullying or stopped schools from imposing civil penalties on students for the off-campus, online speech.

At the turn of the century, few anticipated that so many individuals—minors and adults—would use digital technologies to post, phone, or email crude and caustic comments about others, or transmit sexually provocative or explicit photos of themselves and others. When the public learned through the news media that teens were committing suicide allegedly because they were hounded or embarrassed by hostile social media postings, many were just as shocked to learn that no state specifically banned what became known as cyberbullying.

By early 2014, however, almost every state had enacted laws criminalizing online hostile expression whether it was labeled cyberstalking, cyberharassment, cyberbullying, teen sexting or revenge porn. Some states amended their offline criminal harassment and stalking laws to cover online speech. Others devised new laws. States also passed laws and imposed policies authorizing public schools to punish cyberbullies.

It is widely recognized that cyberbullying can cause harm, mostly emotional distress. But do boorish misuses of social media justify abandoning long-held First Amendment free speech protections to criticize elected officials and public and private figures? In other words, is this current frenzy to censor speech justified under the First Amendment? Of course, advocates, legislators and prosecutors deny that their intentions are to undermine freedom of expression. But as this text will document, many of the new anti-cyberbullying laws, in their language and application, censor constitutionally protected speech.

Defining Cyberbullying

Lock several sociologists and psychologists in a room and, most likely, they will still fail to reach a consensus on cyberbullying's definition. The concept's meaning is still murky and evolving; it is a catchall for various words and conduct. Cyberbullying covers a wide range of speech disseminated via digital and electronic communication and psychologists, sociologists and educators offer several, often vague, and sometimes inconsistent, descriptions of its characteristics. (There is, however, no debate about online bullies' digital tools of choice. For instance, one 2013 literature review identified the following online sites—"email (21%), online chatrooms (20%), social networking sites (20%) and mobile phones (19%) … Other websites (8%) and other forms of texting, such as Twitter (6%), were also reported.)"[14]

In contrast, another literature review identified eight different definitions offered by experts, ranging from "willful and repeated harm inflicted through the medium of electronic text"; to "anything that someone does that upsets or offends someone else"; to "[i]ncludes bullying: (a) through text messaging, (b) through pictures/photos or video clips, (c) through phone calls, (d) through e-mail, (e) in chat rooms, (f) through instant messaging, and (g) through websites. Bullying can happen through text messages/pictures/clips/e-mail/messages/etc. sent to you, but also when text messages/pictures/clips/e-mail/messages/etc. are sent to others about you."[15]

The author of the literature review, Bobby Tokunaga, who studies the social and psychological implications of using communication technologies, rightly argues that, "the need for an integrative definition of cyberbullying is crucial for both conceptual and operational clarity," and offers his corrective definition: "Cyberbullying is any behavior performed through electronic or digital media by individuals or groups that repeatedly communicates hostile or aggressive messages intended to inflict harm or discomfort on others."[16]

As a matter of common sense, none of the above definitions could be codified into a feasible criminal law. Were it so, there would not be enough jails and prisons in the U.S. to house the thousands of online users—citizen bloggers and professional pundits, included—arrested and prosecuted for vitriolic tweeting, blogging and spewing venom on other social media platforms that upset or offended someone, or were intended to inflict discomfort on others. Under the demanding standards of U.S. constitutional law, even Tokunaga's corrective falls short. Neither Tokunaga's nor the other psychological-sociological descriptions would pass constitutionally scrutiny as they are either impermissibly vague[17] or overbroad.[18] How many times does a message have to be repeated to qualify as "repeated?" Is two times sufficient? Is it three, following the baseball tradition of "three strikes your out"? What level of harm is too much? Is annoyance sufficient? Similarly, under the First Amendment student speech doctrine,[19] which recognizes public school students' limited free expression rights, middle and high school classrooms might not be half full if school administrators suspended every student who was caught communicating a hostile or discomforting message.

It has long been settled that offensive language is protected under the First Amendment.[20] Therefore, a cyberbullying definition that includes "offends someone else" cannot be the basis for criminal or civil prosecution of speech. Nevertheless, you can find cyberbullying statutes on the books that include such language and other imprecise definitions and problematic words used by social scientists, psychologists, educators and lay persons mostly because legislators have not heeded the words of civil libertarians and no one has challenged the constitutionality of a particular flawed statute.

A Taxonomy of Cyberbullying Statutes

Generally, statutes regulating hostile online speech fall into six classifications:

1. public school-related laws that impose non-criminal penalties;
2. statutes that impose criminal sanctions on minors;
3. state cyberharassment criminal statutes targeting adults;
4. state and federal cyberstalking statutes;
5. laws targeting sexting by and to minors, including federal child pornography laws, banning the production, distribution, reception, and possession of a sexually explicit image of child; and
6. revenge porn or "non-consensual pornography" statutes.

These categories are fluid. For example, though criminal sanctions to protect minors might not be labeled as "cyberharassment," they are in effect applying harassment law to cyberbullying. Some states and the federal government have statutes that combine the terms of harassment and stalking in a single law, and, depending on the specific terms describing the prohibited conduct such as "a knowing pattern of conduct or a series of acts directed at a specific person," courts may treat them like stalking laws though some legislatures have labeled them harassment.[21] Likewise, cyberstalking and criminal harassment statutes may be used to punish some forms of revenge porn. All, however, depending on their language and applications, raise First Amendment free expression concerns. The U.S. Supreme Court, however, has yet to rule on the constitutionality of any cyberbullying statute.

Free Speech Values

Those who seek to censor cyberbullying say the online version of schoolyard bullying, irreverent contempt for authority, adolescent foreplay (sexting) and expressions of vindictiveness (revenge porn) have little value society should recognize. Yet, virtually all of the statutes criminalizing cyberbullying—contemplated or enacted since since 2007—strike at one or more of the core values of free expression such as self-governance,[22] dissent,[23] self-fulfillment,[24] the right to engage in controversial expression,[25] "to let off steam" or the safety valve function,[26] or the right to express outrageous opinions that violate "common canons of decency."[27]

For example, a teenager who humiliates another teenager online may be responding to previous offline bullying or may have a legitimate belief that he or she has been wronged. Though not the ideal ethical way to respond, isn't it better that the aggrieved teenager throw a verbal jab instead of a physical one in retaliation? That form of cyberbullying would qualify as an exercise of the safety valve function. Though parents might disapprove, a minor who sends a nude selfie to a boyfriend or girlfriend is engaging in self-fulfilling speech, expressing and exploring his or her sexual identity.

As discussed below, prosecutors have used cyberbullying charges to punish adults who have posted parodies of, or vile and hostile statements about elected officials. Such statements are expressions of dissent, the safety valve function and the right to engage in controversial expression. Additionally, political parodies and harsh statements are "political speech," or "speech on public issues which occupies the 'highest rung of the hierarchy of First Amendment values,' and is entitled to special protection."[28]

There is social value even in some revenge porn, the sharing of explicit photos and videos without the victim's consent. Consider if Huma Abedin, the wife of ex-New York Congressman Anthony Weiner, had outed her serial tweeting flashing husband motivated by a feeling of betrayal and spite and posted his revealing selfies as evidence. Such an act would be a form of revenge porn. Yet, despite her motivations, Abedin expressive conduct would have provided voters with valuable information about an elected official. (Many revenge porn statutes provide a "public interest" clause that would exempt such a disclosure.)

Even if we accept the characterization of cyberbullying as low value speech, the U.S. Supreme Court has said that speech lacking "serious" value, a standard used to judge whether sexual explicit content is constitutionally unprotected obscenity, is not applicable to non-sexual expression. "Most of what we say to one another lacks 'religious, political, scientific, educational, journalistic, historical, or artistic value' (let alone serious value), but it is still sheltered from government regulation."[29] Accordingly, the diminished value of some types of cyberbullying expression does not justify censorship.

Free Speech Rights

More legally significant, however, many criminal cyberbullying statutes ban speech that falls outside the well-established categories of constitutionally unprotected expression—true threats,[30] fighting words,[31] incitement,[32] speech integral to criminal conduct,[33] intentional infliction of emotional distress,[34] obscenity, defamation, and fraud.[35] In other words, anti-cyberbullying laws, which are content-based restrictions on expression, can only criminalize speech that falls within the established proscribed categories, unless there is a long tradition of regulating the speech.[36] The Court presumes that new categories of criminalized speech are unconstitutional unless a state can persuade them otherwise.[37]

Cyberbullying laws raise other constitutional concerns. Many cyberbullying criminal statutes are problematic in their entirety, or in part, because legislators have used imprecise terms to define criminal culpability. Without a requirement that the speaker intended to cause serious emotional distress or malicious harm, terms such as "annoy" or "frighten" found in many cyberharassment statutes, are vulnerable to challenges under the substantially overbroad and void for vagueness doctrines. Otherwise, news outlets, particularly tabloids that traffic in sensationalism would be subject to criminal prosecution because a news consumer can be frightened or annoyed by alarming reports about pending hurricanes or Zika-carrying mosquitos, for example.

Overbreadth

Under the First Amendment overbreadth doctrine, a statute is overly broad when it deters individuals from exercising their legitimate rights because it "potentially covers a great deal of constitutionally protected speech," and its constitutionality should not "depend on prosecutorial discretion."[38] Generally, individuals challenging a statute on overbreadth grounds must show that it is unlawful as applied to them.[39] There is an exception. A First Amendment overbreadth challenge can take the form of a preemptive strike—a facial challenge, brought before anyone is charged with violating the statute and by individuals not directly affected by the statute's restrictions.[40] In such an action, plaintiffs argue that the language of the entire statute is substantially overbroad because "no set of circumstances exists under which it would be valid," or that the statute lacks any "plainly legitimate sweep."[41] Plaintiffs may also argue that a great number of a statute's applications are unconstitutional, even though other sections of it may be legitimately enforced.[42] The overbreadth doctrine gives courts the leeway to invalidate an entire statute, or strike down only the offending sections or terms.[43]

Vagueness

Even when speech is not at issue, the Constitution's due process-vagueness doctrine stems from the due process clauses of the Fifth and Fourteenth Amendments, and a court can strike down a statute when a person of ordinary intelligence cannot determine by the language of the statute whether his or her conduct is illegal.[44] The Constitution requires criminal laws to state explicitly what conduct is punishable.[45]

> Vague laws offend several important values. First, because we assume that man is free to steer between lawful and unlawful conduct, we insist that laws give the person of ordinary intelligence a reasonable opportunity to know what is prohibited, so that he may act accordingly. Vague laws may trap the innocent by not providing fair warning. Second, if arbitrary and discriminatory enforcement is to be prevented, laws must provide explicit standards for those who apply them. A vague law impermissibly delegates basic policy matters to policemen, judges, and juries for resolution on an *ad*

> *hoc* and subjective basis, with the attendant dangers of arbitrary and discriminatory application. Third, but related, where a vague statute "abut[s] upon sensitive areas of basic First Amendment freedoms," it "operates to inhibit the exercise of [those] freedoms." Uncertain meanings inevitably lead citizens to "steer far wider of the unlawful zone" … than if the boundaries of the forbidden areas were clearly marked.[46]

Laws that censor cyberbullying regulate the content of speech. Thus, the vagueness of such statutes raises "special First Amendment concerns because of its obvious chilling effect on free speech," the U.S. Supreme Court noted in *Reno v. ACLU* (1997).[47] That "chilling" effect is increased when a statute imposes criminal penalties, the Court said. "The severity of criminal sanctions may well cause speakers to remain silent rather than communicate even arguably unlawful words, ideas, and images … As a practical matter, this increased deterrent effect, coupled with the 'risk of discriminatory enforcement' of vague regulations, poses greater First Amendment concerns than those implicated by the civil regulation. …"[48] In sum, when speech is criminalized, a void-for-vagueness challenge asks: (1) are the terms of the statute sufficiently clear to afford individual or ordinary intelligence a reasonable opportunity to avoid the proscribed conduct, (2) do they provide clear standards for law enforcement and (3) are they clear enough to avoid chilling speech?

Strict Scrutiny

Laws that impose criminal penalties for cyberbullying can be challenged on strict scrutiny grounds. In the First Amendment-free speech context, courts apply strict scrutiny analysis to test the constitutionality of laws that restrict content.[49] Cyberbullying statutes seek to restrict particular types of words and images based on the topic or ideas conveyed, the particular types of words used, or the function or purpose of the message.

The strict scrutiny analysis requires government to show that a statute advances a compelling government interest and that its approach is the least restrictive means of achieving that interest.[50]

For example, cyberharassment laws punish based on a speaker's purpose—an intention to cause physical or serious emotional harm.[51] But do such laws stand up to the strict scrutiny? No doubt, the safety of minors would constitute a compelling government interest. However, there are many far less speech restrictive ways to combat youthful electronic harassment than criminal penalties such as revising Section 230 of the Communications Decency Act to require social media site owners to remove cyberbullying upon notification or sentencing youthful cyberbullies to education reform programs sans a criminal record. Also, in many cases, civil defamation is a more narrowly tailored remedy for many of the harms caused by cyberharasment. Accordingly, in the first ruling of its kind, *People v. Marquan* (2014), New York's highest court struck down a county's anti-cyberbullying law because it was overbroad, vague and did not withstand strict scrutiny, even though the "statute was motivated by the laudable public purpose of shielding children from cyberbullying."[52]

Overcriminalization

Under the related concept of overcriminalization, or "[e]xcessive reliance upon the criminal law to perform tasks for which it is ill-suited,"[53] criminal cyberbullying statutes are at "odds with basic tenets of the criminal law," legal experts argue.[54] A former attorney for the Israel National Police turned law professor, Michal Buchhandler-Raphael, lists the following reasons why "cyberbulling is just not one of the cases justifying criminal sanction":

> First, criminalizing cyberbullying is in tension with criminal law theory that generally rejects negligence as sufficient mens rea ... Second, grounding criminal liability on the endangerment justification raises insurmountable problems of causation ... Suicide is too remote and unforeseeable consequence of bullying. Proving the nexus between the cyberbullying and the ensuing suicide beyond a reasonable doubt is an impossible requirement to meet at a criminal trial ... Finally, criminal statutes against cyberbullying are unwarranted because they are passed in response to public outcry exerting political pressure on legislatures to provide harsh criminal sanctions ... In response to several high-publicized bullying-related suicides, legislatures have adopted excessively severe measures in an attempt to appear "tough on bullying."[55]

Overcriminalization worried U.S. Representative Louie Gohmert (R-TX) during the discussions of the proposed federal Megan Meier Cyberbullying Prevent Act. (The bill, first sponsored by U.S. Rep. Linda Sanchez in 2008, died in committee because of First Amendment concerns.)[56]

> Consider this: The playground still has bullies. When a bully beats up a smaller student and the smaller student goes home, gets on the Internet and says the playground bully is mean, ugly, and stupid, it is the smaller student victim that has now probably committed a Federal felony under this proposed law ... Although it is tempting because the proposal before us would allow me to pursue and seek indictment and arrest for mean-spirited liberals who have been exceedingly mean to me and my family, it appears to be another chapter in overcriminalization.[57]

Though the U.S. Supreme Court has yet to examine the issue of the constitutionality of criminal cyberbullying statutes, a handful of such criminal statutes already have wilted under judicial scrutiny, as discussed in this chapter and elsewhere in this text. The Court also has failed to give specific guidance to states on how to regulate online, off-campus student speech, sexting or revenge porn, though the current efforts to police such expression by state legislatures raise constitutional concerns, leaving state and federal appeals courts to grapple with these emerging free expression controversies.

Cyberbullying: A Concept with Many Faces

We think we know illegal hostile online expression when we see it. But most of us do not. Not really. Leading bullying expert Dan Olweus says an individual is bullied in the traditional in-your-face at-the-playground sense when "he or she is exposed, repeatedly and over time, to negative actions on the part of one or more other persons, and he or she has difficulty defending himself or herself."[58] Of course, traditional playground bullies have always thrown verbal jabs—("Your mother wears combat boots"). Cyberbullying is verbal, except when images are used. Though both types of bullying can cause emotional and psychological trauma, online bullying is never physical. That distinction makes a significant difference in the eyes of the law, as explained below.

Some insist that the medium is what makes cyberbullying different from offline bullying—that cyberspace's anonymity, near permanence and universality ratchets up the message's sting.[59] Others say it is not more psychologically damaging than offline bullying. For instance, one set of researchers was surprised to find "that students who had been *traditionally* bullied rated their bullying experience as harsher than those who had been cyberbullied."[60]

Monica Lewinsky thinks she knows what unacceptable cyberbullying is. The ex-White House intern, who became internationally known for her affair with President Bill Clinton, resurfaced in 2015 and wrapped herself in the mantle of victimhood. "I was branded a tramp, tart, slut, whore, bimbo and, of course, that woman," said Lewinsky in March 2015. "When this happened to me 17 years ago, there was no name for it. Now it's called cyberbullying and online harassment."[61]

Lewinsky has not called for a legislative response to cyberbullying, but rather a return to "a long-held value of compassion—compassion and empathy. Online, we've got a compassion deficit, an empathy crisis."[62]

"Vehement, Caustic, and Sometimes Unpleasantly Sharp Attacks"

Lewinsky, however, is calling for a level of civil public discourse about public officials and figures that the U.S. Supreme Court has never required under the First Amendment. As U.S. Supreme Court Justice William Brennan noted more than 50 years ago in the landmark *New York Times v. Sullivan* (1964) libel ruling, our nation is deeply committed "to the principle that debate on public issues should be uninhibited, robust, and wide-open, and that it may well include vehement, caustic, and sometimes unpleasantly sharp attacks on government and public officials."[63]

Just amend "vehement, caustic, and sometimes unpleasantly sharp attacks" with online and you have another way of describing cyberbullying. The First Amendment free expression principle identified by Justice Brennan was cited in the context of libel law. Yet, some have argued, most notably legal scholars Susan W. Brenner and Megan Rehberg, for resuscitating criminal libel to combat cyberbullying by adolescents aimed at private figures.

> Logically, a cyberbully could be prosecuted for criminal defamation if he or she (i) published information to one or more persons (ii) that was false and (iii) had the capacity to provoke a breach of the peace or expose the person it concerned to public hatred, contempt, or ridicule. Since our definition of cyberbullying assumes that a bully uses modern communications technology to disseminate information about his or her victim, the first requirement should by definition be met in any cyberbullying case. The second and third requirements are similarly unproblematic; the prosecution will have to prove that the information disseminated by the bully was false and that it had the potential for inflicting the requisite harm(s) on the victim.[64]

Yet, it is rare, for prosecutors to bring criminal libel charges for speech that defames a public official, or public or private figures because it has been long recognized that criminal defamation is an out dated concept. In 1961, the American Law Institute, which organizes and clarifies the status of state laws, recommended in a draft of its Model Penal Code that libel not be criminalized:

> Usually we reserve the criminal law for harmful behavior which exceptionally disturbs the community's sense of security. It seems evident that personal calumny falls in neither of these classes in the U.S.A., that it is therefore inappropriate for penal control, and that this probably accounts for the paucity of prosecutions and the near desuetude of private criminal libel legislation in this country.[65]

Today, a minority of states has criminal defamation laws on its books—as of May 2015, only 13—Florida, Idaho, Kansas, Louisiana, Michigan, Montana, New Hampshire, North Carolina, North Dakota, Oklahoma, Utah, Virginia and Wisconsin.[66] If those statutes are to be applied constitutionally, they must conform to the First Amendment defamation law standard of reckless disregard for the truth or knowing falsity standards, or actual malice, for statements concerning public matters and public figures, as required by *New York Times v. Sullivan* and its progeny.[67] Additionally, under *Milkovich v. Lorraine Journal*, the First Amendment protects loose figurative language and rhetorical hyperbole because the average person does not take their meaning to be literal descriptions and opinion or they do not imply a verifiably false factual assertion.[68]

Combined, those two constitutional requirements make it difficult to win a criminal case against online speakers who engage in caustic speech aimed at public figures, such as politicians and celebrities, or about public controversies and events. Consider the venom spewed online at movie actress and University of Kentucky basketball fan Ashley Judd after she tweeted that an opposing team engaged in unsportsmanlike conduct. Judd said individuals tweeted back calling her "a cunt, a whore or a bitch, or telling me to suck a two-inch dick. Some even threatened rape, or 'anal anal anal.'"[69]

Judd, who said, "And by the way, I'm pressing charges,"[70] thinks she knows illegal cyberbullying when she sees it. But her case seems meritless, particularly given her public figure status. The name-calling and slurs are despicably sexist and profane. Yet, each slur is constitutionally protected figurative language, with the possible exception of the threats of rape, which might constitute a true threat.[71] Still, given the context of the tweets—sports trash talk—it is unlikely that a prosecutor could prove that the vile tweeters intended to intimidate her or that a reasonable person would regard the tweets as a serious expression, a standard required under the First Amendment.[72]

What about online private defamers? Could prosecutors use criminal libel to punish cyberbullies who target individuals who are not famous? Brenner and Rehberg cited *Mink v. Knox*, a 2008 federal court ruling, to support their argument that a "criminal libel statute could be applied … 'to private defamers who knowingly publish or disseminate … any statement or object tending … to impeach the honesty, integrity, virtue, or reputation of a private individual, even when no showing of actual malice is made.'"[73]

If that interpretation of the First Amendment is correct, it means that a cyberbully who publishes material defaming a private person (a student or teacher for the purposes of this analysis) can be charged with, and convicted of, criminal defamation as long as he or she published false material that actually inflicted or had the capacity to inflict the harm prohibited by the libel statute at issue. That would open up the possibility of using criminal liability against at least some cyberbullies.[74]

That possibility shrunk quickly. In a 2010 ruling, the U.S. Court of Appeals for the Tenth Circuit ruled that Colorado criminal libel defendants could invoke the opinion-hyperbole defense in cases involving defamers discussing private matters and individuals.[75] In 2012, Colorado decriminalized libel.[76] In 2015, Minnesota did the same in a case involving revenge porn, another form of cyberbullying,[77] leaving Brenner and Rehberg standing on fast sinking precedential ground.

Of note is Albany County legislators' unsuccessful attempt in *People v. Marquan* to save its cyberbullying statute by arguing that it was a defamation statute. Marquan's appeals lawyer, Corey Stoughton of the New York Civil Liberties Union, retorted that,

> The County cites no authority to establish that criminal penalties for defamation are constitutional at all in New York, let alone constitutional in the absence of a showing of "actual malice" (one of very few concepts the County has not attempted to read into the law). Thus, because the Cyber-bullying Law is not a defamation statute—and because, even if it were, it would exceed constitutional boundaries—the law should be struck down on its face as an unconstitutional, content-based regulation of speech.[78]

Accordingly, one would hope that no well-intentioned, clear thinking prosecutor would bring criminal charges against a citizen who makes nasty online statements about public controversies, government officials and other public figures. Yet, that is precisely what has occurred. In effect, prosecutors are using cyberbullying charges in attempts to sidestep First Amendment barriers. In July 2014, a Rhode Island Superior Court Judge overturned a guilty verdict on charges of cyberharassment and cyberstalking against John A. Leidecker, a teachers' union official who had created a fake email address, impersonated a state legislator and sent emails to the state legislature mocking his positions on several political issues.[79] Michael Adams, a former New Britain, Ct., police officer, wasn't as fortunate as Leidecker. Adams reluctantly pled guilty to a charge of breach of the peace and a suspended six-month jail term for saying that he hoped "an angry New Yorker would put a bullet in [Connecticut Governor Dannel] Malloy's head."[80] (See Chapter Five.)

"Without any reference to criminal libel laws, and indeed in jurisdictions where even criminal libel laws limited to false factual assertions have been repealed, some judges and legislatures seem to be responding to the same feeling that drove the old criminal libel laws: people should be legally barred from saying derogatory things (even opinions or true statements) about other people unless they have a good reason to do so," wrote UCLA law professor Volokh who has warned about the use of criminal harassment laws to censor online speech. "Courts should therefore reject the application to one-to-many speech, and legislatures should resist the broadening of such laws."[81]

Public School-related Cyberbullying Statutes

When most people speak of cyberbullying, they think of adolescents. They have a version of the following scenario in mind. A public school student uses social media to communicate, in words or in images, mean-spirited and, sometimes profane, things about school personnel and fellow students. Here is an example from *Snyder v. Blue Mountain School District*, a Pennsylvania case in which an Orwigsburg, Pa., School District suspended two eighth graders for creating a profane and insulting parody of their middle school principal on the home computer.

> HELLO CHILDREN[.] yes. it's your oh so wonderful, hairy, expressionless, sex addict, fagass, put on this world with a small dick PRINCIPAL[.] I have come to myspace so i can pervert the minds of other principal's [sic] to be just like me. I know, I know, youre all thrilled[.] Another reason I came to myspace is because—I am keeping an eye on you students (who[m] I care for so much)[.] For those who want to be my friend, and arent in my school[,] I love children, sex (any kind), dogs, long walks on the beach, tv, being a dick head, and last but not least my darling wife who looks like a man (who satisfies my needs) MY FRAINTRAIN. ...[82]

Terry Snyder and Steven Snyder, parents of one of the students, spent four years in court waging an eventually successful challenge, arguing that the First Amendment did not permit schools to discipline their daughter for her off-campus, online speech.[83] The Snyders were hardly unique. Starting in about 2008, other parents of public school students brought similar legal challenges. But legal precedents provided no clear-cut answers. The law had not caught up to the new social trend because U.S. Supreme Court rulings on students' free speech rights did not address the issue of online expression that is initiated off school grounds and after school hours.

For the most part, precedents in the area of free expression rights of public school students stem from controversies involving censoring public school newspapers or punishment for wearing controversial clothing, delivering vulgar speeches and other offline forms of expression. In 1969, the Court ruled that public school students have First Amendment free speech rights. Those rights, however, can be checked by a school's need to maintain discipline, order, and safety, and to protect the rights of other students. In *Tinker v. Des Moines School District*, the Court said schools could ban and punish speech "by a showing that the students' activities would materially and substantially disrupt the work and discipline of the school."[84] Later, the Court ruled that the First Amendment allows schools to ban lewd, indecent, and offensive speech. In *Bethel School District No. 403 v. Fraser*, the Court said, "The schools, as instruments of the state, may determine that the essential lessons of civil, mature conduct cannot be conveyed in a school that tolerates lewd, indecent, or offensive speech and conduct. …"[85]

In one ruling, *Morse v. Frederick*, the Court set mixed signals about the limits imposed on school administrators' authority to sanction student speech that occurs off school grounds.[86] In *Morse v. Frederick*, a student was suspended for holding up a sign that a principal said was pro-drug—"Bong Hits 4 JESUS"—at a school-supervised public event held on a public street. Because the event occurred in a public forum and not on school grounds, it would seem as though the binding principle of stare decisis—"to stand by that which is decided"—demanded the school show that the display caused a risk of substantial disruption to school activities to deprive the student of his free expression right. That's what the U.S. Court of Appeals for the Ninth Circuit reasoned when it ruled that school principal Deborah Morse had violated the First Amendment rights of Joseph Frederick, then an 18-year-old senior at Juneau-Douglas High School in Juneau, Alaska.[87]

The U.S. Supreme Court, however, upheld the suspension, ruling that the school could ban speech advocating drug use conveyed at school events that were not held on public school property. Yet, the Court noted that "had [the student] delivered the same speech in a public forum outside the school context, it would have been protected."[88] *Morse v. Frederick* is widely viewed as having a narrow application to speech involving the promotion of illegal drug use. In his concurrence, Justice Samuel Alito stressed that the ban on such student speech stands "at the far reaches of what the First Amendment permits."[89]

The Court's lack of guidance on off-campus, school-related cyberbullying led to the following dilemma in the U.S. Court of Appeals for the Third

Circuit. The Snyders lost their appeal before a three-judge panel in that circuit. Yet on the same day, another Third Circuit three-judge panel drew the opposite conclusion in a similar case involving a Pennsylvania public school student who used an off-campus computer to create a vulgar, fictitious MySpace parody profile of his principal. In *Layshock v. Hermitage School District*, the unanimous judicial panel ruled that another Pennsylvania public school district was not empowered to punish a student, Justine Layshock, for his online, off-campus expression.[90]

Precedent requires that cases implicating the same laws with similar facts produce similar legal results. The following year, 2011, the full Third Circuit court ruled, 8-6, that under the First Amendment Pennsylvania public schools could not discipline students for their MySpace parodies of their principals created on their off-campus computers—however lewd or offensive the language of the postings—because they were not likely to cause significant disruptions at school. *Fraser*, the court said, does not apply to off-campus speech, and "because J. S. [Snyder] was suspended from school for speech that indisputably caused no substantial disruption in school and that could not reasonably have led school officials to forecast substantial disruption in school, the School District's actions violated J. S.'s First Amendment free speech rights."[91]

Not every U.S. Court of Appeals Circuit adheres to the Third Circuit's reasoning. Most notably, the U.S. Court of Appeals for the Second Circuit in 2011, which ruled in *Doninger v. Niehoff* that schools could invoke the *Fraser* standard—profane and lewd speech could be banned and punished—even if it is communicated online and off-campus and without a showing of a risk of substantial disruption.[92]

So far, the U.S. Supreme Court has declined to reconcile the conflict between the circuits. Meanwhile, by December 2015, 14 states had passed laws empowering schools to punish off-campus misconduct.[93] Arkansas's anti-bullying statute, for example, prohibits bullying by an electronic act "whether or not the electronic act originated on school property or with school equipment, if the electronic act is directed specifically at students or school personnel and maliciously intended for the purpose of disrupting school, and has a high likelihood of succeeding in that purpose. …"[94] (See Chapter Four for discussion of New Jersey's Anti-Bullying Bill of Rights Act.) Meanwhile, the school administrators who, under newly created laws, may be liable for failure to stop off-campus, online activities by their students,[95] have been turned into snooping Big Brothers, surveillance that can subject them to more liability.[96]

Criminalizing Cyberbullying by School students

Had Pennsylvania teenagers Snyder and Layshock attended North Carolina public schools in 2013, they would have faced the possibility of class 2 misdemeanor charges—"on par with simple assault or resisting arrest and punishable by up to 60 days in jail or a $1,000 fine"[97]—for their online parodies of school officials. North Carolina authorities could have charged them under N.C. Gen. Stat. §14-458.1(a)(1)(d), which makes it a crime to use a computer to create a fake user profile to intimidate and torment or post private and sexual information about a minor, and under N.C. Gen. Stat. §14-458.2, which bans student-on-teacher cyberbullying,[98] the first state law of its kind.[99] N.C. Gen. Stat. §14-458.2 has not been put to the test, but the Supreme of Court of North Carolina struck down N.C. Gen. Stat. §14-458.1(a)(1)(d. as unconstitutional in June 2016. (See "*The Unnecessary and Unjust Creation of Virtual Juvenile Delinquents.*")

First, however, the Court of Appeals of North Carolina upheld the jury criminal conviction of high school student Robert Bishop, who had received a suspended sentence of 30 days and 48 months of supervised probation, for violating the use-of-a computer statute.[100] Bishop and other Southern Alamance High School students posted comments about a classmate, Dillion Price, on the classmate's Facebook page.[101] Price received a notice on his cellphone each time a comment was posted.[102] Here are Bishop's comments deemed criminal, which are responses to other posts: "This is excessively homoerotic in nature. Exquisite specimen;" "Anyone who would be so defensive over Dillion can't be too intelligent;" "And you are equally pathetic for taking the internet so seriously;" "There isn't a fight. We're slamming someone on the open forum that is the internet;" and claiming that Price said "goddamnmotherfucking-pieceofshittyassholefuckingintheanusviolentlywhilelisteningtoBFMV-becauseisuckmassivedicksallthetimegoddammit."[103]

Rejecting Bishop's overbreadth constitutional challenge, the North Carolina appeals court distinguished the use of the Internet to intimidate and torment from the use of words to accomplish the same goal. In other words, the statute is content-neutral, the court said, because it prohibited using a digital tool such as Facebook to torment, which is non-expressive conduct, and not the subject matter of the viewpoint conveyed. "Like the telephone, the Internet can also be used as an instrumentality for communication," the court said. "However, its use for sharing thoughts and ideas does not prevent the Internet from also being used as a mechanism for individuals to engage in harassing or tormenting conduct."[104] The court also rejected Bishop's vagueness argument because the defendant had failed to raise the issue in a motion to dismiss and at the pretrial hearing.[105] The following year, the Supreme Court of North Carolina reversed and threw out Bishop's conviction.

As of mid-2016, N.C. Gen. Stat. §14-458.2, or "2012 School Violence Protection Act," had not been challenged in court. The ACLU of North Carolina, which argued against passage of the statute, listed the following concerns about the statute's constitutionality:

> The terms "intimidate" and "torment" are not fully defined by state law, so it is not clear what types of online speech might be punished. … It threatens to take away students' basic constitutional rights to speak freely and, if necessary, criticize government officials. … The law would criminalize true statements by prohibiting any statement "whether true or false, intending to immediately provoke, and that is likely to provoke, any third party to stalk or harass a school employee." (Example: "Mr. Smith said XYZ in class today.") … In North Carolina, 16 and 17 year olds are charged as adults and could receive up to 60 days in jail under this law. Maturing students often say or post online things without fully understanding the consequences. They should not receive a criminal record and be saddled with a lifetime of damaging consequences simply for posting something on the Internet that a school official finds offensive. … Young people should not be taught that they will be punished for telling the truth, speaking freely or questioning authority. If we make it criminal for students to criticize teachers online, what is to stop the government from making it illegal for any one of us to criticize some other government official, like the city council or state legislature, whether the comments are made online or not?[106]

In July 2014, New York's highest appeals court, the Court of Appeals, struck down Albany County's first anti-cyberbulling law as unconstitutionally overbroad and vague and as a statute that did not hold up under strict scrutiny in *People v. Marquan*.[107] The ruling marked the first time a court had struck down an entire criminal cyberbullying law, followed in four weeks by a similar ruling in Rhode Island in which a judge said a stalking and harassment statute could not used to ban online political speech and parody.[108]

Albany County's statute, adopted in 2010, created a new crime, "cyberbullying," a misdemeanor offense punishable by up to one year in jail and a $1,000 fine.[109] It defined cyberbullying as:

> any act of communicating or causing a communication to be sent by mechanical or electronic means, including posting statements on the internet or through a computer or email network, disseminating embarrassing or sexually explicit photographs; disseminating private, personal, false or sexual information, or sending hate mail, with no legitimate private, personal, or public purpose, with the intent to harass,

annoy, threaten, abuse, taunt, intimidate, torment, humiliate, or otherwise inflict significant emotional harm on another person.[110]

Law professor Volokh, who tracks cyberbullying rulings on his blog, praised the ruling. He said the provision, "wasn't limited to offensive speech *to* a person, but included offensive speech about people; and it wasn't limited to speech that falls within a First Amendment exception (such as threats, or knowing defamatory falsehoods)."[111]

Starting in 2012, Volokh has argued that criminal harassment and stalking laws are misused to target constitutionally protected online speech—with the exception of true threats and defamation—by outlawing hostile speech sent to willing listeners concerning a person, such as a group of students who are bad-mouthing one particular student or teacher in contrast to hostile speech sent directly to that student, say by email.

> "The law is in effect returning to an era when criminal libel laws could impose liability not just for falsehoods, but also for true statements or opinions that were supposedly not said with "good motives". ... Courts should therefore reject the application of these laws to such one-to-many speech, and legislatures should resist the broadening of such laws.[112]

Albany County's first cyberbullying statute and North Carolina's N.G. Gen. Stat. §14-458.1 were similar; both criminalize hostile online speech to protect minors in broad terms. Thus, the Court of Appeals of North Carolina was compelled to address the precedential significance of *Marquan* to *State v. Bishop* by distinguishing N.G. Gen. Stat. §14-458.1 from the Albany County cyber-bullying statute, though its ruling was overturned by the Supreme Court of North Carolina:

> The North Carolina Cyber-bullying Statute does not suffer the same fatal defects as the Albany County cyber-bullying statute. ... The [N.C.] statute only prohibits disclosure of "private, personal, or sexual information pertaining to the minor" on the Internet with the specific intent to intimidate or torment a minor. The statute does not prohibit any other speech or communication on the Internet outside of this context.[113]

In contrast, Albany County legislators never claimed that the original or second cyberbullying laws were content-neutral statutes. At any rate, the New York Civil Liberties Union, which successfully defended Marquan M., a 15-year-old high school student, argued that the revision was still constitutionally infirmed because it "retains the same constitutional flaws that compelled the Court of Appeals to strike down that law: vagueness and overbreadth."[114] Under its current law, Local Laws F of 2014, an adult or minor could face a $1,000 fine and a year in jail, a misdemeanor, if "he or she 'maliciously engages in a course of conduct by electronically transmitting information not of public concern with intent to inflict emotional harm on a minor' … 'private sexual information' about or explicit photos of a minor with the intent to inflict emotional harm would also be a violation, as would maliciously appropriating 'a minor's name or likeness with the intent to inflict emotional harm on the minor."[115]

Criminal Harassment

Before the arrival of social media, offline criminal harassment referred to non-expressive contact such as in-person contact, mailings and telephone calls. Thus, the Modern Penal Code (MPC) § 250.4 (1980) defined harassment "as a petty misdemeanor if, with purpose to harass another, he: (1) makes a phone call without a legitimate purpose; or (2) insults, taunts or challenges another in a manner likely to provoke violent or disorderly response; or (3) calls at inconvenient hours or in offensive language; or (4) subjects another to offensive touching; or (5) engages in any other course of alarming conduct serving no legitimate purpose of the actor."[116] The MPC also recognized that "it may be possible that some instance of harassing conduct is so imbued with expressive content as to implicate first-amendment concerns, but such a case would probably be excluded by the statutory requirements that the action serve no legitimate purpose of the actor and that there be a purpose to harass," the Wisconsin Supreme Court noted in 1987.[117]

In response to cyberbullying, "[s]ome states approach cyberharrassment by including language addressing electronic communications in general harassment statutes, while others have created stand-alone cyberharassment statutes."[118] In total, 48 states targeted "electronic harassment" in their statutes.[119] Meanwhile, the U.S. Supreme Court has yet to address the issue of the constitutionality of harassment statutes that criminalizes online expression.

In the wake of the *Marquan* ruling discussed above, in which the New York Court of Appeals identified the Albany County cyberbullying statute's use of the "no legitimate purpose" intent evidentiary standard as unconstitutionally vague, the MPC is out of step with emerging First Amendment interpretation. Indeed, in a 1975 ruling involving alleged harassment by mail, the Colorado Supreme Court reached a similar conclusion:

> Adding a phrase "without any legitimate purpose" to that subsection injects a vagueness into the statute which cannot withstand First Amendment scrutiny. Such a "limiting construction" disguises the constitutional difficulties of the statute but does nothing to resolve them. A judge or a jury still has to determine whether or not the particular speech of the defendant was "for a legitimate purpose." This delegation of power to judges or juries with no ascertainable standards does not give sufficient breathing room to the constitutionally guaranteed freedoms of speech and press.[120]

Likewise, Loyola Law School Professor Aaron H. Caplan argues that the "no legitimate purpose" clause does not add clarity.

> Another type of intent element often claimed to cure vagueness is "no legitimate purpose" or similar language. While this theory has been accepted by some courts, the ones that reject it have the better of the argument. Labeling a purpose as "illegitimate" is no more definite than labeling an action as "misconduct"—which, by itself, would be unconstitutionally vague. The labeling exercise does not provide notice to the actor or limit discretion by the enforcer. At best, a "no legitimate purpose" element "disguises the constitutional difficulties of the statute but does nothing to resolve them."

Consequently, with the First Amendment limiting the reach of offline and online criminal harassment laws, it is probably impossible to write a statute that criminalizes the vast majority of expression labeled cyberbullying such as taunts, crude jokes, parodies, and manipulative impersonations, denigration, and vulgar and angry sparring. That is a lesson the Missouri legislators who crafted the Meagan Meier law,[121] the Missouri prosecutor who failed to win a conviction under the new law the first time it was employed,[122] and the prosecutor whose trial victory was tossed when a court struck down most of the state statute as unconstitutional should have learned.[123]

The Meagan Meier Law

Missouri's Meagan Meier law is the state's response to the failure to make a criminal conviction against Lori Drew stick,[124] the "impetus for legal reform in Missouri, as in many other states."[125] Drew, then a 49-year-old mother, was charged in 2008 with conspiracy to commit fraud and unauthorized access to a computer under federal law by creating a MySpace account and posting content that drove Megan Meier, 13, to commit suicide in 2006.[126] Prosecutors "touted the case as the first of its kind in the nation."[127]

Meier, who had been under the care of a psychiatrist, hung herself after a "boyfriend" she knew only from contact on MySpace broke up with her.[128] The "boyfriend" was not real; he was Lori Drew, a neighbor of the Meiers and a co-conspirator, all residents of O'Fallon, Missouri.[129] Drew's daughter had been friendly with Meier, but Drew and her daughter came to believe that Meier had spread rumors about the daughter. They created the MySpace account to get information about Meier.[130]

Though all parties were Missouri residents, local prosecutors reportedly said the state had no law that covered the alleged crime.[131] Instead, federal prosecutors indicted Drew in California, where MySpace is headquartered, under the Computer Fraud and Abuse Act of 1986 (CFAA),[132] arguing it covered Drew's misrepresentation of herself in a website registration form. Many legal scholars, however, raised concerns that the prosecutor was stretching the CFAA's meaning and scope. Under the prosecutor's theory it "would be illegal to violate the terms of service of a website, essentially giving individual websites the ability to define crimes under the Act. This, the scholars argue, could not have been Congress's intent."[133]

A jury acquitted Drew of intentionally accessing a computer used in interstate commerce "to obtain information for the purpose of committing the tortious act of intentional infliction of emotional distress."[134] Instead, the jury found Drew guilty of "accessing a computer involved in interstate or foreign communication without authorization or in excess of authorization to obtain information" and violation of a website's terms of service, a misdemeanor.[135] A judge overturned the verdict in 2009 because the statute's language was unconstitutionally vague. The judge noted that, among other shortcomings, the law did not give fair warning to individuals of common intelligence that violating the terms of their contracts with a social networking site to provide truthful information would be criminal, as opposed to a mere breach of contract.[136]

Before Drew's guilty verdict was overturned, several states embarked on amending their harassment and anti-stalking statutes to target electronic and online abusive speech, including Missouri. (The proposed federal Megan Meier Cyberbullying Prevention Act, H.R. 1966, 111th Cong. § 3 (2009) stalled in committee over concerns that the law would not withstand constitutional scrutiny.)[137] Missouri lawmakers amended the state's harassment statute, making it a felony, for an individual who:

(1) Knowingly communicates a threat to commit any felony to another person and in so doing frightens, intimidates, or causes emotional distress to such other person; or

(2) When communicating with another person, knowingly uses coarse language offensive to one of average sensibility and thereby puts such person in reasonable apprehension of offensive physical contact or harm; or

(3) Knowingly frightens, intimidates, or causes emotional distress to another person by anonymously making a telephone call or any electronic communication; or

(4) Knowingly communicates with another person who is, or who purports to be, seventeen years of age or younger and in so doing and without good cause recklessly frightens, intimidates, or causes emotional distress to such other person; or cause recklessly frightens, intimidates, or causes emotional distress to such other person; or

(5) Knowingly makes repeated unwanted communication to another person; or

(6) Without good cause engages in any other act with the purpose to frighten, intimidate, or cause emotional distress to another person, cause such person to be frightened, intimidated, or emotionally distressed, and such person's response to the act is one of a person of average sensibilities considering the age of such person.[138]

Missouri also amended its anti-stalking law to include "a pattern of conduct composed of two or more acts, which *may include communication by any means*, over a period of time, however short, evidencing a continuity of purpose." [italics added][139]

In 2009, Nicole Williams, 21, was one of the first defendants to plead guilty to harassment under the statute, receiving a sentence of two years probation and taking anger management classes.[140] In contrast, a jury acquitted Elizabeth Thrasher, 41, of online harassment.[141] The fault, the prosecutor lamented, was in the statute's wording; the definition of harassment included an "unnecessary and confusing element that states the harassment must be done 'without good cause.'"[142] Thrasher had a good cause and, thereby, a good defense. "It was Pathenos [the alleged victim] who initiated contact with Thrasher via an e-mail that day. In that heated exchange on private e-mails Pathenos called Thrasher a 'fat f**king b**ch.'"[143]

Somewhat ironically, the Supreme Court of Missouri struck down a provision of the Missouri harassment law—565.090.1, subdivision (5)—which criminalized an individual who makes repeated and unwanted communication to another,[144] as unconstitutionally vague and overbroad in a case that had nothing to do with cyberbullying. Danny Vaugh was accused of frightening his ex-wife Retha Vaugh by making repeated telephone calls.[145] The court gave examples of the dangers of the statute's language:

> A few examples illustrate the statute's potential chilling effect upon political speech as well as everyday communications. For instance, individuals picketing a private or public entity would have to cease once they were informed their protestations were unwanted. A teacher would be unable to call a second time on a student once the pupil asked to be left alone. Salvation Army bell-ringers collecting money for charity could be prosecuted for harassment if they ask a passerby for a donation after being told, "I've already given; please don't ask again." An advertising campaign urging an elected official to change his or her position on a controversial issue would be criminalized.[146]

Writing for the American Bar Association's Section of First Amendment & Media Litigation, two Missouri practitioners concluded:

> Whatever legitimate concerns may exist with respect to cyberharassment, they are unlikely significant enough to outweigh the important constitutional rights enjoyed by all Americans to express their views, even to those who do not want to hear them. Blanket rules against anonymous, pseudonymous, or unwanted speech would inevitably chill protected speech, as the Missouri Supreme Court properly pointed out in *Vaughn*. The message of *Vaughn* to citizens is that harassment laws cannot inhibit free speech. Its message to legislatures is that they must combat cyberharassment with careful, tailored laws that target conduct, not speech, or that specifically carve out protected speech from their coverage.[147]

The Missouri court did, however, reverse the lower court's ruling that 565.090.1, subdivision (6)[148] was vague. The statute's words—"'frighten,' 'intimidate,' and 'emotional distress'" are words "with common understanding," and "good cause" provides "sufficient notice as to the criminal conduct proscribed," the court explained.[149] Still, as discussed here, the New York Court of Appeals ruled in two cases in 2014, *People v. Marquan*[150] and *People v. Golb*,[151] that it does not share the Missouri court's view about the constitutional clarity of words such as "good cause" or "harass," which define the requisite criminal intent for harassment. Even before cyberbullying harassment laws, there was no consensus among state courts about the legitimacy of such terms to define the intent standard in harassment statutes.

Missouri revised its harassment statute in 2014.[152] Section 565.090.2 (4) provides that an individual commits harassment if he or she "knowingly communicates with another person who is, or who purports to be, seventeen years of age or younger and in so doing and without good cause recklessly frightens, intimidates, or causes emotional distress to such other person." It appears to have been drafted with the intention to target the kind of communication Lori Drew engaged in with Meagan Meier.

Yet, even under the revised statute Drew would have a strong defense. Initially, Drew intended only to "woo Meier and extract information from her to determine if she had been spreading gossip about her daughter."[153] The prosecutor, however, argued that the scheme "turned into a bid to inflict pain on the girl by having the imaginary boy dump her."[154]

Most significantly, as noted above, the jury acquitted Drew on felony charges for using a computer to commit intentional infliction of emotional distress.[155] Accordingly, the same mens rea, actus reas and causal nexus between the intent and the resultant harm—"the defendant must act intentionally or recklessly; (2) the defendant's conduct must be extreme or outrageous; and (3) the conduct must be the cause (4) of extreme emotional distress"[156]—would apply under the revised harassment statute. Perhaps the latest version of Missouri's cyber-harassment statute might successfully snare some online types of cyber trolls such as those who make malicious statements that amount to true threats, e.g., "I am going to burn your house down and I know where you live, and I know when you are not home."

Drew, however, never engaged in such overtly malicious constitutionally unprotected speech. For example, in the last message to Meier, Drew said Meier was "'cruel' and a 'bad person.'" The message ended by stating: "the world would be a better place without you."[157] The message is mean-spirited, but it does not constitute a message conveying a serious expression of an intent to commit an act of unlawful violence to a particular individual or group of individuals, as the true threat doctrine requires. She did not say she was going to rid the world of Meier, for example. Consequently, the Missouri legislature has not accomplished the goal it embarked upon in 2008, which was to craft a cyberbulling law that would punish unwanted communications.[158]

In New York, You Have the Right to be Annoying

In 2014, New York's highest court struck down the state's aggravated harassment law—a statute that criminalized "in broad strokes, any communication that has the intent to annoy"—as unconstitutionally vague in a case involving adult-to-adult cyberbullying.[159] The defendant, Raphael Golb, used pseudonymous emails and anonymous blogs to discredit scholarly rivals of his father, University of Chicago Professor Norman Golb, a Dead Sea Scrolls scholar.[160]

A jury convicted him on 30 counts, including "14 counts of criminal impersonation in the second degree" and "three counts of aggravated harassment in the second degree."[161] The court vacated some of the criminal impersonation, and all of the aggravated harassment counts, ending the state's criminalization of annoying and alarming speech. (For a full account, see Chapter Five.)

The New York aggravated harassment law required that the state show that a defendant had the "intent to harass, annoy, threaten or alarm another person."[162] In reaching its decision, the court referenced its early ruling, *People v Dietze*,[163] in which it "struck down a similar harassment statute … which prohibited the use of abusive or obscene language with the intent to harass, annoy or alarm another person."[164] "Casual conversation may well be 'abusive' and intended to 'annoy'; so, too, may be light-hearted banter or the earnest expression of personal opinion or emotion," the court ruled. "But unless speech presents a clear and present danger of some serious substantive evil, it may neither be forbidden nor penalized."[165]

Thirty-seven days after the Court of Appeals handed down its decision in *Golb*, the New York State Senate passed an amended version of the flawed aggravated harassment law in an effort to revive the criminal charge.[166] Within a few days, the New York Civil Liberties Union issued its critique:

> The legislation fails to comport with the Court of Appeals ruling in two important respects. First: The legislation purports to criminalize communication that threatens to cause physical harm to another (what the Supreme Court has characterized as a "true threat"). However the amended law would retain from the existing statute the criminal intent to harass. The term "harass" lacks legal precision. What's more, this formulation creates vagueness as to the relation of intent to conduct. This imprecision will lead to the charging and prosecution of communication that does not constitute a true threat, and that is protected speech under the constitution.[167]

While there are several court rulings supporting the NYCLU's position, there are also many rulings supporting the opposing position that the use of terms such as "harass," "alarming," or "annoying" to define offline harassing speech is constitutionally permissible. The follow rulings support the NYCLU's position. In 1975, the Colorado Supreme Court struck down a harassment statute as unconstitutionally overbroad that required intent to harass, annoy, or alarm another person, because, "It would therefore be criminal in Colorado to forecast a storm, predict political trends, warn against illnesses, or discuss anything that is of any significance."[168] The U.S. Court of Appeals for the Fifth Circuit invalidated a Texas telephone-harassment statute as unconstitutionally vague in 1983 because the, "Texas courts have made no attempt to construe the terms 'annoy' and 'alarm' in a manner which lessens their inherent vagueness."[169] A 1984 ruling by the Washington Court of Appeals found that an ordinance criminalizing annoying and alarming telephone communication was overbroad and vague because, "A discussion of any political, social, economic, philosophic or religious topic might well vex, irritate or bother the listener. In addition, the public is constantly being put on the alert with the disastrous effects of everything from vitamin deficiencies in the blood to nuclear obliteration."[170]

In other states, harassing conduct or speech statutes with defining terms such as annoy, harass or intimidate have survived judicial scrutiny. In a 1986 case, in which the Court of Appeals of New Mexico rule that the terms "harass, annoy or offend" were neither unconstitutionally vague or overbroad, the court noted that, "statutes of this type [telephone harassment] have been upheld in twenty-one states."[171]

In later years, other courts have followed suit. Connecticut courts interpreted the language "in a manner likely to course annoyance or alarm" as "unambiguous as a whole by relying on the term 'alarm' to remedy the vagueness of the term 'annoyance.'"[172] Montana's Supreme Court held that its Privacy in Communications statute, which required the state to prove a defendant acted "with the purpose to terrify, intimidate, threaten, harass, annoy or offend" required proof of specific intent and, thus, was not unconstitutionally vague.[173] Iowa's statute contains constitutional safety valve language, meaning its terms cannot be used to punish protected speech.[174] Likewise, Kentucky's harassment statute has safety valve language. That fact and the Kentucky Court of Appeals' finding that telephone communication violates privacy led it to uphold the terms "annoy, alarm, or harass" as constitutionally valid.[175] It must be noted, however, that the safety valve language is the term "without legitimate purpose," and a minority of states courts, including the ruling in *Marquan* in New York, have found the language unconstitutionally vague.

Now, under the theory of *Marquan*, a "no legitimate purpose" provision can be challenged as vague based on *Snyder v Phelps*, which found that, "In most circumstances, 'the Constitution does not permit the legislatures to decide which types of otherwise protected speech are sufficiently offensive to require protection for the unwilling listener or viewer.'"[176] In other words, the "no legitimate purpose" provision allows legislators and juries to determine if otherwise protected speech has no valid communicative purpose, discretion that juries do not have, and legislators have only under limited circumstances.

True Threats and Fighting Words

Additionally, some state courts have struck down criminal harassment laws proscribing harassing speech in part or in full because the statutes failed to meet the standards of the fighting words or true threat doctrines, unprotected categories of expression. To find a defendant guilty, the true threat doctrine, as noted earlier, requires that a speaker intend to pose a threat of violence and that a reasonable person perceive the expression as a serious intention to convey such a threat. The fighting words doctrine applies to face-to-face insults that inflict injury or tend to incite an immediate violent response from the victim.[177] That, of course, does not describe the vast majority of cyberbullying expression, which by definition is not face-to-face or physical. In *City of Billings v. Nelson* (2014), for example, the Supreme Court of Montana ruled that, "Telephone communications are not included within the fighting words doctrine, because there is no possibility the listener will react with immediate violence against the speaker."[178] Thus, if an angry telephone conversation cannot constitute fighting words, online postings, social media comments, and email sent directly to a recipient cannot be criminalized under the fighting words doctrine.

The Supreme Judicial Court of Massachusetts's 2005 ruling in *Common Wealth v. Welch*,[179] made note of several rulings striking down criminal harassment statutes that did not meet the fighting words or true threat standards:

> For example, the Supreme Court of Washington in *State* v. *Williams*, 144 Wash. 2d 197, 208–209 (2001), found constitutional defects in a criminal harassment statute that included threats "to do any other act which is intended to substantially harm the person threatened ... with respect to his or her ... mental health or safety" because it was not limited to "true threats" or "fighting words." The court ultimately struck the term "mental" from the statute in order to save it. Similarly, the Supreme Court of Minnesota, in *State* v. *Machholz*, 574 N.W.2d 415, 417–418 (Minn. 1998), overturned a harassment statute that proscribed "intentional conduct" that causes "a reasonable person ... to feel oppressed, persecuted, or intimidated," including "harassing conduct that interferes with another person or intrudes on the person's privacy or liberty." The court determined that the statute could not be construed as applying only to "fighting words." The Supreme Court of Iowa, in *State* v. *Fratzke*, 446 N.W.2d 781, 784 (Iowa 1989), noted that "in order to uphold the constitutionality of a state statute that attempts to criminalize the use of opprobrious words or abusive language the statute must, by its own terms or as construed by the state's courts, be limited in its application to "fighting words" and must not be susceptible of application to speech that is protected by the [F]irst and [F]ourteenth [A]mendments."[180]

The fighting words doctrine is ill suited for application to online speech. The true threat doctrine, however, is applicable and, as the rulings examined in this text attests, the only practical and constitutionally sound basis for restricting cyberhassment. Unfortunately, for those who wish to impose criminal penalties on cyberbullies, a great deal of cyberbullying expression cannot be banned under the true threat analysis as criminologist Patchin has noted.[181]

State and Federal Cyberstalking Statutes

> Cyberstalking—the use of technology to stalk victims—shares some characteristics with real-life stalking. It involves the pursuit, harassment, or contact of others in an unsolicited fashion initially via the Internet and e-mail. Cyberstalking can intensify in chat rooms where stalkers systematically flood their target's inbox with obscene, hateful, or threatening messages and images. A cyberstalker may further assume the identity of his or her victim by posting information (fictitious or not) and soliciting responses from the cybercommunity. Cyberstalkers may use information acquired online to further intimidate, harass, and threaten their victim via courier mail, phone calls, and physically appearing at a residence or work place.[182]

Based on three recent rulings discussed below and elsewhere in the text, cyberstalking statutes are likely to withstand judicial scrutiny. But here's the rub. The reach of cyberstalking statutes are limited to a single and integrated course of *unwanted* conduct entailing *speech integral to criminal conduct*—such as fraud, extortion, blackmail, perjury, bribery, inciting unlawful conduct, true threats, extortion, criminal conspiracy, aiding and abetting, child pornography—and physical conduct directed at or conveyed directly to a particular individual. Thus, cyberstalking statutes are unsuitable for use against garden-variety cyberbullying engaged in by most adolescents, including most forms of so-called cyberbullicide, which are comprised solely of speech that is not integral to a crime and typically not sent to the target.

Under 18 U.S.C § 2261A(2)(A), the interstate stalking statute, a defendant must have the "intent to kill, injure, harass, or place under surveillance with intent to kill, injure, harass, or intimidate, or cause substantial emotional distress to a person in another State" using "the mail, any interactive computer service, or any facility of interstate or foreign commerce to engage in a course of conduct that causes substantial emotional distress to that person or places that person in reasonable fear of … death … or serious bodily injury. …" Federal court rulings on the interstate stalking statute, part of the Violence against Women's Act (1994), which Congress amended in 2006 to include use of interactive computers, have set the boundaries for the use of cyberstalking laws.

In *U.S. v. Petrovic* (2012), the U.S. Court of Appeals for the Eighth Circuit affirmed the conviction of Jovica Petrovic on four counts of interstate stalking and two counts of interstate extortionate threat, finding that, "The communications for which Petrovic was convicted under § 2261A(2)(A) were integral to this criminal conduct as they constituted the means of carrying out his extortionate threats."[183] Petrovic threatened to distribute sexually explicit photographs of his ex-wife if she refused to continue having sexual relations with him and when she failed to comply he used a website and mail postcards and packages to distribute sexually explicit photographs of his ex-wife, all taken secretly, repeatedly made harassing phone calls to her workplace, physically intimidated her several occasions.[184]

In *U.S. v. Sayer* (2014), Maine resident Shawn Sayer pled guilty to one count of cyberstalking and was sentenced to 60 months' imprisonment, but sought to have a reduced sentence arguing that the interstate stalking law was unconstitutionally vague and overbroad.[185] Sayer created an advertisement on Craiglist that purported to have been posted by his ex-girl friend. Because of the sexually enticing ad, men came to her home for eight months seeking sex.[186] The Court of Appeals for the First Circuit rejected Sayer's appeal, ruling in 2014 that Sayer, "admitted that his conduct, which deceptively enticed men to Jane Doe's home, put Jane Doe in danger and at risk of physical harm. To the extent his course of conduct targeting Jane Doe involved speech at all, his speech is not protected."[187] The court also read the statute to require proof of "serious criminal intent, not just speech that happens to cause annoyance or insult."[188]

Christopher Osinger brought an unsuccessful void-for-vagueness challenge of his conviction for in violation of the federal stalking law in *U.S. v. Osinger* (2014).[189] In a revenge porn scenario similar to Sayer's, Osinger created fake Facebook and Myspace accounts to pose as an ex-girlfriend and he used the sites to post sexually explicit photos of her, which she took voluntarily though she was unaware that he would post them on the Internet.[190] He also stalked her at her home and at her workplace in Illinois, sent emails containing sexually explicit photographs of her to her co-workers there and when she moved to California, he continued unwanted contact with her via text messages.[191] The U.S. Court of Appeals for the Ninth Circuit ruled that, "Because the 'sole immediate object' of Osinger's speech was to facilitate his commission of the interstate stalking offense, that speech isn't entitled to constitutional protection."[192]

In early 2015, three indicted conspirators, David T. Matusiewicz, his mother, Lenore Matusiewicz, and his sister, Amy Gonzalez, argued that the federal cyberstalking statute was unconstitutionally vague and overbroad in a bid to get their indictments for conspiring to stalk and cyberstalk thrown out of court.[193] The conspirators allegedly posted accusations of child abuse against Christine Belford online, sent those accusations to the school one of Belford's children attended and her church, and soliciting their friends' assistance in visiting Belford's home to spy on Belford. The actions stemmed from a kidnapping conviction of their relative, David Matusiewicz, who had taken his children from his ex-wife Belford. Thomas Matusiewicz shot and killed Christine Belford and her companion on February 11, 2013 and took his own life.[194]

Citing *Petrovic*, *Sayer*, and *Osinger*, a federal judge in Wilmington, Del., rejected the defendants' arguments. The judge said though a number of the statements might be protected speech, such as accusations of Belford abusing her children, a substantial number of applications of most of the statements to the statutes were not potentially protected under the First Amendment. In the absence of a pattern of unconstitutional applications of the statute, he could not find the statute unconstitutionally overbroad.[195] The statute did not suffer from unconstitutional vagueness, the judge found, because, "A reasonable person would recognize that taking the actions alleged in the Indictment while possessing the intent to harass or injure required by 18 U.S.C. § 2261A and causing the type of harm described in the statute would expose the person to criminal liability."[196]

The Massachusetts Supreme Judicial Court relied on *Petrovic*, *Sayer*, and *Osinger* to uphold the constitutionality of a state criminal harassment law and its application to cyberbullying in *Commonwealth v. Johnson* (2014).[197] In *Johnson*, a married couple, challenged its conviction on criminal harassment under G. L. c. 265, § 43A (*a*), arguing that the statute was unconstitutionally vague and overbroad. In a campaign directed at a neighboring family, the Lyonses, the Johnsons posted a Craiglist advertising falsely stating that a free golf carts were being given out by the neighboring family and gave its number and address which resulted in numerous phone solicitations and about 40 potential buyers appearing at the home, and the Johnsons engaged in three other similar acts including filing a false child abuse report on the family and sending hostile emails to the family.[198]

Though a criminal harassment statute in name, the terms of G. L. c. 265, § 43A (*a*) read more like a cyberstalking statute. The statute requires for conviction, among other evidence, proof that a defendant engaged in "a knowing *pattern of conduct or speech*, or series of acts, on at least three separate occasions; and that the defendant intended to target the victim with the *harassing conduct or speech, or series of acts*, on each occasion" [emphasis added].[199] Accordingly, the court relied heavily on the recent cyberstalking rulings to uphold the statute's constitutionality.

> The speech here, much as the speech at issue in *Giboney*, *Sayer*, and *Petrovic*, was also "integral to criminal conduct," serving only to implement the defendants' purpose to harass and cause substantial emotional distress to the Lyonses ... To the extent that any of the harassing contacts were composed of words, they were used "so close in time and purpose to a substantive evil as to become part of the ultimate crime itself". ... While the content of the speech in question certainly affected the Lyonses, much of the alarming impact was the product of the frightening number, frequency, and type of harassing contacts with which the defendants bombarded the Lyonses. In these circumstances, the application of § 43A (*a*) to the defendants fully withstands constitutional scrutiny.[200]

In the above cyberstalking cases, the targets were private individuals and the defendants engaged in speech concerning private matters. In contrast, the First Amendment protects a defendant engaged in a pattern of alarming, annoying and bothersome speech about or even directed to a public figure about matters of public concern. At least that is the finding of judges in *U.S. v. Cassidy* (2011)[201] and *State v. Leidecker* (2014).[202] P3/11-2685 (R.I. July 30, 2014). (See Chapter Five for discussion of *Cassidy* and *Leidecker*.)

In *Cassidy*, a federal judge ruled that the federal antistalking law, 18 U.S.C § 2261A(2)(A), could not be applied to convict William Cassidy who tweeted and blogged angry messages about a Buddhist priest, who used the names Alyce Zeoli and Catherine Burroughs, and was well-known in the international Buddhist community and the subject of a published biography. The judge said, the indictment was "directed squarely at protected speech: anonymous, uncomfortable Internet speech addressing religious matters. Tellingly, the Government's Indictment is not limited to categories of speech that fall outside of First Amendment protection—obscenity, fraud, defamation, true threats, incitement or speech integral to criminal conduct."[203]

Likewise, a Rhode Island judge overturned the cyberstalking and cyberharassment conviction of John A. Leidecker, an assistant executive director with the National Education Association of Rhode Island, because his mark was a political candidate and the butt of series of mocking and parodic emails concern campaign issues. Ruling from the bench, the judge said,

> The Supreme Court has consistently classified emotionally disturbing or distressing as protected when the speech touches upon public concerns because "in public debate our own citizens must tolerate insulting and even outrageous speech in order to provide 'adequate breathing space' to the freedoms protected by our First Amendment.[204]

The federal judge in *Cassidy* also took into account that the defendant's tweets were not sent directly to the Buddhist priest and author. Properly construed, stalking laws should not be applicable to speech about someone, only speech communicated directly to the individual. Accordingly, the Georgia Supreme Court blocked an injunction against a message board posts by a community that criticized a poet's copyright enforcement efforts in *Chan v. Ellis* in March 2015.

> The limited evidence in the record shows that Chan and others posted a lot of commentary to his website about Ellis, but it fails for the most part to show that the commentary was directed specifically to Ellis as opposed to the public. As written, most of the posts appear to speak to the public, not to Ellis in particular, even if they are about Ellis. And there is no evidence that Chan did anything to cause these posts to be delivered to Ellis or otherwise brought to her attention, notwithstanding that he may have reasonably anticipated that Ellis might come across the posts, just as any member of the Internet-using public might. The publication of commentary directed only to the public generally does not amount to "contact," as that term is used in OCGA § 16-5-90 (a) (1), and most of the posts about Ellis quite clearly cannot form the basis for a finding that Chan contacted Ellis.[205]

Teen Sexting or "Youth-Produced Sexual Images"

Cyberbullying experts Justine W. Patchin and Sameer Hinduja define sexting as "sending or receiving sexually explicit or sexually suggestive nude or seminude images or video, usually via a cell phone."[206] As described, such communication does not raise issues of legality. Consider ex-New York Congressman Andrew Weiner's notorious sexting obsession.[207] Though sending nude selfies led to a form of political seppuku, the activity was not criminal. The First Amendment protects the possession and distribution of pornography, or sexually explicit content. Obscenity is sexually explicit content that a judge or jury has found to fall outside the First Amendment's protection. The First Amendment does not protect child pornography. So, when adults engage in sexting, the law gets involved only when the images are obscene, they constitute child pornography, harassment, stalking, or, in a minority of states, they can be prosecuted under revenge porn statutes.

In contrast, minors who send nude photos, whether of themselves or of other minors, are subject to federal child pornography laws and "a first time offender convicted of producing child pornography under 18 U.S.C. § 2251, faces fines and a statutory minimum of 15 years to 30 years maximum in prison."[208] Thus, some have suggested that the appropriate term for sexting is "'youth-produced sexual images,' defined as images created by minors (age 17 or younger) that depict minors and that are or could be considered child pornography under criminal statutes."[209]

Under federal law (18 U.S.C. § 2256(2)(A) (2003), child pornography includes visual depictions of minors engaged in "actual or simulated (i) sexual intercourse, including genital-genital, oral-genital, anal-genital, or oral-anal, whether between persons of the same or opposite sex; (ii) bestiality; (iii) masturbation; (iv) sadistic or masochistic abuse; or (v) lascivious exhibition of the genitals or pubic area of any person." The statute U.S.C. § 2256 (8) adds that (B) such visual depiction is a digital image, computer image, or computer-generated image that is, or is indistinguishable from, that of a minor engaging in sexually explicit conduct; or (C) such visual depiction has been created, adapted, or modified to appear that an identifiable minor is engaging in sexually explicit conduct.

In *New York v. Ferber*, the U.S. Supreme Court ruled that the First Amendment did not forbid states from banning the sale of the visual depiction of sexual conduct by minors.[210] Lewd depictions of minors' genitalia are inherently obscene, the Court ruled because the materials' harm to the child "is exacerbated by their circulation"; such a ban helps to limit the child pornography distribution network, the "advertising and selling of child pornography provide an economic motive for and are thus an integral part of the production of such materials"; and the expressive value "of permitting live performances and photographic reproductions of children engaged in lewd sexual conduct is exceedingly modest, if not *de minimis*."[211] In *U.S. v. Williams* (2008), the Court ruled that criminalizing offers to sell fake child pornography—sexually explicit photos featuring adults who appear to be teens—was not impermissibly overboard or vague because digitalization makes it "nearly impossible to prove that a particular image was produced using real children."[212] In short, the Court has said child pornography harms children in the production phase because minors are coerced to pose; the photographs have little or no social value; the distribution of the photos are memorialized records of that coercion; and the photographs, whether they depict real minors or not, are the economic fuel for an illegal industry.

Consensual teen-to-teen sexting, however, does not meet all the judicial rationales for criminal prosecution under federal or state child pornography laws nor the purposes for requiring sex offenders to register as such on publicly accessible files, a significant number of scholars have concluded.[213] Studies have determined that peer pressure[214] and flirting motivate the overwhelming number of teen sexters.[215]

Unlike adult produced child pornography or teen-produced sexting distributed without the original sender's consent and used to embarrass or ridicule, "fun or flirtatious" self-produced teen sexting shared between two consenting teenagers has social value. These types of teens are involved in a conversation and by doing so are defining who they are and will become as sexual beings. University of New Hampshire's Crimes Against Children Research Center scholars, sociologist and lawyer Janis Wolak and sociologist David Finkelhor, categorize this type of sexting as "experimental."[216]

"We use the term 'Experimental' because, while there is no evidence that this behavior is normative, these incidents appear to grow out of typical adolescent impulses to flirt, find romantic partners, experiment with sex and get attention from peers," Wolak and Finkelhor say. "Learning about romantic and sexual relationships is a key task of adolescence in our culture, which provides very mixed messages about appropriate sexual behavior."[217]

"Experimental" teen sexters are simply doing what adolescents have been doing offline—"You show me yours; I'll show you mine"—for as long as the social construct of adolescence has existed, which is about 250 years.[218] We do not impose criminal penalties on teenagers for merely talking about sex with each other offline and in private. Why do we feel compelled to impose criminal felony or misdemeanor charges on "experimental" teen sexters?

Moreover, as law professor JoAnne Sweeny notes, in many states the age of consent for engaging in sex is 17 years or younger yet those same teenagers do not have the right to swop sexually explicit images of themselves under federal law: "Under federal and most state law, the child pornography age is under eighteen even though thirty-nine states have an age of consent of seventeen years or younger."[219] But, as Sweeny points out, it appears that only one defendant has been successful in arguing that it is unconstitutional for a state to prosecute a defendant for sending and receiving images of a teen when that same state allows that teen to engage in sex. In *Salter v. State*, an Indiana defendant sent photos of his genitals to a 16-year-old girl in Delaware, who under Indiana law was old enough to consent to sexual relations. The Indiana Court of Appeals overturned Salter's conviction, ruling:

> By setting the legal age of consent at sixteen, the Indiana legislature has made an implied policy choice that in-person viewing of another person's genitals is "suitable matter" for a sixteen- or seventeen-year-old child. That being so, how could Salter have known that a picture of his genitals would be "harmful," that is, not "suitable," for M.B.? Asked another way, if such images are harmful to sixteen- and seventeen-year-old children, then why would our legislature allow those children to view the same matter in-person, in the course of sexual activity? These questions reveal the flaw in Indiana Code section 35-49-3-3 as applied to Salter: when read in light of well-established Indiana law setting the age of consent, the state did not provide him with fair notice that the State would consider pictures of his genitals harmful to or unsuitable for a sixteen-year-old girl.[220]

Nevertheless, some forms of teen sexting are intended to cause harm. A minority of teens sexually abuse and photograph other youth exists—teens who use sexual pictures to embarrass other teens, or distribute such images without knowledge or permission of the depicted minor. Wolak and Finkelhor classify this type of sexting as "aggravated incidents, youth only," with two subcategories: "intent to harm" and "reckless misuse":

> "Intent to Harm" involved criminal, malicious or other abusive behavior beyond the creation, sending or possession of youth-produced sexual images. In the second subgroup, there did not appear to be any overtly criminal, malicious or other abusive behavior, but someone who was pictured in an image did not willingly or knowingly participate in the taking or sending of a picture. We labeled this sub-group "Reckless Misuse."[221]

There is also additional justification for some level of regulation of teen-produced sexting because there is evidence that a small portion of it gets into the hands of adult child porn purveyors. In 2009, for example, 11% of teen sexting was posted online in contrast to distributing via cellphone to a select group of peers.[222] The 11% of teen-produced and distributed sexual images can cause emotional and psychological harm—shame, humiliation and powerlessness—to the adolescent whose privacy has been violated. Apparently, a portion of self-produced teen sexting ends up as part of online content to satiate pedophiles.

Generally, teens lack the required criminal intent—producing and distributing child pornography was not the goal they had in mind. Also, there is no evidence that teenagers engage in sexting for commercial or financial gain or transmit such images with the intent to gratify pedophiles or fuel the child pornography market. Yet, some images end up as online content for pedophiles. According to the findings of the Internet Watch Foundation-Microsoft study conducted in 2014, 46.1% of 3,803 online teen sexting images and videos studied during a three-month period had been "harvested from 17 different services, including social networks, chat sites and mobile phone apps" and redistributed on 230 third party websites, of which "65 were specifically dedicated to the collection and distribution of youth-produced sexual content."[223]

In sum, though certain types of teen-produced sexting can cause harm even to the consenting sender and recipient, prosecuting "experimental" or "aggravated incidents, youth only," teen sexters is draconian, perhaps unconstitutional, though no such case has reached the U.S. Supreme Court. Similarly, it is unduly harsh to convict "experimental" or "aggravated incidents, youth only" sexters on sex exploitation charges that require them to register as sex offenders, branding them for decades as perverted criminals. As Wolak and Finkelhor concluded, "Our own typological approach suggests that some forms of sexting might well be decriminalized in a de jure or de facto fashion, but that various aggravating conditions might be taken into account in deciding how it is handled."[224]

Others have reached similar conclusions. By early 2015, 17 states had sexting statutes on their books, many of which shielded consensual youthful sharers of sexting from child pornography prosecution.[225] Arizona's "Unlawful use of an electronic communication device by a minor" statute (2011) makes it a misdemeanor to distribute or knowingly send or possess teen sexual images, but no law is broken when: "The juvenile did not solicit the visual depiction" or "took reasonable steps to destroy or eliminate the visual depiction or report the visual depiction to the juvenile's parent, guardian, school official or law enforcement official."[226] New Jersey's law, which permits a "diversionary program for juveniles who are criminally charged for 'sexting' or posting sexual images," gives judges discretion to allow teen sexters to be prosecuted under state child pornography laws or participate in a remedial education or counseling program.[227] Under New York's Cybercrime Youth Rescue Act (2012), a first-time teen sextexter, unaware of the criminal nature of sexting, will have to attend an education reform program.[228] Under Vermont's "Minor electronically disseminating indecent material to another person," statute a first-time offender is treated as a juvenile defendant and not required to register as sex offender.[229]

Meanwhile, in Pennsylvania, Kentucky and other states child rights advocates and others are challenging state prosecutions and convictions of minors on child pornography, sex offender charges or misdemeanor charges—in short, the criminalization of consensual teen sexting—that would stigmatize "adolescents for behaving like adolescents."[230] (For further discussion of the criminalization of teen sexting see Chapter 6.)

Adult Sexting: Revenge Porn, or Non-Consensual Distribution of Intimate Images

There are two key issues raised by banning revenge porn, or non-consensual sharing of intimate images. Can legislators write them narrowly enough to conform to the First Amendment? If so, will a constitutionally permissible revenge porn statute miss the mark? In other words, will it protect women who take photos of themselves and share them with their partners who later distribute them to strangers, a category that includes 80% of revenge porn victims and the impetus for the crusade to ban the activity?[231] (However, Scott Stroud, an assistant professor of communications at the University of Texas, provides results of studies that "indicate that men are slightly more prone to becoming victims of online revenge than women.")[232]

Conceptually, a revenge porn law seeks to ban speech based on content, viewpoint, and against a certain speaker. Thus, it implicates the First Amendment. That is because such a statute, as law professor John A. Humbach explains, is,

> A restriction on speech that is limited to particular content, *e.g.*, sexual exposure, is *content* discrimination. A restriction designed to suppress a particular point of view, *e.g.*, negative or unflattering personal information, is *viewpoint* discrimination. And a restriction that is applicable only to persons who have not received consent is *speaker* discrimination, as well as a *prior restraint*—among the most disfavored of restrictions on speech.[233]

Moreover, revenge porn images are truthful portrayals—they are not photo-shopped, for example—of nude adults and, thus, protected speech. No reasonable person disputes that vindictive ex-partners, devious hackers, and exploitive revenge porn web site owners are reprehensible. But the First Amendment protects morally repugnant speech unless it is defamation, incitement, and speech integral to a crime, true threat, obscene or is a part of a pattern of hostile speech and conduct directed at a victim. Typically, the vindictive ex-partner revenge porn purveyor traffics in truth, however unpleasant. Generally, the website owner is protected under Section 230 of the Communications Decency Act. If the statutes are too broadly written, innocent bystanders—e.g., bookstores, newspapers, photographers, publishers, librarians, parents who text naked photos of infants—will be swept up in their nets.

Therefore, such laws are subject to strict scrutiny, overbreadth and vagueness challenges. Yet, if they are too narrowly drafted, they may not cover the non-consensual distributor's conduct. Thus, the key point of debate among, even among advocates of revenge porn law, has been over the constitutionally appropriate level of mens rea or state of mind criminal culpability. One faction contends that the criminal intent element of revenge porn statutes requires knowledge or recklessness; that the accused knowingly or recklessly broke an agreement of confidentiality. The other side argues that the accused must be found to have intended to cause harm, a position supported by most civil libertarians. Requiring intent to cause harm is more free-speech protective than a knowledge or recklessness standard, but the former, arguably, would allow defendants who post for commercial reasons, such as revenge porn web site owners, a credible defense.

And there is the privacy issue. Those depicted in the photos, the argument goes, wanted the photos to remain private and the ex-intimate partner or strangers knew or should have known that they were private. But if the state has to prove the existence of a reasonable expectation of privacy or the defendant has to show the absence of one, can these new laws effectively protect the prototypical victim—women whose ex-intimate partners share them with third parties?

Mary Anne Franks, law professor and Cyber Civil Rights Initiative (CCRI) board member, an organization that advises legislators on drafting revenge porn statutes, says a constitutionally sound and effective non-consensual pornography statute, the term she prefers, is practicable. In her "Drafting An Effective 'Revenge Porn' Law: A Guide for

Legislators," Franks defines revenge porn, or non-consensual pornography, and the dangers the online speech creates, as:

> The disclosure of sexually explicit images without consent and for no legitimate purpose—popularly but misleadingly referred to as "revenge porn"—causes immediate, devastating, and in many cases irreversible harm. A vengeful ex-partner, opportunistic hacker, or rapist can upload an explicit image of a victim to a website where thousands of people can view it and hundreds of other websites can share it. In a matter of

> days, that image can dominate the first several pages of search engine results for the victim's name, as well as being emailed or otherwise exhibited to the victim's family, employers, co-workers, and peers. Victims are frequently threatened with sexual assault, stalked, harassed, fired from jobs, and forced to change schools. Some victims have committed suicide.[234]

Franks's definition and rationales have logical inconsistencies. For example, does it make sense to treat vengeful ex-partners, hackers, rapists, blackmailing revenge porn web site owners and unwitting third party down loaders equally under the same law? There are, for example, laws in place that criminalize hacking into a private online accounts. Threatening someone with sexual assault is not constitutionally protected speech; it's a true threat. Aren't those threats distinguishable from pornography, which is constitutionally protected speech? Cyberstalking laws would seem to cover many revenge porn scenarios.

Indeed, the defendant in the cyberstalking *U.S. v. Petrovic* was a spurned partner who posted on his website several photographs of his ex performing a sex act. Cyberstalking also would seem to cover the rapist who posts photos of his sexual assault. Computer hacking is a state and federal crime. The website owner who will remove revenge porn photos only if the victim pays is engaging in extortion.

Worse, Franks resorts to the canard of cyberbullicide by referencing the suicides of teenagers Rehtaeh Parsons and Audrie Pott. First, there is no proven link between online hostile speech and suicide.[235] Second, Parsons and Pott were victims of physical sexual assault and hostile sexting.[236] So why do we need to criminalize revenge porn?

Anti-revenge porn advocates say we need criminal laws banning non-consensual pornography "because that is the most accurate and principled characterization of its harm … it is at its base an act of sexual use without consent."[237] Franks adds that victims need a less time consuming and costly alternative to civil actions and "the priority of most victims is to have the material removed, not to recover damages." (To a large degree, Google's revenge porn's right-to-be-forgotten policy undercuts the key basis for criminalizing revenge porn, as it has since June 2015 honored requests to remove sexually explicit non-consensual images from search engine results.)[238]

Between 2013 and early 2015, Franks and the CCRI, the leading anti-revenge porn organization, played a role in the drafting of 15 of 18 state revenge porn statutes that impose felony or misdemeanor penalties, though, as Franks is quick to note, "the final versions of many of these laws may not reflect CCRI's recommendations."[239] That's a disclaimer because Franks is quick to distance CCRI from legislation that does not follow her advice to carefully word statutes to avoid infringing upon First Amendment rights.

For instance, Georgia's state lawmakers ignored her complaints about the language in the draft of Georgia's "Prohibition on nude or sexually explicit electronic transmissions" statue.[240] Franks said the proposed bill was "way overbroad when it comes to constitutional issues—the definition of nudity was so broad that you could go to jail for publicizing a picture of a woman in a wet bathing suit."[241] The anti-revenge porn advocate was referring to the following definition of nudity in the statue: "The showing of the female breasts without any covering or *with less than a full opaque covering*" and the "depiction of covered male genitals in a *discernibly* turgid state" [emphasis added].[242] Nevertheless, critics say that her model revenge porn law and statutes in Texas and New Jersey, for example, that follow its lead, still allow the state to trample on free speech rights.[243]

Under Franks's "Effective Revenge Porn Law":

> An actor may not knowingly disclose an image of another person who is identifiable from the image itself or information displayed in connection with the image and whose intimate parts are exposed or who is engaged in a sexual act, when the actor knows or is reckless with regard to whether that the depicted person has not consented to such disclosure [and under circumstances in which the actor knew that the depicted person had a reasonable expectation of privacy. A person who has consented to the disclosure of an image within the context of a confidential relationship retains a reasonable expectation of privacy with regard to disclosures beyond such a relationship.][244]

The reasonable expectation of privacy standard is met by showing that an individual exhibited an expectation of privacy and that the expectation is one that society is prepared to recognize.[245] In sizing up the New York state revenge porn law, which was influenced by Franks's counsel, law professor Clay Calvert says reliance on the reasonable expectation of privacy standard to show that an ex-intimate partner has violated a victim's privacy is dubious.[246] Calvert argues that studies and media coverage of the issue show a widespread awareness of the likelihood that consensual sexual images might be shared with third parties. Thus, he contends the person depicted in the photograph is highly unlikely to be able to make a persuasive claim that her expectation was reasonable.

> Indeed, scholarly research suggests many people already know of the disclosure risks associated with the consensual taking of sexually explicit images with a partner. A study published in 2013 in *Computers in Human Behavior* found that 26% of those

> surveyed who were in a committed relationship feared their romantic partner would forward the picture or video. When the relationship was merely casual rather than committed, more than half of those surveyed—a whopping 53%—worried that their sexual images would be forwarded. The study was based on a sample of more than 250 college students ranging in age from eighteen to twenty-six years.[247]

Calvert uses Franks's own words to underscore his point. "Most strikingly, during a *Today* show interview in May 2013, Professor Franks admitted as much, stating '[a]nybody who thinks this isn't going to happen to them is just resting on the illusion that people are good people and they are not.'"[248] He points to the popular Snapchat app that destroys sexting images after they are forwarded to the intended recipient. He concludes:

> In fact, all of this collectively undermines, if not eviscerates, the notion that people have a *reasonable* expectation of privacy that their sexual images will not be disclosed beyond the confines of their relationship with a romantic partner. The current wave of news media attention now being paid to revenge porn sites in venues such as the *New York Times*, *Los Angeles Times* and the *Today* show will further raise awareness of the realities of non-consensual disclosure. Arguably, only an *unreasonable* person would take the risk. Thus, New York's bill is flawed to include its "reasonable expectation of privacy" verbiage.[249]

Consider the distinction between an individual's reasonable expectation of privacy when someone secretly films a partner engaged in sex in contrast to the sexter who shares her nude selfie or allows her partner to film her. There is little doubt that the former type of partner enjoys a reasonable expectation of privacy as a New York court rule in *York v. Piznarski*, a case implicating its video voyeurism law handed down before New York enacted its revenge porn act in 2014.[250] The court said, "reasonable people expect to be safe from casual or hostile intrusion within a bedroom" and, when "engaged in sexual relations in a bedroom of a private home[,] expect to be free from surveillance."[251] Secret surveillance denotes lack of consent and an expectation that the bedroom conduct is for the partners' eyes only. In contrast, consensual filming and selfie-sharing denotes ambiguity about the partners' intent and expectations, unless there is evidence to the contrary.

Thus, requiring a finding that disclosure breached a victim's reasonable expectation of privacy would aid juries in sorting through the ambiguity of intimate relationships. Absent the unlikely existence of a written contract or witnesses to testify on either party's behalf, a juror would have no objective evidence to judge veracity. The reasonable expectation test would give jurors an alternative. In each case, a finding of a reasonable expectation of privacy would be judged by the type of evidence Calvert identifies. Statistics and new reports would show that for a particular jurisdiction society does or does not accept that it is reasonable to expect intimate sexual images taken on a cell-phone are likely to remain private.

Nevertheless, tying intent to knowing or reckless violation of a reasonable expectation of privacy does not protect third-party distributors such as book distributors, news organizations and those who unwittingly share sexual explicit photos via email from prosecution or conviction. As a remedy, Franks counsels legislators to include a clause carving out exceptions for "[i]mages involving voluntary exposure in public or commercial settings or [d]isclosures made in the public interest, including but not limited to the reporting of unlawful conduct, or the lawful and common practices of law enforcement, criminal reporting, legal proceedings, or medical treatment."[252] Her solution, however, does not protect the online user who downloads and shares a nude photo that is not marked as non-consensual because, for example, he could be found to have been reckless for failing to check with the web owner about the photo's status. Furthermore, the public interest clause would allow juries and judges to intrude into publishers and librarians' editorial freedom. Also, prosecutors could still go after hackers, photo-taking rapists, and other strangers, who download, send and post nonconsensual sexual images under other criminal statutes.

Arizona's first Revenge Porn law, codified as Arizona Revised Statute 13-1425, failed to include intent-to-harm or public interests exemption provisions.[253] Those omissions apparently led to its demise in July 2015, though, because there was no ruling on its merits, we cannot know with certainty. Arizona agreed to stop enforcing the law as part of a court-approved settlement.[254] Lee Rowland, staff attorney of the ACLU, which brought the lawsuit along with a coalition of booksellers and publishers, says of the court-approved agreement[255] to halt enforcement of the Arizona statute:

> For starters, the law didn't require that the offender actually intend to enact "revenge"—in fact, the law had no intent requirement at all. Nor did the bill require that a person who posted an image *know* it was private, just that they "should have known" they lacked consent. (Pro tip: You *always* lack consent if you haven't asked for it or been told.) Even the most well-intentioned laws can easily run afoul of the First Amendment if they aren't carefully crafted with the Constitution in mind.[256]

What about Illinois Criminal Code Sec. 11-23.5, "Non-Consensual dissemination of private sexual images" law, which became effective June 2015?

CCRI's Carrie Goldberg once said it was one of the best of the new revenge porn laws.[257] Is it constitutionally sound?

The Illinois law makes it a felony to disseminate private sexual images and another section of the criminal code allows the state to void contracts or agreements stemming from the illegal use of the images.[258] Its definition of the banned "intimate parts" includes "transparency clothed genitals" and "partially or fully exposed nipple, including exposure through transparent clothing." 11-23.5(a). As noted earlier, Franks criticized similar language in the Georgia statute as over-inclusive. If challenged, it is likely that such language would be struck.

The statute includes "reasonable expectation of privacy" language similar to the New York statute that Professor Calvert criticized. Again, the likelihood of proving that a victim had a reasonable expectation of privacy beyond a reasonable doubt is a high hurdle for a prosecutor to overcome.

The statute also says an individual is culpable if he knows or should have known that the person in the photograph did not consent. (C)(2)(3). In her "Effective Revenge Porn Law" guidelines, Franks endorses such language and cites the Illinois statute approvingly.[259] The vast majority of criminal charges require a prosecutor to prove that a defendant had knowledge of the facts that made his conduct blameworthy. In *Elonis* the U.S. Supreme Court used a federal statute banning the sale of drug paraphernalia to illustrate the guilty mind requirement, or mens rea, of criminal law. Referring to another case, the Court said, "[W]e held, an individual could not be convicted of selling such paraphernalia unless he 'knew that the items at issue [were] likely to be used with illegal drugs.' Such a showing was necessary to establish the defendant's culpable state of mind."[260]

There is, however, an important distinction between proving that a defendant knew he was engaging in a criminal act and showing he should have known his act was criminal. According to the Model Penal Code, a person acts "knowingly" if "he is aware that his conduct is of that nature or that such circumstances exist … he is aware that it is practically certain that his conduct will cause such a result" even though he doesn't act with the specific intent to cause the result.[261] In contrast, requiring that the state show that a defendant knew he was engaging requires a showing of specific intent.

Law professor Danielle Citron, CCRI advisor and author of *Hate Crimes in Cyberspace*, breaks with Franks on the endorsement of duty-to-know and the absence of intent-to-harm culpability. By Citron's measure, the Illinois statute is far from constitutionally full proof.

> Revenge porn laws should also make clear that to win a conviction, prosecutors must show that the poster of the revenge porn intended to do harm. They should only punish the person who distributes sexually explicit photos knowing that the subject expected them to be kept confidential. We don't want revenge porn statutes to make criminals of teenagers who sext with friends, who then foolishly share them with other friends, without knowing they are breaching someone's confidence and trust. And statutes may need to require proof that the victim suffered harm, emotional, economic, or otherwise, to ensure that they are not too broad.[262]

Citron has her own model revenge porn statute. Notably, her definition of harm includes emotional, reputational and financial loss.[263] The inclusion of reputation is pointless as revenge porn photos are truthful depictions of the targets nude body and sexual activities, even for photos solely concerning private individuals and matters. Moreover, her definition parts with the principle that defamation should not be criminalized. Like Franks, Citron includes a provision immunizing the use of nonconsensual pornography for lawful and other public interest purposes.[264] Citron's model law provides that:

> An actor commits criminal invasion of sexual privacy if the actor intentionally discloses an image of another person whose intimate parts are exposed or who is engaged in a sexual act, knowing that the other person expected the image to be kept private, under circumstances where the other person had a reasonable expectation that the image would be kept private. That the other person has consented to the possession of the image by the actor does not imply consent for the actor to disclose that image more broadly.[265]

By mid-2015, revenge porn laws in California and Wisconsin had led to convictions. Twelve days after Wisconsin Gov. Scott Walker signed Wis. Stat. Ann. §942.09, "Representations Depicting Nudity" act [266] into law on April 7, 2014, Jason W. Sphar of Madison told his ex-girlfriend that he was going to post nude and semi-nude photos of her on the Internet because he believed she had cheated on him.[267] He followed up on his threat by posting the images on Craiglist. Sphar eventually pled guilty to the revenge porn charges and was sentenced to 90 days in jail.[268]

The facts of the Wisconsin case would seem to provide support for the argument that revenge porn laws can effectively snare the prototypical vindictive purveyor that most troubles women. But the evidence is inconclusive. Because the defendant pled guilty, and, there was no appeal, the validity of Wisconsin's law was not tested. The statute, however, contains no requirement that the defendant intended harm. In the eyes of Citron and others, that is a constitutional flaw. Rather, it only provides felony punishment for knowledge of criminality, for an individual who:

> Captures a representation that depicts nudity without the knowledge and consent of the person who is depicted nude while that person is nude in a circumstance in which he or she has a reasonable expectation of privacy, if the person knows or has reason to know that the person who is depicted nude does not know of and consent to the capture of the representation.[269]

California amended its disorderly conduct statute in 2013 and in 2015 to ban individuals from posting nude sexual photos online, "which the persons agree or understand that the image shall remain private," with the intent to "cause serious emotional distress, and the person depicted suffers that distress."[270] First, a Los Angeles jury found Noe Iniguez guilty of three criminal counts including two restraining order violations and the state revenge porn statute.[271] Considering that Iniquez's ex-girlfriend had convinced a judge to issue a restraining order against him for sending harassing texts about two years before he started posting nude photos of her, and that he continued by posting derogatory comments about her on her employer's facebook page, accompanied by name-calling and other harassing language, his conviction isn't surprising.[272] The prosecutor, however, did not need a revenge law to convict Iniguez. Based on the pattern of harassing language and conduct directed at his ex-girlfriend and his speech-based violation of a restraining order, which would constitute speech integral to a crime, the prosecutor would have likely secured a conviction against him under a cyberstalking statute.

Yet, even with the revenge porn statute victory, Franks is not happy with the California statute. "The law is still not perfect; for instance, it requires that the victim demonstrate that she suffered serious emotional distress, which is unnecessary, burdensome and potentially requires the victim to expose even more of her private life to the public eye," she said because many individuals are not motived by intent to cause harm or emotional distress.[273] Of course, as noted above, Franks's colleague, Citron, takes the opposing view.

Literally, California did not need a revenge porn law to convict Kevin Christopher Bollaert, an owner of a revenge porn site, ugotposted.com, who published nude and sexual explicit images of women, posted by ex-boyfriends and husbands, without their consent and charged them as much as $350 to remove the photos.[274] Why? Because a jury found him guilty on charges of identity theft and extortion.[275] After vindictive ex-partners, uncooperative and blackmailing web site owners are the CCRI's second biggest concern and justification for the need to enact revenge porn laws. Section 230 of the Communications Decency Act shields online intermediaries such as web site operators from civil actions such as libel, negligence, fraud, and state law false advertising claims stemming from the content posted by users.[276] Under §230 CDA, online intermediaries who encourage possible illegal content are protected, but not those who directly post illegal content or create their own.[277] The state successfully argued that Bollaert's extortion attempts fell outside the scope of §230 CDA protection.

In a co-written law journal article, "Criminalizing Revenge Porn," Citron and Franks speculated on the impact of Bollaert's conviction on the validity of their argument that revenge porn laws are necessary. "There are countless other sites and blogs that host revenge porn that do not engage in extortion," Citron and Franks wrote. "If these criminal prosecutions are successful, site operators will stop charging for the removal of photos and the phenomenon will still continue."[278]

Citron and Franks also contend that that cyberstalking laws are ineffective tools for snaring site operators:

> Most site operators cannot be said to have engaged in a pattern of harassing conduct vis-à-vis any given victim. They lack the requisite intent to "kill, injure, harass, or place under surveillance with intent to kill, injure, harass, or intimidate, or cause substantial emotional distress" a particular person. Many admitted purveyors of nonconsensual pornography maintain, with some plausibility, that their sole intention is to obtain notoriety, fulfill some sexual desire, or increase traffic for their websites.[279]

Criminal defense attorney and television legal analyst Scott H. Greenfield tracks the revenge porn law debate on his blog, "Simple Justice," and finds the arguments of Franks, Citron and other CCRI advocates unpersuasive.

> Is it possible that the Supreme Court will eventually hold that revenge porn constitutes a new exception to the Constitution, or is somehow shoehorned into an existing exception even though no one has been so bold as to propose that it might be? It's possible. But until then, all the tweaking around the edges of model laws, even if they get to the point where the law has been tightened up such that it passes muster for vagueness and overbreadth, even if that means that someone [Citron and Franks hate] will not be prosecuted so that innocents aren't subject to prosecution as well, the law will still fail to pass muster under the First Amendment.[280]

No doubt, the debate about the constitutionality of revenge porn statutes will continue until the U.S. Supreme Court steps in. Meanwhile, well-intentioned legislators will most likely continue to write constitutionally suspect laws, and who can blame them if they write a bad statute. It's one thing when civil libertarians and censorship-prone prosecutors give conflicting advice about whether a valid revenge porn statute is possible. But what does a legislator do when two advocates from the same camp, Franks and Citron, cannot agree on how to write the ideal revenge porn statute?

Ultimately, the question of the constitutionality of revenge porn laws may come down to the obscenity doctrine. Put another way, can a law that makes pornography illegal, which is otherwise protected under the First Amendment, be constitutionally valid? (This question is taken up in "Image Control: Who Loses When Teen Sexting and Revenge Porn Are Criminalized.")

The Morality of Indignation Makes Bad Law

"It used to be said that 'hard cases make bad law'—a proposition that our less pedantic age regards as doubtful," legal scholar Glanville Williams wrote in the late 1957. "What is certain is that cases in which the moral indignation of the judge is aroused frequently make bad law."[281]

Likewise, the moral indignation of crusaders and legislators frequently leads to the passage of bad statutory laws, and, in turn, a new class of unintended victims, collateral damage, so to speak. Such is the case even in the crusade to criminalize revenge porn in an effort to protect women from reprehensible individuals, who do not deserve anyone's sympathy. It almost happened in Arizona, but for a successful lawsuit brought by a coalition of bookstores, publishers, news media, librarians, and photographers.

Teenagers, though, are the most vulnerable and sympathetic targets of the campaign by the morally outraged to criminalize hostile and sexual online expression. Already, many state legislators have recognized the absurdity and injustice of prosecuting teenage girls who send nude selfies to boyfriends under child pornography and sex offender laws. Yet, prosecutors still treat love-struck, naïve young women as though they were pedophiles and child pornographers.

Similarly, the stampede by legislators to crack down on online teenager cyberbullies by prosecuting them as criminals under hastily devised cyberharassment statutes is misguided because most teenage cyberbullies are engaging in constitutionally protected speech. Using cyberharassment statutes to crush political dissent, parody and uninhibited criticism of government officials is beyond the pale because the U.S. Supreme Court has protected such expression for more than 60 years. Yet, that is precisely what some prosecutors have done, forcing defendants to spend money and time to secure free speech rights that would obviously be theirs if they had made the same statements standing on a soap box, circulated them in a pamphlet, or broadcasted them on radio and television.

Finally, the unsettled state and inconsistent interpretation of the First Amendment student speech doctrine by the courts puts public school students needlessly and arbitrarily at risk of suspension. Depending on the interpretation of the doctrine by a particular federal or state court, a student in one state or jurisdiction who posts "*&^*^%&^% to my horrible teachers" on his social media site risks suspension, while a student in another state or jurisdiction is protected by the First Amendment. Yet, if either student shouted, "*&^*^%&^% to my horrible teachers," at the top of his lungs while walking home from school, the chances are nil that school administrators would take action against the student. Banning cyberbullying is a complicated and nuanced undertaking. It is made more difficult when one chooses to ignore the well-established rights of adult speakers to offend, to offer truthful criticism, and to possess and distribute sexually explicit content without fear of criminal prosecution, and the rights of public school students to be free from censorship unless their online, off-campus speech substantial disrupts the school environment or violates the rights of other students.

Notes

1. U.S. v. Elonis, 730 F.d 321, 325–25 (3d Cir. 2013).
2. Lyle Denniston, "Opinion Analysis: Internet Threats Still in Legal Limbo?," *Scotusblog*, June 1, 2015, 1:49 PM, http://www.scotusblog.com/2015/06/opinion-analysis-internet-threats-still-in-legal-limbo/ (accessed August 11, 2016).
3. U.S. v. Elonis, 730 F.ed 321, 326.
4. "What is Cyberbullying," U.S. Department of Health & Human Services, http://www.stopbullying.gov/cyberbullying/what-is-it/index.html (accessed August 11, 2016).
5. Virginia v. Black, 538 U.S. 343, 360 (2003).
6. Elonis v. U.S., 135 S. Ct. 2001, 2016 (2015).
7. Jessica Valenti, "Free Speech is a Bad Excuse for Online Creeps to Threaten Rape and Murder," *The Guardian*, June 18, 2014 7:30 EDT, https://www.theguardian.com/commentisfree/2014/jun/18/free-speech-online-creeps-cyberbullying-laws (accessed August 11, 2016).
8. Elonis v. U.S., 135 S. Ct. 2001, 2004.
9. Ibid., 2012.
10. Justin W. Patchin, "The Challenge of Criminalizing Threatening Online Speech (Elonis v. United States)," Cyberbullying Research Center, August 7, 2015, http://cyberbullying.org/criminalizing-online-threatening-speech-elonis (accessed August 11, 2016).

11. Eugene Volokh, "The Supreme Court Doesn't Decide When Speech Becomes a Constitutionally unprotected 'True Threat,'" *The Volokh Conspiracy* (blog), June 1, 2015, https://www.washingtonpost.com/news/volokh-conspiracy/wp/2015/06/01/the-supreme-court-doesnt-decide-when-speech-becomes-a-constitutionally-unprotected-true-threat/?utm_term=.89ad45adf05d (accessed August 12, 2016).
12. U.S. v. Elonis, 841 F. 3d 589, 598 (2016).
13. People v. Walter Relerford, 2016 IL App (1st) 132531 (June 24, 2016), http://www.illinoiscourts.gov/Opinions/AppellateCourt/2016/1stDistrict/1132531.pdf (accessed July 5, 2016).
14. Charles E. Notar, Sharon Padgett, and Jessica Roden, "Cyberbullying: A Review of Literature," *Universal Journal of Educational Research* 1 (2013): 1–9, http://files.eric.ed.gov/fulltext/EJ1053975.pdf (accessed July 5, 2016).
15. Robert S. Tokunaga, "Following You Home from School: A Critical Review and Synthesis of Research on Cyberbullying Victimization," *Computers in Human Behavior* 26 (2010): 282.
16. Ibid., 278.
17. "Under the due process vagueness doctrine, a court can strike down a statute when a 'person of ordinary intelligence' cannot determine whether his or her conduct falls within the prohibition. The Constitution requires criminal laws to state explicitly what conduct is punishable." Grayned v. City of Rockford, 408 U.S. 104, 108 (1972).
18. The First Amendment overbreadth doctrine prohibits a statute from criminalizing otherwise legal and constitutionally protected conduct. See New York v. Ferber, 458 U.S. 747, 769–73 (1982).
19. Tinker v. Des Moines School District, 393 U.S. 503, 513 (1969) (The U.S. Supreme Court ruled that it was an unconstitutional abridgement of a public school student's First Amendment free speech right to ban student speech, "if it could not be justified by a showing that the students' activities would materially and substantially disrupt the work and discipline of the school."); Bethel School District No. 403 v. Fraser, 478 U.S. 675, 683 (1986), The Court said, "The schools, as instruments of the state, may determine that the essential lessons of civil, mature conduct cannot be conveyed in a school that tolerates lewd, indecent, or offensive speech and conduct …").
20. "If there is a bedrock principle underlying the First Amendment, it is that the government may not prohibit the expression of an idea simply because society finds the idea itself offensive or disagreeable." Texas v. Johnson, 491 U.S. 397 (1989).
21. Commonwealth v. William P. Johnson, 470 Mass. 300 (2014).
22. Thomas I. Emerson, "Toward a General Theory of the First Amendment," *Yale Law Journal* 72 (1963): 877, 882–84.
23. Ibid., 888.
24. Ibid., 879–81.
25. Texas v. Johnson, 491 U.S. 397, 414 (1989).
26. Emerson, "Toward a General Theory of the First Amendment," 885.
27. Robert C. Post. "The Constitutional Concept of Public Discourse: Outrageous Opinion, Democratic Deliberation, and Hustler Magazine v. Falwell," *Harvard Law Review* 103 (1989–1990): 602, 625, http://digitalcommons.law.yale.edu/cgi/viewcontent.cgi?article=1209&context=fss_papers (accessed July 5, 2016).

28. Connick v. Myers, 461 U.S. 138, 145 (1983).
29. U.S. v. Stevens, 130 S. Ct. 1577, 1591 (2010).
30. See U.S. v. Jeffries, 692 F.3d 473 (2012).
31. Gooding v. Wilson, 405 U.S. 518 (1972).
32. Brandenburg v. Ohio, 395 U.S. 444 (1969).
33. Giboney v. Empire Storage & Ice Co., 336 U.S. 490 (1949).
34. Avlana K. Eisenberg, "Criminal Infliction of Emotional Distress," *Michigan Law Review* 113 (2015): 607, http://repository.law.umich.edu/mlr/vol113/iss5/1 (accessed July 5, 2016).
35. U.S. v. Alvarez, 132 S.Ct. 2537, 2544 (2012).
36. Ibid., 2547.
37. Ibid.
38. U.S. v. Stevens, 533 F. 3d 218, 235, n. 16 (2008).
39. United States v. Raines, 362 U.S. 17, 21 (1960)
40. People v. Marquan, 24 N.Y.3d 1, 8 (2014).
41. Stevens, 130 S. Ct. 1577, 1587(2012).
42. Ibid.
43. See Broadrick v. Oklahoma, 413 U.S. at 601, 613 (1973). ("[A]ny enforcement of a statute thus placed at issue is totally forbidden until and unless a limiting construction or partial invalidation so narrows it as to remove the seeming threat or deterrence to constitutionally protected expression.")
44. Papachristou v. Jacksonville, 405 U.S. 156, 162 (1972); Winters v. New York, 333 U.S. 507, 515–16 (1948).
45. Grayned v. City of Rockford, 408 U.S. 104, 108 (1972).
46. Ibid., 109.
47. Reno v. ACLU, 512 U.S. 844, 872 (1997).
48. Ibid.
49. Reed v. Town of Gilbert, 135 S. Ct. 2218, 2222 (2015).
50. Ibid.
51. Eugene Volokh, "One-to-One Speech vs. One-to-Many Speech, Criminal Harassment Laws, and 'Cyberstalking,'" *Northwestern University Law Review* 107 (2013): 731, 767–68, http://scholarlycommons.law.northwestern.edu/nulr/vol107/iss2/9 (accessed August 19, 2016).
52. People v. Marquan, 24 NY 3d 1, 11 (2014).
53. Stanford H. Kadish, "The Crisis of Overcriminalization," in *Crime and Criminal Justice*, ed. David W. Patterson (New York: MSS Information Corporation, 1972), 66.
54. Michal Buchhandler-Raphael, "Overcriminalizing Speech," *Cardozo Law Review* 36 (2015): 29 (Forthcoming, Volume (5)), http://ssrn.com/abstract=2421254 (August 17, 2016).
55. Ibid., 30–32.
56. Justin W. Patchin, "Public Radio Discussion on Proposed Cyberbullying Legislation," Cyberbullying Research Center, May 13, 2009, http://cyberbullying.org/public-radio-discussion-on-proposed-cyberbullying-legislation (August 17, 2016).
57. *Cyberbullying and Online Safety for Children: Hearing Before the Subcomm. on Crime, Terrorism, and Homeland Security of the H. Comm. on the Judiciary*, 111th Cong. 22 (2009)

(statement of Rep. Louie Gohmert, Committee on the Judiciary), http://www.gpo.gov/fdsys/pkg/CHRG-111hhrg52547/html/CHRG-111hhrg52547.htm (August 17, 2016).
58. Olweus Bullying Prevention Program, "Bullying Frequently Asked Questions," Violence Prevention Works.org, http://www.violencepreventionworks.org/public/faqs.page (accessed August 17, 2016).
59. Marilyn A. Campbell, "Cyber-bullying: An Old Problem in a New Guise?" *Australian Journal of Guidance and Counselling* 15 (2005): 68–76; Justin W. Patchin and Sameer Hinduja, "Bullies Move Beyond the Schoolyard: A Preliminary Look at Cyberbullying," *Youth Violence and Juvenile Justice* 4 (2006): 148–169.
60. Marilyn A. Campbell et al., "Victims' Perceptions of Traditional and Cyberbullying, and the Psychosocial Correlates of their Victimisation," *Emotional and Behavioural Difficulties* 17 (2012): 389–401, 397.
61. Brian Alexander, "Monica Lewinsky Talk hits Cyberbullying," *USA Today*, March 21, 2015, 6:20 PM EDT, http://www.usatoday.com/story/life/people/2015/03/21/monica-lewinsky-ted-talks-culture-of-humiliation/25148717/ (accessed August 17, 2016).
62. Alexandra Schwartz, "Monica Lewinsky and the Shame Game," *The New Yorker*, March 16, 2015, http://www.newyorker.com/culture/cultural-comment/monica-lewinsky-and-the-shame-game (accessed August 17, 2016).
63. New York Times v. Sullivan, 376 U.S. 254, 270 (1964).
64. Megan Rehberg and Susan W. Brennan, "'Kiddie Crime?' "The Utility of Criminal Law in Controlling Cyberbullying," *First Amendment Law Review* 8 (2009): 50, http://ssrn.com/abstract=1537873 (accessed August 17, 2016).
65. Model Penal Code §250.7 comment at 44 (Tentative Draft No. 13, 1961).
66. Eric P. Robinson, "Another One Bites the Dust: Minnesota's Criminal Libel Law Struck Down," *Blog Law Online* (blog), May 28, 2015, http://bloglawonline.blogspot.com/2015/05/another-one-bites-dust-minnesotas.html (August 17, 2016).
67. State v. Turner, 863 NW 2d 204, 208 (2015).
68. Milkovich v. Lorraine Journal, 497 U.S. 1 (1990).
69. Ashley Judd, "Forget Your Team: Your Online Violence Toward Girls and Women Is What Can Kiss My Ass," *Identities.Mic*, March 19, 2015, http://mic.com/articles/113226/forget-your-team-your-online-violence-toward-girls-and-women-is-what-can-kiss-my-ass (accessed August 17, 2016).
70. David Just, "Video: Ashley Judd says She's Pressing Charges after Twitter Threats," *Chicago Sun-Times*, March 17, 2015, 12:44 PM, http://chicago.suntimes.com/basketball/7/71/447881/video-ashley-judd-says-shes-pressing-charges-twitter-threats (accessed August 19, 2016).
71. Virginia v. Black, 538 U.S. 343, 360 (2003).
72. Ibid., 343.
73. Rehberg and Brenner, "'Kiddie Crime?' The Utility of Criminal Law in Controlling Cyberbullying," 58.
74. Ibid.
75. Mink v. Knox, 613 F. 3d 995, 1006–07 (10th Cir. 2010).
76. Mikel J. Sporer, "Colorado Repeals Criminal Libel Law," *Silha Center for the Study of Media Ethics & Law*, http://www.silha.umn.edu/news/Spring2012/SILHACENTER DefamationLawsuitsUniversityofMinnesota.html (accessed August 19, 2016).

77. Minnesota v. Timothy Robert Turner, A14-1408 (Minn. Ct. App. 2015), http://scholar.google.com/scholar_case?case=7182565365062452882&q=State+v.+Timothy+Robert+Turner&hl=en&as_sdt=4,200,201&as_ylo=2015 (accessed August 19, 2016).
78. Appellant's Reply Brief at 2, People v. Marquan, 24 NY 3d 1 (2014) (No. 332-12 APL #2013-00231), http://www.nyclu.org/files/releases/2013-12-18_AppellantReplyBrief.PDF (accessed August 19, 2016).
79. State v. Leidecker, P3/11-2685 (R.I. July 30, 2014), http://www.washingtonpost.com/news/volokh-conspiracy/wp-content/uploads/sites/14/2014/10/Leidecker.pdf (accessed August 19, 2016).
80. Lisa Backus, "Cop gets Suspended Sentence for Facebook Threat," *The Bristol Press*, December 5, 2011 12 AM, http://www.centralctcommunications.com/bristolpress/news/article_807ce9c0-d444-5842-8282-50f0fb73eef6.html (accessed August 19, 2016).
81. Volokh, "One-to-One Speech vs. One-to-Many Speech, Criminal Harassment Laws, and 'Cyberstalking,'" 738–39.
82. Snyder v. Blue Mountain, 650 F. 3d 915, 921 (3d Cir. 2011).
83. Ibid., 920.
84. Tinker v. Des Moines School District, 393 U.S. 513.
85. Bethel School District, No. 403 v. Fraser, 478 U.S. 675, 683 (1986).
86. Morse v. Frederick, 551 U.S. 393 (2007).
87. Frederick v. Morse, 439 F. 3d 1114 (9th Cir. 2006).
88. Morse v. Frederick, 551 U.S. 393, 404 (2007).
89. Ibid., 425.
90. Layshock v. Hermitage School District, 593 F.3d 249, 263 (2010).
91. Snyder v. Blue Mountain, 650 F. 3d at 920.
92. Doninger v. Niehoff, 642 F. 3d 334, 346 (2d Cir. 2011).
93. Sameer Hinduja and Justin W. Patchin, "A Brief Review of State Cyberbullying Laws and Policies," Cyberbullying Research Center, January 2016, http://www.cyberbullying.us/Bullying-and-Cyberbullying-Laws.pdf (accessed August 19, 2016).
94. Arkansas Code Annotated §6-18-514, http://law.justia.com/codes/arkansas/2012/title-6/subtitle-2/chapter-18/subchapter-5/section-6-18-514 (accessed August 19, 2016).
95. See Simon v Bellmore-Merrick Central High School District, 2015 NY Slip Op 08654 (November 24, 2015), http://law.justia.com/cases/new-york/appellate-division-first-department/2015/16236-13901-13.html (accessed January 13, 2016); Hunter Schwarz, "Schools Can Require Students to Hand Over their Social Media Passwords," *The Washington Post*, January 22, 2015, http://www.washingtonpost.com/blogs/govbeat/wp/2015/01/22/schools-can-require-students-to-hand-over-their-social-media-passwords-under-illinois-law/ (accessed January 13, 2016); Emily Suski, "Beyond the Schoolhouse Gates: The Unprecedented Expansion of School Surveillance Authority Under Cyberbullying Laws," Case Western Reserve Law Review 65 (2014), http://papers.ssrn.com/sol3/papers.cfm?abstract_id=2573390 (accessed January 13, 2016).
96. Curt Brow, "ACLU Wins Settlement for Sixth Grader's Facebook Posting," *Star Tribune*, March 25, 2014, http://www.startribune.com/minnewaska-student-wins-70k-from-school-over-facebook-post/252263751/?c=y&page=all&prepage=1#continue (accessed January 13, 2016).

97. American Civil Liberties Union of North Carolina, "Factsheet—Criminalizing Online Speech," http://acluofnorthcarolina.org/files/ACLU_FACTSHEET-Criminalizing-Online-Student-Speech.pdf (accessed January 13, 2016); See also Arkansas Code Annotated. § 5-71-217 (2005 & Supp. 2013), and Louisiana Revised Statutes Annontated. § 14:40.7 (2007 & Supp. 2013).
98. 2014 North Carolina General Statutes, Chapter 14-Criminal Law. Article 60-Computer Related Crime, http://law.justia.com/codes/north-carolina/2014/chapter-14/article-60 (accessed January 13, 2016).
99. American Civil Liberties Union of North Carolina, "Factsheet—Criminalizing Online Speech."
100. State v. Bishop, COA14-1227 (N.C. Ct. App. June 16, 2015), http://caselaw.findlaw.com/nc-court-of-appeals/1705020.html (accessed August 17, 2016).
101. Ibid.
102. Ibid.
103. Ibid.
104. Ibid.
105. Ibid.
106. American Civil Liberties Union of North Carolina, "Factsheet—Criminalizing Online Speech."
107. People v. Marquan, 24 NY 3d 1 (2014).
108. State v. Leidecker, No. P3/11-2685 (R.I. July 30, 2014), http://www.washingtonpost.com/news/volokh-conspiracy/wp-content/uploads/sites/14/2014/10/Leidecker.pdf (accessed August 19, 2016)
109. People v. Marquan, 24 NY 3d at 6.
110. Ibid.
111. Eugene Volokh, "New York's Highest Court Strikes down Cyber-bullying Law," *The Volokh Conspiracy* (blog), July 1, 2014, http://www.washingtonpost.com/news/volokh-conspiracy/wp/2014/07/01/new-yorks-highest-court-strikes-down-cyber-bullying-law/ (accessed August 19, 2016).
112. Volokh, "One-to-One Speech vs. One-to-Many Speech, Criminal Harassment Laws, and 'Cyberstalking,'" 731.
113. State v. Bishop, COA14-1227 (N.C. Ct. App. June 16, 2015).
114. E-mail sent to Daniel McCoy, Albany County Executive from Robert A. Perry, NYCLU Legislative Director, October 2, 2014, http://www.nyclu.org/files/releases/Cyberbullying_Albany_Letter_County_Executive_10_2_2014.pdf (accessed August 19, 2016).
115. Ibid.
116. Bachowski v. Salamone, Wis. 2d 397, 417 n.2 (1987)
117. Ibid., 418 n. 3.
118. Press Release. National Conference of State Legislatures, "State Cyberstalking and Cyberharassment Laws," Rhode Island Bar.Com, January 26, 2011, https://www.ribar.com/UserFiles/law%20day-%20cyber%20laws.pdf (accessed August 19, 2016).
119. Hinduja and Patchin, "A Brief Review of State Cyberbullying Laws and Policies."
120. Bolles v. People, 541 P.2d 80, 83 (Colo. 1975).
121. See Mo. Rev. Stat. §§ 565.225.1(3), 565.090.1(3).

122. Shane Anthony, "Jury in Cyber Harassment Trial Found No Proof of 'Emotional Distress,'" *St. Louis Dispatch*, February 19, 2011, http://www.stltoday.com/news/local/stcharles/article_5990583f-8aad-5b74-a85c-4dfde5bf4637.html (August 19, 2016).
123. See State v. Vaughn, 366 S.W.3d 513, 521 (Mo. 2012).
124. U.S. v. Drew, 259 F.R.D. 449 (C.D. Cal. 2009).
125. Lyrissa B. Lidsky and Andrea P. Garcia, "How Not to Criminalize Cyberbullying," *Missouri Law Review* 22 (2012), 701.
126. See Drew, 259 F.R.D. at 452.
127. Scott Glover, "MySpace Goes to Trial," *Los Angeles Times*, November 25, 2008, http://articles.latimes.com/2008/nov/25/local/me-myspace25 (accessed August 19, 2016).
128. See Drew, 259 F.R.D. at 452.
129. Ibid.
130. Fox News, "No Criminal Charges in MySpace Suicide," December 3, 2007, http://www.foxnews.com/story/2007/12/03/prosecutor-no-criminal-charges-in-myspace-suicide/ (accessed August 19, 2016).
131. Lidsky and Garcia, "How Not to Criminalize Cyberbullying," 701, n. 43.
132. Drew, 259 F.R.D. at 452.
133. William Tasch, "'MySpace Mom' Asks Court Not to Stretch Federal Crime Beyond Congress' Intent," *Public Interest Law Reporter* 14 (2009): 172, 173, http://lawecommons.luc.edu/pilr/vol14/iss2/10 (accessed August 19, 2016).
134. Drew, 259 F.R.D. at 453.
135. Ibid., 457.
136. Ibid., 467.
137. Harvey Silvergate, "What You Don't Know *Can* Hurt You," *Reason.com*, July 2011, http://reason.com/archives/2011/06/21/what-you-dont-know-can-hurt-yo (accessed August 19, 2016).
138. 2008 Mo. Laws 812 (codified at Mo. Rev. Stat. § 565.090.1(5) (6) (Supp. 2011)).
139. Ibid.
140. Thomas A. Jacobs, *Teen Cyberbullying Investigated: Where Do Your Rights End and Consequences Begin* (Minneapolis: Free Spirit, 2010), 162.
141. Steve Pokin, *St. Peters Woman Found Not Guilty in Cyber Harassment Case*, *St. Louis Today* (February 17, 2011, 12:00 AM, http://www.stltoday.com/suburban-journals/stcharles/news/st-peters-woman-found-not-guilty-in-cyber-harassment-case/article_6dac3355-56dc-505e-922c-9d62b7e1080f.html (accessed August 21, 2016).
142. Ibid.
143. Ibid.
144. "Section 565.090.1(5) defines 'harassment' to occur when a person '[k]nowingly makes repeated unwanted communication to another person.'" State v. Vaugh, 366 S.W.3d 513 at 519 (Mo. banc 2012).
145. Ibid., 516.
146. Ibid., 519.
147. Michael L. Nepple and Mark Sableman, "Missouri Recognizes Right to Deliver Unwanted Speech," ABA Section of Litigation, First Amendment & Media Litigation, July 26, 2012, http://www.thompsoncoburn.com/Libraries/Firm_Documents/Sableman-Nepple_article.pdf (accessed August 21, 2016).

148. 2008 Mo. Laws 812.
149. Vaugh, 336 S. W. 3d 513 at 522.
150. Marquan, 24 N.Y.3d 1.
151. People v. Golb, 23 NY 3d 455 (2014).
152. Mo. Rev. Stat. § 565.090.2, http://www.moga.mo.gov/mostatutes/stathtml/56500000902.html (accessed August 21, 2016).
153. United Press International, "Cyberbullying Case goes to Jury," *UPI.com*, November 25, 2008, 9:40 AM, http://www.upi.com/Top_News/2008/11/25/Cyberbullying-case-goes-to-jury/57271227624011/#ixzz3UZX5Zf00 (accessed August 21, 2016).
154. Ibid.
155. Drew, 259 F.R.D. at 457.
156. Ibid.
157. Internet Business Law Services Editor, "Internet Law-Missouri Governor Signs Cyber-Bullying Bill into Law," *IBLS.com*, http://www.ibls.com/internet_law_news_portal_view.aspx?s=latestnews&id=2095 (accessed August 21, 2016).
158. See Lidsky and Garcia, "How Not to Criminalize Cyberbullying,", 711, 712.
159. Golb, 23 NY 3d 455, 467 (2014).
160. Ibid., 459.
161. Ibid., 459–60 (2014).
162. Ibid., 466–67 (2014).
163. People v Dietze, 75 NY2d 47 (1989).
164. Golb, 23 NY 3d 455 at 467.
165. Dietze, 75 NY 2d 47 at 51.
166. The New York State Senate, Bill S7869-2013, June 6, 2014, http://open.nysenate.gov/legislation/bill/S7869-2013 (accessed August 21, 2016).
167. New York Civil Liberties Union, Legislative Memo: In Opposition of an ACT to Amend the Penal and Executive Law, in relation to aggravated harassment in the second degree (June 19, 2014), http://www.nyclu.org/content/support-of-act-amend-penal-and-executive-law (accessed August 21, 2016).
168. Bolles v. People, 541 P. 80, 83 (1975).
169. Kramer v. Price, 712 F.2d 174, 178 (5th Cir. 1983).
170. Everett v. Moore, 37 Wash. App. 862, 864 (1984).
171. State v. Gattis, 730 P. 2d 497, 501 (1986).
172. State v. LaFontaine, 16 A. 3d 1281 (2011).
173. State v. Dugan, 303 P. 3d 775, 774 (2013).
174. State v. Button, 622 NW 480, 485 (Iowa 2001).
175. Yates v. Com., 753 S.W. 2d 874, 875 (1988).
176. Snyder v Phelps, 131 S Ct 1207, 1220 (2011), quoting Erznoznik v Jacksonville, 422 US 205, 210–11 (1975).
177. Gooding v. Wilson, 405 U.S. 518.
178. City of Billings v. Nelson (2014), 322 P. 3d 1039, 1045 (2014).
179. Common Wealth v. Welch, 444 MA 80 (2005).
180. Ibid., 96.
181. Patchin, "The Challenge of Criminalizing Threatening Online Speech (Elonis v. United States)."

182. National Institute of Justice, "Stalking," October 25, 2007, http://www.nij.gov/topics/crime/stalking/pages/welcome.aspx (accessed August 21, 2016).
183. U.S. v. Petrovic, 701 F. 3d 849, 855 (8th Cir. 2012).
184. Ibid., 853–55.
185. U.S. v. Sayer, 748 F. 3d 425 (1st Cir. 2014).
186. Ibid., 428.
187. Ibid., 434.
188. Ibid., 435.
189. U.S. v. Osinger, 753 F. 3d 939 (9th Cir. 2014)
190. Ibid., 942.
191. Ibid.
192. Ibid., 953.
193. U.S. v. Matusiewicz, 13–83 (US. Dist. Ct. Del, March 26, 2015), http://www.ded.uscourts.gov/sites/default/files/Chambers/OtherOpinions/GAM/Opinions/Mar2015/13-83.pdf (accessed August 21, 2016).
194. Ibid., *1–2.
195. Ibid., *5–6
196. Ibid., *17.
197. Commonwealth v. William P. Johnson, 470 MA 300 (2014).
198. Ibid., 304–05.
199. Ibid., 307.
200. Ibid., 310–11.
201. U.S. v. Cassidy, 814 F. Supp. 2d 574 (D. Md. 2011).
202. State v. Leidecker, P3/11-2685 (R.I. July 30, 2014).
203. Cassidy, 814 F. Supp. 2d 574, 583.
204. Leidecker, No. P3/11-2685, *17.
205. Chan v. Ellis, S14A1652,*7 (Ga. Supreme Ct. Mar. 27, 2015).
206. Sameer Hinduja and Justin Patchin, "State Sexting Laws," Cyberbullying Research Center, July 9, 2013, http://cyberbullying.us/summary-of-state-sexting-laws/ (accessed August 21, 2016).
207. Michelle Kim, "A Timeline of Weiner's Sexting Scandal," *WNBCNY*, 2015, Updated at 1:54 PM EDT, Jul 29, 2013, http://www.nbcnewyork.com/news/local/Weiner-Timeline-Photo-Scandal-Women--123266188.html (accessed August 21, 2016).
208. U.S. Department of Justice, Citizen's Guide to U.S. Federal Law on Child Pornography, July 6, 2015, http://www.justice.gov/criminal-ceos/citizens-guide-us-federal-law-child-pornography(accessed August 21, 2016).
209. Kaitlin Lounsbury, Kimberly J. Mitchell, and David Finkelhor, *The True Prevalence of 'Sexting* (Durham: Crimes against Children Research Center, University of New Hampshire, April 2011), 4, http://www.unh.edu/ccrc/pdf/Sexting%20Fact%20Sheet%204_29_11.pdf (accessed August 21, 2016).
210. New York v. Ferber, 458 U.S. 747 (1982).
211. Ibid., 756–65.
212. U.S. v. Williams, 128 S. Ct. 1830, 1837 (2008).
213. See Shannon Shafron-Perez, "Average Teenager or Sex Offender? Solutions to the Legal Dilemma Caused by Sexting," *John Marshall Journal of Information Technology & Privacy Law*

26 (2009), 431; Robert Richards and Clay Calvert, "When Sex and Cell Phones Collide: Inside the Prosecution of a Teen Sexting Case," *Hastings Communication & Entertainment Law Journal* 32, no. 1 (2009–2010): 1. Julia Halloran McLaughlin, "Crime and Punishment: Teen Sexting in Context," 115 *Penn State Law Review*, (2010): 135, http://www.pennstatelawreview.org/115/1/115%20Penn%20St.%20L.%20Rev.%20135.pdf; Amy Adele Hasinoff, *Sexting Panic: Rethinking Criminalization, Privacy, and Consent* (Champaign: University of Illinois Press, 2015); Shaheen Shariff, *Sexting and Cyberbullying: Defining the Line for Digitally Empowered Kids* (New York: Cambridge University Press, 2015).

214. Ysolt Usigan, "Teen Sexting Driven by Peer Pressure, says Study," *CBSNews.com*, September 30, 2011, 4:47 PM, http://www.cbsnews.com/news/teen-sexting-driven-by-peer-pressure-says-study/ (accessed August 21, 2016).
215. Kathy Martinez-Prather and Donna M. Vandiver, "Sexting Among Teenagers in the United States: A Retrospective Analysis of Identifying Motivating Factors, Potential Targets and the Role of a Capable Guardian," *International Journal of Cyber Criminology* 8 (January–June 2014): 21–35, 24, 26, http://www.cybercrimejournal.com/pratherVandiverijcc2014vol8issue1.pdf (accessed August 17, 2016).
216. Janis Wolak and David Finkelhor, *Sexting: A Typology* (Durham: Crimes against Children Research Center, University of New Hampshire, March 2011), 3, http://www.unh.edu/ccrc/pdf/CV231_Sexting%20Typology%20Bulletin_4-6-11_revised.pdf (accessed August 17, 2016).
217. Ibid., 7.
218. Eastwood Atwater, *Adolescence* (Englewood Cliffs: Prentice-Hall, 1992).
219. JoAnne Sweeny, "Do Sexting Prosecutions Violate Teenagers' Constitutional Rights?," *San Diego Law Review*, 48 (November 6, 2010): 953, http://ssrn.com/abstract=1703964 (accessed August 17, 2016).
220. Salter v. State, 906 NE 2d 212, 223 (Ind. Ct. App. 2009).
221. Wolak and Finkelhor, *Sexting: A Typology*, 4.
222. Janis Wolak, David Finkelhor, and Kimberly J. Mitchell, *Trends in Arrests for Child Pornography Production: The Third National Juvenile Online Victimization Study* (Durham: Crimes against Children Research Center, University of New Hampshire, 2012), 3, http://www.unh.edu/ccrc/pdf/CV270_Child%20Porn%20Production%20Bulletin_4-13-12.pdf (accessed August 17, 2016).
223. *Emerging Patterns and Trends #1: Youth Produced Sexual Content* (Cambridge, UK: Internet Watch Foundation, March 10, 2015), 3, 11, https://www.iwf.org.uk/assets/media/resources/Emerging%20Patterns%20and%20Trends%20Report%201%20-%20Youth-Produced%20Sexual%20Content.pdf (accessed August 17, 2016).
224. Wolak and Finkelhor, *Sexting: A Typology*, 9.
225. Sameer Hinduja and Justin W. Patchin, "State Sexting Laws," Cyberbullying Research Center (2015), http://www.cyberbullying.us/state-sexting-laws.pdf (accessed August 17, 2016).
226. AZ Rev Stat § 8-309, http://law.justia.com/codes/arizona/2011/title8/section8-309 (accessed August 17, 2016).
227. New Jersey Statute Annotated 2A: 4A-71.1 (2012), http://www.njleg.state.nj.us/2010/Bills/AL11/128_.PDF (accessed August 17, 2016).
228. NY A01203, General Assembly Bill 1203, Reg. Sess. (NY 2013), http://legiscan.com/NY/text/A01203/id/676258 (accessed August 17, 2016).

229. Vermont Statute Annotated Title 13 § 2802b (2009), http://www.leg.state.vt.us/docs/2010/Acts/ACT058.pdf (accessed August 17, 2016).
230. Marsha Levick, "Sexting Bill Victimizes Pennsylvania Teens," *PennLive*, October 23, 2012, 12:22 AM, http://www.pennlive.com/opinion/2012/10/sexting_bill_victimizes_pennsylvania_teens.html (accessed August 17, 2016).
231. Heather Kelly, "New California 'Revenge Porn' Law May Miss Some Victims," *CNN.com*, October 3, 2013, 3:01 PM, http://www.cnn.com/2013/10/03/tech/web/revenge-porn-law-california/ (accessed August 17, 2016).
232. Scott R. Stroud, "The Dark Side of the Online Self: A Pragmatist Critique of the Growing Plague of Revenge Porn," *Journal of Mass Media Ethics: Exploring Questions of Media Morality*, 29 (2014): 168, 179.
233. John A. Humbach, "The Constitution and Revenge Porn," *Pace Law Review* 35 (2014): 215, 217–18, http://digitalcommons.pace.edu/plr/vol35/iss1/8 (accessed August 17, 2016).
234. Mary Ann Franks, *Drafting An Effective "Revenge Porn" Law: A Guide for Legislators* (Coral Gables: Cyber Civil Rights Initiative, June 17, 2015), http://www.endrevengeporn.org/guide-to-legislation/ (accessed August 17, 2016).
235. See Bridget Roberts-Pittman, Julie M. Slavens, and Bradley V. Balch, "Cyberbullying and the Complex Relationship between Bullying and Suicide," *Illinois School Board Journal* (January–February 2015), https://www.iasb.com/journal/j010215_02.cfm (accessed August 17, 2016); News Staff, "Cyberbullying Does Not 'Cause' Teen Suicide," *Science 2.0*, October 20, 2012, 10:13 AM.
236. Emily Bazelon, "Another Sexting Tragedy," *Slate*, April 12, 2013, http://www.slate.com/articles/double_x/doublex/2013/04/audrie_pott_and_rehtaeh_parsons_how_should_the_legal_system_treat_nonconsensual.html (accessed August 17, 2016).
237. Mary Anne Franks, "Why We Need a Federal Criminal Law Response to Revenge Porn," *Concurring Opinions* (blog), February 15, 2013, http://concurringopinions.com/archives/2013/02/why-we-need-a-federal-criminal-law-response-to-revenge-porn.html; http://concurringopinions.com/archives/2013/02/why-we-need-a-federal-criminal-law-response-to-revenge-porn.html (accessed August 22, 2016).
238. Amit Singhal, "'Revenge Porn' and Search," *Google Public Policy Blog*, June 19, 2015, http://googlepublicpolicy.blogspot.com/2015/06/revenge-porn-and-search.html (accessed August 22, 2016).
239. Franks, *Drafting An Effective "Revenge Porn" Law: A Guide for Legislators*, 4.
240. GA Code16-11-90, http://law.justia.com/codes/georgia/2014/title-16/chapter-11/article-3/part-3/section-16-11-90/ (accessed August 22, 2016).
241. Michelle Goldberg, "Revenge Porn Is Malicious and Reprehensible. But Should It Be a Crime?" *The Nation*, October 20, 2014, http://www.thenation.com/article/war-against-revenge-porn/ (accessed August 22, 2016).
242. GA Code16-11-90.
243. Mark Bennett, "2015.61: Unlawful Disclosure or Promotion of Intimate Visual Material," *Defending People* (blog), July 7, 2015, http://blog.bennettandbennett.com/2015/07/2015-61-unlawful-disclosure-or-promotion-of-intimate-visual-material/ (accessed August 21, 2016); Scott H. Greenfield, "Rhode Island Revenge Porn Crime Gets Vetoed," *Simple Justice* (blog), July 22 2016, http://blog.simplejustice.us/2016/06/22/rhode-island-revenge-porn-crime-gets-vetoed/ (accessed August 22, 2016).

244. Franks, *Drafting An Effective "Revenge Porn" Law: A Guide for Legislators*, 8.
245. Katz v. U.S., 389 U.S. 347, 361 (1967).
246. Clay Calvert, "Revenge Porn and Freedom of Expression: Legislative Pushback to an Online Weapon of Emotional and Reputational Destruction," *Fordham Intellectual Property, Media & Entertainment Law Journal* 24 (Spring 2014): 673: 697–99.
247. Ibid., 698.
248. Ibid., 697–98.
249. Ibid., 699.
250. Senate Bill S5946A-2013, Creates the crimes of unlawful dissemination of an intimate image in the first and second degrees as a class E felony and class A misdemeanor, respectively, http://open.nysenate.gov/legislation/bill/S5946A-2013 (accessed August 22, 2016).
251. New York v. Piznarski, 113 AD 3d 166, 176 (N.Y. App. Div., 2013).
252. Franks, *Drafting An Effective "Revenge Porn" Law: A Guide for Legislators*, 9.
253. American Civil Liberties Union (Press Release), "ACLU, Bookstores, Publishers, News Media, Librarians, and Photographers Charge Law Violates Freedom of Speech," September 23, 2014, https://www.aclu.org/news/first-amendment-lawsuit-challenges-arizona-criminal-law-banning-nude-images (accessed August 1, 2016).
254. American Civil Liberties Union (Press Release), "Judge Halts Enforcement of Unconstitutional Nude Photo Law in Arizona," July 10, 2015, https://www.aclu.org/news/judge-halts-enforcement-unconstitutional-nude-photo-law-arizona (accessed July 28, 2016).
255. Antigone Books v Mark Brnovich, 2:14-cv-02100-PHX-SRB (July 10, 2015), http://mediacoalition.org/files/litigation/antigone-books-brnovich-final-decree.pdf (accessed August 1, 2016).
256. Lee Rowland, "Victory! Federal Judge Deep-Sixes Arizona's Ridiculously Overbroad 'Nude Photo Law,'" American Civil Liberties Union (Press Release), July 10, 2015, 6:45 PM, https://www.aclu.org/blog/speak-freely/victory-federal-judge-deep-sixes-arizonas-ridiculously-overbroad-nude-photo-law (accessed August 1, 2016).
257. Carrie Goldberg, "Seven Reasons Illinois is Leading the Fight Against Revenge Porn," *Cyber Civil Rights Initiative*, December 31, 2014, http://www.cybercivilrights.org/seven-reasons-illinois-leading-fight-revenge-porn/ (accessed August 22, 2016).
258. Ill. Criminal Code Sec. 11-23.5 (2) (f); Sec. 11-23.5 (1).
259. Franks, *Drafting An Effective "Revenge Porn" Law: A Guide for Legislators*, 5.
260. Elonis, 135 S.C., 2001, 2010.
261. Vernellia R. Randall, Model Penal Code § 2.02. General Requirements of Culpability, University of Dayton Law School, http://academic.udayton.edu/legaled/crimlaw/02-Elements/04MPC2-02.htm (accessed August 1, 2016).
262. Danielle Citron, "How to Make Revenge Porn a Crime," *Slate.com*, November 7, 2013, http://www.slate.com/articles/news_and_politics/jurisprudence/2013/11/making_revenge_porn_a_crime_without_trampling_free_speech.html (accessed August 22, 2016).
263. Danielle Citrton, *Hate Crimes in Cyberspace* (Cambridge, MA: Harvard University Press, 2014), 152.
264. Ibid., 152–53.

265. Ibid., 152.
266. Wisconsin Statute 942.09, Wisconsin State Legislature, https://docs.legis.wisconsin.gov/statutes/statutes/942/09 (accessed August 22, 2016).
267. Bruce Vielmetti, "Woman's Ex-Headed for Trial under New Wisconsin Revenge Porn Law," *Milwaukee-Wisconsin Journal Sentinel*, January 1, 2015, http://www.jsonline.com/news/crime/womans-ex-headed-for-trial-under-new-wisconsin-revenge-porn-law-b99415745z1-287314261.html (accessed August 22, 2016).
268. Kate Stein, "Man Gets 90 Days in Jail in 'Revenge Porn' Case," *Wisconsin State Journal*, July 17, 2015, 10:15 AM, http://host.madison.com/news/local/crime_and_courts/man-gets-days-jail-in-revenge-porn-case/article_a6bde6ce-85e1-59ba-8577-c0c3a589ef31.html (accessed August 22, 2016).
269. Wisconsin Stat. 942.09(2)(am)1., https://docs.legis.wisconsin.gov/statutes/statutes/942/09 (accessed August 22, 2026).
270. California Penal Code §647(j)(4), https://leginfo.legislature.ca.gov/faces/codes_displaySection.xhtml?sectionNum=647.&lawCode=PEN (accessed April 27, 2017).
271. "City Attorney Feuer Secures Conviction Under State's 'Revenge Porn' Law," *Monrovia Weekly*, December 4, 2014, http://www.monroviaweekly.com/crime/city-attorney-feuer-secures-conviction-under-states-revenge-porn-law/ (accessed August 19, 2016).
272. Megan Geuss, "LA Man First to Be Sentenced Under California's "Revenge Porn" Law," *Arstechnia*, December 2, 2014, 10:46 AM EST, http://arstechnica.com/tech-policy/2014/12/la-man-one-of-first-to-be-sentenced-under-californias-revenge-porn-law/ (accessed August 19, 2016).
273. Veronica Rocha, "'Revenge Porn' Conviction is a First Under California Law," *Los Angeles Times*, December 4, 2014, 8:00 PM, http://touch.latimes.com/#section/-1/article/p2p-82189930/ (accessed August 22, 2016).
274. Tony Perry, "San Diego Man Guilty in 'Revenge Porn' Case," *Los Angeles Times*, February 2, 2015, 8:39 PM, http://touch.latimes.com/#section/-1/article/p2p-82705264/ (accessed August 22, 2016).
275. Ibid.
276. 47 U.S.C. § 230 (2000).
277. Fair Housing Council of San Fernando Valley v. Roommates.com, 521 F. 3d 1157 (2008).
278. Danielle Keats Citron and Mary Anne Franks, "Criminalizing Revenge Porn," *Wake Forest Law Review* 49 (2014): 345, 369, http://papers.ssrn.com/sol3/papers.cfm?abstract_id=2368946 (accessed August 22, 2016).
279. Ibid., 369–70.
280. Scott H. Greenfield, "The New Model Revenge Porn Law; Better, But … (Update x2)," *Simple Justice* (blog), October 6, 2014, http://blog.simplejustice.us/2014/10/06/the-new-model-revenge-porn-law-better-but/ (accessed August 22, 2016).
281. Glanville Williams, *The Sanctity of Life and the Criminal Law* (New York: Knopf, 1957), 105.

· 3 ·

THE UNNECESSARY AND UNJUST CREATION OF VIRTUAL JUVENILE DELINQUENTS

When Robert Bishop was a high school student, his words made Dillion Price cry, beat himself in the head and throw things.[1] He "slammed" (teased him harshly) Price on Facebook and encouraged schoolmates to do likewise. For this, they said Bishop was a criminal.

Bishop was accused of cyberbulling when he was called into the assistant principal's office of Southern Alamance High School in Graham, North Carolina.[2] Soon after, in February 2012, the police said he was a criminal when they arrested him.[3]

Bishop, however, never believed he deserved the arrest and stigma. "If these comments were so serious as to cause Price to have fits, why didn't his mother confront me directly and privately?" Bishop says. "Why did she not reach out to my family? Why was it that the first time I learned of this was in a media report about my case? I'm not a heartless, evil bully. If someone had come to me personally and said, 'Hey, this is bad/wrong/hurtful,' maybe law enforcement wouldn't have needed to be involved."[4]

The criminal justice system, however, was very much involved. Two years later at a criminal trial, Alamance County Assistant District Attorney Brooks Stone told a jury that Bishop should be convicted because he violated the state's cyberbullying law.[5] The jury returned a verdict of guilty, making Bishop, then 18, the first person in North Carolina to be convicted by a jury under the state's cyberbullying statute.[6] The "Protecting Children of this State by Making Cyber-Bullying A Criminal Offense Punishable as a Misdemeanor" law, adopted in 2009, prohibited the use of a computer or computer network to post or "encourage others to post on the Internet private, personal or sexual information pertaining to a minor" with "the intent to intimidate or torment a minor."[7]

In June 2015, Bishop failed to shake the "cyberbully criminal" stigma when the Court of Appeals of North Carolina upheld his convictio n.[8] He had received a suspended sentence of 30 days, 48 months of supervised probation and was banned from social media sites for a year, though the probation and ban were suspended while he appealed.[9] A local newspaper took note.

> Robert Bishop is saddled with a grownup criminal record because he wrote some things that weren't very nice while he was a high school sophomore ... The comments ranged from the vulgar to the nonsensical, but they're the same kind of boyhood barbs and schoolyard putdowns that can be heard every day in locker rooms, cafeterias and playgrounds.[10]

Things changed on June 10, 2016, when the North Carolina Supreme Court struck down a provision of the statute as unconstitutional under the First Amendment.[11] After a four-year struggle, Bishop was no longer a cyberbully in the eyes of the law. Bishop celebrated by phone calling and messaging friends and thanking all of his attorneys.

"I didn't know how to respond at first," Bishop says. "I was absolutely perceived as a criminal from the time I was arrested to today [June 10, 2016] ... For the last four years, I've had to think about how my status as a criminal affects my future; how to explain a count of cyberbullying to future friends, employers, or schools. Suddenly my life felt more free."[12]

Yet, despite the overturned conviction, he believes he is still tainted by the conviction. "I'm sure there are some people I went to high school with who believe I still am a criminal in spite of my victory (They might say something along the lines of, "You got off on a technicality.")"[13]

Because his conviction was overturned, Bishop, now a community college student, enjoyed the right to petition to have his record expunged.[14] Some or all of the other five former teens arrested the same day as Bishop for cyberbullying on Facebook stood to benefit from Bishop's victory, though they played no role in his First Amendment challenge.[15] "Under G.S. 15A-1415(b)(5), a noncapital defendant may file a motion for appropriate relief at any time after a verdict, alleging that '[t]he conduct for which the defendant was prosecuted was protected by the Constitution of the United States,'" noted Jeffrey B. Welty, of the North Carolina School of Government, who wrote about the ruling on the North Carolina Criminal Law blog.[16,17]

Beyond the local impact, the ruling marked the second time, after the New York Court of Appeals ruling in *People v. Marquan* M. (2014),[18] a state high court struck down as unconstitutional in part or in its entirety a criminal cyberbullying statute designed to protect minors by banning aggravating or irritating online speech. Is it likely that the North Carolina ruling would mark a turning point; that it would decelerate the call to criminalize hostile and abusive teen-to-teen online speech begun in the aftermath of the Meagan Meier suicide in 2008?[19] Given the fervor that drives anti-bullying advocates and their legislative and prosecutorial allies, the significance of the New York and North Carolina rulings were not likely to be game changers.

Other state lawmakers and prosecutors are likely to contend that their statutes are distinguishable from New York and North Carolina's. To that point, reflect upon the winning argument the North Carolina Department of Justice made in its brief before the North Carolina Court of Appeals.

> The North Carolina cyberbullying statute does not suffer from the same defects as the ordinance invalidated in *People v. Marquan* M. Section 14-458.1(a)(1)d narrowly tailors the law to criminalize only those electronic communications aimed at minors. The statute applies only to "posts" on the Internet regarding private, personal, or sexual information pertaining to that minor, and the scope of criminal liability is constrained by the specific intent requirement. The text of section 14-458.1(a)(1)d adequately restricts its reach to discrete types of electronic bullying designed to cause psychological and emotional harm to minors.[20]

The two statutes, however, were strikingly similar. The state's argument, and the appeals court's adoption of it, was near-reality defying. The court said the statute regulated non-expressive conduct, i.e., the act of *posting* on the Internet was not communicative. Ultimately, that argument proved unpersuasive to the seven justices of North Carolina's highest court.[21]

Proponents, however, are likely to argue that they can still draft a criminal statute that effectively targets teenagers' harsh and insulting online criticism of each other without offending the First Amendment. The Albany County Legislature responded to the judicial invalidation of its cyberbullying crime law by adopting a revision that civil libertarians denounced as unconstitutional.

Similarly, North Carolina Attorney General Roy Cooper, whose office defended the law in court, encouraged legislators to re-examine the issue after the ruling. "Just because violence happens online doesn't make it any less real or less hurtful," Cooper said the day of the ruling. "Cyberbullying can lead to physical harm, depression in its victims and even suicide and it's troubling to see this law overturned."[22]

But the lesson lawmakers, prosecutors and anti-bullying advocates should draw from the highest courts in North Carolina and New York is that it cannot be done; a cyberbullying crime law designed to protect minors from other minors cannot be constitutionally valid and effective. That's because criminal harassment laws banning online speech are content-restrictive, requiring that a speaker have the intent to threaten an unwilling listener with bodily harm. Speech that merely annoys, pesters, intimidates, torments or alarms is unlikely to meet that standard because of the inexact meanings of such terms and because prosecution based on such types of speech would allow the state to restrict First Amendment-protected expression. Furthermore, banning the disclosure of broadly interpreted terms such as "personal" or "sexual" information only adds to the murkiness of the already uncertain concept of cyberbullying.

The First Amendment and criminal law require clarity and precision. But a clearly defined and narrowly restricted statute designed to protect minors from hostile online speech would severely hamstring the state's authority to police the hyperbolic and uncivil barbs, putdowns and insults that characterize the vast majority of teen-generated cyberbullying.

Accused and Convicted

What are we to make of teens like Bishop and Marquan Mackey-Meggs? For instance, when Mackey-Meggs was a student at Cohoes High School in Albany County, N.Y., he created a Facebook page where he "anonymously posted photographs of high-school classmates … with detailed descriptions of their alleged sexual practices and predilections, sexual partners and other types of personal information. The descriptive captions, which were vulgar and offensive, prompted responsive electronic messages that threatened the creator of the website with physical harm."[23] Albany County Attorney Thomas Marcelle characterized the comments as vicious, life-altering attacks on fellow students for the express purpose of humiliating them.[24]

We don't know fully what Mackey-Meggs was thinking. He has never talked publicly about the Facebook page. We do know, however, that he was 15 when he created the page in 2011.[25] We know from his mug shot that he is

African American, though there is no reason to believe that racial conflicts in school drove him to insult his schoolmates. We do know that Mackey-Meggs told the police, "He intended the pages to be funny."[26] If that is true, he was extremely immature.

Still, there seems to be an admirable trait that he and Bishop shared, one that separated them from the majority of teens targeted by criminal cyberbullying statutes that raised obvious free speech concerns—well, at least to civil libertarians and First Amendment lawyers. They had the resolve to challenge the laws in court.

"The other students all decided to be represented by one attorney," Bishop recalls. "This attorney, whose name I do not know, told the students that trying to fight the charge would involve repercussions, such as personal belongings related to the case confiscated or searched. This was obviously false—at no point was my computer or anything else conceivably related to the case taken and at no point did that appear to be a possibility. I feel the other students were wrong for hiring the attorney, as I was offered the same plea bargain that they took even prior to deciding to get court-appointed counsel."[27]

New York

Mackey-Meggs created his social media page, "Cohoes Flames," in December 2010 when Albany Local Law 11 was but a month old.[28] The Albany County Legislature voted to make cyberbullying a misdemeanor crime "punishable by a fine of up to $1,000 and/or up to one year imprisonment" to protect minors and adults because, among things, "forty two percent of children in the fourth through eighth grade surveyed in a recent poll reported being bullied online … victims attempt or commit suicide in part because of the cyber-bullying they've endured,"[29] and because New York State had failed to regulate student online speech.[30] (New York legislators, however, amended The Dignity for All Students Act to empower schools to ban cyberbullying in 2012.)[31]

Albany Local Law 11 defined cyberbullying as

> any act of communicating or causing a communication to be sent by mechanical or electronic means, including posting statements on the internet or through a computer or email network, disseminating embarrassing or sexually explicit photographs; disseminating private, personal, false or sexual information, or sending hate mail,

> with no legitimate private, personal, or public purpose, with the intent to harass, annoy, threaten, abuse, taunt, intimidate, torment, humiliate, or otherwise inflict significant emotional harm on another person.[32]

The Cohoes Flame posting did not reveal the author's identity, but a police investigation led to Mackey-Meggs arrest in June 2011. Police charged him with 10 counts of harassment and 10 counts of cyberbullying.[33] At the start, before a city judge, the teen argued that the statute violated his First Amendment free speech rights, but to no avail.[34] On December 1, 2011, Cohoes City Court denied his motion to dismiss the case.[35] So, the teen pled guilty to only "one count of violating the Cyber-bullying Law, conditioned on his right to appeal."[36] Mackey-Meggs suffered another setback in 2013 when the Albany County Court upheld the constitutionality of statute on the grounds that its application to speech targeting minors was constitutional, though applying it to adults was not.[37]

Mackey-Meggs, however, prevailed at the New York Court of Appeals. The court ruled that the statute was unconstitutionally vague and overbroad; that its reach extended well beyond its asserted goal to protect minors from harmful online speech. That was so, the court said, because the statute criminalized all electronic means of communication, "such as telephone conversations, a ham radio transmission or even a telegram … a broad spectrum of speech outside the popular understanding of cyberbullying, including, for example: an email disclosing private information about a corporation or a telephone conversation meant to annoy an adult."[38]

The court noted that under New York rulings, "the First Amendment protects annoying and embarrassing speech even if a child may be exposed to it."[39] Therefore, the court reasoned, a criminal cyberbullying statute cannot punish any one for expressing annoying, taunting or humiliating speech. The Court said, "it is well established that prohibitions of pure speech must be limited to communications that qualify as fighting words, true threats, incitement, obscenity, child pornography, fraud, defamation or statements integral to criminal conduct."[40]

What of Mackey-Meggs's claim that he was attempting to be funny?[41] The court did not directly address the issue, but his claim goes to the question of mens rea[42] or intent and the use of cyberbullying laws to criminally prosecute defamation. In other words, had the court ruled against Marquan-Meegs, expression that a speaker intended to be funny could have been legitimately censored to protect minors and adults from harm. Imagine the impact such a ban would have had on insult comedians, parodists and satirists, particularly those who leave a record of their jokes on websites and social media. At the very least, many would have been discouraged, or to put it in First Amendment terms, there right to speech would have been chilled.

Of course, humorous expression that poses a true threat can be criminalized. In *U.S. v. Cothran* (2002), for example, the U.S. Court of Appeals for the Third Circuit ruled that a potential airline traveler who told a flight reservation agent that he was upset with U.S. Air for not letting him bring explosives on the plane, and that he wanted to blow a plane out at 35,000 feet was not protected as a joking, but was a criminal threat unprotected by the First Amendment.[43] The New York statute, however, did not require a prosecutor to show that the accused met the true threat test of criminal intent—"a speaker means to communicate a serious expression of an intent to commit an act of unlawful violence to a particular individual or group of individuals."[44] Therefore, Marquan-Meeks would have prevailed had he used the "I was just being funny" defense.

Were Marquan-Meeks's humorous comments defamatory? "Of all the dignitary harms, defamation is probably the most common theory plaintiffs invoke to remedy hurt flowing from a joke."[45] If they were, prosecution of Marquan-Meeks under a criminal statute still could not survive judicial scrutiny because New York, like the overwhelming majority of states, does not recognize defamation as a criminal action.[46] Thus, his humor motive claim reveals that the statute was a criminal libel law cloaked in cyberbullying clothing.

Some anti-bullying advocates salvage hope from the New York ruling because the court said, "Even if the First Amendment allows a cyberbullying statute of the limited nature proposed by Albany County, the local law here was not drafted in that manner."[47] Justin Patchin, a co-chair of the research center and a professor at the University of Wisconsin-Eau Claire, said that he was encouraged that the court said cyberbullying laws were not automatically unconstitutional. "The problem is, it's going to be really tricky to write a law that is comprehensive in its coverage of bullying and at the same time passes constitutional muster," he said.[48]

Others, such as Haley E. Phillips, a law student writing for the *North Carolina Law Review*, categorized the North Carolina law as representative of several statutes that are unconstitutional, and predicted,

> If the reasoning used in *Marquan* M. is applied to other criminal cyberbullying statutes, several statutes that currently exist are likely to be found unconstitutional, including North Carolina's. Because these statutes criminalize online speech in very general ways, like Albany County's did, it will be difficult for courts and legislators to

rewrite them in a way that is both constitutional and comprehensive in addressing bullying.[49]

North Carolina

Though the North Carolina Supreme Court's reasoning was similar, its doctrinal analysis was somewhat different because it struck down a statutory provision based on strict scrutiny and not vagueness or overbreadth. Vagueness or overbreadth analysis focus on due process, in other words, fair treatment. In contrast, courts use strict scrutiny analysis to determine the constitutionality of a statute or regulation that targets the words and images of a message or the viewpoint conveyed. Because the North Carolina high court said the statutory provision targeted certain types of expression, strict scrutiny was applied. Under the provision, it was unlawful to "post or encourage others to post on the Internet private, personal, or sexual information pertaining to a minor" with the "intent to intimidate or torment a minor."[50]

Oddly enough, the comments that got Bishop arrested and charged with one count of cyberbullying on February 9, 2012 were indirectly generated by Price, the object of the online mockery. In September 2011, Price had inadvertently sent a "sexually themed" text to a classmate.[51] That student posted his own Facebook page a screenshot of Price's apparently embarrassing message, which sparked a spate of verbal jousting among a number of schoolmates, including responses from Price, more than 30 comments in all.[52]

Generally, students expressed their dislike for Price—"Can we just kick his ass already?"—and intimated that he was gay.[53] Bishop volunteered to "tag" Price so that he would be notified of the posts, an action that triggered the provision's ban on encouraging others to post personal information with the intent to intimidate or torment.[54] Bishop also posted his own insults and comments about Price and other students: "This is excessively homoerotic in nature; Exquisite specimen; Anyone who would be so defensive over [Price] can't be too intelligent; And you are equally pathetic for taking the internet so seriously; There isn't a fight. We're slamming someone on the open forum that is the [I]nternet; and I heard that his anus was permanently stressed from having awkwardly shaped penises in it."[55]

Bishop says his comments were in retaliation to things Price had said to two friends, all part of a longstanding feud between Price, his family, and friends versus his family members. "I made many comments that were intended at the time to be nothing more than nonsensical and weird humor, which I was known for in high school. It still bewilders me that some of these comments were ever considered evidence."[56]

The middle level appeals court ruled for the state because it said the portion of the statute did not target expression, only the act of posting. The court viewed the law as a criminal harassment statute and it cited precedent in which the sending of repeated unwanted telephone calls or mail was deemed unprotected conduct, unworthy of First Amendment protection. "Like the telephone, the Internet can also be used as an instrumentality for communication" the appeals court analogized. "However, its use for sharing thoughts and ideas does not prevent the Internet from also being used as a mechanism for individuals to engage in harassing or tormenting conduct."[57]

The telephone analogy, however, is flawed. Even if one treats the "tagging" as comparable to telephoning someone repeatedly, the analogy falls apart once Price willingly engaged in the online exchange. Generally, those who send messages have a right to do so unless the recipient says otherwise. As Chief Justice Warren Burger explained in a ruling upholding a law requiring mail recipients to give notice when they did not wish to receive commercial mailings, "the right of every person 'to be let alone' must be placed in the scales with the right of others to communicate."[58]

The N.C. Supreme Court had no need to address that precedent because it ruled that the statute targeted speech. Reversing the lower court, the N.C. Supreme Court ruled that, "Posting information on the Internet, whatever the subject matter, can constitute speech as surely as stapling flyers to bulletin boards or distributing pamphlets to passersby, activities long protected by the First Amendment."[59] To determine the appropriate level of judicial scrutiny to apply, the court asked whether the statute language's purpose was to ban speech because of expression or for a purpose having little or nothing to do with the content of a message. The statute, the court said, was content-based because it "criminalizes some messages"—private, personal, or sexual information pertaining to a minor—"but not others, and makes it impossible to determine whether the accused has committed a crime without examining the content of his communication."[60]

The statute met the first prong of the strict scrutiny test—"protecting children from online bullying is a compelling governmental interest."[61] It failed the second prong of the test. The state did not use means that were sufficiently narrow enough to protect free speech rights to advance its interest in protecting minors because (1) it "contained no requirement that the subject of an online posting suffer injury as a result, or even that he or she become aware of such a posting;"[62] (2) its failure to define "intimidate" or "torment," conduct that annoys, pesters or harasses cannot justify protecting minors by imposing criminal penalties for online annoyance;[63] (3) it failed to define "private, personal, or sexual information pertaining to a minor;" and the statute would mandate civility.[64]

"Civility, whose definition is constantly changing, is a laudable goal but one not readily attained or enforced through criminal laws," the court noted.[65]

Blogger Eugene Volokh, a UCLA First Amendment law professor who co-authored a friend of the court brief opposing the statute, illustrated why the law was written too broadly to survive strict scrutiny. Under the undefined term of "personal information," a North Carolinian could be prosecuted for "talking about friends … and what they're doing" and "their love life. The law was billed as a ban on bullying, but bullying is not a well-defined term," Volokh says. "I think a lot of members of the legislature haven't fully figured out what they're trying to ban."[66]

What Not to Criminalize When Banning Cyberbullying

Guided by the New York and North Carolina rulings, anti-bullying legislators should avoid banning expression that annoys, intimidates, abuses, torments, pesters or discusses an individual's personal matters. Even in the pre-Internet era, courts struck down criminal harassment statutes banning annoying, intimidating, abusive or pestering expression as vague or overbroad or limited their application to conform with First Amendment principles.

The U.S. Supreme Court struck down as vague and a violation of the constitutional right of free assembly and association a Cincinnati ordinance which created a "criminal offense for 'three or more persons to assemble … on any of the sidewalks … and there conduct themselves in a manner *annoying* to persons passing by'" in a 1971 ruling [emphasis added].[67] *Coates* implies that annoying expression could not be legitimately criminalized since annoying non-expressive conduct is unconstitutionally vague. Generally, the Constitution protects expression, but it does not protect non-expressive conduct from criminalization, *Coates* ruled.

> Conduct that annoys some people does not annoy others. Thus, the ordinance is vague, not in the sense that it requires a person to conform his conduct to an imprecise but comprehensible normative standard, but rather in the sense that no standard

of conduct is specified at all. As a result, "men of common intelligence must necessarily guess at its meaning."[68]

In *Virginia v. Black*, the U.S. Supreme Court, in defining what constitutes an unprotected expressive threat said, "Intimidation in the constitutionally proscribable sense of the word is a type of true threat, where a speaker directs a threat to a person or group of persons with the intent of placing the victim in fear of bodily harm or death."[69] Therefore, to penalize for online intimidating expression, the communication must amount to a true threat, "a serious expression of an intent to commit an act of unlawful violence to a particular individual or group of individuals."[70]

Under the Court's ruling *in Elonis v. U.S.* (2015), the state must prove that a speaker knew or truly believed that his conduct was illegal or had the purpose to intimidate to be held criminally culpable under the true threat doctrine.[71] For instance, a defendant cannot be convicted under a statute criminalizing the sale of drug paraphernalia unless the state shows "he 'knew that the items at issue [were] likely to be used with illegal drugs.'"[72] Thus, it would seem, that under a cyberbullying law proscribing intimidating speech, a state would have to show that a teen knew he was engaging in illegal conduct or he had the intent to place the target of his banter in fear of bodily harm or death. As so much of teens' online taunts are nonsensical hyperbole, meeting the true threat standard is likely to occur in only rare cases.

Abusive language is constitutionally proscribable only when it constitutes "fighting words," those that, "have a direct tendency to cause acts of violence by the person to whom, individually, the remark is addressed," the Court ruled in *Gooding v. Wilson* (1972).[73] The fighting words exception to the First Amendment, however, is unsuitable for application to social media or email because recipients are not captive audiences caught in face-to-face confrontations.[74]

On the other hand, legislators contemplating banning cyberbullying by targeting pestering speech may find refuge in rulings such as *Wagner v. Texas* (2015). "A statute is not vague or overbroad simply because a word or phrase is not specifically defined … A person harasses another when he persistently disturbs, bothers continually, or pesters that person."[75] Accordingly, *Wagner v. Texas* would require that a criminal harassment cyberbullying statute ban only a series of messages sent to an individual.

Many states ban annoying, alarming, intimidating and tormenting expression in the criminal harassment context and require a persistent effort. For example, by January 2015, 37 states had online harassment laws.[76] As the U.S. Court of Appeals for the Third Circuit noted, "(t)here is no categorical 'harassment exception' to the First Amendment's free speech clause."[77] Nevertheless, criminal harassment statutes banning expression must be carefully written to avoid successful overbreadth, vagueness or strict scrutiny challenges.

UCLA law professor Volokh says carefully drafted criminal harassment statutes tend to limit speech restrictions to "what one may call 'unwanted one-to-one' speech—speech said to a particular person in a context where the recipient appears not to want to hear it, whether because the recipient has expressly demanded that the speech stop or because the speaker intends to annoy or offend the recipient."[78]

But cyberbullying criminal statutes do not limit their scope to "one-to-one" speech such as email or a messages posted on the social media page of a targeted individual, who has the ability to limit who accesses his or her Facebook or Tweet account, or avoid a social media site that features teen gossip and badmouthing. Why not? Because that is not where the action is. Narrowing the statute's scope in such a manner would greatly decrease the state's authority to deter and punish teens for exchanging the types of barbs and putdowns that rankle anti-bullying advocates. Moreover, merely narrowing the reach of criminal cyberbullying laws just does not seem to send a tough enough message to appease the anti-cyberbullying crowd.

More Flawed Statutes

Civil libertarians, particularly the Electronic Frontier Foundation and state chapters of the ACLU, have informed lawmakers of the constitutional defects of their proposed cyberbullying bills in just about every state with little or no impact. The Albany County Legislature ignored warnings in 2010 and in 2015 when it passed a revision of its invalidated "Local Law Prohibiting Cyberbullying."[79]

In another instance, despite advice and protest from civil libertarians, Pennsylvania's governor signed into law a "Cyberharassment of a Child" statute in 2015.[80] The statute outlaws cyberharassment intended "to harass, annoy or alarm" and makes a "seriously disparaging statement or opinion about the child's physical characteristics, sexuality, sexual activity or mental or physical health or condition … which is intended to and under the circumstances is reasonably likely to cause substantial emotional distress to a child of the victim's age and which produces some physical manifestation of the distress."[81]

In a letter to the Pennsylvania House Judiciary Committee, The ACLU of Pennsylvania, acknowledged that lawmakers had revised early drafts, but lamented that, "Unfortunately, those revisions cannot address the fundamental problems [with the proposed law] … Phrases … like 'with the intent to harass, annoy or alarm' and 'seriously disparaging' are vague and subjective … At its core [the proposed law] criminalizes rude speech."[82]

The Pennsylvania statute also criminalizes disparaging statements of opinion. As noted in the above discussion about *Marquan*, criminalization of defamation is an outdated concept and any such statute should not survive a constitutional challenge based on *New York Times v. Sullivan* and *Milkovich v. Lorraine Journal*.[83]

Colorado's lawmakers believe they passed a criminal harassment law that does not infringe upon First Amendment rights, yet effectively combats harmful cyberbullying.[84]

They are overly optimistic.[85] "Kiana Arellano's Law," effective July 2015, restricts conduct and expression, including unwanted offline and online speech. The speaker must have intent to "harass, annoy, or alarm another person" with repeated "insults, taunts, challenges," or make "communications in offensive coarse" ways.[86] Though "annoying" and "alarming" speech is protected under the First Amendment according to several court rulings, including the New York Court of Appeals,[87] the Colorado statute requires that the banned expression be "likely to provoke a violent or disorderly response."

Arguably, the inclusion of intent on the speaker's part and a likelihood causality standard invokes the incitement exception—speech calculated to produce unlawfulness and is highly likely to.[88] But does the incitement doctrine fit comfortably with the elements of a cyberbullying harassment statute? Only if the bullied individual's lawless action were rationally connected to the bully's exhortation and the victim committed the act immediately or soon after reading or hearing it.

In *Hess v. Indiana*, (1973), the Court ruled that incitement required that there be "evidence, or rational inference from the import of the language" that a defendant's "words were intended to produce imminent disorder" and that it was not enough that "speech had a tendency to lead to violence."[89] Therefore, the individual who exhorts a target to attack someone or tells others to attack the target, as Bishop did, would be protected under the First Amendment unless message recipients engaged in lawlessness described by the exhorter. Bishop's messages, for example, did not encourage lawlessness; slamming is constitutionally protected criticism. Thus, were the Colorado statute to survive judicial scrutiny, it is highly unlikely it would snare typical so-called cyberbullies.

The statute also bans the use of online technologies "to harass or threaten bodily injury or property damage, or makes any comment, request, suggestion, or proposal by telephone, computer, computer network, computer system, or other interactive electronic medium that is obscene."[90] The phrase "to harass or threaten bodily injury or property damage," invokes the true threat exception to the First Amendment.

The statute, however, bans direct and indirect online communication.[91] In other words, an online posting need not be sent directly to an individual victim. Here the statute reaches too far by proscribing speech about someone rather than speech sent directly to someone. It makes the initial sender criminally culpable for harm even though he or she may never have intended to expose the injured party to the message.

The statute careens off track by proscribing obscenity, defined as "a patently offensive description of ultimate sexual acts or solicitation to commit ultimate sexual acts, whether or not said ultimate sexual acts are normal or perverted, actual or simulated, including masturbation, cunnilingus, fellatio, anilingus, or excretory functions."[92] The U.S. Supreme Court has established a three-prong test to determine if speech is obscene: An average person, applying contemporary community standards, must find that the material, as a whole, appeals to the prurient interest; the material must depict or describe, in a patently offensive way, sexual conduct specifically defined by applicable law; and the material, taken as a whole, must lack serious literary, artistic, political or scientific value.[93] Beyond that, the production, sale and possession of sexual depictions of minors is obscene.[94] The definition of obscenity in the Kiana Arellano's Law, however, does not comply with the constitutional standard of obscenity.

The definition of obscenity in the Kiana Arellano's Law parrots the indecency exception to the First Amendment to a large degree. Indecent content is "language or material that, in context, depicts or describes, in terms patently offensive as measured by contemporary community standards for the broadcast medium, sexual or excretory organs or activities."[95] The statute's obscenity ban cannot be saved by converting it to an indecency standard because the indecent expression ban applies only to broadcast media. Moreover, the Internet enjoys full First Amendment protection and online sexual expression can be banned only if it is obscene.[96] The obscenity provision of the Colorado statute is constitutionally overbroad because it targets constitutionally protected expression.

The statute has a "savings clause"—"This section is not intended to infringe upon any right guaranteed to any person by the first amendment to the United States constitution or to prevent the expression of any religious, political, or philosophical views."[97] Professor Volokh, quoting the Minnesota Supreme Court, reminds us that saving clauses "cannot substantively operate to save an otherwise invalid statute."[98]

Even if all or most of the statute survived judicial scrutiny, it is unlikely that its scope would cover the type of statements that supposedly drove the eponymous Kiana Arellano to attempt suicide by hanging. Anonymous online texters called her "pathetic," and, "Nobody likes you at school."[99] Though annoying and alarming, those statements would not be proscribed under the ambit of the statute because they are not obscene, do not incite lawlessness or constitute a threat to bodily injury or property damage.

Her mother, Kristy Arellano, testified that the anonymous online posts that "pushed her to the breaking point … called her horrible names" and "stated that she deserved to die."[100] Does telling someone they deserve to die constitute a true threat? On its face, it is not certain that it does. It is not equivalent to saying, "I'm going to kill you," which, under most circumstances, is a true threat. As noted above, *Elonis v. U.S.* requires that the state prove a speaker knew or truly believed that his conduct was illegal or had the purpose to intimidate to be held criminally culpable under the true threat doctrine. That might be a difficult task considering the loopiness of many teens.

It is not mere theoretical conjecture to question the statute's enforceability. About four months after its enactment, Mesa County (Colorado) District Attorney Dan Rubinstein said, "I don't think this law is facially unconstitutional, but I certainly think it has the potential to be abused Law enforcement agencies seem quite aware that this law has the potential to be handled over-broadly."[101]

Conclusion

With the fall of a provision of the North Carolina statute in June 2016, 17 states criminalized cyberbullying and legislators in five other states were considering similar statutes.[102] There is always the chance that these laws will not be enforced and no one will challenge them. For example, criminal harassment cyberbullying statutes designed to protect minors have been on the books of Albany and Monroe counties in New York for two years, yet no one has been prosecuted under them.[103] Yet, bullying experts do not categorically dismiss the value of criminalizing teen cyberbullying.[104] So, there appears to be incentive and justification to try to draft a constitutionally sound cyberbullying criminal harassment statute to protect minors. No doubt, the legislative experiment will continue until a critical mass of state courts strike down criminal harassment laws targeting teen cyberbullying. Until then, the prospect that more teens will be unjustifiably charged under such statutes remains.

Robert Bishop has some advice for them. When the authorities arrest you, don't just know your rights, you must use them, he says. "You have the right not to speak to police. You have the right to ask for an attorney, and as a minor, ask for your parents. Using these rights will not hurt you. It may be the only thing that keeps you free."[105]

Using your rights, he says, includes challenging your conviction on First Amendment grounds.

> Become intimately familiar with the text of the law you're accused of violating. Become intimately familiar with some of the cornerstone cases of First Amendment law. So far, the two cyberbullying statutes that have been overturned were so vague that almost anything posted about a minor was likely to result in a successful conviction. To gain your innocence, you may have to make your own First Amendment challenge.[106]

Notes

1. Brief for the State, North Carolina v. Robert Bishop at 3 (COA14-1227 (N.C. Ct. App. June 16, 2015).
2. Ibid., 4.
3. Ibid. (accessed August 22, 2016).
4. Robert Bishop, e-mail message to author, June 18, 2016, 2:42 PM.
5. Michael D. Abernethy, "Testimony Begins in Cyberbullying Trial," *The Times News*, Updated February 4, 2014, 6:30 PM, http://www.thetimesnews.com/article/20140204/News/302049833 (accessed August 22, 2016).
6. Ibid.
7. N.C.G.S. § 14-458.1(a)(1)(d), http://www.ncleg.net/EnactedLegislation/Statutes/HTML/BySection/Chapter_14/GS_14-458.1.html (accessed August 22, 2016).
8. State v. Bishop, COA14-1227 (N.C. Ct. App. June 16, 2015), http://caselaw.findlaw.com/nc-court-of-appeals/1705020.html (accessed August 22, 2016).
9. Ibid.

10. "Our View: Teen Taunts, 'Cyberbullying' and Free Speech", *Richmond County Daily Journal*, June 27, 2016, http://yourdailyjournal.com/opinion/editorials/1474/our-view-teen-taunts-cyberbullying-and-free-speech (accessed August 22, 2016).
11. State v. Robert Bishop, 223PA15 (June 10, 2016), https://appellate.nccourts.org/opinions/?c=2&pdf=32867 (accessed August 22, 2016).
12. Bishop, e-mail.
13. Ibid.
14. North Carolina General Statutes § 15A-146, http://law.justia.com/codes/north-carolina/2005/chapter_15a/gs_15a-146.html (accessed August 22, 2016).
15. Devon Swartz and Lindsey Eaton, "Six Alamance Co. Teens Charged in Facebook Cyberbullying Cases," *Fox 8*, February 10, 2012, 7:12 PM, http://myfox8.com/2012/02/09/five-alamance-co-teens-arrested-in-cyberbullying-cases/ (accessed August 22, 2016).
16. Jeffrey B. Welthy, "Cyberbullying Statute Struck Down," *North Carolina Criminal Law*, June 13, 2016, 8:52 AM, http://nccriminallaw.sog.unc.edu/cyberbullying-statute-struck/ (accessed August 22, 2016).
17. Bishop, e-mail.
18. People v. Marquan, 24 N.Y.3d 1 (2014).
19. Lyrissa B. Lidsky and Andrea P. Garcia, "How Not to Criminalize Cyberbullying," *Missouri Law Review* 22 (2012): 701.
20. Brief for the State, North Carolina v. Robert Bishop, 23.
21. State v. Robert Bishop, 223PA15 (June 10, 2016), https://www.washingtonpost.com/news/volokh-conspiracy/wp-content/uploads/sites/14/2016/06/BishopOpinion.pdf (accessed August 22, 2016).
22. Gary D. Robertson, "Citing Free Speech, NC Cyberbullying Law Struck Down," *Associated Press*, June 10, 2016, 3:00 PM, http://www.chicagotribune.com/news/sns-bc-nc--supreme-court-cyberbullying-20160610-story.html (accessed August 22, 2016).
23. Marquan, 24 NY 3d 1, 6.
24. Robert Gavin, "Highest Court to take on Bullying," *Times Union*, June 3, 2014, 8:39 PM, http://www.timesunion.com/local/article/Highest-court-to-take-on-bullying-5526444.php (accessed August 22, 2016).
25. Dave Canfield, "Marquan Mackey-Meggs of Cohoes Charged with Cyber-Bullying for Cohoes Flame Facebook Group," *Troy Record*, June 17, 2011, 12:06 PM EDT, http://www.troyrecord.com/article/TR/20110617/NEWS/306179972 (accessed August 22, 2016).
26. Brief of Appellant Marquan W. Mackey-Meggs, State v. Marquan W. Mackey-Meggs, CA-332-12 (2103), 4, New York Civil Liberties Union, http://www.nyclu.org/files/releases/2013-10-17_RedactedCourtofAppealsBrief.PDF (accessed August 22, 2016).
27. Bishop, e-mail.
28. Marquan, 24 NY 3d 1, 6.
29. Albany Local Law 11: A Local Law Prohibiting Cyber-Bullying in Albany County (2010), http://www.albanycounty.com/Libraries/Crime_Victims_and_Sexual_Violence_Center/LocalLaw_No_11_for_2010_CyberBullying.sflb.ashx (accessed August 22, 2016).
30. Marquan, 24 NY 3d 1, 5–6.
31. Ibid., 5.

32. Albany Local Law 11.
33. Dave Canfield, "Marquan Mackey-Meggs of Cohoes Charged with Cyber-Bullying for Cohoes Flame Facebook Group."
34. Marquan, 24 NY 3d 1, 7.
35. Brief of Appellant Marquan W. Mackey-Meggs, State v. Marquan W. Mackey-Meggs, CA-332-12 (2103), 4.
36. Ibid.
37. Ibid., 5.
38. Marquan, 24 NY 3d 1, 9.
39. Ibid., 11.
40. Ibid., 7.
41. Brief of Appellant Marquan W. Mackey-Meggs, State v. Marquan W. Mackey-Meggs, CA-332-12 (2103), 4.
42. Henry Campbell Black, *Black's Law Dictionary* (St. Paul: West Publishing, 1979), 889.
43. U.S. v. Cothran, 286 F. 3d 173, 175–76 (3d Cir. 2002).
44. Virginia v. Black, 538 U.S. 343, 358 (2003).
45. Laura Little, "Just a Joke: Defamatory Humor and Incongruity's Promise," *Southern California Interdisciplinary Journal* 21 (2011): 115, http://ssrn.com/abstract=1701290 (accessed August 5, 2016).
46. People v. Golb, 23 NY 3d 455, 471 (N.Y. Court of Appeals, 2014); Golb v. New York, 135 S. Ct. 1009 (January 12, 2015) cert denied.
47. Marquan, 24 NY 3d 1, 11.
48. Daniel Wiessner, "N.Y. Top Court says Cyberbullying Law Violates Free Speech," *Reuters*, July 1, 2014, 11:14 AM EDT, http://www.reuters.com/article/us-new-york-cyberbully-idUSKBN0F64N420140701 (accessed June 22, 2016).
49. Haley E. Phillips, "Online Bullying and the First Amendment: State Cyberbullying Statutes after People v. Marquan M," *North Carolina Law Review* 93 (2014–2015): 179, 181.
50. G.S. §14-458.1(a)(1)(d), North Carolina General Assemby, http://www.ncleg.net/EnactedLegislation/Statutes/HTML/BySection/Chapter_14/GS_14-458.1.html (accessed August 22, 2016).
51. North Carolina v. Robert Bishop, 223PA15 *2.
52. State v. Bishop, 774 SE 2d 337, 341.
53. Ibid.
54. Ibid.
55. Ibid.
56. Bishop, e-mail.
57. State v. Bishop, 774 SE 2d 337, 343.
58. Rowan v. U.S. Post Office Department, 397 U.S. 728, 736 (1970).
59. North Carolina v. Robert Bishop, 223PA15 *8.
60. Ibid., *13
61. Ibid.
62. Ibid., *16.
63. Ibid., 16–17.

64. Ibid., *18.
65. Bishop, *18.
66. David Donovan, "State Supreme Court Strikes Down Anti-Cyberbullying Law," *Detroit Legal News*, http://www.legalnews.com/detroit/1426625, http://www.legalnews.com/detroit/1426625 (accessed August 22, 2016).
67. Coates v. Cincinnati, 402 US 611-612 (1971)
68. Ibid., 614.
69. Virginia v. Black, 538 US 343, 360.
70. Ibid.
71. Elonis v. US, 135 S. Ct. 2001, 2009-2011 (2015).
72. Ibid., 2011.
73. Gooding v. Wilson, 405 U.S. 518 (1972).
74. Common Wealth v. Welch, 444 Mass. 80, 96 (2005).
75. Wagner v. Texas 05-13-01329-CR *6-7 (Tex. App. May 5, 2015), https://casetext.com/case/wagner-v-state-152 (accessed August 22, 2016).
76. Dia Kayyali, "Facing the Challenge of Online Harassment," Electronic Frontier Foundation, January 8, 2015, https://www.eff.org/deeplinks/2015/01/facing-challenge-online-harassment (accessed August 22, 2016).
77. Saxe v. State College Area School Dist., 240 F.3d 200, 206 (3d Cir. 2001).
78. Eugene Volokh, "One-to-One Speech vs. One-to-Many Speech, Criminal Harassment Laws, and 'Cyberstalking,'" *Northwestern University Law Review* 107 (2013): 731, 741, http://www2.law.ucla.edu/volokh/crimharass.pdf
79. E-mail sent to Daniel McCoy, Albany County Executive from Robert A. Perry, NYCLU Legislative Director, October 2, 2014, New York Civil Liberties Union, http://www.nyclu.org/files/releases/Cyberbullying_Albany_Letter_County_Executive_10_2_2014.pdf (accessed August 22, 2016).
80. 18 Pa. C.S.A. § 2709 (a.1)., Pennsylvania General Assembly, http://www.legis.state.pa.us/WU01/LI/LI/CT/HTM/18/00.027.009.000..HTM (accessed August 22, 2016).
81. Ibid.
82. ACLU of Pennsylvania, Memorandum: Opposition to House Bill 229 ((MARSICO), February 1, 2015, https://www.aclupa.org/files/9814/2800/6442/memo_HB_229_H-Jud_Feb_2015.pdf (accessed August 22, 2016).
83. Milkovich v. Lorraine Journal, 497 U.S.1 (1990).
84. Colorado Revised Statutes. § 18-9-111 (2015). Harassment—Kiana Arellano's Law, http://www.lpdirect.net/casb/crs/18-9-111.html (accessed August 22, 2016).
85. Kevin Simpson, "How A Cyberbullying Law in Colorado was Tweaked …," *The Denver Post*, July 13, 2015, http://www.denverpost.com/2015/07/13/how-a-cyberbullying-law-in-colorado-was-tweaked-to-be-more-effective/ (accessed August 22, 2016).
86. Colo. Rev. Stat. § 18-9-111(1)(h).
87. People v. Golb, 23 N.Y.3d 455, 467 (2014).
88. Brandenburg v. Ohio, 395 U.S. 444 (1969).
89. Hess v. Indiana, 414 U.S. 105, 109 (1973).
90. Colo. Rev. Stat. § 18-9-111 (1) (e).
91. Ibid.

92. Colo. Rev. Stat. § 18-9-111(1.5).
93. Miller v. California, 413 U.S. 15 (1973).
94. New York v. Ferber, 458 U.S. 747 (1982).
95. "Obscene, Indecent and Profane Broadcasts," Federal Communications Commission, https://www.fcc.gov/consumers/guides/obscene-indecent-and-profane-broadcasts (accessed June 21, 2016).
96. Reno v. ACLU, 521 U.S. 844 (1997).
97. Colo. Rev. Stat. § 18-9-111(1.5) (8).
98. Volokh, "One-to-One Speech vs. One-to-Many Speech, Criminal Harassment Laws, and "Cyberstalking," 766.
99. Anne Trujillo, "Bulled by Text Messages: The Story of Hope Behind Kiana's Law," *Denver Channel 7*, ABC, 9:50 PM, Jun 30, 2015, 10:56 PM, June 30, 2015, http://www.thedenverchannel.com/news/local-news/bullied-by-text-messages-the-story-of-hope-behind-kianas-law (accessed August 22, 2016).
100. Associated Press, "Cyberbullying Bill Clears Hurdle In Colorado Senate After Mother's Emotional Story," *CBSDenver.com*, March 4, 2015, 5:18 PM, http://denver.cbslocal.com/2015/03/04/cyberbullying-bill-faces-tough-road-in-colorado-senate/ (accessed August 22. 2016).
101. Paul Shockley, "State's New Cyberbullying Law Vexing for Police," *The Daily Sentinel*, November 8, 2015, http://www.gjsentinel.com/news/articles/states-new-cyberbully-law-vexing-for-police (accessed August 22, 2016).
102. Sameer Hinduja and Justin Patchin, "A Brief Review of State Cyberbullying Laws and Policies," Cyberbullying Research Center," http://www.cyberbullying.us/Bullying-and-Cyberbullying-Laws.pdf (accessed August 22, 2016).
103. Kaelyn Rich, New York Civil Liberties Union-Capital Region Chapter, e-mail message to author, June 22, 2016, 10:19 AM.
104. S. Hinduja and J. W. Patchin, "Cyberbullying Identification, Prevention, and Response," Cyberbullying Research Center (www.cyberbullying.us), http://cyberbullying.org/Cyberbullying-Identification-Prevention-Response.pdf (accessed August 22, 2016).
105. Bishop, e-mail.
106. Bishop, e-mail.

· 4 ·

"ENCLAVES OF TOTALITARIANISM"

> In our system, state-operated schools may not be enclaves of totalitarianism. School officials do not possess absolute authority over their students. Students in school as well as out of school are "persons" under our Constitution. They are possessed of fundamental rights which the State must respect, just as they themselves must respect their obligations to the State. In our system, students may not be regarded as closed-circuit recipients of only that which the State chooses to communicate. They may not be confined to the expression of those sentiments that are officially approved. In the absence of a specific showing of constitutionally valid reasons to regulate their speech, students are entitled to freedom of expression of their views.
>
> —*Tinker v. Des Moines Independent Community School District* (1969)[1]

If New Jersey had a properly worded anti-bullying law on its books in late 2015, chances are Bethany Koval would have retained her near obscurity as just another highly opinionated and prolific tweeter.[2]

In December 2015, Koval, a 16-year-old of Jewish descent, and resident of Fair Lawn, N.J., tweeted frequently about political and social controversies, particularly the Israeli-Palestinian conflict, from a leftist perspective.[3] During the winter school-break, Koval's pro-Palestinian tweets drew the attention of her Fair Lawn High School peers. Offended by Koval's political opinions, one pro-Israel classmate unfollowed her.[4] In response, Koval tweeted, "i'm sooooo glad that pro-Israel girl from my school unfollowed me! I'm so FREE now like ...[expletive] ISRAEL."[5]

In response, the classmate complained to their high school principal and Koval was called to the principal's office,[6] the start of an investigation to determine whether she had violated New Jersey's Anti-Bullying Bill of Rights Act (the Act), which became effective in the 2011–2012 school year.[7] The Act, widely considered the nation's toughest and most comprehensive anti-bullying statute directed at schools, mandates among other requirements, that school officials report all alleged bullying and cyberbullying incidents, occurring on or off-school grounds, "within one school day of the report of the incident."[8]

The Nation's Toughest and Most Comprehensive Anti-Bullying Statute Directed at Schools

Under the Act, bullying and cyberbullying are categorized as, "Harassment, intimidation or bullying (HIB)." HIB misconduct is defined as:

> any gesture, any written, verbal or physical act, or any electronic communication, whether it be a single incident or a series of incidents, that is reasonably perceived as being motivated either by any actual or perceived characteristic, such as race, color, religion, ancestry, national origin, gender, sexual orientation, gender identity and expression, or a mental, physical or sensory disability, or by any other distinguishing characteristic, that takes place on school property, at any school-sponsored function, on a school bus, or off school grounds as provided.[9]

In an apparent attempt to conform to the seminal public school students' free speech rights ruling, *Tinker v. Des Moines School District*,[10] the Act requires school officials to show that a single incident or pattern of harassment, intimidation or bullying, "substantially disrupts or interferes with the orderly operation of the school or the rights of other students."[11] In *Tinker*, a pre-Internet ruling, the U.S. Supreme Court set the limits on school authority to discipline students under the First Amendment. In the absence of a High Court ruling specifically on student speech on the Internet, *Tinker*'s doctrinal analysis is controlling: to discipline a student for speech, a school must show that the speech materially disrupted the school activities, created substantial disorder in the school, or violated the rights of others.[12]

The Act also directs school administrators to apply reasonableness in determining how to identify alleged banned misconduct. According to the statute, harassment, intimidation or bullying are the types of misconduct that,

> a reasonable person should know … will have the effect of physically or emotionally harming a student or damaging the student's property, or placing a student in reasonable fear of physical or emotional harm to his person or damage to his property; has the effect of insulting or demeaning any student or group of students; or creates a hostile educational environment for the student by interfering with a student's education or by severely or pervasively causing physical or emotional harm to the student.[13]

Each school district board of education is required to adopt a harassment, intimidation or bullying policy and may give school administrators authority to determine if an accusation warrants investigation.[14] But the Act's definition of harassment, intimidation or bullying misconduct is so broad—"emotionally harming a student … insulting or demeaning any student"—and the reporting requirements so severe, an administrator's discretion, and use of common sense, is greatly restrained.[15] Actually, the Fair Lawn Public Schools superintendent claimed he didn't have a choice other than to initiate an investigation once a student complained: "We are obligated by New Jersey's anti-bullying statute—one of the strictest in the nation—to investigate any such allegation to determine whether an act of HIB occurred under statute."[16]

Unconstrained by such mandated protocols, a sensible school administrator would not have started an investigation once it was clear that his students had voluntarily engaged in an online, off-campus political debate unrelated to school curriculum that caused no substantial threat to the safety and peace of the school environment, or infringed upon the rights of another student.[17]

Moreover, by its nature political discourse and debate, the highest form of constitutionally protected speech, often offends, insults and demeans. That's a probability New Jersey legislators appeared to have ignored or discounted when they banned speech that is emotionally harming, insulting and demeaning. Consequently, law and policy gave Fair Lawn school officials no choice but to investigate Koval, contrary to the letter and spirit of *Tinker*.

As soon as the investigation got underway, Koval tweeted her story to more than 6,000 followers: "Threatened to file a bully case against me. It's against state law to express unpopular political views on the Internet, now."[18] She drew a great deal of news media attention and support from free expression and pro-Palestinian advocates. Some of her backers emailed and called the school, "demanding that she not be punished, and in some cases referring to the school's management as 'Zionist' and the investigation as 'harassment.'"[19]

The responses, however, weren't all good. She drew the ire of some classmates—"Just couldn't make it through the school day. Too much aggression amongst classmates here."[20] A pro-school administrator faction took to the streets, holding a rally in the high school's parking lot: "As a parent, I fully support the school for doing the best that they can to keep our children safe from harm, on and off school grounds," the leader of the rally said. "I think we parents have a duty to show our support and not allow the school staff to be persecuted by the media for simply attempting to protect our children."[21]

Reportedly, comments on the pro-school group's Facebook page were more personal. A Fair Lawn parent Lior Cohen called her stupid, a bully and "claimed she had a 'terrorist organization supporting her.'" "When u hate for no reason you need to be punished and your place is in prison!!"[22]

Koval told a local reporter that she had received online and offline messages calling her a Nazi, that she should kill herself and that she would be physically assaulted in the school parking lot as retribution.[23] But she declined to report the name-calling and threats to school authorities. "I don't like the law. I don't want to contribute to it," she explained. "I believe the law is enforced arbitrarily and it's too vague to uphold any moral standards."[24]

Ultimately, Koval was cleared. School investigators found that the "incident involved 'peer conflict' but did not meet the standard for harassment, intimidation or bullying under New Jersey state law."[25] The public controversy raised by the investigation, however, brought to light much more.

Perhaps no other set of circumstances underscores the potential for misuse and abuse resulting from a poorly drafted school anti-bullying statute better than Koval's three months under scrutiny for voicing her political views. Here was yet another incident where the application of an anti-bullying statute wrongly stigmatized an individual for exercising her right to free speech and turned the wrongly accused bully into a target of insults, intimidation and threats. Moreover, the high-profile controversy underscored previous complaints by school officials that the law's strict reporting requirements were counterproductive. Soon after, the New Jersey Board of Education weighed granting school principals clear authority to decide whether to embark on a full investigation after receiving a complaint.[26] A major state newspaper ran an editorial emphatically opposed to the statute, citing the Koval incident: "On N.J. Bullying Law: Can We Get Off the Crazy Train?"[27]

Exonerated, Koval had no need to challenge the law's constitutionality in court. But the Act's defects run far deeper than inflexible reporting demands. Like so many anti-cyberbullying statutes—criminal or civil—the Act's language is highly vulnerable to challenges of constitutional overbreadth and vagueness. (In fact, as discussed later in this chapter, one set of parents challenged the law as unconstitutional, though the suit was settled out of court). As Koval's attorney, ACLU-NJ Senior Staff Attorney Alexander Shalom, put it,

> In some cases, the anti-bullying law is being read so broadly that perfectly constitutional free speech can easily be placed under a microscope, contrary to the spirit of the law. It's not going to be the bland, inoffensive speech that tests the strength of the First Amendment; it's going to be the words that spark controversy and inflame people's passions. Students shouldn't have to fear that their thoughts on politics, or anything else, could be taken out of context and have them branded as a bully, especially when the consequences can be so serious.[28]

Beyond the Tinker Analysis

Unfortunately, New Jersey's anti-bullying school statute is not unique. It is representative of the school anti-bullying statutes explicitly authorizing jurisdiction over off-campus speech found in the District of Columbia and 32 other states.[29] This chapter offers an argument against New Jersey's Anti-Bullying Bill of Rights Act, and state laws like it that target off-campus cyberbullying by severely restricting school administrators' discretion, conflating insensitivity and rudeness with harassment and intimidation, among other dubious terms; failing to consider First Amendment protection for truthful statements; and in practice, ignore or stretch the boundaries of the *Tinker* substantial disruption and infringement rights test.

Nevertheless, it is argued here that the pre-online-era *Tinker* analysis is an inadequate tool for protecting student political speech—arguments, discussions and rants about political and social issues, or even personal insults—distributed in a medium unanticipated by the U.S. Supreme Court. Consider, for example, how the analysis, applied by two federal Third Circuit panels on similar cases, produced two conflicting outcomes that had to be reconciled by an en banc panel in *JS Ex Rel. Snyder v. Blue Mountain School District* (2011).[30]

Therefore, staking out a position against the prevailing view which holds that schools must ban off-campus online speech to police on-campus bullying and related student conflicts, this chapter argues that the proper balance between school authority and student free speech rights is best kept when schools do not discipline students for off-campus, online speech. In other words, schools should play no role in policing off-campus, online or offline speech. Colorado takes such an approach.[31]

Moreover, five federal Third Circuit judges, writing in the concurring opinion of *JS Ex Rel. Snyder v. Blue Mountain School District* (en banc, 2011), warned against extending *Tinker*'s reach to off-campus, online speech.

> Applying *Tinker* to off-campus speech would create a precedent with ominous implications. Doing so would empower schools to regulate students' expressive activity no matter where it takes place, when it occurs, or what subject matter it involves—so long as it causes a substantial disruption at school. *Tinker*, for example, authorizes schools to suppress political speech—speech "at the core of what the First Amendment is designed to protect," … if it substantially disrupts school activities … Suppose a high school student, while at home after school hours, were to write a blog entry defending gay marriage. Suppose further that several of the student's classmates got wind of the entry, took issue with it, and caused a significant disturbance at school. While the school could clearly punish the students who acted disruptively, if *Tinker* were held to apply to off-campus speech, the school could also punish the student whose blog entry brought about the disruption. That cannot be, nor is it, the law.[32]

The Rise of Anti-Bullying School Laws

Psychologists Dewey Cornell and Susan P. Limber identify the Columbine High School shooting massacre, supposedly conducted by vengeful bullied students in 1999, and *Davis v. Monroe County Board of Education*,[33] which established that schools could be liable for their deliberate indifference to know acts of severe, pervasive, and objectively offensive student-to-student sexual harassment, as "turning points in the recognition of school bullying as an important societal problem in the United States."[34] Not doing more to root out bullying among the student body, it seems left school administrators vulnerable to a double whammy of violence and legal liability. So, between 1999 and January 2016, all of the states and the District of Columbia passed anti-bullying school legislation.[35]

Meanwhile, the move by legislatures to mandate that schools target off campus, off-hours cyberbullying had its own driving forces[36]—mostly a combination of moral panics fueled by suicide-related cyberbullying incidents and the U.S. Supreme Court's failure to reconcile the conflicting circuit court rulings on off-campus, online speech. The New Jersey Legislature, for example, passed the Act with nearly unanimous backing in response to activism and "national media coverage surrounding multiple student suicides,"[37] most notably the suicide of New Jersey's Rutgers University freshman Tyler Clementi, whose roommate secretly video taped Clementi in a gay romantic encounter and streamed it over the Internet.[38] Similar to the moral panic leading to the crusade to criminalize cyberbullying, the unscientifically proven nexus between cyberbullying and suicide loomed as a bogeyman. For instance, the state-created New Jersey Commission on Bullying in Schools—which "heavily influenced the drafting" of the Act[39] with a 66-page report—mentioned "suicide prevention" or referenced a causal connection between bullying and suicide 24 times.[40]

In 2011 and 2012, the U.S. Supreme Court declined to hear appeals of four online, off campus student speech cases.[41] In the absence of guidance from the high court,[42] state legislatures and school administrators have relied on lower court rulings to identify the limits of school authority to discipline off-campus, online speech. But there is no unanimity amount the courts on the issue. Thus, schools' attempts to control students' online speech have been contested in the courts, joining the queue of student speech cases starting with *Tinker*.[43]

Catherine Ross, professor of law at George Washington University Law School, identifies three approaches that appellate judges have fashioned to test the constitutionality of school authority to punish students for off-campus, online speech: The dominant approach which requires that schools show a "'nexus,' or close connection, between the speech and that school, or that it was 'reasonably foreseeable' that the speech would reach the school community. Foreseeability requires schools to show that the speaker should have anticipated that someone would share the speech on campus."[44]

A second approach, devised by two appellate circuits, requires schools show a nexus and "serious, identifiable threat directed toward the campus."[45] Ross identifies the aforementioned concurring opinion in the Third Circuit's *JS Rel Snyder v. Blue Mountain* School District in which a majority of judges sitting en banc "reject[ed] out of hand any suggestion that schools can police students' out-of-school speech," as the third approach.[46]

In three rulings involving plaintiffs' challenges of the constitutionality of school mandated anti-bullying statutes, courts applied the first and second approaches. In *Sagehorn v. Independent School District* (2015),[47] a federal Fifth Circuit trial court judge in Minnesota and federal Fifth Circuit appellate panel in *Bell v. Itawamba County School Board* (2015) applied the dominant approach.[48] In *Wynar v Douglas County School District* (2013),[49] the U.S. Court of Appeals for the Fifth Circuit applied Ross's second approach.

New Jersey is located in the federal Third Circuit and the majority opinion in JS Rel *Snyder v. Blue Mountain*—in contrast to the concurrence—endorsed the dominate approach calling for showing a close link between student online speech and the school or that the communication's substantially disruptive impact on the school environment is reasonably foreseeable.[50] Therefore, its anti-bullying statute and, more important, Fair Lawn High School's decision to embark upon an investigation of Koval should have conformed to the Third Circuit's standard. It does not appear to have done so, though the city's school superintendent insisted at the outset that, "at no time have District officials sought to censor or reprimand any pupils for their online speech. The Fair Law School District recognizes and respects individuals' First Amendment rights to free speech."[51]

Harmless Tweets

According to the news accounts, here are some of the offending tweets, posted in December 2015, when school was not in session.

A. OOOOOOOOO THESE KIDS ARE TALKIGN SMACK ABOUT ME AT SCHOOL BECAUSE OF MY ANTI-ISRAEL POSTS I SEE Y'ALL, SUPPORTING GENOCIDE AND ALL!!!!! [52]
B. I want to @ one of them soooo bad but that would be too cruel.[53]
C. @bbyboytroyee I'm so tempted it hurts but I feel like they're just uneducated and I should talk to them in person first.[54]
D. @bendykoval look at you being a nice moral person i woulda taken a different approach.[55]
E. im sooooo glad that pro-Israel girl from my school unfollowed me! I'm so FREE now like. … FUCK ISRAEL FUCK ISRAEL FUCK ISRAEL FUCK ISRAEL[56]

Though in tweet "A" Koval notes that her peers are talking smack about her in school (belittling her), such talk by itself does not add up to substantial disruption in school or the reasonable likeliness of oral or physical confrontation. *Tinker* counsels that "a mere desire" by schools "to avoid the discomfort and unpleasantness that always accompany an unpopular viewpoint," does not amount to substantial disruption.[57] Consider also that the federal Third Circuit appellate court has said that, "*Tinker* requires a specific and significant fear of disruption not just some remote apprehension of disturbance."[58] Though the *Tinker* standard does not require that schools show certainty, "the forecast of substantial disruption must be reasonable."[59]

What level of activity amounts to substantial disruption? There is no definitive answer. Ross says the U.S. Supreme Court provided some guidance by identifying conduct the "*Tinker* protestors did *not* engage in. They weren't 'aggressive.' They did not lead 'group demonstrations.' They 'neither interrupted school activities nor sought to intrude in the school affairs or the lives of others' and caused 'no interference with work and no disorder.'"[60] In another pre-Web era ruling, a lower court found that the after-class, on campus use of a typewriter to compose an occasional article for a *National Lampoon*-like publication amounted to "insignificant school contact" as most of the student work was conducted "exclusively in their homes, off campus and after school hours."[61]

In *Doninger v. Niehoff* (2011), a ruling by the federal Second Circuit dealing with alleged cyberbullying, the student's "blog post directly pertained to a [school event] … it invited other students to read and respond to it by contacting school officials … students did in fact post comments on the post, and that school administrators eventually became aware of it"—demonstrated "that it was reasonably foreseeable that … the post would reach school property and have disruptive consequences there."[62] In *Bell v. Itawamba County School Board* (2015), the U.S. Court of Appeals for the Fifth Circuit used an expansive application of the *Tinker* analysis to support the disciplining of a high school student who recorded a rap song on his Facebook page criticizing two sports coaches because the song was directed at the school community and reasonably understood by school officials to be threatening, harassing, and intimidating to a teacher.[63]

In contrast, in the federal Third Circuit's *J.S. ex rel. Snyder v. Blue Mountain School District* (2011) ruling, in which off-campus, online speech also was at issue, the following events did not constitute substantial disruption: "general 'rumblings'" regarding a Myspace posting; a student report of the posting to the principal; students' discussion of the posting during classes; a teacher's multiple request to students to stop discussing the matter; a school counselor's interrupted counseling sessions; and a group of students reporting of the online communication to a teacher.[64]

By the measure provided by precedents above, Koval's tweets and responses to them did not amount to prima facie evidence of substantial disruption. Koval's tweets did not address school matters or affairs, and she did not send them to school officials. None of her tweets threaten school employees or fellow students. She did not invite her classmates to debate her or contact the school.

Though Koval was bullied by other classmates in retaliation for her political views, such a retaliation cannot constitute substantial disruption as it would endorse the "heckler's veto," the censoring of a speaker to appease angry listeners.[65] At the outset, other than the one complaining student, there were no other reports of students' discussion of Koval's tweets in class of oral or physical confrontation that required teachers to intervene. After the principal heard Koval and other student's testimony, it should have been apparent that Koval did not engage in harassment, intimidation or bullying.

Moreover, tweets B–D are evidence that Koval had rejected resorting to face-to-face confrontation with her critics at school, further evidence that it was unreasonable to conclude that the online debate would spill over into the classrooms, hallways or school yards of the high school. Moreover, there does not seem to be *Wisniewski*-like evidence of Koval making serious or violent threats.[66]

Tinker holds that schools may discipline students for "colliding with the rights of others"[67] or for invading the rights of others. In other words, students have the right to be free of physical and verbal assaults from other students. The U.S. Court of Appeals for the Ninth Circuit, for example, ruled that verbal assaults targeting race, religion or sexual orientation could cause psychological damage which would amount to an infringement of a student's rights under a *Tinker* analysis.[68]

Based on that analysis, Koval's words in tweet "E" did not infringe upon the rights of the complaining student. First, the student dropped out of the debate on her own free will. Second, there does not appear to be threats directed at her. Koval used profanity, but it was not directed at the student.

Finally, in *Snyder v. Blue Mountain*, the federal Third Circuit rejected the application of the *Fraser* profanity standard to off-campus, online speech.[69] Therefore, Koval's use of profanity online was beyond the purview of the New Jersey school, which is located in the jurisdiction of the Third Circuit.

Perhaps Fair Lawn school officials also engaged in a similar calculus in reaching their finding that Koval tweets did not constitute harassment, intimidation and bullying under state law? The Act requires that "at a minimum" … schools must show a "reason to believe that the alleged" harassment, intimidation or bullying "has substantially disrupted or interfered" with school operations or the rights of other students when investigating off-campus misconduct.[70] Fair Lawn school officials, however, declined to make their analysis public.

Some might argue that if any damage was done, Koval created it because she publicized the matter. But even if we had never learned about the controversy, the potential for damage existed. The U.S. Supreme Court has recognized that certain types of state action can impose a "'chilling' effect that would be antithetical to the First Amendment's protection of true speech on matters of public concern."[71] The Act's flaws, particularly its lack of clarity about school administrator's discretion to investigate, may result in arbitrary actions that signal to students to steer clear of expressing innocuous and political statements protected under the First Amendment. But Koval, clearly not the average American teen judging by her engagement in public political discourse, was not intimidated.

"A more timid high school student would just shut down and not be involved in Twitter anymore at all," ACLU of New Jersey attorney Shalom said. "And so I think we need to be real concerned about bringing people in when you read their controversial political speech to ask them questions about it because the real concern is that it will chill them from speaking in the future."[72]

"Get Off the Crazy Train?"

In the immediate aftermath of the Koval controversy, The *New Jersey Star-Ledger*, the largest circulating paper in the state, called for legislators to fix what it characterized as the unclear and broad language of the statute that led to an unwarranted investigation of Koval. It argued that the statute's flawed language reflected that it was passed in haste "in the wake of Rutgers bullying victim Tyler Clementi's suicide … not well drafted … Too often … badly enforced … This problem was entirely foreseeable. Yet legislators left it up to the Department of Education to work out the fundamental details—like sharpening its vastly broad definition of bullying so it makes some common sense."[73]

The editorial declared that, "kids like Koval are being threatened with bullying investigations for no good reason, not to mention a potential black mark on their permanent records. This must stop, immediately. The law is being applied so broadly that it's threatening perfectly constitutional free speech."[74]

Meanwhile, the state Department of Education contemplated shoring up the defects in the statute's language brought to the forefront by the Koval controversy and recommended by the state's Anti-Bullying Task Force. Each district school board would amend the harassment, intimidation and bullying regulations to include power imbalance; that bullying is unwanted, aggressive behavior that may involve a real or perceived power imbalance.[75] Presumably, had it been in place, such a directive would have signaled early on that Koval had not bullied her peer because, for one thing, the complaining student was not coerced to join in the online debate and could leave at her own free will, as she eventually chose to do.

Another proposed revision would empower the school principal to decline to start an investigation when "the facts presented, if true, do not satisfy the definition in law."[76] Accordingly, the Fair Lawn High School principal would have seen the wisdom in not investigating Koval.

In a retort to the *Star-Ledger* editorial and the task force recommendations, Assemblywoman Valerie Vainieri Huttle, one of statute's sponsors, defended the statute's language. "The definition of HIB in the law is broad for two reasons. First it seeks to define something that is as broad as human behavior itself and can differ vastly from case-to-case. Secondly, HIB—how we understand what it is, what it looks like and how we deal with it—is still an emerging field."[77]

Defining "Harassment, Intimidation and Bullying"

Unwittingly, the assemblywoman suggests an argument for never having passed the Anti-Bullying Bill of Rights Act or repealing it: When legislators rush to regulate an emerging and inadequately understood social phenomenon, they produce broad and vague laws subject to abuse and highly vulnerable to constitutional legal challenges. A federal lawsuit brought by Tenalfy, N.J., parents of a fourth-grader who in 2011 embarrassed a classmate by explaining to students that the classmate had dyed her hair because she had head lice, apparently an accurate assessment, was one such a challenge.[78]

Before the lawsuit was filed, an administrative law judge upheld the finding of bullying, ruling that the local board's decision was not "unreasonable, arbitrary or capricious," but noted that the Commissioner of Education said, the "case may stretch the definition of [harassment, intimidation and bullying] to the outer edge of legislative intent" noting that "districts are struggling to find the right balance between common sense and the highly prescriptive provisions of the law."[79]

Justifiably, the student's parents, Woi Cheng Lim and Linwen Mao, believed the ruling allowed the school to exert its authority beyond constitutional limits. It filed a federal lawsuit in 2012, arguing that the statute should be struck because the statute's language was constitutionally overbroad and vague on its face, and as applied, and their son's single face-to-face incident did not constitute substantial disruption, or deprive the student of any protected right because the class lesson continued after their son apologized.[80] In 2015, the Tenafly, N.J., Board of Education reached a settlement with Lim and Mao that did not necessarily favor the school.[81]

Like many other states, New Jersey's anti-bullying law's definitions muddy the legal distinctions between the terms bullying, harassment and intimidation,[82] which raises concerns of unconstitutional overreach and vagueness. According to one study,

> 22 states use the terms "harassment," "intimidation," and "bullying" interchangeably. Fourteen states restrict their definitions only to the term bullying and another eight states include the terms harassment and bullying but define them separately ... In only 13 states must the aggressive behavior be a continuous pattern to be considered bullying and in one state alone (Delaware) the aggressive behavior must not only be repeated, but it must be repeated against the same student. In 16 states, the behavior must be severe, persistent or pervasive, leaving open the possibility that single episodes meet the bullying threshold. Additionally, 15 states specify that single, serious acts can be considered bullying ... power imbalance is largely overlooked, with only three states referencing power differential in their definition of bullying. Moreover, only three states (Delaware, New Hampshire, and Utah) include all three elements in their definition: intention, repetition, and power imbalance.[83]

In the criminal law context, impermissible non-expressive harassment typically entails unwanted conduct directed at an individual that is likely to provoke an immediate reaction of fright, intimidation, or emotional distress.[84] Under New Jersey law, generally harassment is only a criminal violation, "and has not been recognized in New Jersey as a tort action for damages."[85] Instead, New Jersey plaintiffs must allege intentional infliction of emotional harm—that the defendant engaged in intentional and outrageous conduct that caused "'physical illness or serious' or an abnormal 'psychological'" condition.[86]

The statute bars intimidation, a term that typically invokes the true threat doctrine. A true threat places an individual in fear of bodily harm or death.[87] The doctrine, however, applies to criminal prosecutions of unprotected speech. New Jersey's anti-bullying law imposes civil penalties. Thus, it would be inappropriate to punish students based on criminal law principles. However, as discussed below, "intimidation" has a specific meaning in student free speech doctrine.[88]

"Bullying," has no specific legal denotation. In most statutes, bullying is defined by referencing other forms of misconduct. For instance, Under Illinois's Bullying Prevent statute, 105 ILCS 5/27-23.7, definition of bullying includes "harassment, threats, intimidation, stalking, physical violence, sexual harassment, sexual violence, theft, public humiliation, destruction of property, or retaliation for asserting or alleging an act of bullying."

> Most states define bullying in terms of its intent to harm and severity of impact, but only four states include a power imbalance in their criteria and only eight define bullying as a repetitive behavior ... Perhaps the statute that is closest to the scholarly understanding of bullying is found in Virginia law (Va. Code Ann. §22.1–276.01): "Bullying" means any aggressive and unwanted behavior that is intended to harm, intimidate, or humiliate the victim; involves a real or perceived power imbalance between the aggressor or aggressors and victim; and is repeated over time or causes severe emotional trauma. "Bullying" includes cyberbullying. "Bullying" does not include ordinary teasing, horseplay, argument, or peer conflict.[89]

Nevertheless, the Act's definition of "harassment, intimidation or bullying" is tethered to New Jersey student free speech rights rulings and state and federal rulings upholding the right of students to sue schools for failing to stop gender-based bullying and the development of a hostile educational environment under state and federal laws, according to a New Jersey government document.[90] Those ruling, discussed below, are: *Davis v. Monroe County Board of Education, LW v. Toms River Regional Schools Board of Education, and Saxe v. State College Area School District.*

In *Davis v. Monroe County Board of Education* (1999), the U.S. Supreme Court ruled that schools could be held liable for student-to-student, gender-based harassment under Title IX of the Education Amendments of 1972.[91] The Court said harassment must be "so severe, pervasive, and objectively offensive that it effectively bars the victim's access to an educational opportunity or benefit."[92] In contrast to *Davis v. Monroe*, the New Jersey Anti-Bullying Reporting statute allows for a "single incident or a series of incidents" of harassment, intimidation or bullying.[93]

Davis v. Monroe County Board of Education spurred public schools to adopt similar anti-harassment policies as a means of shielding themselves from liability for failure to stop gender-based, student-on-student harassment.[94] The New Jersey Supreme Court addressed the constitutionality of one such policy in *LW v. Toms River Regional Schools Board of Education*. The court ruled that schools are liable for failing to police a hostile school environment created by bullying under the New Jersey Law Against Discrimination (LAD).[95]

> We do not suggest, however, that isolated schoolyard insults or classroom taunts are actionable. Rather, in the educational context, to state a claim under the LAD, an aggrieved student must allege discriminatory conduct that would not have occurred

> "but for" the student's protected characteristic, that a reasonable student of the same age, maturity level, and protected characteristic would consider sufficiently severe or pervasive enough to create an intimidating, hostile, or offensive school environment, and that the school district failed to reasonably address such conduct.[96]

Again, a court warns against targeting single incidents of bullying—advice New Jersey lawmakers failed to heed when they revised the anti-bullying statute in 2011. Nor did they take the advice of widely recognized bullying expert Dan Olewus who defines bullying as involving "a pattern of behavior repeated over time" and "an imbalance of power or strength."[97]

Note also that the scope of the Anti-bullying Rights Act exceeds the prohibitions of the New Jersey LAD statute[98] by banning statements and actions against "any other distinguishing characteristic." LAD identifies only "race, creed, color, national origin, nationality, ancestry, age, sex, familial status, marital status, domestic partnership or civil union status, sexual orientation, gender, atypical hereditary cellular or blood trait, genetic information, liability for military service, and mental or physical disability, perceived disability, and AIDS and HIV status."[99] As education law professors Joseph O. Oluwole and Preston C. Green note in *Censorship and Student Communication in Online and Offline Settings*, "Neither the legislature nor judiciary has clearly delineated what constitutes a distinguishing characteristic; accordingly, this determination will have to be based on the subjective judgments of school officials until there are definitive and limpid guidelines from the judiciary and/or the legislature."[100]

In *Saxe v. State College Area School District*, the U.S. Court of Appeals for the Third Circuit struck down as constitutionally overbroad a Pennsylvania school anti-harassment policy restricting speech considered a threat to individuals and the school environment that had an excessively long reach.[101] The school went too far, the court said, by banning disparaging speech directed at "clothing, physical appearance, social skills, peer group, intellect, educational program, hobbies, or values."[102] Thus, the court said,

> the Policy prohibits harassment based on personal characteristics that are not protected under federal law. Titles VI and IX, taken together with the other relevant federal statutes, cover only harassment based on sex, race, color, national origin, age and disability. The Policy, in contrast, is much broader, reaching, at the extreme, a catch-all category of 'other personal characteristics' (which, the Policy states, includes things like "clothing," "appearance," "hobbies and values," and "social skills"). Insofar as the policy attempts to prevent students from making negative comments about each others' "appearance," "clothing," and "social skills," it may be brave,

> futile, or merely silly. But attempting to proscribe negative comments about "values," as that term is commonly used today, is something else altogether. By prohibiting disparaging speech directed at a person's "values," the Policy strikes at the heart of moral and political discourse—the lifeblood of constitutional self government (and democratic education) and the core concern of the First Amendment. That speech about "values" may offend is not cause for its prohibition, but rather the reason for its protection: "a principal function of free speech under our system of government is to invite dispute …"[103]

The New Jersey statute, however, treats characteristics as though they are values. Case in point, *C.C. v. Board of Education* (2016), a ruling involving a six-grader who was punished for criticizing another student's vegetarianism.[104] Yet, vegetarianism is a strongly held set of values. It can be rooted in religion, morals, ethics, ecological beliefs, or the values of compassion and fairness. On the other side of the coin, meat eating is often a strongly held culturally practice and value, as any vegetarian who has tried to persuade a steak eater to consume tofu can attest. Thus, under the *Saxe v. State College Area School District* rationale, New Jersey has no authority to ban disparaging remarks about "characteristics" when the term can be used to censor speech about personal values.

Equally significant, the *Saxe* court said, the policy defined harassment as "(1) verbal or physical conduct (2) that is based on one's actual or perceived personal characteristics and (3) that has the purpose or effect of either (3a) substantially interfering with a student's educational performance or (3b) creating an intimidating hostile, or offensive environment."[105] The court ruled that the policies were overbroad under the *Tinker* substantial disruption and the infringement of rights analysis.[106] The New Jersey Act's definition of harassment, intimidation or bullying encompasses the same elements. It follows, that by the measure of the *Saxe* ruling, the Act is also unconstitutional. Though the state references the aforementioned cases in its "Model Policy and Guidance for Prohibiting Harassment, Intimidation and Bullying on School Property, at School-Sponsored Events and on School Buses,"[107] there is a strong argument that precedents do not support the constitutionally of the Act in part, or in its entirety.

Moreover, the term "intimidation" holds a narrowly applied meaning in the context of public school student speech doctrine. As noted earlier, under the U.S. Court of Appeals Fifth Circuit ruling in *Bell v. Itawamba County School Board*, handed down after the Act's enactment, off-campus student speech may be restricted without offending the First Amendment "when a student intentionally directs at the school community speech reasonably understood by school officials to threaten, harass, and intimidate a teacher, even when such speech originated, and was disseminated, off-campus without the use of school resources."[108] In contrast, the Act makes no such distinction. It doesn't address student-to-teacher cyberbullying. It talks only of harm to students by students. Therefore, "intimidation" as defined by the statute, cannot justifiably support a finding of "HIB" unless the student engages in threatening or violent non-verbal conduct or speech directed at teachers. Otherwise, the use of the term "intimidation" is overbroad, allowing schools to proscribe constitutionally protected speech.

Constitutional Challenges

Courts will strike down a statute as constitutionally overbroad when its language prohibits individuals from exercising their legitimate rights because the statute "potentially covers a great deal of constitutionally protected speech."[109] Under the constitutional vagueness doctrine, courts may strike down a statute when a person of ordinary intelligence cannot determine by the language of the statute whether his or her conduct is illegal.[110] Based on the above precedents, it would seem that the Anti-Bullying Rights Act is overly broad and vague. That's what Lim and Mao, the parents of the Tenafly students, argued in their lawsuit against the school board.[111]

The Act also allows schools to exceed their constitutional authority, the parents argued, by punishing speech that "has the effect of insulting or demeaning any student or group of students" and allowing schools to discipline students for a "single incident."[112] Consequently, any truthful declaration or innocent question about a student's identifying characteristics, proclivities, quirks or habits are subject to punishment, the parents argued.

> The Act could be used to stifle student discussion on divisive topics like sincerely held religious beliefs … religious practices, ethnic or cultural customs, or even observations about differing physical attributes as innocuous as hair color or length, eye color, or height differences, if such discussions had the effect of "insulting or demeaning" a student or "creat[ing] a hostile educational environment." Historical discussions about German atrocities committed during the Holocaust, or observations about the relationship between terrorism and radical Islam might justifiably "insult or demean" German or Muslim students respectively, providing adequate grounds for speech suppression on the basis that the statements disrupt the rights of other students.[113]

Thus, the parents questioned how it is possible for the reasonable grade-school student to identify in advance, or the school official to correctly determine after the fact, that remarks about a "distinguishing characteristic" would be interpreted as an "insulting," demeaning, or hostile environment-creating? "As a practical matter, the Act is unreasonable in its expectations and the standard that it purports to hold school children to,"[114] the complaint argued.

About the same time Fair Lawn High School cleared Koval in early March 2016, a New Jersey administrative law judge upheld a finding of "harassment, intimidation or bullying" against an 11-year-old Montgomery Township sixth-grader.[115] The pre-teen's transgression? During a lunchtime cafeteria conversation, the student made the mistake of telling another six-grader, a vegetarian, "it's not good to not eat meat" and "he should eat meat because he'd be smarter and have bigger brains."[116]

The ruling underscores the argument of the Tenafly parents. It is unreasonable to expect a six-grader to know that criticizing and giving advice to a vegetarian is the same as criticizing someone about their "race, color, religion, ancestry, national origin, gender, sexual orientation, gender identity and expression, or a mental, physical or sensory disability." Moreover, as noted above, criticism or ridicule of an individual's lifestyle choice is not banned under Title VII of the Civil Rights Act of 1964, Title I of the Americans with Disabilities Act of 1990 or Title IX of the Education Act of 1972. On the other hand, the First Amendment protects the right to criticize others for their values and beliefs.

But that's not what the administrative law judge ruled, even though there was no finding of substantial disruption to the classroom. It was not "arbitrary, capricious or unreasonable" to find that the "state of being a vegetarian can constitute 'any other distinguishing characteristic.'"[117] He cited precedents:

> In *W.C.L. and A.L. o/b/o L.L. v. Board of Education of the Borough of Tenafly*, a student's comments relating to head lice on another student was perceived as being motivated by a distinguishing characteristic. *In R.G.B. v. Village of Ridgewood Bd. Of Ed.* … a student calling another student a "horse" and a "fat-ass" was found to constitute HIB and reasonably perceived as motivated by the distinguishing characteristic of appearance or body-type. In *C.C. o/b/o/ S.C. v. Bd. of Ed. Of Twp. Of Jefferson* … a student's comments that another student "sucks at basketball" was found to constitute HIB because the comments were reasonably perceived as motivated by the distinguishing characteristic of height, intelligence and sports proficiency.[118]

Conclusion

Though the proper application of the *Tinker* analysis should have and, apparently did, block school authorities from disciplining Koval, the test is generally poorly suited to address off-campus online speech. In *Snyder v. Blue Mountain School District* U.S. Court of Appeals Third Circuit Judge D. Brooks Smith and four other judges have staked out such a position. Smith's first rationale from distinguishing *Tinker* from cases involving off-campus online speech was that *Tinker* is grounded in the "special characteristics of the school environment."[119] That is to say, students' free speech rights are greatly limited on school property in recognition that educators' have the responsibility to maintain safety. Those special characteristics, however, do not apply to off-campus forums where students should be treated as adults under the First Amendment and free to express political opinions, among other topics, without fear of censorship. Smith warned,

> ... if *Tinker* were applied to off-campus speech, there would be little reason to prevent school officials from regulating *adult* speech uttered in the community ... Adults often say things that give rise to disruptions in public schools. Those who championed desegregation in the 1950s and 60s caused more than a minor disturbance in the southern schools. Of course, the prospect of using *Tinker* to silence such speakers is absurd. But the absurdity stems not from applying *Tinker* to off-campus speech uttered by adults and students alike, but from the antecedent step of extending *Tinker* beyond the public-school setting to which it is so firmly moored.[120]

Smith also voiced concerns about school officials applying the highly elastic foreseeability standard to determine substantial disruption. Smith argued, "speech originating off campus does not mutate into on-campus speech simply because it foreseeably makes its way onto campus ... A bare foreseeability standard could be stretched too far, and would risk ensnaring any off-campus expression that happened to discuss school-related matters."[121] Likewise, substantial disruption based on foreseeability allows schools to punish students for speech even if its impact develops years after it was first posted. In contrast, speech that incites lawlessness can be censored only when it poses an imminent and serious threat or is likely to and the speaker intended to create the specific lawlessness or disorder.[122]

What's Smith's alternative to *Tinker*? Treat the alleged off-campus cyberbully like an adult citizen under the First Amendment—subject the speech to defamation, obscenity "or otherwise unprotected speech" tests.[123]

Back in New Jersey, the Anti-Bullying Taskforce quietly offered another, though largely ignored, alternative. "Research supports that creating a positive school climate is the single best way to prevent [harassment, intimidation or bullying]."[124]

Notes

1. *Tinker v. Des Moines Independent Community School District*, 393 U.S 503, 511(1969).
2. Bethany Koval, benny • בית, https://twitter.com/bendykoval (accessed August 22, 2016).
3. Hannah Adely, "Fair Lawn High School Looks into Whether Student's Anti-Israel Political Tweets are Bullying," *NorthJersey.com*, January 7, 2016, 2:17 PM, Last updated: Friday, January 8, 2016, 6:56 AM, http://www.northjersey.com/news/fair-lawn-superintendent-says-he-was-following-the-law-in-questioning-student-over-anti-israel-tweets-1.1487045 (accessed August 22, 2016).
4. Ibid.
5. Yanan Wang, "A N.J. Teen Who Tweeted 'Israel is a Terrorist Force' was Called to the Principal's Office for 'Bullying,'" *Washington Post*, January 8, 2016, https://www.washingtonpost.com/news/morning-mix/wp/2016/01/08/a-n-j-teen-who-tweeted-israel-is-a-terrorist-force-was-called-to-the-principals-office-for-bullying/ (accessed August 22, 2016).
6. Ibid.
7. New Jersey Statutes Ann. § 18A:37-13.2 & 37-14 (2011), New Jersey Permanent Statutes Database, 2015, http://lis.njleg.state.nj.us/cgi-bin/om_isapi.dll?clientID=33828468&Depth=2&advquery=%2218A%3a37-13%22&depth=4&expandheadings=on&headingswithhits=on&hitsperheading=on&infobase=statutes.nfo&rank=%20%20&record={8627}&softpage=Doc_Frame_PG42&wordsaroundhits=10&zz= (accessed June 30, 2016).
8. New Jersey Department of Education, "Anti-Bullying Rights Act (N.J.S.A 18A:37-13 *et seq*) Questions and Answers," November 2015, http://www.state.nj.us/education/genfo/faq/AntiBullyingQA.pdf, 3 (accessed August 22, 2016).
9. 18A:37-14, "Definitions Relative to Adoption of Harassment and Bullying Prevention Policies," New Jersey Permanent Statues Database, 2015, http://lis.njleg.state.nj.us/cgi-bin/om_isapi.dll?clientID=297373751&Depth=4&TD=WRAP&advquery=%2218A%3a37-14%22&headingswithhits=on&infobase=statutes.nfo&rank=&record={864B}&softpage=Doc_Frame_Pg42&wordsaroundhits=2&x=40&y=10&zz= (accessed August 22, 2016).
10. Tinker v. Des Moines School District, 393 U.S. 503, 513 (1969).
11. 18A:37-14, "Definitions Relative to Adoption of Harassment and Bullying Prevention Policies."
12. Tinker v. Des Moines School District, 393 U.S. 503, 513.
13. 18A:37-14. "Definitions Relative to Adoption of Harassment and Bullying Prevention Policies."
14. "Questions and Answers," November 2015, http://www.state.nj.us/education/genfo/faq/AntiBullyingQA.pdf, 3
15. Hannah Adley, "State Board of Education Considers letting Principals Decide Whether to Investigate Bullying Allegations," *NewJeresy.com*, April 6, 2016, 7:04 PM, http://www.northjersey.com/news/state-board-of-education-considers-letting-principals-decide-whether-to-investigate-bullying-allegations-1.1539473 (accessed August 22, 2016).
16. Nathan Tempey, "ACLU: Schools Bullying Case Against 'F--- Israel' Teen is Egregious," *Gothamist*, January 7, 2016, 4:35 PM, http://gothamist.com/2016/01/07/nj_school_bullying_teen_israel.php (accessed August 22, 2016).

17. Tinker v. Des Moines School District, 393 U.S. 503, 513.
18. Liam Stack, "Tweets About Israel Land New Jersey Student in Principal's Office," *New York Times*, January 7, 2016, http://www.nytimes.com/2016/01/07/nyregion/anti-israel-tweets-land-new-jersey-student-in-principals-office.html?_r=0 (accessed August 22, 2016).
19. Nathan Temply, "Parents Protest in Support of School Administrators Investigating 'F--- ISRAEL' Teen," *Gothamist*, January 10, 2016, 2:00 PM, http://gothamist.com/2016/01/10/httpfairlawndailyvoicecomschoolsfai.php (accessed August 22, 2016).
20. Stack, "Tweets About Israel Land New Jersey Student in Principal's Office."
21. Temply, "Parents Protest in Support of School Administrators Investigating 'F--- ISRAEL' Teen."
22. Hannan Adely, "Fair Lawn Teen at Center of Tweets Uproar Tells of Retribution," *The Record*, March 17, 2016, http://www.northjersey.com/news/fair-lawn-teen-at-center-of-tweets-uproar-tells-of-retribution-1.1528602?page=all (accessed August 22, 2016).
23. Ibid.
24. Ibid.
25. ACLU of New Jersey, "Student's Political Tweets Not Bullying, School Officials Rule," *American Civil Liberties Union of New Jersey*, March 8, 2016, https://www.aclu-nj.org/news/2016/03/08/students-political-tweets-not-bullying-school-officials-rule (accessed August 22, 2016).
26. Hannan Adely, "State Board of Education Considers Letting Principals Decide Whether to Investigate Bullying Allegations," *The Record*, April 6, 2016, 7:04 PM, http://www.northjersey.com/news/state-board-of-education-considers-letting-principals-decide-whether-to-investigate-bullying-allegations-1.1539473 (accessed June 30, 2016).
27. Star-Ledger Editorial Board, "On N.J. Bullying Law: Can We Get Off the Crazy Train?" March 14, 2016, 5:42 PM, http://www.nj.com/opinion/index.ssf/2016/03/on_nj_bullying_law_can_we_get_off_the_crazy_train.html (accessed August 22, 2016).
28. ACLU of New Jersey, "Student's Political Tweets Not Bullying, School Officials Rule."
29. Joseph O. Oluwole and Preston C. Green, *Censorship and Student Communication in Online and Offline Settings* (Hershey: IGI Global, 2016), 377, 379.
30. JS Ex Rel. Snyder v. Blue Mountain School District, 650 F.3d 915 (en banc 3d Cir. 2011).
31. Colorado Revised Statutes §22-32-109 (a)(I), http://cdpsdocs.state.co.us/safeschools/Legislation/C.R.S.22-32-109.1-2015.pdf (accessed August 22, 2016).
32. JS Ex Rel. Snyder v. Blue Mountain School District, 650 F.3d 915, 939.
33. Davis v. Monroe County Board of Education, 526 U.S. 629 (1999).
34. Dewey Cornell and Susan P. Limber, "Law and Policy on the Concept of Bullying at School," *American Psychologist* (May–June 2015), 332, 333, http://www.apa.org/pubs/journals/releases/amp-a0038558.pdf (accessed August 22, 2016).
35. Sameer Hinduja and Justin W. Patchin, "A Brief Review of State Cyberbullying Laws and Policies," Cyberbullying Research Center, January 2016, http://www.cyberbullying.us/Bullying-and-Cyberbullying-Laws.pdf (accessed August 19, 2016).
36. Emily F. Suski, "Beyond the School House Gates: The Unprecedented Expansion of School Surveillance Authority Under Cyberbullying Laws," *Case Western Reserve Law Review* 65 (2014): 63, 66.
37. New Jersey Education Association, "Anti-Bullying," (2010–2016), http://www.njea.org/issues-and-political-action/anti-bullying (accessed August 22, 2016).

38. Matt Friedman, "Near Jersey Senate, Assembly Pass 'Anti-Bullying Bill of Rights' in Wake of Tyler Clementi's Death," *NJ.com*, November 23, 2010, 5:27 AM, http://www.nj.com/news/index.ssf/2010/11/nj_assembly_passes_anti-bullyi.html (accessed August 22, 2016).
39. Education Law Center, "Bullying," (2011–2016), http://www.edlawcenter.org/issues/bullying.html (accessed August 22, 2016).
40. New Jersey Commission on Bullying in Schools, *There Isn't A Moment to Lose: An Urgent Call for Legal Reform and Effective Practices to Combat Bullying in New Jersey Schools* (Newark: Education Law Center, December 15, 2009), http://www.edlawcenter.org/assets/files/pdfs/bullying/Bullying%20Report%20December%202009%20-%20%20Final.pdf (accessed August 22, 2016).
41. Doninger v. Niehoff, 642 F.3d 334 (2d Cir. 2011), 132 S.Ct. 499 (2011), *cert denied*; Kowalski v. Berkeley County Schools, 652 F.3d 565 (4th Cir. 2011), *cert. denied*, 80 U.S.L.W. 3427 (2012); Layshock v. Hermitage School District, 650 F.3d 205 (3d Cir.2011) *cert denied*, 132 S. Ct. 1097 (2012); J.S. ex rel Snyder v. Blue Mountain School District, 650 F.3d 915 (3d Cir. 2011) (en banc), *cert. denied*, 132 S. Ct. 1097 (2012).
42. Ray Tarinelli, "Supreme Court Denies Review of Taylor Bell Case on Student Off-Campus, Online Speech," *SPLC*, February 29, 2016, 9:45 AM, http://www.splc.org/article/2016/02/supreme-court-denies-review-of-taylor-bell-case (accessed August 22, 2016); Bell v. Itawamba County School Board, 799 F 3d 379 (5th Cir. 2015), *cert cenied*, No. 15-666 (2016).
43. Catherine Ross, *Lessons in Censorship: How School and Courts Subvert Students' First Amendment Rights* (Cambridge, MA: Harvard University Press, 2015).
44. Ibid., 224.
45. Ibid., 225.
46. Ibid.
47. *Sagehorn v. Independent School District*, No. 728, 14-1930 (JRT/BRT) (2015).
48. Bell v. Itawamba County School Board, 799 F 3d 379.
49. Wynar v Douglas County School District, 728 F. 3d 1062 (9th Cir. 2013).
50. *JS Rel Snyder v. Blue Mountain* School District, 650 F. 3d 915, 931–32.
51. Yanan Wang, "A N.J. Teen Who Tweeted 'Israel is a Terrorist Force' was Called to the Principal's Office for 'Bullying.'"
52. ACLU of New Jersey, "Student's Political Tweets Not Bullying, School Officials Rule."
53. Bethany Koval @bendykoval, December 23, 2015, https://twitter.com/bendykoval/status/679829455100080128 (accessed August 22, 2016).
54. Bethany Koval @bendykoval, https://twitter.com/bendykoval/status/679841782591569921 (accessed August 22, 2016).
55. rama @saviorsivan, December 23, 2015, https://twitter.com/saviorsivan/status/679845201595121664?replies_view=true&cursor=AMAWmtJLbwk (accessed August 22, 2016).
56. Bethany Koval. @Bendykoval, December 27, 2015, 1:06 AM, https://twitter.com/bendykoval/status/681038459360948224 (August 22, 2016).
57. Tinker v. Des Moines School District, 393 U.S. 503, 509.
58. Saxe v. State College Area School District, 240 F.3d 200, 211 (3d Cir. 2001).
59. LaVine v. Blaine School District, 257 F.3d 981, 989 (9th Cir. 2001).

60. Ross, *Lessons in Censorship: How School and Courts Subvert Students' First Amendment Rights*, 151.
61. Thomas v. Board of Education, Granville Central School District, 607 F.2d 1043, 1045 (2d Cir. 1979).
62. Doninger v. Niehoff, 642 F.3d 334, 348.
63. Bell v. Itawamba County School Board, 799 F 3d 379.
64. J.S. ex rel. Snyder v. Blue Mountain School District, 922–23.
65. Bible Believers v. Wayne County, Michigan, 805 F.3d 228 (2015).
66. Wisniewski v. Board of Education of Weedsport Central School District, 494 F.3d 34, 38 (2d Cir. 2007).
67. Tinker v. Des Moines School District, 393 U.S. 503, 513.
68. Harper v. Poway Unified School District, 445 F. 3d 1166, 1178 (2006).
69. J.S. ex rel. Snyder v. Blue Mountain School District.
70. *Model Policy and Guidance for Prohibiting Harassment, Intimidation and Bullying on School Property, at School-Sponsored Functions and on School Buses* (Trenton: New Jersey Department of Education, April 2011), 24, http://www.state.nj.us/education/parents/bully.htm (accessed August 9, 2016).
71. Philadelphia Newspapers, Inc. v. Hepps, 475 U.S. 767, 777 (1986).
72. Adely, "Fair Lawn High School Looks into Whether Student's Anti-Israel Political Tweets are Bullying."
73. Star-Ledger Editorial Board, "On N.J. Bullying Law: Can We Get Off the Crazy Train," *Newark Star-Ledger*, March 14, 2016, 5:42 PM, http://www.nj.com/opinion/index.ssf/2016/03/on_nj_bullying_law_can_we_get_off_the_crazy_train.html (accessed August 9, 2016).
74. Ibid.
75. New Jersey Anti-Bullying Taskforce, *Annual Report* (Trenton: State of New Jersey, January 26, 2016), www.state.nj.us/education/students/safety/behavior/hib/task/AnnualReport16.pdf, 10–11 (accessed August 9, 2016).
76. Ibid.
77. Valerie Vaneiri-Huttle, "Nothing Vague About Being the 1st to Tackle Bullying," *Star-Ledger*, February 5, 2016, 11:41 AM, http://www.nj.com/opinion/index.ssf/2016/02/nothing_vague_about_nj_being_the_1st_to_tackle_bul.html (accessed August 9, 2016).
78. Brief for Plaintiff in Opposition to Defendant Commissioner of Education's Motion to Dismiss, W.C.L. and A.L. v. Board of Education of the Borough of Tenafly, 2:13-CV-07399 (U.S.D.C. NJ (2014), https://www.rutherford.org/files_images/general/04-08-2014_Lim_Brief.pdf (accessed April 30, 2017).
79. Ibid., 1.
80. Ibid., 30.
81. John W. Whitehead of the Rutherford Institute, e-mail message to author, June 3, 2016, 11:48 AM.
82. See Cornell and Limber, "Law and Policy on the Concept of Bullying at School," 333–43, http://www.apa.org/pubs/journals/releases/amp-a0038558.pdf (accessed August 9, 2016).
83. Michele Cascardi et al., "The Problem with Overly Broad Definitions of Bullying: Implications for the Schoolhouse, and the Ivory Tower," *Journal of School Violence* 13 (2014): 253, 265.

84. Bachowski v. Salamone, Wis.2d 397, 417 no. 2 (1987); *State v. Vaughn*, 366 S.W. 3d 513 (Mo. 2012).
85. Love v. New Jersey Department of Corrections, 2:2015cv04404 *28 (D.N.J. 2016), http://law.justia.com/cases/federal/district-courts/new-jersey/njdce/2:2015cv04404/320899/34/ (accessed August 22, 2016).
86. Ibid., *27.
87. U.S. v. Elonis, 135 S. Ct. (2001).
88. Bell v. Itawamba County School Board, 799 F 3d 379, 396.
89. Cornell and Limber, "Law and Policy on the Concept of Bullying at School," 339.
90. *Model Policy and Guidance for Prohibiting Harassment, Intimidation and Bullying on School Property, at School-Sponsored Events and on School Buses*, Part 1: Background, 201.
91. Davis v. Monroe County Board of Education, 526 U.S. 629 (1999).
92. Ibid., 633.
93. New Jersey Education Association, "Anti-Bullying."
94. Nan Stein, *Classrooms & Courtrooms: Facing Sexual Harassment in K-12 Schools* (Williston: Teachers College Press, 1999).
95. *About the NJ Law Against Discrimination(LAD)* (Trenton: Office of the Attorney General, Department of Law & Public Safety, 1996–2007), http://www.nj.gov/oag/dcr/law.html#LAD (accessed August 22, 2016).
96. LW v. Toms River Regional Schools Board of Education, A-111-05 *14 (2007), http://www.edlawcenter.org/assets/files/pdfs/bullying/LW%20decision.pdf (accessed August 22, 2016).
97. Dan Olewus, "Recognizing Bullying," *ViolencePreventionWorks.org*, 2016, http://www.violencepreventionworks.org/public/recognizing_bullying.page (accessed June 30, 2016).
98. "About the N J Law Against Discrimination," http://www.nj.gov/oag/dcr/law.html#LAD (accessed August 22, 2016).
99. "About the N J Law Against Discrimination."
100. Oluwole and Green, *Censorship and Student Communication in Online and Offline Settings*, 362.
101. Saxe v. State College Area School District, 240 F. 3d 200 (3d Cir. 2001).
102. Ibid., 210.
103. Ibid.
104. C.C. v. Board of Education (2016), 2016 WL 958848, oral decision, http://njlaw.rutgers.edu/collections/oal/html/initial/edu12103-15_1.html (accessed August 22, 2016).
105. Saxe, 240 F. 3d 200, 216.
106. Ibid., 217.
107. *Model Policy and Guidance for Prohibiting Harassment, Intimidation and Bullying on School Property, at School-Sponsored Events and on School Buses*, Part 1.
108. Bell v. Itawamba County School Board, 799 F 3d 379, 396.
109. U.S. v. Stevens, 533 F. 3d 218, 235, no. 16 (2008).
110. Papachristou v. Jacksonville, 405 U.S. 156, 162 (1972); Winters v. New York, 333 U.S. 507, 515–16 (1948).
111. W.C.L. and A.L. v. Board of Education of the Borough of Tenafly, 2:13-CV-07399 (U.S.D.C. NJ (2012), https://www.rutherford.org/files_images/general/04-08-2014_Lim_Brief.pdf (accessed April 30, 2017).

112. Ibid., 13.
113. Ibid., 14.
114. Ibid., 20.
115. C.C. v. Board of Education (2016) 2016 WL 958848, oral decision.
116. Ibid.
117. Ibid.
118. Ibid.
119. J.S. Ex Rel, Snyder v. Blue Mountain School Board, 937.
120. Ibid., 940.
121. Ibid., 941.
122. Brandenburg v. Ohio, 395 U.S. 444 (1969); Hess v. Indiana, 414 U.S. 105 (1973).
123. J.S. Ex Rel, Snyder v. Blue Mountain School Board, 940–41.
124. New Jersey Anti-bullying Taskforce, *Annual Report*, 20.

· 5 ·

CENSORSHIP REDUX

The 21st Century Attack on the First Amendment Right of Public Criticism by the Use of Cyberharassment, Cyberstalking and Online Impersonation Laws

> Fear of serious injury cannot alone justify suppression of free speech and assembly. Men feared witches and burnt women. It is the function of speech to free men from the bondage of irrational fears. To justify suppression of free speech there must be reasonable ground to fear that serious evil will result if free speech is practiced. There must be reasonable ground to believe that the danger apprehended is imminent. There must be reasonable ground to believe that the evil to be prevented is a serious one.
>
> —*Whitney v. California* (1927)[1]

Raphael Haim Golb, 49, did not sleep well in the early morning of Thursday, March 5, 2009, and he found no comfort in his waking hours that day, either.[2] The lawyer and literary scholar did not get to bed until 5 AM because he had been working on a blog posting called, "Antisemitism and the Dead Sea Scrolls." About 7 AM, he awoke, startled to see a New York City policeman standing over him wielding a gun. He was baffled until the police officer announced that he was under arrest because of "the Dead Sea Scrolls and your computer." I am being arrested for "making fun of a professor on the Internet," he thought with disbelief.[3]

Bewilderment turned into near paralyzing fear and then disorientation that morning as several law enforcement officers watched him dress, cuffed him, and took him from his Greenwich Village apartment to the underground holding pens of the Tombs, the Manhattan Detention Complex, already full of hundreds of other arrestees. Released from the Tombs on the following day, Golb promised he would be vindicated on 51 counts stemming from an alleged online harassment scheme.[4]

Now, he recalls the harrowing day with a degree of irony, remarking that, "I commend the district attorney for his ability to demonstrate his authority and terrorize people."[5]

Golb, the authorities charged, harassed several Dead Sea Scrolls scholars, most notably Lawrence Schiffman of New York University, by impersonating and criticizing them in an email and blog campaign. At his trial, Golb said he had, indeed, targeted his father's scholarly rivals, but with no intent to defraud or commit any other crime. Rather, he argued, he took on the identities of the scholars to mock and criticize them by parody and satire. It was his contribution to a long-running and heated scholarly debate over the origins of the Dead Sea Scrolls in which his father, Norman Golb, had been ostracized, he said.

Going back to the 1980s, Norman Golb, professor of Near Eastern languages and civilization at the University of Chicago, was treated as something of a heretic when he developed a theory of the origins of the scrolls, ancient religious texts discovered in caves in the Judaean Desert, that contradicted the then prevailing view. During the ensuing struggle, Golb played a highly publicized role in opposing the well-known academic monopoly that controlled access to the Scrolls.[6] The *New York Times'* coverage of a scholarly conference on the controversial scrolls held at Brown University in 2002 gives some indication of the acrimony in this field.[7] Some scholars refused to attend the conference, if scholars from the opposing camp were invited, and Norman Golb was not invited, the *Times* reported. "Others don't want to acknowledge that mine is the best hypothesis," Golb said.[8]

A jury, however, was not persuaded that Raphael Golb's online campaign was a parodic and satirical retort. In 2010, Golb was convicted on 30 criminal counts—two counts of identity theft in the second degree; 14 counts of criminal impersonation in the second degree; 10 counts of forgery in the third degree; three counts of aggravated harassment in the second degree; and one count of unauthorized use of a computer.[9] He was sentenced to six months in jail and five years of probation.[10]

In the summer of 2016, Golb, a lawyer with a degree from New York University and a doctorate in comparative literature from Harvard, resigned himself to the certainty that by the same time in the following year he would be serving a two-month sentence in New York's notorious Riker's Island jail.[11]

Golb, however, doesn't believe he is a criminal, and he is neither delusional nor disingenuous to think so.

First, he no longer can be considered guilty on the three counts of aggravated harassment. The aggravated harassment charges were the core foundation supporting the other criminal charges of impersonation, forgery and unauthorized use of a computer. However, In *People v. Golb* (2014), New York's highest court, the Court of Appeals, threw out of all of his convictions for aggravated harassment along with the statute that criminalized the behavior.[12] His purpose, law enforcement argued, was to harass his father's rivals. Posing as them in emails and online—hence the criminal impersonation, forgery and unauthorized use of a computer charges—were the means and methods to carry out the alleged harassment. He was not guilty of harassment, therefore he should not still be guilty of impersonations, forgeries and unauthorized use of computers.

"The aggravated harassment charges," Golb says, "allowed the prosecution to poison the trial atmosphere by casting a negative pall over my entire campaign, including the blogs. That was the 'criminal context' forming the background for the other charges."[13]

Second, the court also vacated the convictions on five of the 14 counts of criminal impersonation; the one remaining count for identity theft in the second degree (the other had been previously vacated by the intermediate appellate court); and the conviction for unauthorized use of a computer.[14] Later, Golb won the right to a retrial on two criminal impersonation counts.[15] So, by mid-2016, he stood convicted of the two closely related crimes of 10 counts of forgery and seven counts of criminal impersonation.

Golb says his emails, particularly one that had Schiffman "confessing" to plagiarizing his father were "an academic send-up, in the tradition of all sorts of well-known satirical texts like the *Letters of Obscure Men* [1515–1517]. The *Letters* notoriously fooled gullible readers around Europe. They are credited with setting the stage for the Protestant reformation. They are a key humanistic text from which the term 'obscurantism' is derived. But they would be illegal if written and published in New York today."[16]

His view cannot be dismissed as merely an esoteric historical point from a literary scholar. The Electronic Frontier Foundation, for example, argues that criminalizing online impersonation threatens protected speech such as parody Twitter accounts, used for satire and social commentary.[17] Though the possibility was discussed in the media, no charges were brought against conservative political pundit Tucker Carlson of the *Daily Caller* when he bought the web address www.keitholbermann.com and sent emails out in the name of the liberal pundit, Keith Olbermann.[18]

Also, consider that the U.S. Supreme Court in *U.S. v. Alvarez* (2012) struck down the Stolen Valor Act, which made it a crime to lie about receiving military medals or honors—arguably, a form of impersonation—as an unconstitutional restriction on speech.[19] To legitimately criminalize deception, the Court said, government must prove that the deception of speech was integral to a crime such as fraud or posing as a law enforcement official. Moreover, deceptive speech on public matters must be addressed by civil action, subject to defamation's reckless disregard for the truth or knowing falsity standards, and by negligence when private individuals are defamed.[20]

> Were the Court to hold that the interest in truthful discourse alone is sufficient to sustain a ban on speech, absent any evidence that the speech was used to gain a material advantage, it would give government a broad censorial power unprecedented in this Court's cases or in our constitutional tradition. The mere potential for the exercise of that power casts a chill, a chill the First Amendment cannot permit if free speech, thought, and discourse are to remain a foundation of our freedom.[21]

Lastly, had Court of Appeals Chief Judge Jonathan Lippman had his way, none of the convictions would have survived. Dissenting in *Golb*, he said the criminal impersonation statute was constitutionally overbroad and the entire indictment should have been dismissed. "[I]n an age in which pseudonymous communication has become ubiquitous, particularly on the Internet, this [criminal impersonation] statute, literally understood, criminalizes a vast amount of speech that the First Amendment protects."[22]

Fear of the Internet's One-to-Many Communicative Powers

Starting in about 2008, prosecutors, juries and judges chose to make criminals out of adults who used online media to mock, scorn and vilify individuals engaged in matters of public concern by misapplying harassment, stalking and criminal impersonation laws, or by relying on new but badly drafted statutes. Many of these alleged and convicted cyber-criminals were exercising their First Amendment free speech rights. They made that claim when they were arrested, they asserted that claim at trial and they argued that before judges. Though not as overt or on the same scale, the current effort to criminalize objectionable speech on matters of public concern has disturbing similarities to the speech-repressive period of World War I and the Red Scare of the early 1920s.[23]

But this time the perceived threat to social stability isn't leftwing radicals and immigrants. It is the fear of the one-to-many communicative powers of the Internet. As never before, cyberspace technologies enable a wide swath of individuals, from jilted lovers to so-called trolls to political activists, to share their pranks and grievances anonymously, pseudonymously and repeatedly with millions with the push of a few buttons or keys. But our understanding of First Amendment principles has changed dramatically in the near 100 years since the post-WWI period. Starting in the late 1920s, the U.S. Supreme Court embarked on an effort to expand the scope of free speech protections and U.S. Supreme Court Justice Louis Brandeis's concurrence in *Whitney v. California*, quoted in part at the chapter's start, was one of the seminal steps in that direction.

That is why the campaign to criminalize adult cyberbullying should disturb all of us. The legislators who pass repressive cyberbullying laws, the district attorneys who prosecute online impersonators such as Golb or John Leidecker,[24] and the judges who issue cyberstalking-based injunctions against individuals such as web site owners like Chan should be well aware that they are trampling on firmly established free speech rights. Instead, accused cyberbullies have had to file appeals to protect their rights. From 2011 to mid-2016, eight such defendants proved that they were wrongly charged or convicted for criminal cyberbulling by persuading judges that they were indeed engaged in traditionally protected free expression.

- In the federal cyberstalking case, *U.S. v. Cassidy* (2011), a federal judge ruled that the First Amendment protects anonymous and abusive tweets about a religious leader sent to willing followers of the tweet account.[25]
- In *People v.* Golb (2014), the New York Court of Appeals struck down the state's aggravated harassment statute and vacated in part a conviction for identity theft, five convictions for online criminal impersonation and a conviction for unauthorized use of a computer, though it affirmed in part convictions for nine counts of criminal impersonation in the second degree and convictions for forgery.[26]
- In *Chan v. Ellis* (2015), the Georgia Supreme Court blocked an anti-stalking statute-based restraining order imposed on an online message board operator because mean and insulting comments about someone, as opposed to comments directed to them, cannot constitute stalking.[27]
- In *State v. Leidecker*, a judge overturned a criminal cyberharassment/stalking conviction of a union administrator who sent emails to an elected official under a pseudonym.[28]

- In *Scott v. Blum* (2016), a Florida appeals court reversed a trial court's order imposed on a process server because he sent emails only to third parties and not directly to the subject of the emails.[29]
- In *People v. Relerford* (2016), an Illinois appeals court struck portions of the state's stalking and cyberstalking statutes on Fourteenth Amendment due process grounds because they failed to require mens rea or guilty mind culpability.[30]
- In three separate rulings from May 2015 to June 2016, Texas judges struck down Texas Penal Code §33.07, a seven-year-old harassment-through-impersonation law, as unconstitutional because it failed to adequately define the proscribed harm.[31] A state appeals court, however, reversed two of the rulings in August 2016.[32]

Combined, the rulings send a message about individuals' rights to engage in public discourse—we will not allow the First Amendment to be refashioned to suit the hysteria of the times. In effect, the rulings remind us that under the First Amendment, adults who engage in abusive and outrageous online criticism should be treated no differently than their offline counterparts whose speech that is "'outrageous' or 'offensive'; that is filled with 'exaggeration' or 'vilification'; that is 'indecent'; that ruptures the 'dignity' of the recipient; or that is perceived as an instrument of 'aggression and personal assault'"[33] has been protected for more than 70 years.

In other words, the First Amendment does not shield true online harassers and stalkers from criminal prosecution. Instead, it protects from criminal prosecution individuals, such as Golb, Leidecker and Chan, who engage in allegedly abusive public discourse by drawing a line between expression that is sent to third parties or the world at large *about* individuals, institutions, or artistic creations and ideas, in contrast to expression directed *to* an individual intended to intimidate by causing fear of violence to the target. If these accused and convicted cyberbullies had not prevailed, powerful precedents supporting government's authority to exclude online speakers from longstanding First Amendment free speech standards of proof of harm—intent on the speaker's part and the immediate or high likelihood of a serious adverse impact—would have been established.[34]

More to the point, to deprive online speakers of the right to hyperbole, ridicule and vilification would cripple the Internet as a medium for exercising political dissent and criticism and discussion of matters of public concern, forms of expression vital for the democratic exchange of ideas and individual expression. Despite the widespread presence of adult-to-adult name-calling, particularly obnoxious and profane speech about women,[35] the arguments justifying lesser free speech protection for those charged with cyberharassment or cyberstalking are unconvincing. Aspects of the Internet that arguably make online stalking more disturbing than traditional stalking—anonymity, the ability of a perpetrator to urge others to participate in verbal mob action, and the ability of the perpetrator to mask his proximity—can be minimized or checked through technology or the law without undermining free speech rights. For example, though Section 230 of the Communications Decency Act (CDA) has been interpreted to shield online intermediaries from cyberstalking claims and anonymous users enjoy limited First Amendment protection from disclosure, the law also gives parties the right to unmask online pseudo- or anonymous speakers in *Subpoena Duces Tecum* proceedings.[36]

Even outspoken feminists, rightly troubled by disproportionately high amounts of verbal abuse heaped on female Internet users, suggest only civil actions as solutions, such as imposing liability on online intermediaries, requiring intermediaries to take down offending expression after a cyberstalking conviction and civil rights lawsuits.[37] Similarly, there is no legitimate reason to criminally punish individuals for assuming others' identities online or creating fictional online identities when their purpose is merely political or social commentary or parody. As criminal impersonation law has long recognized, an impersonator must have the intent "to unlawfully gain a benefit for himself or another or to injure or defraud another."[38] Moreover, because the U.S. Supreme Court has severely limited the ability of public figures to prevail in actions for defamation and intentional infliction of emotional distress caused by parody, satire or caricature, criminal prosecution for such speech should be unacceptable under the First Amendment.

Nevertheless, as the legal struggles of Ralphael Golb, John Leidecker, John William Cassidy, Matthew Chan, and Randy Scott attest, prosecutors, judges and juries have sent emailers, tweeters, e-impersonators and web site owners to jail, prison or imposed restraining orders for cyberstalking and cyber harassment without giving due consideration to the First Amendment and criminal evidentiary principles.

People v. Golb

Golb's email and online posting campaign, which started in 2006, was a response to a San Diego Natural History Museum sponsored Dead Sea Scrolls exhibit which traveled to other museums and was presented online.

Conflicting interpretations of the older Golb were excluded, along with the evidence supporting them.[39] "This is a system where [museums and scholars] silence people by excluding them," said Mr. Golb, explaining his motivation. "The Scroll exhibits were a *public farce that deserved a satirical Internet campaign*."[40] By 2009, Golb gradually created more than 80 online aliases "to criticize what he saw as a concerted effort to exclude the research conclusions of his father and others who agree with him from the exhibits."[41] Golb used virtually all of these pseudonyms to post comments online, however, rather than to directly contact Schiffman or the other scholars involved in the exhibits. For instance, from the email account that he created in Schiffman's name, larry.schiffman@gmail.com, Golb sent emails to the New York University (NYU) dean and provost, where Schiffman worked, and to the NYU Department of Hebrew and Judaic Studies where Schiffman had been chair.[42]

Schiffman, one of the older Golb's more determined adversaries[43] and then chairman of NYU's Hebrew and Judaic studies department, was scheduled to speak at the exhibit in New York in 2008, while Norman Golb and his allies were again excluded. Raphael also sent emails to Schiffman's students. One said the following: "Apparently, someone is intent on exposing a minor failing of mine that dates back almost 15 years ago," the e-mail read. "You are not to mention the name of the scholar in question to any of our students, and every effort must be made to prevent this article from coming to their attention. This is my career at stake."[44]

In that email, Golb alluded to an inquiry made by *Haareetz* newspaper journalist Dr. Avi Katzman in an interview with Schiffman that was reproduced partially in *Who Wrote the Dead Sea Scrolls* (1995), authored by Norman Golb. "Schiffman was asked by the journalist why it was in that 'in different articles you have published, you have not hesitated to take over portions of Golb's theory without acknowledging as much, and without giving him credit.'"[45] The charges were ignored at NYU, and Schiffman never rebutted them.[46] In further emails, Raphael Golb sharpened his parody of academic "politics." For example, he portrayed Schiffman as justifying himself with these two sentences: "But this is simply the politics of Dead Sea Scrolls studies. If I had given credit to this man I would have been banned from conferences around the world."[47]

"No reasonable academic," Golb said, "would take such preposterous admissions by a distinguished department chairman at face value."[48] In fact, Schiffman told *Tablet* he "suffered no harm; 'the opposite, I got a big raise out of it,' he said—noting his recent move from NYU to YU, where he makes more money than he did at NYU—'though emotionally it was very difficult.'"[49]

A jury found Golb guilty of violating New York Penal Law § 240.30 (1) (a) which provides that "[a] person is guilty of aggravated harassment in the second degree when, with intent to harass, annoy, threaten or alarm another person, he or she … communicates with a person, anonymously or otherwise, by telephone, by telegraph, or by mail, or by transmitting or delivering any other form of written communication, in a manner likely to cause annoyance or alarm."[50] The Court of Appeals, however, ruled that the statute was unconstitutionally vague and overbroad.[51]

What's the problem with criminalizing annoying or alarming speech? The court did not provide much rationale for its ruling. Its reasoning was based largely on three rulings by federal judges on the constitutionality of the statute—two overturning convictions, and one striking it as unconstitutional as applied—and one New York ruling stemming from a challenge of a similarly worded harassment statute, *Vives v. New York City* (2003).[52] In *Vives*, the defendant mailed "27,000 copies of his political and religious materials to various people."[53]

At the outset of her ruling in *Vives* (2003), U.S. District Court Judge Shira Scheindlin describes the near ubiquity of annoying communication technologies. The implication, of course, is that all of the forms of communication the judge identified would be in jeopardy if government could ban speech that either the defendant intended to be alarming and annoying or that the recipient found alarming or annoying.

> In this Information Age, Americans are bombarded daily with unsolicited communications, by telephone, fax, email, and mail. The vast majority view these communications as, at a minimum, annoying—email boxes filled with spam, prerecorded advertisements left on telephone answering machines, mail slots jammed with credit card applications, catalogs and brochures. Some of the communications go beyond annoying, and rise to the level of alarming—emails that threaten the recipient with harm if the email is not forwarded to a certain number of people, or warn the user that the contents of a computer are not secure from hackers and viruses unless a particular product is purchased and downloaded.[54]

Perhaps the following exchange during oral arguments between Court of Appeals Judge Eugene P. Pigott's and New York City Assistant District Attorney Vincent Rivellese better illustrates the disquieting potential for censorship terms such as alarm and annoy hold. Rivellese argues that the statute allowed him to bring harassment charges against a speaker even though the target of his criticism did not receive the message.

Judge Pigott: So if—well, that's I—you get—you get three college kids—you get some college kid who write—who e-mails the girlfriend of his roommate saying, you know, he really is a useless person. Is that aggravated harassment with respect to the victim, boyfriend/roommate?

Mr. Rivellese: Yes, because it's got—

Judge Pigott: Really?
Mr. Rivellese: It meets all the elements. It does not require that the person that you send the communication to is the same person that you intend to harass, annoy and alarm.[55]

Identity Theft, Fraud and Online Impersonation

Freelance investigative reporter Violent Blue claimed that, "One thing that reached new heights of both stupidity and tragedy in 2010 was the trend of online impersonation."[56] In an article speculating on the impact of California's first online impersonation law, scheduled to go into effect in January 2011, Blue said, "This past year saw a sharp spike in a much more personal kind of impersonation: when people abuse the anonymity of the Internet to cyber-harass individuals."[57]

Whether incidents of harassment-by-e-personation increased dramatically in 2010 cannot be determined, and Blue offered no statistical proof for her claim. By 2016, however, some were calling the misuse of twitter, Craiglist, emails, instagrams, blogs and Facebook accounts to assume someone else's identity or create fake ones an "epidemic."[58] Online impersonation implicates at least two types of crimes: identity theft and fraud, and criminal harassment and cyberstalking. Identity theft and fraud occur when someone wrongfully obtains another's personal data—such as a social security number, passwords to online account, bank account, credit card number or telephone calling card number—to deceive or defraud, typically for economic gain such as the purchase of thousands of dollars of items by credit card purchases.[59] Criminalization of such conduct raises no free speech concerns.

A charge of online impersonation is another matter. For example, California's criminal online impersonation statute is a harassment law banning communication. Under it, a "person who knowingly and without consent credibly impersonates another actual person through," for example, "opening an e-mail account or an account or profile on a social networking Internet Web site in another person's name … for purposes of harming, intimidating, threatening" faces felony charges.[60]

In 2010, the Electronic Frontier Foundation (EFF) failed to persuade California lawmakers that their proposed law raised serious free speech concerns. It argued that the law would provide corporations and politicians with a tool to criminally punish artists and political activists who spoofed and parodied them solely for social and political ends, for example, "'identity correction,' posing as business and government representatives and making statements on their behalf to raise popular awareness of the real effects of those entities' activities."[61] It also argued that existing laws against fraud and defamation covered constitutionally unprotected harms that might result from online impersonation.

In New York, a charge of criminal impersonation in the second degree requires that the defendant have "intent to obtain a benefit or to injure or to defraud."[62] The statute provides no examples or definitions of "injury" or "harm." Golb argued unsuccessfully that scholarly debate was constitutionally exempted from fraud; that reputational harm could not be the basis of injury in a criminal impersonation case because New York, along with the vast majority of states, had abandoned criminal libel and that the truth of the contents of the criminalized "confessions" should have been allowed as a defense.[63] An intermediate-level appeals court, however, rejected those arguments.[64]

Reviewing precedents and creating another of its own, the New York Court of Appeals held that harm could come in the form of monetary fraud, interference with government operations and loss of reputation.[65] "Many people, particularly with a career in academia ... value their reputations at least as much as their property, and we believe the legislature intended that the scope of the statute be broad enough to capture acts intended to cause injury to reputation."[66]

In contrast, there was no harm in creating email accounts under someone else's name that went unused, or sending messages and queries from accounts that did not defraud or harm reputations. "The mere creation of email accounts that are not used does no substantial harm to anyone. Additionally, the email sent from the Seidel email address to Dr. Kohn, asking her opinion on the differing theories about the Scrolls and whether she was planning to answer Professor Golb's critique, is insufficient to support a conviction for criminal impersonation in the second degree."[67]

Golb's sending of emails from accounts in the names of Schiffman, Seidel and Cross deceived others, the court said. Thus, the court affirmed his conviction for forgery in the third degree, which is defined as falsely making, completing or altering a written instrument "with intent to defraud, deceive or injure another."[68] Because Golb, as a New York University alumnus, had legitimate access to its computers, and because there was no evidence he intended to "falsify the business records" of the university, the court vacated his convictions for unauthorized use of a computer and identity theft in the second degree.[69] (The intermediate appeals court had already vacated another felony conviction on identity theft premised on the charge that Golb had schemed to earn $1,000 because "there was no evidence that defendant intended to defraud one or more persons of property in excess of $1,000 or that he attempted to do so."[70]

Chief Judge Lippman dissented from part of the majority's ruling allowing the criminalization of reputational harm stemming from criminal impersonation and forgery. He rightly questioned how the statute could be constitutionally sound when,

> Criminal libel has long since been abandoned … not least of all because of its tendency in practice to penalize and chill speech that the constitution protects … and it has been decades since New York's criminal libel statute was repealed. The use of the criminal impersonation and forgery statutes now approved amounts to an atavism at odds with the First Amendment and the free and uninhibited exchange of ideas it is meant to foster.[71]

The forgery charges also were constitutionally flawed for much the same reason, Lippman argued. "Treating pseudonymous emails as forgeries when they are made with some intent to 'injure' in some undefined way is no different than penalizing impersonation in Internet communication for the same amorphous purpose. Both treatments give prosecutors power they should not have to determine what speech should and should not be penalized."[72]

The *Golb* majority's argument—"Many people, particularly with a career in academia, as relevant to this case, value their reputations at least as much as their property"[73]—is an unconvincing and clumsy sidestepping of First Amendment and New York state precedents. In effect, the court carved out in cursory fashion an exemption from the First Amendment for speech with academic value—or scholarly debates.

But why stop with scholars? Don't, say, authors, priest and Buddhists monks, ethicists and artists, political and ideological purists value their reputations as much as their property, oftentimes more so? They do, of course, but the court did not consider them. It drew a constitutional line with little justification. Moreover, if the reputations of Schiffman and others were injured, civil actions—libel lawsuits were the constitutionally appropriate recourse.

(But, as noted above, Schiffman said Golb's email campaign caused him emotional difficulty, a type of harm not recognized in libel law.)[74]

In January 2016, Golb won the right to a retrial on two criminal impersonation counts.[75] A federal trial judge found that it was "unreasonable for the Court of Appeals to conclude that overbroad jury instructions" on those two counts "were harmless beyond a reasonable doubt" and "had substantial and injurious effect or influence in determining the jury's verdict."[76]

> Because it is not clear that Petitioner sent the emails with the intent to cause 'substantial harm,' or to obtain more than a 'slight' benefit, it was unreasonable for the Court of Appeals to conclude that the overbroad jury instructions on Counts 33 and 37 were harmless beyond a reasonable doubt. For the same reason, the Court finds that the overbroad jury instructions 'had substantial and injurious effect or influence in determining the jury's verdict' on Counts 33 and 37.[77]

"The charade of the trial and appellate proceedings, the collaboration between an academic clique and probably the nation's most prominent prosecutor's office—the always disastrous intervention of legal authorities into a scientific controversy—is itself a gross violation of the civility that's ostensibly being defended," Golb said. "If the system is so corrupt as to have allowed this to unfold, it's hard to see why the same kind of thing can't happen to anybody else who 'crosses the line' in the wrong circumstances. How much money has the city spent on this nonsense?"[78]

Texas Courts Wrestle with Criminalizing Online Impersonation

In 2009, Texas criminalized online impersonation.[79] Under the Texas statute, an individual commits criminal online impersonation when he creates an online page or site, or posts or sends email or post electronic messages, without consent and with intent to cause harm or to defraud.[80] The online impersonation provision is part of Texas's computer crimes statute which defines harm as including "partial or total alteration, damage, or erasure of stored data, interruption of computer services, introduction of a computer virus, *or any other loss, disadvantage, or injury that might reasonably be suffered as a result of the actor's conduct*" [emphasis added].[81] That does not, for example, specify fraud, threats or impersonation of a police office as proscribed harms. Thus, arguably, "harmful" includes virtually any type of expressive and non-expressive conduct and level of harm from annoyance to serious emotional distress.

In three separate rulings from May 2015 to June 2016, Texas judges struck down the statute as unconstitutional precisely because it failed to define "harm" adequately. In February 2016, a Waco judge ruled that because the statute failed to define "harm," it was unconstitutionally vague and did not pass strict scrutiny analysis. The judge struck down the statute and dismissed an indictment against an ex-husband who used his former wife's name to create a Facebook profile.[82] In May 2015, a Harris County district judge struck the statute as overbroad.[83] But in August 2016, two Texas Court of Appeals panels reversed, ruling in *State v. Abigail Marie Stubbs* [84] and *Ex Parte Michael Dwain Bradshaw*[85] that the impersonation/harassment statute targeted a substantial amount of constitutionally unprotected speech and was neither unconstitutionally vague or overbroad.

The gap between the trial and intermediary appeals court rulings centered mostly on what constitutes expressive conduct in cyberspace, and it mirrors the conflicting arguments of the North Carolina courts in *State v. Bishop* (2015) and *State v. Bishop* (2016), examined in Chapter Three. Like the intermediary Texas appeals court in *Stubbs* and *Ex Parte Michael Dwain Bradshaw*, an intermediary North Carolina appeals court in *Bishop* ruled that an online posting was non-expressive conduct and that a cyberbullying harassment statute targeted non-expressive conduct.[86] The North Carolina Supreme Court, however, reversed, ruling that the cyber harassment statute targeted expressive conduct, an online posting was speech, and, consequently, under strict scrutiny analysis the statute was unconstitutional.[87] The North Carolina Supreme Court and the Texas Court of Appeals panel invoked the same precedent, the U.S. Supreme Court's ruling in *Reed v. Town of Gilbert* (2015),[88] but offered conflicting characterizations of the expressive nature of the act of online posting.

In *Reed*, a six-justice majority created a broad standard for determining when a regulation restricts content. The *Reed* Court held that, "[g]overnment regulation of speech is content based if a law applies to particular speech because of the topic discussed or the idea or message expressed."[89] The Court also recognized "a separate and additional category of laws that, though facially content neutral, will be considered content-based regulations of speech: laws that cannot be 'justified without reference to the content of the regulated speech'. ... Those laws, like those that are content based on their face, must also satisfy strict scrutiny."[90] If, however, they restrict non-expressive conduct, courts will apply the less speech-protective intermediary scrutiny.

The North Carolina Supreme Court ruled that the act of posting online met the first *Reed* standard, and, consequently, the "Cyber-bullying Statute,"

North Carolina General Statutes § 14-458.1, prohibited "the use of a computer or computer network to '[p]ost or encourage others to post on the Internet private, personal or sexual information pertaining to a minor' with 'the intent to intimidate or torment a minor.'"[91] In other words, the cyberbullying statute targeted speech because, "Posting information on the Internet—whatever the subject matter—can constitute speech as surely as stapling flyers to bulletin boards or distributing pamphlets to passerby—activities long protected by the First Amendment."[92]

The U.S. Court of Appeals for the Fourth Circuit used a similar analogy in *Bland v. Roberts* (2013), when it held that "liking" someone on Facebook was protected speech. "In sum, liking a political candidate's campaign page communicates the user's approval of the candidate and supports the campaign by associating the user with it. In this way, it is the Internet equivalent of displaying a political sign in one's front yard, which the Supreme Court has held is substantive speech."[93]

The two Texas intermediary courts, however, conducted the second *Reed* line of inquiry. They held that the impersonation/harassment statute was not content specific but was "connected to" and tended "to involve expression."[94] In other words, the statute only implicated speech.

But the implicated speech is constitutionally unprotected because it is integral to criminal conduct, the courts held. The courts arrived at the conclusion by considering the "specific types of criminal intent delineated by the statute and the conduct such intent requirements seek to proscribe."[95] Both found, in the words of the *Bradshaw* court, "Almost all conceivable applications of section 33.07(a) to speech associated with the proscribed conduct fall within the categories of criminal, fraudulent, and tortious activity that are unprotected by the First Amendment."[96] Likewise, the *Stubbs* court noted that, "When the intent is to do something that, if accomplished, would be unlawful and outside First Amendment protection, such as the intent to threaten or intimidate, such an intent might help to eliminate First Amendment concerns."[97]

Both courts found that the plain language of the law did not evince viewpoint discrimination nor did the legislature seek to favor or disfavor any particular viewpoint or restrict protected speech.[98] The *Stubbs* court said, for example, "Consistent with the text of the statute, the Legislature did not appear to be targeting or expressing its disagreement with any particular topic or viewpoint, but rather sought to address malicious usage of someone else's name or persona to create a web page or post a message online without her permission."[99]

Based on the foregoing, the *Stubbs* court reasoned that the statute did not implicate a sufficient amount of protected speech to warrant defining it as content-restrictive.

> Moreover, just because the content of the web page or the message may need to be examined does not render the law content based. "It is common in the law to examine the content of a communication to determine the speaker's purpose. Whether a particular statement constitutes a threat, blackmail, an agreement to fix prices, a copyright violation, a public offering of securities, or an offer to sell goods often depends on the precise content of the statement". … We cannot conclude that this is a situation where the Legislature has proscribed speech in order "to limit discussion of controversial topics and thus to shape the agenda for public debate."[100]

The North Carolina Court interpreted *Reed* broadly, and, arguably, more sensibly than the Texas appeals courts because, among other flaws, the Texas court's analysis does not appear to provide a "clear and firm rule governing content neutrality" which "is an essential means of protecting the freedom of speech, even if laws that might seem 'entirely reasonable' will sometimes be 'struck down because of their content-based nature.'"[101]

It is, for example, reasonable to distinguish the acts of posting, distribution or publishing from the message itself based on a time, place and manner proscription such as limiting distribution of leaflets to drivers on a fast-moving highway. But the Texas impersonation/harassment statute is not a time, place or manner regulation. It bans a certain type of expression, which is the message one's image or persona signals, and its purpose, which is to use it to defraud and intimidate. What the North Carolina Supreme Court said about its cyberbullying law, is also true about the Texas impersonation/harassment statute, "Here, it is clear that the cyberbullying statute is content based, on its face and plain text, because the statute 'defines regulated speech by [its] particular subject matter.'"[102] An analogy used in *Reed* Court is instructive. A law banning the use of sound trucks for political speech "is content based even if it does not discriminate among viewpoints within that subject matter."[103]

Of course, true threats and fraud do not enjoy constitutional protection. But to define the statute as non-content specific because it can be used to ban constitutionally unprotected speech, as the Texas courts did, allows the state to sweep up in its prosecutorial net speech that is constitutionally protected, until the criminal justice system finds otherwise. Thus, the statute has potential to chill speech and is overbroad. The more speech-protective approach would have been to test the Texas statute under strict scrutiny.

The Texas courts, however, ruled that the statute was not overbroad and did not chill protected speech because the vast majority of speech restricted by the statute is not protected under the First Amendment. "In other words," as the Stubbs court ruled, looking retroactively rather than prospectively, "there is no indication that a substantial number of section 33.07(a) cases involve persons who are engaging in the legitimate communication of ideas, opinions, or information rather than acting upon and expressing their criminal intent to defraud or inflict fear of danger."[104]

Both courts also rejected unconstitutional vagueness challenges. The defendants argued that the statute's intent to harm standard—"anything reasonably regarded as loss, disadvantage, or injury, including harm to another person in whose welfare the person affected is interested"[105]—was vague. But the courts held that the statute's intent to harass requirement could not be interpreted to include, for example, constitutionally protected annoying or embarrassing speech because it is linked to proscribing only unconstitutionally protected speech.

> Beyond the fact that "harm" is sufficiently defined, and considering the entirety of section 33.07(a) as we must, the statute includes three other proscribed intents ... Considered in context, the inclusion of these other operative intents listed in the statute reflects the Legislature's intent to target more intense rather than less intense mental states ... This reading is consistent with the Legislature's replacement of the original intents of "harass" and "embarrass," which clearly implicate low-intensity emotional states ... Unlike such a standard involving "harassing" or "embarrassing" conduct, which arguably would lend itself to arbitrary enforcement and chilling of protected speech, the "harm" standard does not present a situation requiring wholly subjective judgments not subject to any definition or narrowing context.[106]

The Texas courts ruling on vagueness appear to be on solid constitutional grounds. But their ruling on overbreadth is questionable because they do not acknowledge the obvious possibility that the statute may be misused to charge a speaker with illegal impersonation, even if such a case has yet to surface. More important, by implication, and in contrast to the ruling in *Bishop*, they appear to have assigned less First Amendment protection for cyberspace expression than for offline expression, which, of course, is impermissible under the First Amendment.[107]

Rhode Island v. John Leidecker

> It is indeed not true that all ridicule, or all disagreeable comment, is actionable; a man must not be too thinskinned or a self-important prig.[108]

In September 2010, Walter Flatus and Doug Gablinski exchanged several emails, and Flatus corresponded electronically with Douglas W. Gablinske.[109] At the time, Douglas W. Gablinske, a two-term Democrat, was waging a hard-fought primary campaign for re-election as a Rhode Island state representative.[110] In the email exchanges, Gablinske tried in vain to convince his constituent Flatus that he did not vote to impose a toll on a bridge and that rude emails coming from Doug Gablinski were not from him.

> Some monkey business is going on here. I do not have a personal email address. I have a state e-mail address and my business e-mail address. I just noticed that you had corresponded with what is obviously (to me, not you) a bogus address … How did you get that? You'll also notice that my name is misspelled. How did that happen? I need to know more about how this happened. Please call me. …[111]

The Rhode Island representative lost the primary election that month and continued his bid for re-election in a write-in campaign.[112] Flatus re-emerged. His name appeared on two street signs opposing Gablinske's write-in campaign. "The Winds of Change for District 68" and "11, Flatus, Write or Wrong." The state representative said Flatus's email and sign campaign caused him to suffer from "sleeplessness, nervous, nauseated stomach and was just physically and emotionally worn out from what happened to him with the e-mails and signs."[113]

Given the meaning of flatus—flatulence—it should not come as a surprise that the irate constituent was fictional. The e-mailer and political placard poster and Gablinski were really John Leidecker, a 54-year-old a lawyer and assistant executive director with the National Education Association of Rhode Island (NEARI), a teachers' union.[114] It was all a dirty tricks campaign organized by thugs, Gablinske claimed. "To the average person they have no idea of the stuff that goes on in election campaign[s]. It s very nasty, particularly when you tangle with organized labor. The leadership, which I refer to as organized crime, has a practice of thuggery. They are a master of dirty tricks. I have no doubt this goes to the very top."[115]

Like Golb, Leidecker argued it was it was parody, not dirty political tricks. "What I did was give a poke in the eye to an elected representative by mocking his worst conduct in a series of patently fake emails. I made fun of him," Leidecker says. "I had about as much influence on the election as the fan in the stand has on the outcome of a baseball game when he yells at the batter that he stinks."[116]

Nevertheless, Leidecker was first charged under the state's Use of False information statutes.[117] The police changed the charge to a violation of the cyberharasment/cyberstalking statute.[118] ("Many statutes include stalking-type language in their definitions of harassment, or vice versa.")[119]

Why the change of criminal charges? Leidecker offers a theory. "They knew they wanted to charge me with something, but weren't sure what. They quickly dropped the 'false information' idea because it just didn't fit," he says. "I didn't send the emails for the 'purpose of submitting a claim for payment, or makes, presents, or uses or causes to be made, presented, or used any data for the purpose of submitting a claim for payment with knowledge of its falsity and with knowledge that it will be used for any claim for payment, shall be guilty of a felony. …'"[120]

In 2011, a trial judge found Leidecker guilty of criminally cyberstalking and fined him $100 for the misdemeanor.[121] In 2014, a state judge overturned the verdict on First Amendment grounds.[122]

Cyberharassment and Cyberstalking

As discussed in Chapter Two, and elsewhere in this text, constitutionally unprotected cyberharassment is best understood as repeated unwanted online speech directed to an individual that poses a credible threat, though not every state statute complies with this standard. Constitutionally unprotected cyberstalking is a single and integrated course of unwanted conduct entailing speech integral to criminal conduct and non-expressive conduct directed at individual. Because the virtual world reflects the best and worst of offline reality, the dynamic of men—ex-acquaintances and husbands and strangers—relentlessly tracking, contacting and threatening women frequently mars cyberspace.

In response to the murder of six women that took place in 1989, California enacted the nation's first "stalking" law in 1990.[123] By 1993, 48 states had similar legislation on the books,[124] and in 1996, the federal government adopted 18 U.S.C. 2261A Interstate Stalking.[125] As early as 1999, U.S. Attorney General Janet Reno identified cyberstalking as a growing problem.

> Although online harassment and threats can take many forms, cyberstalking shares important characteristics with offline stalking. Many stalkers—online or off—are motivated by a desire to exert control over their victims and engage in similar types of behavior to accomplish this end. As with offline stalking, the available evidence (which is largely anecdotal) suggests that the majority of cyberstalkers are men and the majority of their victims are women, although there have been reported cases of women cyberstalking men and of same-sex cyberstalking … In addition, the ease

> of use and non-confrontational, impersonal, and sometimes anonymous nature of Internet communications may remove disincentives to cyberstalking. Put another way, whereas a potential stalker may be unwilling or unable to confront a victim in person or on the telephone, he or she may have little hesitation sending harassing or threatening electronic communications to a victim. Finally, as with physical stalking, online harassment and threats may be a prelude to more serious behavior, including physical violence.[126]

Harmful and lethal cyberstalking is real.[127] Yet, there is still no clear explanation why cyberstalking and harassment bans and related restraining orders have been "morphing," to use UCLA law professor Volokh's term, into bans against public criticism.[128] Perhaps it is attributable to law enforcement's clumsy responses to an unanticipated new phenomenon—the widespread use of email and social media to vilify anonymously and repeatedly.

That might be one way to explain the curious case of *Rhode Island v. John Leidecker*. Based on the plain language of the then existing Connecticut's Computer Crime statute 11-52-4.2, it is difficult to see how charging Leidecker was justified. The statute required that a "course of conduct must be of a kind that causes a reasonable person to suffer substantial emotional distress, or be in fear of bodily injury."[129] If "conduct" is interpreted to mean the mere sending of an estimated 12 emails, it is difficult to see how the receiving of them could cause the requisite emotional distress. If that were true, then junk email senders would be charged routinely with cyberstalking or cyberharassment.

If "conduct" means the emails' content, there does not appear to be anything Leidecker said that approached the level of seriously alarming or threatening that would cause "a reasonable person to suffer substantial emotional distress or fear of bodily injury." Also, the statute's savings clause—"Constitutionally protected activity is not included within the meaning of 'course of conduct'"—should have signaled to prosecutors and the trial judge that the emails and signs were protected speech because they concerned an elected official and political campaign issues.[130]

Those obvious facts and First Amendment principles were lost on the prosecutor and trial judge, but were glaring to Rhode Island Superior Court Judge Susan E. McGuirl who overturned Leidecker's conviction. This was not an analytically difficult case to decide: no Gordian knot to unravel to see that the criminal charges were directed at expression substantively relevant to democratic self-governance—Leidecker's emails and signs concerning an elected official and political campaign issues.

Lacking "Civic Courage"

One of the provisions of the Rhode Island statute required that Leidecker's sole intent was to harass.[131] Referencing rulings from Minnesota, Florida and Pennsylvania to interpret the meaning of "solely to harass," McGuirl said, the emails were not threatening. Leidecker sent them merely to annoy and to obtain information about a political campaign issue, she said.

In *Whitney v. California*, Justice Louis Brandeis developed the First Amendment theory of civic courage.[132] Eighty-three years later, U.S. Supreme Court Justice Antonin Scalia invoked that theory when, saying, "And in light of the fact that for the first century of our existence, even voting was public … the fact is that running a democracy takes a certain amount of civic courage. And the First Amendment does not protect you from criticism or even nasty phone calls when you exercise your political rights to legislate or to take part in the legislative process.[133]

McGuirl did not cite the civic courage theory or quote Brandeis or Scalia. But the theory was implied when she said that, "During a campaign I assume a candidate can expect and does receive communication and criticism, I assume annoying at times from constituents and voters who have an interest in the outcome of the election."[134]

The statute also applied a reasonable victim's standard. The National Center for Victims of Crime explains that context is important in applying a reasonable person standard: "A 'reasonable person' standard of fear asks the question, 'Would the perpetrator's conduct cause a reasonable person in similar circumstances to be afraid?'"[135] McGuirl identified the political campaign as the relevant context.

> And I think in this case we're looking at a reasonable person that is actually a public figure. A reasonable person standard would be that who is running in a political campaign and a reasonable standard would have to apply to somebody in which these issues were so-called hot issues at the time or issues that were being discussed both in the General Assembly and in the course of the political campaign.[136]

Another provision required that the defendant have a legitimate purpose in engaging in the alleged illegal conduct. In the *Marquan* cyberharassment ruling (2014), the New York Court of Appeals said, "the First Amendment forbids the government from deciding whether protected speech qualifies as 'legitimate.'"[137] But that ruling followed Leidecker by 29 days, so McGuirl could not cite it. Rather she ruled that comment on political campaign issues and about a public figure satisfied the "legitimate purpose" provision.[138]

Finally, noting the constitutional savings clause, McGuirl said, precedents hold that uncomfortable political online speech and political signs are protected under the First Amendment, and that federal stalking laws require a showing that a cyberstalker have a "serious criminal intent, not just speech that happened to cause annoyance or insult."[139]

"I think the public is astute enough to get [the free speech violations], if they saw the police coming down on non-violent protesters—even people like the Westboro Church," says Leidecker, reflecting on the use of harassment and stalking laws to restrict caustic online political speech and parody. "I think they even get it when it comes to symbolic action like flag burning. But it is not hard to miss the First Amendment point when there is a confluence of media and government casting someone in a negative light and the parody is more oblique. Emails, Facebook, Snapshot … these are all new vehicles. I have no doubt that had I printed the 'dialogue' between Flatus and Gablinski on a single page (much like a t.v. script) and handed out my flyer to passersby, people (and the trial judge) would have understood what I was doing and saying."[140]

U.S. v. Cassidy

In 1988, the U.S. Supreme Court ruled that the First Amendment protected pornography publisher Larry Flynt from a lawsuit for intentional infliction of emotional distress, stemming from a vulgar parody, and brought by Televangelist Reverend Jerry Falwell.[141] A public figure, the Court said, may not recover damages for emotional harm caused by the publication of an "ad parody offensive to him, and doubtless gross and repugnant in the eyes of most" because "in the world of debate about public affairs, many things done with motives that are less than admirable are protected by the First Amendment."[142] The Court noted that caustic political cartoons have played a meaningful role in public political discourse. "Despite their sometimes caustic nature, from the early cartoon portraying George Washington as an ass down to the present day, graphic depictions and satirical cartoons have played a prominent role in public and political debate … From the viewpoint of history it is clear that our political discourse would have been considerably poorer without them."[143]

Accordingly, why should a Buddhist spiritual leader be treated differently from Rev. Falwell under the First Amendment? Or, as UCLA's Volokh argues, citing *Snyder v. Phelps* and *Hustler Magazine, Inc. v. Falwell*, the U.S. Supreme

Court had held that [deliberately offensive and annoying speech on civic matters] "can't lead to civil liability even when it is 'outrageous' and purposefully causes severe emotional distress (historically a highly demanding standard). It thus can't lead to criminal liability under the considerably lower standards imposed by criminal harassment laws."[144]

Yet, federal authorities in Maryland charged William Lawrence Cassidy under a federal stalking statute, 18 U.S.C. § 2261A(2)(A), for blog postings and sending more than 350 tweets about a Buddhist religious leader, Alyce Zeoli, "an enthroned tulku or reincarnate master who was enthroned in 1988 as a reincarnate llama."[145] At first, federal authorities said Cassidy's tweets caused Zeoli substantial emotional distress, but later argued that the tweets were true threats. But the federal district judge who dismissed the case noted that, "the Government, did not seek an Indictment on the basis that Defendant intentionally used the Internet to put A.Z. in reasonable fear of death or serious bodily injury."[146] Here is a sample of Cassidy's tweets: "ya like haiku? Here's one for ya: 'Long, Limb, Sharp Saw, Hard Drop;'" ROFLMAO. "(A.Z.) is a demonic force who tries to destroy Buddhism." "(A.Z.) you called me a 'sick low life pig' oh great Mandarava? Go kill yourself."[147]

Cassidy's mocking and caustic tweets and blogs about the religious figure, well-known in the Buddhist American community, cannot be distinguished in any meaningful constitutional way from *Hustler* magazine's mocking parody of Rev. Falwell, a fundamentalist Christian leader who sought the Republican Party presidential nomination. Indeed, the judge in *Cassidy*, cited the *Hustler* ruling and others for the proposition that, "the Supreme Court has consistently classified emotionally distressing or outrageous speech as protected, especially where that speech touches on matters of political, religious or public concern. This is because 'in public debate our own citizens must tolerate insulting, and even outrageous, speech in order to provide "adequate breathing space" to the freedoms protected by the First Amendment.'"[148]

Implicitly, the judge rejected any notion of Internet exceptionalism: that tweets and blog postings were more harmful than offline forms of communication and, therefore, should be treated differently under the law. Potential recipients of tweets and postings, he noted, do not have to read them, and may never know they exist, unless they choose to receive the tweets or access a specific blog.

> Because this case involves First Amendment issues, terms that were in use by citizens when the Bill of Rights was drafted may help in understanding the legal context of Blogs and Twitter. Suppose that a Colonist erects a bulletin board in the front yard

> of his home to post announcements that might be of interest to others and other Colonists do the same. A Blog is like a bulletin board, except that it is erected in cyberspace rather than in one's front yard. If one Colonist wants to see what is on another's bulletin board, he would need to walk over to his neighbor's yard and look at what is posted, or hire someone else to do so. Now, one can inspect a neighbor's Blog by simply turning on a computer. Twitter allows the bulletin board system to function so that what is posted on Colonist No. 1's bulletin board is automatically posted on Colonist No. 2's bulletin board for Colonist No. 2 to see. The automatic postings from one Colonist to another can be turned on or off by the owners of the bulletin boards, but there is no mandatory aspect of postings on one Colonist's bulletin board showing up on the other's. It is entirely up to the two Colonists whether their bulletin boards will be interconnected in such a manner.[149]

Leidecker and *Cassidy* tell us that the First Amendment will not abide the use of cyberharassment or cyberstalking laws to ban antagonistic and offensive direct (emails) or non-direct (tweets and blogs) electronic messages when they concern civic matters or are about public figures such as religious leaders and elected officials. Likewise, the ruling by the Supreme Court of Georgia in *Chan v. Ellis* stands for the principle that cyberstalking law-based injunctions cannot be legitimately used to ban the First Amendment right of an online intermediary to provide a public forum for criticism of people—including private individuals engaged in matters of public concern—not directly sent to the target, unless the criticism is unprotected speech.

Chan v. Ellis

Matthew Chan is a Columbus, Georgia-based real estate investor, book, audiotape and web publisher, and self-styled advocate for individuals who believe that they have been unfairly hounded by copyright infringement notices demanding take downs of copyrighted content and payment.[150] Chan says settlement letters demanding payment for alleged copyright infringement are "extortion letters" and his website, ExtortionLetterInfo.com, provided a message board where he and others posted their complaints about receiving copyright infringement notices and settlement demands.[151] By 2012, Linda Ellis, author of the motivational poem "The Dash," had become a popular target of complaints, accusations and threats about her enforcement of her copyright to her poem—"nearly 2,000 posts … many of which are mean-spirited, some of which are distasteful and crude," and at least one that threatened to disclose information about her family.[152]

Ellis sued, alleging that the electronic publication of the posts was a violation of Georgia's stalking statute, OCGA § 16-5-90(a)(1), and following an evidentiary hearing a trial court judge issued an injunction in February 2013, ordering Chan to delete all posts concerning Ellis.[153] (Though it was not addressed in the Georgia Supreme Court ruling, the restrictive order violates §230 of the Communication Decency Act. The federal provision shields online intermediaries like Chan from liability for users' unlawful speech such as defamation, "infliction of emotional distress, negligence, public nuisance, civil theft, invasion of privacy, securities law violation, fraud, and cyberstalking.")[154]

In addition to the censorship, the injunction ordered Chan to stay 1,000 yards from Ellis and have no direct or indirect contact with her or her family. The Georgia statute provides in part:

> A person commits the offense of stalking when he or she follows, places under surveillance, or contacts another person at or about a place or places without the consent of the other person for the purpose of harassing and intimidating the other person. For the purpose of this article, the terms "computer" and "computer network" shall have the same meanings as set out in Code Section 16-9-92; the term "contact" shall mean any communication including without being limited to communication in person, by telephone, by mail, by broadcast, by computer, by computer network, or by any other electronic device; and the place or places that contact by telephone, mail, broadcast, computer, computer network, or any other electronic device is deemed to occur shall be the place or places where such communication is received.[155]

Briefs by Chan and others made a handful of arguments in his defense—among them, the online speech was protected under the First Amendment, and the postings did not put Ellis in reasonable fear.[156] But the most compelling and, perhaps, most obvious argument that they asserted was that Chan never made contact with Ellis online or offline as the statute requires. And the failure to meet a basic element of stalking or cyberstalking is why the Georgia Supreme Court reversed the court injunction against Chan.

> … most of the posts appear to speak to the public, not to Ellis in particular, even if they are about Ellis. And there is no evidence that Chan did anything to cause these posts to be delivered to Ellis or otherwise brought to her attention, notwithstanding that he may have reasonably anticipated that Ellis might come across the posts, just as any member of the Internet-using public might. The publication of commentary directed only to the public generally does not amount to "contact," as that term is used in OCGA § 16-5-90(a)(1), and most of the posts about Ellis quite clearly cannot form the basis for a finding that Chan contacted Ellis.[157]

Similar to *Cassidy* and *Chan v. Ellis*, a Florida appeals court in *Scott v. Blum* (2016) rejected an attempt to convert constitutionally protected online communication into criminal cyberstalking by requiring evidence that the alleged victim was the recipient of communications sent to him from the defendant.[158] "The emails sent to 2200 NAPPS members do not constitute words 'directed at a specific person' for purposes of the cyberstalking statute simply because they are about Mr. Blum."[159]

Like *Leidecker*, the court found that the target's alleged level of suffering did not meet a reasonable person standard. The ruling suggests that Frederic A. Blum may have had a defamation action, though he certainly did not have grounds to impose an injunction on Scott. "A reasonable person would not suffer substantial emotional distress over the emails, articles, blog posts, and videos at issue," the judge ruled. "That the articles written by Mr. Scott contain false allegations or embarrassing information is not a basis for a cyberstalking injunction."[160]

The U.S. Supreme Court's ruling in *Elonis v. U.S* (2015),[161] proved dispositive in *People v. Walter Relerford* (2016). In *Elonis*, the Court ruled that a defendant could not be criminally culpable under 18 U.S.C. § 875(c), which makes it a federal crime, punishable by up to five years in prison and a $250,000 fine, to transmit any communication in interstate or foreign commerce containing a threat to injure the person of another, unless government proves the defendant knew or truly believed that his conduct was illegal or had the purpose to intimidate.[162] Illinois stalking and cyberstalking statutes, an appeals court panel ruled, did not meet the *Elonis* standard for criminal culpability. Consequently, those portions of the statutes were facially unconstitutional under the due process clause of the Fourteenth Amendment and the court reversed the defendant's conviction.[163]

Is "Cyberbullying" Ethical?

There is a tendency by some to justify the imposition of restraining orders on accused cyberbullies, or the criminal prosecution of them, on ethical grounds, as though the First Amendment were a mere technicality. Such critics are offended by cyberbullying speech and the methods used to express them. The *Providence Journal*'s condemnation of Leidecker after his exoneration is representative. Mischaracterizing "the line between free speech and Internet harassment" as "a fine one," the newspaper said, "If Rhode Island teachers are serious about sending the message that Internet bullying and harassment are wrong—and we think they are—they need to rid themselves of a top union official. Punishing children who are still learning right from wrong while lucratively rewarding, with their union dues, an adult lawyer who crudely harassed a state representative is the height of hypocrisy."[164]

The courts, however, said Leidecker and Golb, for example, did not harass, and others did not directly cause harm or intend to. Consequently, there is an argument that the speech that the exonerated cyberbullies engaged in was ethical, at least by Millian ethical standards. In *On Liberty*, 19th century British philosopher and seminal utilitarian ethical philosopher John Stuart Mill argued that government could only rightfully restrict speech when it caused harm, a theory later incorporated into First Amendment free speech doctrine, such as the right of government to prevent and punish speech that causes imminent harm. "An opinion that corn-dealers are starvers of the poor, or that private property is robbery, ought to be unmolested when simply circulated through the press, but may justly incur punishment when delivered orally to an excited mob assembled before the house of a corn-dealer, or when handed about among the same mob in the form of a placard."[165] Mill also argued that speech should be protected, "so long as what we do does not harm them, even though they should think our conduct foolish, perverse, or wrong."[166]

Accordingly, some may condone Leidecker and Golb's online campaigns as foolish, perverse and wrong, but under a Mill's harm principle they are ethically defensible. Moreover, applying the utilitarian "greatest good for the greatest number" ethical tenet,[167] parody, satire and other forms of outrageous speech have the capacity to reveal truths that provide valuable information and wisdom about the human condition that may yield great benefit to substantial portions of any community.

Connecticut: Harassment and Breach of Peace in Cyberspace

In May 2011, Michael Adams was charged with incitement (Connecticut General Statutes§ 53a-179a),[168] harassment (Connecticut General Statutes 53a-183 (2011) and breach of peace (Connecticut General Statutes § 53a-181) for posting the following statement about Connecticut Governor Daniel Malloy who was visiting New York City for a ceremony at Ground Zero in memory of those who died in the 9/11 attacks. "I hope that Governor Malloy will be shot by an angry New Yorker during his visit to New York."[169] His ACLU-Connecticut lawyers argued that the charges flouted "core First

Amendment principles as well as principles of statutory construction that Connecticut courts have long observed. Properly construed, the statutes in question do not apply to Mr. Adams's posting and would be unconstitutional, as applied, if they did."[170]

Under General Statutes section 53a-183 (a) (2), a defendant is guilty of harassment in the second degree when he operates with "intent to harass, annoy or alarm another person, he communicates with a person by telegraph or mail, by electronically transmitting a facsimile through connection with a telephone network, by computer network, as defined in section 53a-250, or by any other form of written communication, in a manner likely to cause annoyance or alarm."[171] General Statutes section 53a-181(4) provides "A person is guilty of breach of the peace in the second degree when, with intent to cause inconvenience, annoyance or alarm, or recklessly creating a risk thereof, such person … publicly exhibits, distributes, posts up or advertises any offensive, indecent or abusive matter concerning any person. …"[172]

To be culpable for incitement, the state must prove that speech poses a serious and imminent threat and that the speaker intended the specific harm to occur.[173] Adams's lawyers argued,

> The posting is constitutionally protected because there is no allegation that Mr. Adams specifically intended to incite violence, or that he threatened violence, or that there was any likelihood that violence would imminently occur, and all of the allegations in the warrant indicate that the posting was merely an offensive joke. The posting itself establishes only an intent, on Mr. Adams's part, to engage in hyperbole and humor—both of which are completely within the First Amendment's guarantees.[174]

The lawyers also argued that his Facebook posting did not fall within the categories of unprotected speech such as true threats, obscenity or fighting words and, therefore, were protected, and the statute was unconstitutionally vague as applied. "The absence of any speech exception in the present case therefore establishes, at one and the same time, *both* that the posting is constitutionally protected *and* that Connecticut's incitement, harassment and breach of peace statutes do not prohibit Mr. Adams's posting. Mr. Adams's posting consists only of protected hyperbole and humor, which no valid statute could or does proscribe."[175]

Ultimately, Adams pled guilty to the breach of peace charge "to end the ordeal for himself and his family."[176] One of his attorneys, Martin B. Margulies, Professor of Law Emeritus at Quinnipiac School of Law, says Adams agreed to the plea because he was "a single parent with a twelve-year-old kid and couldn't risk prison time. The plea offer of no time was a gun to his head. The gun worked. The system did not."[177] Margulies added, "It was clear from the beginning that the prosecutor and judge knew little about the First Amendment and cared less. His agenda was to win convictions and hers was to move the docket. The notion that a judge's job is to protect important freedoms seems never to have entered her mind."[178]

Of course, a plea bargain left the merits of Adams's First Amendment arguments unresolved. Yet, even a ruling in *State v. Buhl* (2016),[179] a case in which the harassment and breach of peace statutes were invoked by the state to convict a freelance journalist who created a fake Facebook profile—she maintains that she was not the owner of the account—did not offer clarity about the constitutionality of the two statutes as applied to cyberbullying.

In June 2016, the Connecticut Supreme Court affirmed a harassment conviction, but reversed a lower court's ruling, which found insufficient evidence of a breach of peace conviction[180] of online journalist Teri A. Buhl.[181] Ultimately, Buhl served 30 days in jail, ended in August 2016.[182] The state intermediate and high courts said Buhl's First Amendment arguments were inadequately briefed and declined to consider them.[183]

After the ruling, Buhl's counsel, Stephan E. Seeger, said,

> We stand firmly by our claim that Ms. Buhl's constitutional arguments were presented in a cognizable manner, however novel or unique, and the Court appears to have avoided the First Amendment question in part, by establishing an abuse of discretion standard applicable to its ability to review the lower Court's ruling on the adequacy of a constitutional claim. Here, the argument is simple, and it was explained simply; Ms. Buhl is not similarly situated to other criminal defendants. Because she is a reporter, and has an obligation to protect her sources, her behavior in communicating anonymously, or at all for that matter, cannot be viewed in the same way as it might be for non-reporters. She took her obligation to protect her source over an opportunity to explain how she is innocent of the charges and that they have the wrong person.[184]

In the absence of judicial clarity on the matter, what follows is a First Amendment analysis of Connecticut General Statutes, section 53a-183 (a) (2), harassment in the second degree, and section 53a-181(4), breach of peace in the second degree, applied to the facts of *State v. Buhl*. First, the analysis shows that, though Connecticut courts purport to treat expressive and non-expressive harassment differently to devote appropriate constitutional protection to speech, in practice they often weigh the impact of speech to determine whether a telephone call or a mail delivery, for example, constitutes harassing speech. Thus, it is argued, in reality, the courts are criminalizing speech unconstitutionally. Properly analyzed, cases such as *Buhl* require the application of the *Reed* content-specific analysis, discussed above, to determine whether the Connecticut harassment statute bans expression or regulates non-expressive conduct.

Secondly, Connecticut law seems to have no doctrinal measure for gauging when a defendant publicizes private information in a breach of peace action, yet the statute criminalizes the exhibition, distribution, posting and advertising of offensive, indecent or abusive information about an individual. The court in *Buhl* arrived at the conclusion that a defendant intended to make public the content of a private Facebook account based almost entirely on testimony from the victim and without exploring doctrines shedding light on privacy-public disclosure precedents. Thus, it would seem that the state's breach of peace statute is vulnerable to vagueness and overbreadth challenges because it fails to make clear under what circumstances an online private forum would become public.

A jury convicted journalist Buhl of harassment and breach of privacy, finding that she anonymously posted the diary of a teenager, the daughter of her boyfriend, a divorcé, on Facebook and mailed copies of the diary anonymously to his home.[185] The harassment charged stemmed from the posting and the mailing, but the online posting alone was the basis for the breach of peace charge.[186] The diaries revealed that the daughter had participated in local underage drinking parties in which teenagers also engaged in sexual acts.

Buhl, who had written for several publications, including *Group Capital Investor* and *Forbes* magazine, maintained she came upon the diary while investigating a story on local teenage binge drinking and sex parties in New Canaan, Ct., and an anonymous source posted them on Facebook.[187] The court, however, ruled there was sufficient evidence to show that she posted the diary.[188] She did, however, admit to mailing the diaries to her boyfriend, the teenage girl's father.[189]

The precedents established by the Connecticut Supreme Court in *State v. Moulton* (2013) address the First Amendment limits imposed on the two statutes.[190] In *Moulton*, the court ruled that the harassment statute, section 53a-183 (a), banned harassing non-expressive and expressive conduct.[191] When expressive conduct is at issue, the court ruled, a conviction must be based on a violation of unprotected categories of speech such as true threats.[192] The true threat standard requires that the state show beyond a reasonable doubt that a speaker's communication was a "serious expression of intent to commit an act of unlawful *violence* [emphasis added] to a particular individual or group of individuals"[193] and, under *Elonis*, that the speaker intended to intimidate.[194] Likewise, the court in *Moulton* ruled that a conviction on breach of peace in the second degree, section 53a-181(4), must meet the true threat standard.[195] Thus, by that measure, Connecticut's approach to criminalizing harassing speech is constitutionally sound.

Non-expressive harassment is treated differently under Connecticut law. When the harassing conduct is considered non-expressive—the act of sending the diaries via mail or posting online, for example—the state is required to prove that a speaker intended to communicate in a manner likely to cause annoyance or alarm.[196] Generally, imposing criminal penalties for non-expressive harassing conduct based on a mens rea of intent to harass, annoy or alarm raises no constitutional questions. "State and federal telephone harassment laws have long banned calls made to people with the intent to 'abuse,' 'annoy,' 'harass,' or 'offend' (sometimes with the limitation that the calls must be repeated or anonymous)," Volokh notes.[197] Still, as discussed below, it is not clear that Connecticut judges are punishing only non-expressive conduct when they target the use of communicative technologies.

Did Buhl Intend to Intimidate by Threatening Violence?

None of the evidence or testimony suggests that Buhl intended to intimidate her boyfriend or his daughter with a threat of violence to meet the true threat standard. The content of the diary and the Facebook posting concerned the daughter's self-described sexual and drinking activities. "The package contained copies of M's private diary entries, which described her drinking heavily at a party and performing oral sex on a boy. As the trial court noted, any parent receiving such a mailing would reasonably find it 'incredibly distressful, disturbing, and abhorrent.'"[198] That characterization, however, falls far short of even a suggestion of violence because neither Buhl nor the content of the diary explicitly said or suggested that Buhl should have foreseen that her speech would be reasonably interpreted as a serious expression of intent to harm.

The court noted that, "The anonymous nature of the mailing served to increase P's and M's anxieties because they did not know who had intruded into M's bedroom and copied her diary entries, how the mailer had obtained the entries, or who else might have access to them … P, in fact, testified that he felt 'violated' that M's diary entries were in 'someone else's hands.'"[199] Since M, the daughter, felt violated, can Buhl's mailing of copies of the diary be reasonably interpreted as signaling that violence would follow?

Buhl's claims aside, objectively, it is highly unlikely that Buhl's expressive conduct would amount to a true threat. The objective test requires an examination of "the entire factual context of the statements including: the surrounding events, the listeners' reaction, and whether the words are conditional," noted the U.S. Court of Appeals in the Ninth Circuit in *U.S. v. Bagdasarian* (2011), a ruling in which the court overturned the conviction of Walter Bagdasarian after he posted hostile online messages against Barack Obama on the Internet in 2008.[200] The Ninth Circuit ruled that anonymity by itself is insufficient to meet a true threat intent test.[201] Thus, the anonymous postings and mailings in the *Buhl* case would be weighed accordingly. The Ninth Circuit also considered that the postings appeared on a financial message board as part of a "non-violent discussion forum that would tend to blunt any perception that statements made there were serious expressions of intended violence."[202] Similarly in *Buhl*, there is no indication that the Facebook account was a space for discussion of violence.

Consider that in *Bagdasarian*, the following words were ruled not to constitute a true threat: "'Re: Obama fk the niggar, he will have a 50 cal in the head soon' and (2) 'shoot the nig.'"[203] The court said the Bagdasarian failed "to express any intent on his part to take any action."[204] The same could be said to be true of Buhl's expressive actions. (Accordingly, Adams's attorneys correctly invoked the true threat doctrine as a defense because Adams said, "I hope that Governor Malloy will be shot by an angry New Yorker during his visit to New York,"[205] as opposed to, "I am going to shoot Governor Malloy.")

In contrast, in *U.S. v. Jeffries*, (2012), a defendant, who posted a video online in which he declared in song that he would kill a specific judge, was ruled to have made a true threat. His words showed an intent to engage in a specific act of violence: "I have been to war and killed a man/I don't care if I go to jail for 2,000 years/'Cause this is my daughter we're talkin' about/*And when I come to court this better be the last time/I'm not kidding at all, I'm making this video public/'Cause if I have to kill a judge or a lawyer or a woman I don't care*/'Cause this is my daughter we're talking about."[206]

Non-Expressive Harassment

At first, it seems, the state would have a strong case if Buhl's conduct were viewed as non-expressive. But on closer inspection, cracks appear. First, though

Buhl fails to address whether a conviction for non-expressive harassment can be based on a single action, it is not entirely clear whether *Moulton* supports such a standard. The single ringing of a target's telephone was the non-expressive conduct at issue in *Moulton*. But, the court acknowledged, "Although it is not impossible for a single telephone call to be harassing or alarming based solely on the circumstances surrounding the physical placing of the call, it is far more likely that a lone telephone call will be found to be harassing or alarming on the basis of the offensive or abusive *content* [emphasis added] of the call."[207]

Additionally, *Moulton* cites five harassment rulings in which repeated phone calls were at issue in defining a harassing, annoying or alarming telephone calls.[208] On its face, the two sections of the harassment statute are indistinguishable regarding the communicative medium. Section 531a-183 (2) identifies "telephone network" and (3) identifies "telephone call." Thus, it would seem that a fair reading of section 531a-183 (2) would require that use of communication technologies to harass be repeated. The *Buhl* court, however, did not tackle the relevance of its own implied standard. More significant, is that in *Moulton* the Connecticut Supreme Court voiced a preference for a finding of non-expressive harassment based on repeated non-expressive conduct and took into account the nature of the accompanying speech, too.

Though the Connecticut courts have ruled that the harassment statute is to be read to distinguish speech from non-expressive conduct, the facts of *Buhl* and others cited in *Moulton* blur such a distinction. In *Buhl*, the Connecticut Supreme Court appeared to have placed great weight on expressive conduct even though it applied an intent standard reserved for non-expressive conduct. It rejected Buhl's argument that, for example, the letter accompanying the mailed diaries showed concern for the well-being of the father and daughter.

But the court ruled that the letter "does not change the disturbing *contents* of the mailing or the fact that someone, even an apparent 'friend,' had gone through M's nightstand, read her private diary entries, and made copies of them."[209] Again, the court weighed the impact of expressive conduct of both the letter accompanying the mailing and the content of the mailing to reach the conclusion that Buhl intended to harass, annoy or alarm, a standard supposedly to be applied to only non-expressive conduct.

Here is another portion of the court's rationale for finding that the supposedly non-expressive conduct of mailing constituted harassment. The court clearly references "diary entries" describes them, and says the father, "P," learned "this information" and he was shocked "by the contents of the mailing."

> The contents of the mailing also show an intent to harass, annoy, or alarm P or M. The package contained copies of M's private diary entries, which described her drinking heavily at a party and performing oral sex on a boy. As the trial court noted, any parent receiving such a mailing would reasonably find it "incredibly distressful, disturbing, and abhorrent." P not only learned this information from a purportedly anonymous stranger, but realized that an unknown person had been in his home--specifically, his daughter's bedroom—rifled through her belongings, and made copies of her private diary entries. He was reasonably "shocked," "surprised," and "outraged" by the contents of the mailing, and felt "violated" that an unknown person had been in his home. Additionally, with respect to M, mailing such content to a person's parents could reasonably evince the intent to harass, annoy, or alarm that person, especially if the person is a minor.[210]

Consequently, there is strong evidence that the statute, even when ostensibly applied to non-expressive conduct, is actuality a statute that cannot be "justified without reference to the content of the regulated speech," and, thus must face strict scrutiny, as *Reed* dictates.[211] At least that is how the North Carolina Supreme Court would have handle the issue, as we have seen in the discussion of the Texas impersonation/harassment statute. Would the content-based Connecticut harassment statute survive strict scrutiny? No doubt, the state would articulate a compelling government interest to criminalize expressive harassment. But civil injunctions, for instance, provide less speech-restrictive alternatives. Therefore, it is unlikely that General Statutes § 53a-183 (a) (2) would survive constitutional scrutiny.

The approach taken by the Texas courts to determine when conduct is "certainly connected to and will tend to involve speech"[212] is not likely to yield a favorable result for the prosecution primarily because the harassment statute, as interpreted by the courts, links the intent standard to unconstitutionally vague terms of harass, alarm or annoy. In contrast, the Texas courts held that impersonation/harassment statute's intent standard was linked to constitutionally unprotected speech and could not be interpreted to include prosecution for annoying or embarrassing speech.[213] The Texas approach, however, does leave wiggle room to save the statute from strict scrutiny. The Connecticut court could find that the statute targets non-expressive conduct because it "does not reach a substantial amount of constitutionally protected speech in furthering the state's significant interest in proscribing criminal."[214]

Breach of Peace

Writing for the Technology & Marketing Law Blog, Seattle-based privacy, social media and intellectual property litigator Venkat Balasubramani remarked about *Buhl*. "It's disappointing that the court passes up an opportunity to strike down a statute criminalizing speech intended to cause annoyance," Balasubramani said, contrasting *Buhl* with the North Carolina Supreme Court's ruling in *State v. Bishop*. "A loose test for a criminal breach of the peace conviction sounds like a recipe for censorship."[215]

In finding that Buhl was guilty of a breach of peace, the court, inexcusably, did not fully grasp how Facebook's privacy controls operate, nor did it invoke the appropriate precedent to determine what constitutes a public exhibition or distribution of private information. The intermediary appeals court, however, concluded that there was insufficient evidence to support the defendant's breach of the peace conviction because the state bore the burden of proving that the posts were publicly exhibited and had failed to present testimony from a person with suitable knowledge of privacy settings on Facebook.[216]

The state supreme court, however, said it relied "primarily" on the daughter's testimony to determine whether the Facebook account was accessible to the public.[217] At first, the daughter testified correctly that, "a user's profile may be accessible to the public, or only to his or her network of 'friends,' depending on the user's privacy settings."[218] The daughter said she first viewed the page through the account of someone who had "friended" Tasha Moore, the pseudonym for the owner of the account, but later she could access the posts from her own Facebook account. Therefore, the daughter said, she "believed the profile was 'unprivate' and, thus, any member of the public could view the profile and the posts about" her.[219] The daughter's belief is at odds with *Wired* magazine's "Here's How to Use Facebook's Mystifying Privacy Settings,"[220] for example. She, or any other "unfriended" individuals, should not have been able to access the profile unless the owner of account allowed her to do so. Unless the privacy settings are set to default, a Facebook post is accessible only to a user's network of friends by "tagging."[221] Balasubramani argued that the court should have brought in experts to corroborate or contradict the teenager's testimony.

"Given the difficulty courts and litigants have had with Facebook's privacy settings, it was surprising to see the court conclude that the accessibility of the page was a matter of sufficient common knowledge and experience that anyone could testify about it," Balasubramani said. "At a minimum, the court could have said that the state failed to carry its burden on this element of the offense."[222]

The daughter also testified that as many as eight individuals were invited to view the profile.[223] Thus, based solely on such testimony, the court ruled that the account was public and met the statutory requirement of publicly exhibiting, distributing, posting or advertising the offending speech. A more rigorous rationale would have included a doctrinal touchstone to gauge whether the account was a public forum, such as the tort of public disclosure of private facts.

Because the law on Facebook privacy settings is emerging and unsettled, the court should have considered other rulings in which analog-era privacy doctrines have been applied to online forums. The public disclosure of private facts doctrine, for example, would have shed some light. The invasion of privacy tort provides that, "One who gives publicity to a matter concerning the private life of another is subject to liability to the other for invasion of his privacy, if the matter publicized is of a kind that (1) would be highly offensive to a reasonable person, and (2) is not of legitimate concern to the public," according to the Restatement of Torts.[224] The Restatement explains that "publicity … means that the matter is made public, by communicating it to the public at large, or to so many persons that the matter must be regarded as substantially certain to become one of public knowledge."[225] Only "a minority of jurisdictions allow[s] recovery for disclosures to small numbers of people."[226] Consequently, under the majority application of the tort, eight invited viewers would not have met the publication test.

For example, circumstances in *Buhl* dramatically contrast with those of Cynthia Moreno who unsuccessfully argued that that the republication of content taken from her Myspace page constituted a public disclosure of private facts that were not of legitimate public concern and thus was an invasion of privacy. In contrast to *Buhl* Facebook account, Moreno's account was made "available to any person with a computer and thus opened it to the public eye. Under these circumstances, no reasonable person would have had an expectation of privacy regarding the published material," a California appeals court ruled.[227]

Seeger, Buhl's attorney, argued that a small number of invitees cannot turn a private forum public, offline or online.

> We must catch up with the technology when it comes to our consideration of analogs. We have to begin not by abandoning well know and traditional definitions of legal and logical concepts but by attempting to marry them consistently with their functional equivalents in cyberspace. Today I am not so sure that my Facebook status or the idea of a Facebook invitation is so clearly analogous to real world instantiations of the same that my inferences upon them can be treated identically. For me, I still believe that if I specifically invite six people to my private yard party by written invitation noting the same, and an uninvited guest walks through an open gate to my yard, my private party doesn't morph into a public affair.[228]

Conclusion

It can be reasonably said that the crusade to ban hostile online speech, or cyberbullying, emerged in 2008 in response to the cyberbullying-related suicide of teenager Megan Meier.[229] To combat the new phenomenon, legislatures passed laws that criminalized online speech in ways that would surely be unconstitutional if applied to offline speech. As this book attests, those laws have been misused to punish minors and adults. This chapter focused on adults as victims of poorly drawn cyberharassment, cyberstalking and online impersonation/harassment statutes, and flawed prosecutorial and judicial decision-making in the enforcement of such laws to squelch harsh criticisms of adults by adults.

Prosecutorial discretion and judicial interpretation, and not the new laws, pose the greater threat to the right of adults to criticize. There is no rule requiring prosecutors to enforce constitutionally dubious laws. "It is well known that prosecutors possess nearly unfettered discretion to charge or to decline to charge, and thus are the most powerful actors in the criminal justice system."[230] Yet, in *U.S. v. Cassidy*, federal prosecutors in Maryland, who apparently did not appreciate the distinction between non-directed and directed tweets, filed cyberstalking charges against a defendant who had blogged and sent non-directed tweets about a publicly known individual. The case had no merit. A federal trial judge dismissed the indictment.[231]

Judges, required to follow precedent, have, nevertheless, deviated from well-settled First Amendment principles in restricting online obloquy and vituperation. Such were the circumstances of *State v. Leidecker*. Leidecker's emails concerned traditional constitutionally protected political speech and he sent the emails to an elected official running for re-election. Yet, as noted above, despite the U.S. Supreme Court's nearly 100-year-old commitment to giving political speech the highest level of constitutional protection, a prosecutor and trial judge expressed no reservations about Leidecker's conviction. An appeals court judge had to reverse the conviction.

A court's lack of familiarity with online technologies can skew the outcome of a cyberbullying case, disfavoring defendants. That is one plausible explanation for the rulings in *State v. Buhl*, *State v. Stubbs* and *Ex Parte Michael Dwain Bradshaw* in which the offline understanding of what constitutes constitutionally protected publication, distribution and privacy did not apply to online conduct.

This chapter has examined a flurry of rulings from 2011 to 2016 in which courts have reined in the use of cyberbullying harassment, stalking, and impersonation/harassment statutes to protect online expression produced by adults about adults. Historian Eric Foner observed that, "In the name of a 'new freedom for the individual,' the 1920s saw the birth of a coherent concept of civil liberties, and with it the beginnings of meaningful legal protection for freedom of speech against the actions of the state."[232] Perhaps, the six rulings, and even the Texas rulings that were reversed, signal a turning point—the beginnings of meaningful legal protection for freedom of speech for Internet users engaged in speech addressing matters of public concern or speech harshly critical of public figures.

Notes

1. Whitney v. California, 274 U.S. 357, 376 (1927).
2. Raphael Haim Golb, e-mail, July 14, 2016, 1:37 PM.
3. Ibid.
4. Laura Italiano, "'Dead' Man Walking from Jail," *The New York Post*, March 7, 2009, 12.
5. Ibid., Golb, e-mail.
6. See Sara S. Hodson, "Freeing the Dead Sea Scrolls: A Question of Access," *The American Archivist* 56 (Fall, 1993): 690–703, 693, http://americanarchivist.org/doi/pdf/10.17723/aarc.56.4.w213201818211541 (accessed August 22, 2016).
7. John Noble Wilford, "Debate Erupts Over Authors of the Dead Sea Scroll," *New York Times*, December 24, 2002, http://www.nytimes.com/2002/12/24/science/debate-erupts-over-authors-of-the-dead-sea-scrolls.html?pagewanted=all (accessed August 22, 2016).
8. Ibid.
9. People v. Golb, 23 NY 3d 455, 459–60 (N.Y. Court of Appeals, 2014); Golb v. New York, 135 S. Ct. 1009 (January 12, 2015) cert denied.
10. Golb, 23 NY 3d 455, 459–60.
11. Golb, e-mail.
12. People v. Golb, 23 NY 3d 455, 460.
13. Golb, e-mail.
14. Ibid.
15. Golb v. The Attorney General of the State of New York, 1:2015cv01709—Document 25 (S.D.N.Y. 2016), http://law.justia.com/cases/federal/district-courts/new-york/nysdce/1:2015cv01709/439393/25/ (accessed July 12, 2016).
16. Golb, e-mail.
17. Corynne McSherry, "'E-Personation' Bill Could Be Used to Punish Online Critics, Undermine First Amendment Protections for Parody," Electronic Frontier Foundation, August 22, 2010, https://www.eff.org/deeplinks/2010/08/e-personation-bill-could-be-used-punish-online (accessed July 12, 2016).
18. Sydney Smith, "Tucker Carlson Hoaxed Philadelphia Daily News in Fake Olbermann Inteview," *ImediaEthics.com*, November 11, 2010, 4:20 AM EST, http://www.imediaethics.org/tucker-carlson-hoaxed-philadelphia-daily-news-in-fake-keith-olbermann-interview/ (accessed August 7, 2016).

19. U.S. v. Alvarez, 132 S. Ct. 2537 (2012).
20. Ibid., 2553.
21. Ibid., 2547–48.
22. Golb, 23 NY 3d 455, 470.
23. Christopher M. Finan, *From the Palmer Raids to the Patriot Act: A History of the Fight for Free Speech in America* (Boston: Beacon Press, 2007).
24. State v. Leidecker, P3/11-2685 (R.I. July 30, 2014), https://www.washingtonpost.com/news/volokh-conspiracy/wp-content/uploads/sites/14/2014/10/Leidecker.pdf?tid=a_inl (accessed September 5, 2016).
25. U.S. v. Cassidy, 814 F. Supp. 2d 574, 583 (D. Md. 2011).
26. Golb, 23 N.Y.3d 455, 467.
27. Chan v. Ellis, S14A1652 (Ga. Supreme Ct. March 27, 2015).
28. Leidecker, P3/11-2685.
29. Scott v. Blum, 2D15-3412 (Florida 2d District Court of Appeal, April 29, 2016), http://www.2dca.org/opinions/Opinion_Pages/Opinion_Pages_2016/April/April%2029,%202016/2D15-3412.pdf (accessed July 5, 2016).
30. People v. Walter Relerford, 2016 IL App (1st) 132531 (June 24, 2016), http://www.illinoiscourts.gov/Opinions/AppellateCourt/2016/1stDistrict/1132531.pdf (accessed July 5, 2016).
31. Tommy Witherspoon, "Waco Judge Rules Texas Online Impersonation Law Unconstitutional, Violates First Amendment," *Waco Tribune*, February 26, 2016, 6:01 PM (accessed July 7. 2016).
32. State v. Abigail Marie Stubbs, 2016 Tex. App. LEXIS 8553 (Tex. App. 2016); Ex Parte Michael Dwain Bradshaw, 2016 Tex. App. Lexis 9203 (Tex. App. Dallas [5th Dist.] August 23, 2016).
33. Robert Post, "Reconciling Theory and Doctrine in First Amendment Jurisprudence," *California Law Review* 88 (2000): 2353, 2370, http://scholarship.law.berkeley.edu/cgi/viewcontent.cgi?article=1478&context=californialawreview (accessed July 7. 2016).
34. Wilson Huhn, "Scienter, Causation, and Harm in Freedom of Expression Analysis: The Right Hand Side of the Constitutional Calculus," *William. & Mary Bill Rights Journal* 125 (2004), http://scholarship.law.wm.edu/wmborj/vol13/iss1/4 (accessed July 7. 2016).
35. Maeve Duggan, "Part 1: Experiencing Online Harassment," Pew Research Center, October 22, 2014, http://www.pewinternet.org/2014/10/22/part-1-experiencing-online-harassment/ (accessed July 7, 2016).
36. Samuel J. Morley, "Unmasking Anonymous Internet Posters: Can Civil Procedure Rules Adequately Protect Online Speech," *Communications Lawyer* 30 (November 2013), http://www.americanbar.org/publications/communications_lawyer/2013/november/unmasking_anonymous_internet_posters_can_civil_procedure_rules_protect_online_speech.html (accessed July 7, 2016).
37. John Wihbey and Leighton Walter Kille, "Internet Harassment and Online Threats Targeting Women: Research Review," Shorenstein Center on Media, Politics and Public Policy, July 13, 2015, http://journalistsresource.org/studies/society/gender-society/internet-harassment-online-threats-targeting-women-research-review (accessed July 7. 2016).
38. "Criminal Impersonation Law & Legal Definition," *USLegal.Com*, http://definitions.uslegal.com/c/criminal-impersonation/ (accessed June 30, 2016).

39. John Leland, "Online Battle Over Sacred Scrolls, Real-World Consequences," *New York Times*, February 16, 2013, http://www.nytimes.com/2013/02/17/nyregion/online-battle-over-ancient-scrolls-spawns-real-world-consequences.html (accessed June 30, 2016).
40. Golb, e-mail.
41. Ibid.
42. Batar Ungar-Sargon, "Dead Sea Scrolls Go to Court," *Tablet*, January 14, 2013, http://www.tabletmag.com/jewish-arts-and-culture/books/121361/dead-sea-scrolls-go-to-court (accessed August 7, 2016).
43. See Norman Golb, "Response: The Confidential Letter Composed by Prof. Lawrence Schiffman of New York University," November 30, 2010, https://oi.uchicago.edu/sites/oi.uchicago.edu/files/uploads/shared/docs/schiffman_response_2010nov30.pdf (accessed August 7, 2016).
44. Steve Kolowich, "The Fall of an Academic Cyberbully," *The Chronicle of Higher Education*, March 20, 2009, 1.
45. Norman Gold, *Who Wrote the Dead Sea Scrolls* (New York: Charles Scribner's Sons, 1995), 215.
46. Leland, "Online Battle Over Sacred Scrolls, Real-World Consequences."
47. Ungar-Sargon, "Dead Sea Scrolls Go to Court."
48. Golb, e-mail.
49. Batar Ungar-Sargon, "Dead Sea Scrolls Go to Court."
50. Golb, 23 NY 3d 455, 466–67.
51. Ibid., 467.
52. Ibid., 467.
53. Vives v. New York City, 305 F.Supp.2d 289, 299 (2003).
54. Ibid., 292–93.
55. Tim Cushing, "NY Prosecutor: Annoying Someone Is A Criminal Act, Especially If It's in Writing," *Techdirt.com*, April 11, 2014, 7:45 AM, https://www.techdirt.com/articles/20140409/15223626862/ny-prosecutor-annoying-someone-is-criminal-act-especially-if-its-writing.shtml (accessed August 7, 2016).
56. Violent Blue, "Analysis: California's Online Impersonation Law, Effective January 1," *ZDNet.com*, December 30, 2010, 06:00 GMT (22:00 PST), http://www.zdnet.com/article/analysis-californias-online-impersonation-law-effective-january-1/ (accessed July 7, 2016).
57. Ibid.
58. Lisa Evers, "Fighting Online Impersonation," *Fox* 5, March 23, 2016, 10:45 PM EDT, http://www.fox5ny.com/news/112850308-story (accessed July 7, 2016).
59. U.S Department of Justice, "Identity Theft," November 2, 2015, https://www.justice.gov/criminal-fraud/identity-theft/identity-theft-and-identity-fraud (accessed July 7, 2016).
60. California Penal Code §528.5, http://www.leginfo.ca.gov/cgi-bin/displaycode?section=pen&group=00001-01000&file=528-539 (accessed July 7, 2016).
61. McSherry, "'E-Personation' Bill Could be Used to Punish Online Critics, Undermine First Amendment Protections for Parody."
62. New York State Penal Law § 190.25 (June 2014), https://www.nycourts.gov/judges/cji/2-PenalLaw/190/190.25%281%29.pdf (accessed July 7, 2016).

63. People v. Golb, 102 AD 3d 601, 602–03 (2013).
64. Ibid.
65. Golb, 23 NY 3d 455, 466.
66. Ibid.
67. Ibid.
68. Ibid., 468.
69. Golb, 23 NY 3d 469.
70. People v. Golb, 192 AD 601, 603 (2013).
71. Golb, 23 NY 3d 471.
72. Ibid.
73. Ibid., 466.
74. Restatement (2d) of Torts, § 559, http://www.columbia.edu/~mr2651/ecommerce3/2nd/statutes/RestatementTorts.pdf (accessed August 8, 2016).
75. Golb v. The Attorney General of the State of New York, 1:2015cv01709—Document 25 (S.D.N.Y. 2016), http://cases.justia.com/federal/district-courts/new-york/nysdce/1:2015cv01709/439393/25/0.pdf?ts=1453555434 (accessed July 7, 2016).
76. Ibid., 29.
77. Ibid.
78. Golb, e-mail.
79. Texas Penal Code Ann. §33.07(a)(2), http://www.statutes.legis.state.tx.us/Docs/PE/htm/PE.33.htm#33.07 (accessed August 8, 2016).
80. Ibid.
81. Ibid., 33.01(14).
82. Tommy Witherspoon, "Waco Judge Rules Texas Online Impersonation Law Unconstitutional, Violates First Amendment," *Waco Tribune*, February 26, 2016, 6:01 PM, http://www.wacotrib.com/news/courts_and_trials/waco-judge-rules-texas-online-impersonation-law-unconstitutional-violates-first/article_d633811c-86d0-5dce-a3f5-924ff6591ba0.html (accessed April 30, 2017).
83. Craig Malisow, "Notorious Ex-Judge Chris Dupuy Free After Charges Dismissed," *Houston Press*, June 22, 2016, 5 AM, http://www.houstonpress.com/news/notorious-ex-judge-chris-dupuy-free-after-charges-dismissed-8501861 (accessed July 7, 2016).
84. Stubbs, 2016 Tex. App. LEXIS 8553.
85. Ex Parte Michael Dwain Bradshaw, 2016 Tex. App. Lexis 9203.
86. State v. Bishop, COA14-1227 (N.C. Ct. App. June 16, 2015), http://caselaw.findlaw.com/nc-court-of-appeals/1705020.html (accessed August 22, 2016).
87. Ibid.
88. Reed v. Town of Gilbert, 135 S. Ct. 2218 (2015).
89. Ibid., 2227.
90. Ibid.
91. Bishop, 774 SE 2d 337, 342 (2015).
92. Bishop, 223PA15 *8.
93. Bland v. Roberts, 730 F. 3d 368, 386 (4th Cir. 2013).
94. Stubbs, 2016 Tex. App. LEXIS 8553, *3; See Ex Parte Michael Dwain Bradshaw.
95. Stubbs, *11; Ex Parte Michael Dwain Bradshaw, *11.

96. Bradshaw, *11.
97. Stubbs,*14.
98. Stubbs, *18–22; Bradshaw, *7.
99. Stubbs, *21–22.
100. Stubbs, *22–23; See Bradshaw, *17.
101. Reed, 135 S. Ct. 2218, 2231.
102. Bishop, 223PA15 *12
103. Reed, 135 S. Ct. 2218, 2230.
104. Stubbs, *31; Bradshaw, *11.
105. Bradshaw, *21.
106. Stubbs, *37–38; Bradshaw, *22.
107. Reno v. ACLU, 521 US 844 (1997).
108. Burton v. Crowell Publishing Co., 82 F.2d 154, 155 (2d Cir. 1936).
109. "Email from Rep. Douglas W. Gablinske," *The Volokh Conspiracy* (blog), October 21, 2014, https://www.washingtonpost.com/news/volokh-conspiracy/wp-content/uploads/sites/14/2014/10/LeideckerEmail.pdf (accessed July 7, 2016).
110. Mark Reynolds, "NEA Deputy Director Guilty of Cyber-stalking," *Providence Journal*, September 20, 2011, 6.
111. Ibid., e-mail from Rep. Douglas W. Gablinske.
112. State v. Leidecker, P3/11-2685 at *4 (R.I. July 30, 2014).
113. Ibid., *6.
114. Ibid., *1.
115. Tom Mooney and Tatiana Pina, "Political Dirty Tricks Alleged," *Providence Journal*, December 1, 2010, 1.
116. John Leidecker, e-mail to author, June 12, 2016, 12:02 PM.
117. Rhode Island General Laws. §11-52-7 Use of false information, http://law.justia.com/codes/rhode-island/2010/title11/chapter11-52/11-52-7.html (accessed August 23, 2016).
118. Rhode Island General Laws. §11-52-4.2 Cyberstalking and cyberharassment prohibited, http://webserver.rilin.state.ri.us/Statutes/title11/11-52/11-52-4.2.htm (accessed August 23, 2016).
119. Aaron H. Caplan, "Free Speech and Civil Harassment Orders," *Hastings Law Journal* 64 (April 2013): 781, 794, http://www.hastingslawjournal.org/wp-content/uploads/2014/03/Caplan-64.3.pdf (accessed August 23, 2016).
120. Leidecker, e-mail.
121. Mark Reynolds, "NEA Deputy Director Guilty of Cyber-stalking."
122. Leidecker, P3/11-2685 (R.I. July 30, 2014).
123. Robert N. Miller, "Stalk Talk': A First Look at Anti-Stalking Legislation," *Washington & Lee Law Review* 50 (1993): 1303, http://scholarlycommons.law.wlu.edu/wlulr/vol50/iss3/11 (accessed July 22, 2016).
124. Ibid.
125. 18 U.S. Code § 2261A-Stalking, Legal Information Institute, https://www.law.cornell.edu/uscode/text/18/2261A (accessed July 12, 2016).
126. Janet Reno, *Cyberstalking: A New Challenge for Law Enforcement and Industry* (Washington, DC: United States Department of Justice, August 1999), http://www.cyber-rights.org/documents/cyberstalkingreport.htm (accessed July 12, 2016).

127. Libor Jany, "In Electronic Era, Stalkers, Abusers Can be Hard to Track," *Star Tribune*, June 8, 2016, 11:13 PM, http://www.startribune.com/in-electronic-era-stalkers-abusers-can-be-hard-to-track/382278371/ (accessed July 12, 2016).
128. Eugene Volokh, "Court Order Banning Speech about a Person (and Banning Gun Possession) Reversed," *Washington Post* (blog), May 2, 2016, https://www.washingtonpost.com/news/volokh-conspiracy/wp/2016/05/02/court-order-banning-speech-about-a-person-and-banning-gun-possession-by-speaker-reversed/ (accessed July 12, 2016).
129. Rhode Island General Laws § 11-52-4.2 Cyberstalking and cyberharassment prohibited, http://webserver.rilin.state.ri.us/Statutes/title11/11-52/11-52-4.2.htm (accessed July 12, 2016).
130. Ibid.
131. Leidecker, P3/11-2685, *9.
132. Whitney v. California, 274 US 357, 375 (1927).
133. Doe v. Reed, 09–559 (April 28, 2010), http://www.supremecourt.gov/oral_arguments/argument_transcripts/09–559.pdf (July 12, 2016).
134. Leidecker, P3/11-2685, *13.
135. National Center for Victims of Crime, *The Model Stalking Code Revisited: Responding to the New Realities of Stalking* (Washington, D.C., January 2007), 35, https://victimsofcrime.org/docs/default-source/src/model-stalking-code.pdf?sfvrsn=12 (accessed July 4, 2016).
136. Leidecker, P3/11-2685, *14.
137. People v. Marquan, 24 NY 3d 1,14 (2014).
138. Leidecker, P3/11-2685, *16.
139. Leidecker, P3/11-2685, *18–19.
140. Leidecker, e-mail to author, June 12, 2016, 12:02 PM.
141. Hustler Magazine, Inc. v. Falwell, 485 U.S. 46 (1988).
142. Ibid., 50, 53.
143. Ibid., 55.
144. Eugene Volokh, "One-to-One Speech vs. One-to-Many Speech, Criminal Harassment Laws, and 'Cyberstalking,'" Northwestern University Law Review, 107 (2013): 731, 789, http://www2.law.ucla.edu/volokh/crimharass.pdf (accessed July 12, 2006).
145. Cassidy, 814 F. Supp. 2d 574, 578–79.
146. Ibid., 592, n. 11.
147. Ibid., 590.
148. Ibid., 582.
149. Ibid., 577.
150. Matthew Chan, "My Case by Matthew Chan," *ExtortionLetterInfo* (blog), http://www.extortionletterinfo.com/my-case-by-matthew-chan/ (accessed July 5, 2016).
151. Ibid.
152. Chan v. Ellis, 770 SE 2d 851, 852 (Ga. Supreme Ct. March 27, 2015).
153. Ellis v. Chan, SU 13409 (Georgia Superior Court, 2013), http://www.dmlp.org/sites/dmlp.org/files/2013-02-13-Ellis%20Petition%20for%20Personal%20Protective%20Order.pdf (accessed July 5, 2016).
154. Samuel J. Morley, "How Broad Is Web Publisher Immunity Under §230 of the Communications Decency Act of 1996?," *The Florida Bar Journal*, February, 2010, 8, https://www.floridabar.org/divcom/jn/jnjournal01.nsf/c0d731e03de9828d852574580042ae7a/94

fda41e804565ac852576b9006af919!OpenDocument&Highlight=0,* (accessed April 30, 2017).
155. OCGA § 16-5-90(a)(1) (2010), http://law.justia.com/codes/georgia/2010/title-16/chapter-5/article-7/16-5-90 (accessed July 5, 2016).
156. Matthew Valor (Chan), "Chan v. Ellis: Essential Appellate Court Case Documents," *Defiantly.com* (blog), October 1, 2015, http://defiantly.net/chan-v-ellis-essential-appellate-court-case-documents/ (accessed July 5, 2016).
157. Chan v. Ellis, 770 SE 2d 851, 855.
158. Scott v. Blum, 2D15-3412 (Florida 2d District Court of Appeal, April 29, 2016), http://www.2dca.org/opinions/Opinion_Pages/Opinion_Pages_2016/April/April%2029,%20 2016/2D15-3412.pdf (accessed July 5, 2016).
159. Scott v. Blum, 2D15-3412, *5.
160. Ibid., *5.
161. Elonis v. US, 135 S. Ct. 2001, (2015).
162. Ibid., 2009–2011.
163. People v. Walter Relerford, 2016 IL App (1st) 132531*13 (June 24, 2016), http://www.illinoiscourts.gov/Opinions/AppellateCourt/2016/1stDistrict/1132531.pdf (accessed July 5, 2016).
164. "Harassment and Hypocrisy," *Providence Journal*, August 5, 2014, 12:01 AM, http://www.providencejournal.com/article/20140805/NEWS/308059604 (accessed July 5, 2016).
165. John Stuart Mill, "The Project Gutenberg EBook of On Liberty," *On Liberty* (Salt Lake City: Project Gutenberg, 2011): 104, https://www.gutenberg.org/files/34901/34901-h/34901-h.htm (accessed July 5, 2016).
166. Ibid., 23.
167. John Stuart Mill, *Utilitarianism* (1863), http://www.utilitarianism.com/mill1.htm (accessed July 5, 2016).
168. Connecticut General Statutes Annotated, Sec. Sec. 53a-179a, http://law.justia.com/codes/connecticut/2005/title53a/sec53a-179a.html (accessed August 24, 2016).
169. Memorandum in Support of Michael Adams's Motion to Dismiss, State v. Michael Adams, H15N-CR11-0258251-S *1 (Superior Ct. of Connecticut, September 9, 2011).
170. Ibid.
171. Connecticut General Statutes § 53a-183 (a) (2).
172. Connecticut General Statues, Sec. 53a-181.
173. Brandenburg v. Ohio, 395 U.S. 444 (1969).
174. Memorandum in Support of Michael Adams's Motion to Dismiss, *2.
175. Ibid., *7.
176. ACLU of Connecticut Legal Docket, Free Speech, 2013, https://www.acluct.org/wp-content/uploads/2013/08/UPDATEDLegalDocket.pdf (accessed August 8, 2016).
177. Martin B. Margulies, e-mail to author, Aug 27, 2016, 10:25 AM.
178. Ibid.
179. Buhl, 321 Conn. 688 (Conn. Supreme Court 2016).
180. Ibid.
181. Teri Buhl, *Smashmouth Investigative Journalism* (blog), http://www.teribuhl.com/ (accessed August 24, 2016).

182. Ibid., "Update 8.7.16—I am Free."
183. Buhl, 321 Conn. 688, 691.
184. Venkat Balasubramani, "St. Sup. Ct. Affirms Harassment and Breach of Peach Conviction for Posting Pages from Diary to Facebook," *Technology & Marketing Law Blog*, June 16, 2016, http://blog.ericgoldman.org/archives/2016/06/state-sup-ct-affirms-harassment-and-breach-of-peace-conviction-for-posting-pages-from-diary-to-facebook.htm (accessed August 28, 2016).
185. Ibid., 710–11.
186. Ibid., 714–15.
187. Teri Buhl, State v. Buhl, *Smashmouth Investigative Reporting*.
188. Buhl, 321 Conn. 688, 691.
189. Ibid., 694.
190. State v. Moulton, 78 A. 3d 55 (Conn. Supreme Court, 2013).
191. Ibid., 64.
192. Ibid., 72.
193. Virginia v. Black, 538 U.S. 343, 359 (2003).
194. Elonis, 135 S. Ct. 2001, 2012.
195. Ibid., 74.
196. State v. Book, 109 A. 3d 1027, 1034 (Conn. App. Ct. 2015)
197. Volokh, "One-to-One Speech vs. One-to-Many Speech, Criminal Harassment Laws, and 'Cyberstalking,'" 740.
198. Buhl, 321 Conn. 688,721.
199. Ibid., 720.
200. U.S. v. Bagdasarian, 652 F. 3d 1113, 1119 (9th Cir. 2011).
201. Ibid., 1121.
202. Ibid.
203. Ibid., 1115.
204. Ibid., 1123.
205. Memorandum in Support of Michael Adams's Motion to Dismiss.
206. U.S. v. Jeffries, 692 F. 3d 473, 475 (6th Cir. 2012).
207. Moulton, 78 A. 3d 55, 70, n. 21.
208. Ibid., 69, n. 18.
209. Buhl, 321 Conn. 688,722.
210. Buhl, 321 Conn. 688,721.
211. Reed, 135 S. Ct. 2218, 2227.
212. Stubbs, 2016 Tex. App. LEXIS 8553, *3; See Ex Parte Michael Dwain Bradshaw.
213. Ibid., *31
214. Ibid., *2–3.
215. Venkat Balasubramani, "St. Sup. Ct. Affirms Harassment and Breach of Peach Conviction for Posting Pages from Diary to Facebook."
216. Buhl, 321 Conn. 688, 696.
217. Ibid., 698, 699, 702.
218. Ibid.
219. Ibid., 699.

220. Gordon Gottsegen, “Here’s How to Use Facebook’s Mystifying Privacy Settings,” *Wired.com*, August 18, 2016, 5:55 AM, http://www.wired.com/2015/08/how-to-use-facebook-privacy-settings-step-by-step/ (accessed August 28, 2016).
221. “How Tagging Works,” *Facebook*, https://www.facebook.com/about/tagging (accessed September 5, 2016).
222. Balasubramani, “St. Sup. Ct. Affirms Harassment and Breach of Peach Conviction for Posting Pages from Diary to Facebook.”
223. Buhl, 321 Conn. 688,705.
224. Restatement of Law, Second, Torts, §652D, http://cyber.law.harvard.edu/privacy/Privacy_R2d_Torts_Sections.htm (accessed August 28, 2016).
225. Ibid.
226. Mark D. Robbins, “The Rights of Privacy and Publicity under Massachusetts Law,” *Massachusetts Law Review* 86 (2002), http://www.massbar.org/publications/massachusetts-law-review/2002/v86-n4/the-rights-of-privacy-and (accessed August 28, 2016).
227. Moreno v. Hartford Sentinel, Inc., 172 Cal.App.4th 1125, 1130 (2009).
228. Balasubramani, “St. Sup. Ct. Affirms Harassment and Breach of Peach Conviction for Posting Pages from Diary to Facebook.”
229. Richard Koman, “Megan’s Law: Mo. Prosecutors Using New Cyberbullying Laws,” *Zdnet.com*, December 21, 2008, http://www.zdnet.com/article/megans-law-mo-prosecutors-using-new-cyberbullying-laws/ (accessed December 30, 2015).
230. H. Babe Howell, “Prosecutorial Discretion and the Duty to Seek Justice in an Overburdened Criminal Justice System,” *Georgetown Journal of Legal Ethics* 27 (2014): 285, 286, http://policeandcommunity.org/pdfs/Archives/2014/Archives-Legality/2014_ProsecutorialDiscretionandDutyToSeek_Howell.pdf (accessed September 5, 2016).
231. Cassidy, 814 F. Supp. 2d 574.
232. Eric Foner, *The Story of American Freedom* (New York: W.W. Norton, 1999), 183.

· 6 ·

IMAGE CONTROL

Who Loses When Teen Sexting and Revenge Porn Are Criminalized?

> In the next decade, the proliferation of digital visual capacity will regularly require legal decision-makers to come to grips with the status of pervasive image capture under the First Amendment.
>
> —Seth F. Kreimer, University of Pennsylvania Law School (2011)[1]

In early 2016, New Mexico traveled further along the path to decriminalizing teen sexting than any other state. Its Republican governor, signed legislation, albeit reluctantly, which included an amendment exempting from prosecution for child pornography teens between 14 and 17 years old who send explicit images of themselves to one another.[2]

To put the New Mexico statute into some context, consider that Nebraska doesn't go as far as New Mexico because a teen sexter charged with child pornography and possession of sexually explicit conduct for consensual sexting in that state is provided the right to an affirmative defense. In other words, instead of the prosecutor carrying the burden of proving guilt beyond a reasonable doubt, the teen sexter in Nebraska must persuade a jury that he or she meets several possible exemptions.[3] Elsewhere, Florida provides an exemption if a teen (1) did not solicit the image, (2) took reasonable steps to report the image to a legal guardian, school or law enforcement, (3) did not distribute the image to a third party.[4] Consequently, one-to-one consensual sharing would still be punishable as child pornography distribution. In other sexting law reform states, teens of specified ages can argue as a defense that they are of the age of consent, or prosecutors retain the discretion to pursue child pornography, sex offender charges, or impose mandatory education[5] against teen sexters.[6]

Meanwhile, Rhode Island Governor Gina M. Raimondo played the contrarian to the revenge porn law adoption movement that edged toward mainstream acceptance that year. By May 2016, 34 states had criminalized revenge porn,[7] and a U.S. Congresswoman rolled out the Intimate Privacy Protection Act (IPPA), proposed federal revenge porn bill that summer.[8] But that June, Raimondo vetoed a bill, which was, she said, "apparently intended to curb the dissemination of private sexual material over the Internet, but its sweep is much broader."[9] She became the first governor to veto a revenge porn bill.[10]

Teen sexting and revenge porn have sprouted from the same technological tree. They are sexting—the use of digital technologies—smartphones, email, social media and other web sites—to transmit or display a photographic or video image that depicts nudity, semi-nudity or sexually provocative poses typically for non-commercial purposes. They are distinguishable, however, mostly by two factors—the age of the depicted person and the online user's motivation.

"Most commonly when people use the term 'sexting,' it is to refer to incidents where minors take pictures of themselves when they are nude or nearly nude and send them to others," explains criminal justice professor and cyberbullying authority Justin W. Patchin.[11] In *Miller v. Skumanick* (2009), one of the earliest, if not the first ruling involving sexting, a Pennsylvania court defined it as "the practice of 'sexting,' which has become popular among teenagers in recent years."[12]

The question has been asked by parents, psychologists, law enforcement officers and just about anyone over 21: Why do teens sext? "The most oft-cited survey, by the National Campaign to Prevent Teen and Unplanned Pregnancy, suggests peer pressure influences girls who sext: Some 51% of teen girls say pressure from a male is a factor, compared with 18% of boys who blame the opposite sex, according to the on-line survey last year of 1,280 people 26 and under," *The Wall Street Journal* reported in 2009. "When surveyed, by far the most common reason kids give for sexting is that their boyfriend or girlfriend wanted the picture," Hanna Rosin reported, also identifying peer pressure as a motivation.[13] A survey of studies from 2008 to 2012 revealed the vast majority of teens sext to flirt.[14]

There is some evidence, however, that a small portion of teen self-produced sexting ends up online and is exploited by child pornographer distributors[15] and, unfortunately, there have been incidents in which consensual one-to-one teen sexting resulted in hurtful non-consensual one-to-many distribution.[16] But the overwhelming majority of teen sexters are not motivated by anger, retribution or mendacity.

In contrast, many individuals who post sexually explicit photos of former spouses or lovers are motivated by anger, hence the colloquial term "revenge porn," or, in the case of online intermediaries, to gain payment to remove the photos[17] or sheer idiotic spitefulness. The generic revenge porn perpetrator wishes to embarrass or humiliate his target, in some cases cause great damage to the reputations and emotional well-being of those who have spurned him.

Many see blameworthy criminal misconduct in both types of sexting and demand that guilty sexters face felony or misdemeanor charges. A growing minority, however, such as New Mexico lawmakers and Rhode Island Governor Raimondo, are troubled by the harm that such laws pose to free expression and say education and civil penalties are the appropriate responses.

This chapter examines the constitutionality of teen sexting prosecutions and revenge porn criminal laws. It takes the position that it is unjust to prosecute teens for engaging in the consensual sharing of self-produced sexually provocative or explicit images because such minors lack the intent to cause harm to themselves or others. It also argues against the constitutional legitimacy of state revenge porn statutes and the proposed IPPA, as they existed in 2016, which is to say all of the laws. All share the flaw of criminalizing the distribution by adults of indecent or sexually explicit content, expressive activity that is constitutionally protected until it has been adjudged obscene. Thus, the unjust victimization of sexting teens and adults will end only when prosecutors cease charging teens engaged in consensual, non-commercial sexting with misdemeanor and felony offenses, and legislators draft constitutionally sound revenge porn statutes.

Free Speech, Teen Sexting and Revenge Porn

Statutes that criminalize teen sexting and revenge porn implicate the First Amendment. In *Kaplan v. California* (1973), the U.S. Supreme Court noted that constitutional limits on criminalizing content as obscene applied "to moving pictures, to photographs, and to words in books ... As with pictures, films, paintings, drawings, and engravings, both oral utterance and the printed word have First Amendment protection."[18] In *Texas v. Johnson* (1989), the Court established a test that can be applied to support First Amendment protection for photography, "In deciding whether particular conduct possesses sufficient communicative elements to bring the First Amendment into play, we have asked whether [a]n intent to convey a particularized message was present, and [whether] the likelihood was great that the message would be understood by those who viewed it."[19] Thus, bans on the publication and distribution of photographic images are content restrictive and subject to traditional First Amendment tests such as void-for-vagueness, overbreadth, strict scrutiny and obscenity analyses.

As noted above, revenge porn laws implicate the First Amendment obscenity doctrine because they criminalize what is otherwise protected speech—adults distributing sexually explicit, but not obscene, images. If a statute defined revenge porn as consistent with the standards of the three-prong obscenity test, it would stand a far greater chance of withstanding constitutional scrutiny.[20] But none of the state statutes or the proposed federal law demands such consistency. Thus, they are content-restrictive laws, presumed to be unconstitutional unless they survive strict scrutiny analysis.

They would likely satisfy the first prong of the strict scrutiny analysis—they advance a compelling government interest by protecting an individual's privacy. It is doubtful, however, that government would be able to show that a criminal ban is narrowly tailored. Typically, states provide other constitutionally approved ways to target revenge porn, including invasion of privacy torts, copyright actions, and criminal cyberstalking laws.

There is another constitutional impediment. Bans on nonconsensual distribution of intimate images do not fall into any of the traditional constitutionally unprotected speech categories—defamation, obscenity, fighting words, incitement, speech integral to a crime, fraud or true threats. Thus, revenge porn is a newly created category of unprotected speech and in *U.S. v. Stevens* (2010), the U.S. Supreme Court signaled its reluctance to add more categories of unprotected speech.

> When we have identified categories of speech as fully outside the protection of the First Amendment, it has not been on the basis of a simple cost-benefit analysis … Our decisions in *Ferber* and other cases cannot be taken as establishing a freewheeling authority to declare new categories of speech outside the scope of the First Amendment.[21]

Under the First Amendment overbreadth doctrine, a statute is overly broad when its scope "potentially covers a great deal of constitutionally protected speech," and its constitutionality should not "depend on prosecutorial discretion."[22] And as the Court noted in *Erznoznik v. Jacksonville* (1975), "minors are entitled to a significant measure of First Amendment protection, and only in relatively narrow and well-defined circumstances may government bar public dissemination of protected materials to them."[23] These rulings suggest that prosecuting teens who sext to flirt under criminal statutes would be an unconstitutional overbroad application of the law because they do not possess the requisite intent or mens rea. Still, *Clark v. Roccanova* (2011) suggests that using child porn laws to prosecute sexting by minors is constitutional.[24]

Criminal Intent, Teen Sextng and Revenge Porn

The criminalization of non-consensual revenge porn raises questions about what level of mens rea, or "a guilty or wrongful purpose,"[25] element of revenge porn statutes is appropriate for fairness and due process. In criminal law, the "'central thought' is that a defendant must be 'blameworthy in mind' before he can be found guilty, a concept courts have expressed over time through various terms such as *mens rea*, scienter, malice aforethought, guilty knowledge, and the like," the U.S. Supreme Court said in *Elonis v. U.S.* (2015). "Although there are exceptions, the 'general rule' is that a guilty mind is 'a necessary element in the indictment and proof of every crime.'"[26]

As discussed in Chapter Two, leading proponents of revenge porn laws disagree about the value of requiring prosecutors to prove that a speaker intended to harass or intended malice. Danielle Citron, Cyber Civil Rights Initiative (CCRI) advisor and author of *Hate Crimes in Cyberspace*, argues for its inclusion.[27] But the CCRI, the group that has taken the lead on advocating and ghostwriting revenge porn statutes for legislators, argues that including an intent-to-harass requirement would provide an escape clause for third parties such as revenge porn site owners and people who hack and then post intimate and private photos of celebrities. They also point to *People v. Marquan*[28] and *People v. Bishop*[29] (See "The Unnecessary and Unjust Creation of Cyber Delinquents") in courts struck down statutes because they contained vague and overbroad intent-to-harass language and conclude that it is better to omit a malice intent requirement.[30]

The absence of an intent-to-harm requirement troubled Gov. Raimondo. The Motion Picture Association of America raised the same concern about Minnesota's proposed revenge porn early bill in 2016.[31] (At the end, the terms of the Minnesota bill, signed into law in August 2016, required only a showing of negligence.)[32]

The proposed federal IPPA, which the CCRI helped to draft, would hold defendants criminally culpable when they knowingly distribute sexually explicit material with reckless disregard for the victim's lack of consent.[33] The IPPA's recklessness standard appears to comport with one plausible reading of the Court's ruling in *Elonis v. U.S.*—"the *Elonis* majority left the 'recklessness door' conspicuously open, and yet provided almost no guidance to lower courts on whether to walk through it or how to confront the constitutional challenges to the statute on the other side."[34] Still, as discussed below, the IPPA's constitutionality has been widely questioned.

For teen sexting, there are two questions: (1) Are Fourteenth Amendment due process and First Amendment overbreadth and vagueness rights of teens violated by charging sexting teens under child pornography laws, an indictment that implies they have the guilty purpose of exploiting minors, which can mean themselves. In other words, is it fair to hold hormonally driven and foolish teen sexters blameworthy for the creation and distribution of child pornography? (2) If teens are of legal age to consent to sexual activities, though younger than 18, is it a violation of their constitutional rights to prosecute them for sexting? In other words, if one 17-year-old correctly believes he has the right to engage in sexual relations with a 16-year-old, is it reasonable for him to believe he has the right to exchange self-produced sexually revealing photos with the other teen? If it is a reasonably held belief, how is it possible that the teen formed the mental intent required to violate child pornography or criminal sexting laws?

Teen Sexting, Revenge Porn: Privacy and Consent

Prosecution of revenge porn and teen sexting implicate concepts of consent in the criminal and civil law contexts. Joseph Henry Beale, Jr., the first dean of University of Chicago Law School, tells us that, "An act which consists of an injury to an individual may, however, be of a criminal act only if done without the consent of the individual."[35] Stephen J. Schulhofer, criminal justice scholar at New York University Law School, notes that, "wherever sexual consent has been formally defined and required—whether in criminal law, government-mandated codes of student conduct, or codes of conduct initiated by universities themselves—it has been described as an expression of willingness or assent, communicated by all behavior, including both words and actions."[36]

Accordingly, if a revenge porn defendant is to be found guilty, a prosecutor must prove that an ex-partner or the alleged victim did not give consent to have her sexually explicit photo shared publicly, or knew that consent to distribute was not given. That's an easy task when an online intermediary or other third party, unrelated to the victim in any intimate way, is in the dock, and the law is clear on criminal liability under such circumstances. When photos are taken surreptitiously, stolen, acquired by fraud, misrepresentation, or coercion, the victim has not given consent.[37]

But how does one untangle the truth in a he-said, she-said scenario? Some revenge porn law activists say that defining consent as affirmative consent, or "a direct expression of willingness, permission or agreement,"[38] and shifting the burden of proof on the defendant eases prosecutors' tasks considerably.[39] For example, North Carolina's Disclosure of Private Images statute, under which a woman was the first to be charged, provides that, "the person discloses the image without the affirmative consent of the depicted person."[40] (The accused woman revenge porn perpetrator did not have a former intimate relationship with the alleged victim.) The proposed federal IPPA, however, would not require the prosecutorial-favorable affirmative defense. Under the IPPA, the state would have a somewhat more difficult burden of proving reckless disregard for consent. Courts' definitions of recklessness vary and the term is frequently equated to willful, wanton and grossly negligent misconduct.[41]

In the teen sexting context, consent raises a slew of questions. Are minors capable of understanding the consequences of consent? If the answer is no, then a teen who receives a sexual explicit photo from another is precluded from arguing consent as a defense. Taken to its logical conclusion, if minors are incapable of giving consent, consensual sharing of intimate photos between teens would be illegal under any circumstance. That illegal category would include circumstances in which a teen, who is of the age of sexual consent, distributes or accept photos from another teen, who is not of the age to consent to sex. There is, of course, another way of viewing a teen's supposedly diminished capacity to consent—the teen is incapable of forming the required criminal state of mind necessary for child pornography and other child exploitation offenses. (In contrast, the right of two adults to engage in the consensual sharing of sexual explicit photos of themselves is protected under the First Amendment as long as the content is not obscene.)[42]

Though consent was not directly addressed in *Clark v. Roccanova*, a federal judge dismissed a motion to dismiss a lawsuit under a sexual exploitation of a minor statute brought by a 14-year-old against other 14-year-olds because of her incapability of ignoring peer pressure to share intimate photos of herself. The plaintiff, a girl, sent sexually explicit photos to a boy who shared them with other teen boys. Essentially, the judge ruled that the girl teen could sue for sexual exploitation because her age made her an easy target to manipulate. The court ruled that male teens Roccanova, Rudy and Lynch "coerced, enticed and persuaded Clark to produce a sexually explicit video" by making "several telephone calls from Roccanova asking for the video in question and threatening to withhold his friendship if the video was not produced."[43] Apparently, the court assumed that Clark did not have the capacity to make a sound decision. "For an adult, the threat to 'not be her friend' would not suffice to vitiate consent, but for a vulnerable eighth-grade girl it evoked something quite different from a passing request or romantic inquiry."[44]

Professor Kreimer, of the University of Pennsylvania Law School, and one of three attorneys who represented Mary Jo Miller[45] in a case involving the use of child pornography charges against teens who arguably did not transmit sexually revealing images of themselves, argues that criminal law is poorly suited to handle the complexities of minors' ability to consent. "On the other hand, the spectrum running from Roccanova's conduct through sexual negotiation, experimentation and flirtation to generalized peer pressure is tinged with shades of gray too subtle for the criminal justice system."[46]

So far, other than under the New Mexico statute, teen consent is not given full weight. Among the 30 states where the legal minimum age of consent for sexual activity is below 18,[47] only Indiana allows defendants, who are not more than four years apart in age and engaged in a dating or a personal relationship, to argue as a defense that child pornography charges should not apply to them.[48] Moreover, in *A. H. v. Florida* (2007), a Florida district court has ruled prosecutors do not have to recognize the privacy interest of two consenting teen sexters who transmit their nude images to a third party.[49]

In *Regina Tyrrell* (1894), 1 Q.B. 710, the British Court established a common law and statutory construction principle to which American courts subscribe. "… when the legislature has imposed criminal penalties to protect a class of persons, it can hardly have meant that a member of that very class should be punishable either as an aider or abettor or as a co-conspirator."[50] Thus, the *Tyrell* principle guarding against criminalizing a victim should apply equally to modern teen sexters. Yet, the principle does not seem to have given prosecutors reason to pause.

Teen Sexting, the Age of Consent and Victims of Incoherent Laws

Surely, teens, who can legally engage in sexual relationships but cannot legally share sexual explicit photos of themselves, are yet another class of victims of the cyberbullying moral panic and incoherent laws. Cormega Copening, then 17, and Brianna Denson, then 16, of Fayetteville, N.C, were such victims. In September 2014, the prosecution of Copening and Denson on sexual exploitation charges drew international attention to the legal absurdity of simultaneously treating teen sexters as adults and minors. "The decisions by the Cumberland County Sheriff's Office to charge the teens and the District Attorney Office to prosecute the teens for sexting outraged many people, who commented on the charges in social media and elsewhere. The case made national news in the past few weeks and generated headlines as far away as Russia," the local *Fayetteville Observer* noted.[51]

The *Daily Mail* in the United Kingdom remarked, "The age of consent to have sex in North Carolina, however, is 16 years old, which means the couple could have sex with one another, but could not send nude photos to one another."[52] There was another paradox, the local *Fayetteville Observer* newspaper noted. "Copening was charged as an adult who exploited himself sexually because North Carolina criminal law classifies teens aged 16 and 17 as adults when they commit crimes, yet also defines them as minors under the age of 18 when they are the victims of crime."[53]

The photos were private. Copening and Denson never intended to share them with anyone else and they did not transmit them to a third party. Instead, police found them when Copening had to hand over his cellphone at his high school as part of an investigation of an alleged rape. He was never a suspect; police thought that someone might have sent photos of the assault to his phone.[54]

Both Copening and Denson reached a plea agreement with the local prosecutor. Initially, they were charged with sexual exploitation of a minor under a state law targeting individuals who sexually exploit and abuse children and with creating child porn.[55] If convicted for the felonies, the couple would have faced prison time and registration as sex offenders for possibly as long as 30 years.[56] Instead, under the plea agreement, Copening admitted to two misdemeanor counts of disseminating harmful material to minors because he sent his girlfriend nude photos of himself, and he was sentenced to a year's probation.[57] Similarly, Denson, charged with two counts of felony sexual exploitation of a minor for making and possessing her photo, was sentenced to a year's probation after pleading guilty to a single count of disseminating harmful material to minors.[58] Copening and Denson completed their probations and all charges against them were dismissed by July 2016.[59]

The *Fayetteville Observer*, noting that Copening was planning to attend a university on a partial scholarship to play football, opined that the prosecution of the teens was "a stunning case of law-enforcement overzealousness. A lot more prosecutorial common sense was in order but it went missing in this case. For the sake of others who could fall into the same trap, our lawmakers need to fine-tune the child-porn statutes to make sure something like this doesn't happen again."[60]

Did Copening and Denson have grounds to challenge the prosecution's handling of the cases? As discussed in "Cyberbullying and Free Speech," a ruling by the Indiana Court of Appeals in *Salter v. State* (2009) suggests that they could have challenged the incoherency of the charges as unconstitutionally vague.[61] In *Salter*, the court reversed Herbert W. Salter's convictions for 40 counts of child exploitation and five courts of disseminating harmful content to minors for receiving, storing and sharing nude photos with a 16-year-old.[62] Under several Indiana statutes, however, the age of consent was 16.[63] The court ruled that Indiana Code section 35-49-3-3, which banned the dissemination of harmful content to minors, was unconstitutionally vague because it did not give an individual of ordinary intelligence fair notice that sending sexually explicit photos of himself to a 16-year-old, old enough to consent to sexual relations in Indiana, was banned under the law.

> By setting the legal age of consent at sixteen, the Indiana legislature has made an implied policy choice that in-person viewing of another person's genitals is "suitable matter" for a sixteen- or seventeen-year-old child. That being so, how could Salter have known that a picture of his genitals would be "harmful," that is, not "suitable," for M.B.? Asked another way, if such images are harmful to sixteen- and seventeen-year-old children, then why would our legislature allow those children to view the same matter in-person, in the course of sexual activity? These questions reveal the flaw in Indiana Code section 35-49-3-3 as applied to Salter: when read in light of well-established Indiana law setting the age of consent to sexual relations, it did not provide him with fair notice that the State would consider pictures of his genitals harmful to or unsuitable for a sixteen-year-old girl.[64]

Age of consent issues aside, the constitutionality of prosecuting a teen sexter on child pornography or exploitation of minor charges is an unresolved question. So far, two courts have reached opposite conclusions. *In re CS, 2012* (2012), a Pennsylvania trial court held that applying child pornography statutes to teen sexting failed to provide a teenager of ordinary intelligence fair notice that her activity would violate the state's Sexual Abuse of Children statute (18 Pa.C.S.A. § 6312) because the purpose behind the child porn law had little to do with teen sex.[65]

The Court of Appeals of Ohio (In Re JP (2012)), however, rejected a 13-year-old girl's attempt to have her conviction on disseminating matter harmful to juveniles in violation of a state statute reversed.[66] The teen sent nude photos of her self to an incarcerated male teen, whose age was not identified.[67] She argued that the statute was unconstitutionally vague because it failed "to provide guidelines designating which party is the victim and which party is the offender."[68] When two minors are involved it "criminalizes consensual conduct between two members of the statute's protected class, producing an absurd result, she contended."[69]

The Ohio court, however, said the application of the statute did not treat the teen as both a victim and an offender.

> The statute requires only *one* person to act in order to be culpable ... Here, only appellant engaged in the unlawful act. Further, had appellant sent *any* nude photograph to a juvenile, e.g., a nude photograph of an adult, she would still have disseminated harmful material. Simply because the image was of her does not make her any less culpable of the offense. In this case, appellant recklessly disseminated harmful material.[70]

Teen Sexting: Criminalizaton or Decriminalization?

One way to decrease the likelihood that teens engaged in harmless consensual texting are not unjustly treated by the legal system is to reduce the possibility that they can be subjected to the harsh penalties of child porn or related sexual abuse of minors charges is to classify the conduct as a misdemeanor. But that approach typically still gives prosecutors the discretion to pursue penalties disproportionate to the offense. Because in states that have chosen reform, "statutes uniformly provide for reduced penalties for teenagers who sext, relative to sentences under child pornography laws. However, they also preserve the possibility of prosecution, either in the juvenile justice system or in adult criminal court."[71]

A better way to reduce greatly the possibility that an innocuous teen-to-teen sexter is not victimized by law enforcement is to do as New Mexico has done and decriminalize one-to-one teen consensual texting. The way to eliminate the possibility all together, however, is to decriminalize distribution by teen third parties who have permission to disseminate, an approach no state has adopted.

Here is another example of why decriminalization is a more sensible and just approach than mere reform—the prosecution of Levar Allen, a 17-year-old athlete at Parkway High School in south Bossier City, La.,[72] a case that drew 32,445 supporters of a Change.org-sponsored petition sent to the city's police chief in 2016.[73] People were outraged that the Black star athlete was charged with child pornography, when a white female classmate, 16, who sent a sexually explicit photo first, was not. However, it was later reported that the girl was also charged, but only under the state's sexting law.[74]

Still, there was cause for outrage. Under Louisiana law, it is a felony for someone 17 or older to have consensual sex with someone between the ages 12 to 15. It is a misdemeanor, however, for someone age 17 to 19 to have sex with someone between the ages of 15 to 17. Therefore, if Allen, 17, and had sex with the 16-year-old classmate, he would have faced only misdemeanor charges. Yet, he was charged under the hasher felony of child pornography for engaging in virtual sexual posing with the 16-year-old.[75] That's because, the state's sexting law does not shield 17-year-olds from child pornography prosecution. Yet, it shields minors 16 years and younger from felony prosecution by providing misdemeanor fines "not less than one hundred dollars nor more than two hundred fifty dollars, imprisoned for not more than ten days, or both" and probation under certain circumstances for individuals 16 or younger.[76]

Arguing that race still might have played a role in Allen's arrest, Robby Soave, an associate editor at *Reason.com*, said no one should have been arrested.

> The worst consequence of sexting is the one that law enforcement agents carry out: arrest. If young people seeing each other's naked bodies was such a horrible crime, surely the state of Louisiana would prohibit them from having actual sex as well. And yet, it does no such thing. In Louisiana, the age of consent is 17, but people younger than 17 can consent if they are within two years of age of their partner. For people younger than 15, they can consent if the gap is three years. A 13-year-old can consent to sex with a 16-year-old for instance, but a 15-year-old cannot consent to sex with an 18-year-old. I don't understand the logic behind such a law, but then again I don't understand the logic of criminalizing consensual sexting between teenagers who are approximately the same age, either.[77]

About a year earlier, communications professor Amy Adele Hasinoff warned of arrests like Allen's in *Sexting Panic: Rethinking Criminalization, Privacy, and Consent* in support of her argument that all forms of teen sexting should be decriminalized and removed from the bias of prosecutorial discretion. "Evidence from studies of other types of crimes strongly suggests that the criminalization of sexting will have a disproportionate effect on girls, youth of color, queer youth, and low-income youth," she wrote.[78]

Hasinoff also contends that consensual sharing of sexting should be protected because the exchange is private and harmless, whereas nonconsensual texting violates privacy and is harmful.

> The problem with viewing sexting as simply deviant and criminal for everyone involved is that it makes the malicious distribution of private images seem like a normal and inevitable part of sexting. If the typical sexting scenario is instead viewed as consensual exchange of images, then it is obvious that sexting is not inherently harmful, but that malicious distribution of private images certainly is.[79]

Revenge Porn

Whether a revenge porn felony or misdemeanor statute potentially victimizes may depend almost entirely on how narrowly it is drawn. But there are major points of departure among revenge porn law activists, scholars, civil libertarian activists and defense attorneys on how best to write a statute that would pass constitutional scrutiny.

To summarize the discussion of the two schools of feminist thought, their key point of departure is over the legal standard of punishment. One side led by Mary Anne Franks, law professor and Cyber Civil Rights Initiative (CCRI) board member, does not want statutes to require intent to cause emotional distress or harassment.[80] They prefer the standard to be knowledge, reckless disclosure or the negligence. In other words, they do not want revenge porn laws to have to meet the intent standards of cyber harassment statutes, though the inclusion of such a mens rea would fortify their claim to constitutionality as opposed to the creation of a new species of unprotected speech based solely on lack of consent.[81] Nevertheless, Franks argues:

> "Intent to cause emotional distress" or "intent to harass" requirements arbitrarily distinguish between perpetrators motivated by personal desire to harm and those motivated by other reasons. Motive requirements ignore the reality that many perpetrators are motivated not by an intent to distress but by a desire to entertain, to make money, or achieve notoriety. The 2014 distribution of over a hundred celebrities' private, intimate photos on various websites makes this point abundantly clear: the disclosers in that case were hoping for Bitcoin (online currency) donations, and likely had no personal relationship to their victims at all.[82]

The other faction, led by Danielle Citron, Case Western University Law professor, contends that revenge porn laws must require a speaker to cause harm, including "emotional harm, reputational harm and financial loss," by knowing disclosure.[83]

> Revenge porn laws should apply only if a defendant disclosed another person's nude image knowing the person expected the image to be kept private and knowing the person did not consent to the disclosure. By clarifying the mental state in this way, legislation would punish only intentional betrayal of someone's privacy. Carelessly or foolishly posting someone's nude image would not constitute criminal behavior. It would not be a crime, for instance, to repost a stranger's nude photos having no idea that person intended them to be kept private.[84]

Citron believes illegal disclosure must be found to violate the victim's reasonable expectation of privacy.[85] Franks, however, prefers to omit that requirement because,

> of the benefits and drawbacks of including it. The benefit of including such language is to emphasize that the statute does not apply to images voluntarily created in commercial or public settings ... The drawback of this approach is twofold: 1. The term "reasonable expectation of privacy" might create more ambiguity than it resolves, especially considering the doctrinal baggage of the term from Fourth Amendment jurisprudence and 2. The term is an awkward fit for cases involving sexual assaults in public or semi-public settings, as well as for hacking scenarios. If privacy is included as an element, it would be prudent to address these issues explicitly.[86]

Both sides appear to agree that the statutes must carve out exemptions for disclosures that relate to newsworthiness, or the public interest, and nude photos voluntarily taken in public or in commercial settings.[87]

Other critics of revenge porn laws identify a range of concerns about their constitutionality. At minimum, the laws must require intent to harm culpability for all parties, including third parties who unknowingly redistribute posted images, intentional violation of the reasonable expectation of privacy of the victim, and exempt online intermediaries, many argue. They also put little faith in the inclusion of matters-of-public concern exemptions if the statute doesn't include a malicious intent provision. The malicious intent standard would exclude most news organizations, publishers, booksellers and libraries. The "public interest" exemption has the drawback of involving juries and judges second-guessing editorial decision-making, which many in news and publishing see as an intrusion of editorial autonomy.[88] But constitutional law heavyweight Erwin Chemerinsky argues that allowing juries to decide newsworthiness or what is in the public interest will not chill speech if a law says, "No videos of people having sex should be made public unless all of the participants consent.")[89]

Then there are critics, such as Texas defense lawyer Mark Bennett who has blogged about the revenge porn since 2013, and contends that the odds are exceedingly slim that the U.S. Supreme Court would rule in favor of a revenge porn law. In two of his blog posts, he questioned whether criminalizing pornography could be squared with the obscenity doctrine, an argument that formed the basis of *State v. Vanburen* (2016),[90] a ruling by a Vermont judge striking down the state's revenge porn law on First Amendment grounds.

> It may be true: the Court *could* rewrite the obscenity exception to cover not only what is today recognized as obscenity—works that appeal to the prurient interest; depict or describe, in a patently offensive way, sexual conduct; and lack serious literary, artistic, political, or scientific value—but also mere nudity, even if it is not patently offensive and does have serious artistic value. If it did that, then revenge porn could be obscene. But this amounts to speculative legal fiction. It could happen, but it is not, I think, likely.[91]

As Bennett reads *U.S. v Stevens*[92] and *U.S v. Alvarez*,[93] "For a revenge-porn statute to be constitutional, it would have to either not be content-based; restrict speech only in one of the nine recognized categories of unprotected speech; or restrict speech only in a newly recognized category of unprotected speech."[94] In short, Bennett does not believe a constitutionally valid revenge porn statute can be written because, "A restriction on speech is content-based if the content of the speech matters. By definition, a revenge-porn statute will be content-based: posting sexual images of a person will be restricted, but posting grumpy-cat pictures will not be. Revenge porn does not fall into one of the nine recognized categories of unprotected speech."[95] Addressing the merits of a proposed Texas law and an earlier version of the proposed federal revenge porn law, Bennett predicted victimization.

> Do-gooders will support the criminalization of bad conduct without consideration of its effect on good conduct. We'll wind up with another revenge-porn penal statute that can't be justified under current constitutional law. Fortunately, getting the U.S. Supreme Court to recognize a new category of unprotected speech is not an easy proposition. Unfortunately, people will be arrested and prosecuted, timid do-gooder trial and appellate courts will uphold the bad statute, and the government will destroy more lives before the issue hits the U.S. Supreme Court, or even the Texas Court of Criminal Appeals.[96]

Mens Rea and the First Amendment

Unfortunately, First Amendment doctrine provides no crystal clarity on the issue of intent-to-harm. On one hand, there are doctrines such as incitement requiring that a speaker intended to cause a specific type of lawlessness that resulted from his speech.[97] On the other hand, expression can be censored for national security reasons under the prior restraint doctrine when it poses only a serious and imminent threat.[98] The fighting words doctrine is another example of a free speech restriction in which the speaker's state of mind is not material because fighting words "are characterized by their tendency to provoke a violent response."[99]

According to a small number of scholars who have published on the issue, such as Larry Alexander, of University of San Diego School of Law, precedents show that a speaker's intent is not essential to speech protection. "I have argued that a speaker's mental state with respect to whether her words will cause harms that the government can legitimately seek to prevent should be immaterial to whether her speech is protected by the First Amendment—except to the extent her mental state bears on whether sanctioning her will chill others' protectable speech."[100]

Acknowledging that many free speech doctrines do not require a finding of the speaker's intent, Leslie Kendrick, of the University of Virginia School of Law, however, contends that intent matters in free speech.

> A guilty mind alone is not sufficient to render speech unprotected. Some ill-intentioned speech will receive protection as a result of other free-speech considerations, such as listener interests. Nor is intent necessary to the regulation of certain speech categories, such as speech involving special duties and commercial speech. These exceptions are consistent with an autonomy-based account of free speech. Outside of such categories, speaker's intent is one important factor in the question of whether speech is protected. Where other free-speech considerations have been satisfied, it forms a final barrier between speech and regulation. The fact that First Amendment doctrine often makes it so is not an accident or mistake, but rather a reflection of the intuitive relationship between speaker interests and protection for expression, between autonomy and freedom of speech.[101]

Arizona

In 2014, Arizona passed a statute that did not include an intent-to-harass requirement or a public interests exemption provision.[102] In 2015, the ACLU, representing a coalition of bookstores, newspapers, photographers, publishers, and librarians, reached a settlement with Arizona to halt enforcement of its revenge porn statute.[103] Does the settlement indicate that the CCRI/Frank's position is invalid? No, because the judge made no ruling on the merits of the statute. The 2016 revision of the statute, however, rejects the CCRI-Frank's approach because its terms include an intent-to-harass standard.

The original statute did not require intent to harass or to cause emotional harm. Instead, a speaker had to act intentionally and with knowledge that consent was not given: "It is unlawful to intentionally disclose, display, distribute, publish, advertise or offer a photograph, videotape, film or digital recording of another person in a state of nudity or engaged in specific sexual activities if the person knows or should have known that the depicted person has not consented to the disclosure."[104] According to the Model Penal Code, a person acts "knowingly" if "he is aware that his conduct is of that nature or that such circumstances exist … he is aware that it is practically certain that his conduct will cause such a result" even though he doesn't act with the specific intent to cause the result.[105]

In short, knowing culpability is based on negligence, just about the least defendant-protective culpability standard, with strict liability being the least protective. "Purposeful" intent is the most defendant-protective level of mens rea—"the first and most serious of the mental states…. If a criminal acts with the goal of bringing about the harmful consequences that result from his behavior, "Sherry F. Colb, of Cornell Law School explains, then he has acted with purpose …" if Ben set fire to Dan's home in order to cause Dan's death, then Ben has killed Dan 'purposely.'"[106] Still, "knowing" culpability has been considered an acceptable level of criminal blame-worthiness along with purpose, recklessness, and negligence. "If, for example, Ben had no desire to kill Dan but nonetheless set fire to Dan's occupied home (perhaps because Ben wanted to destroy documents that happen to be located there), then Ben would have killed Dan knowingly."[107]

In support of its argument, the CCRI correctly argues that many privacy violations do not require a defendant to intend harm because "the bad act is the disclosure of private material without consent, so the statute should require that a person do this intentionally."[108] Therefore, because a revenge porn statute protects privacy, an intent to disclose without consent standard is constitutionally sufficient, it contends. Still, all-party eavesdropping statutes, for example, such as Illinois's PA 98-1142, require that a breach of consent be based on a reasonable expectation of privacy.[109] Accordingly, revenge porn statutes should include similar terms, but the original Arizona statute did not. (Clay Clavert, of the University of Florida College of Journalism and Communications, however, argues that the inclusion of "'reasonable expectation of privacy' verbiage" in a revenge porn law undermines the motive of revenge porn law advocates because it is fairly clear now that "only an unreasonable person would take the risk" of sharing nude photos with intimate partners.[110]

The statute's public interest provision did not specifically protect booksellers, librarians and newspapers, such as the plaintiffs who brought the lawsuit in 2014. It also failed to exempt disclosure of images in the bona fide public interest, or similar language, which would, arguably, cover photos used by the Arizona plaintiffs. Instead, it exempted, "Lawful and common practices of law enforcement, reporting unlawful activity, or when permitted or required by law or rule in legal proceedings. Lawful and common practices of medical treatment; images involving voluntary exposure in a public or commercial setting."[111] That standard left open the strong possibility that a bookseller or librarian would not have stocked certain books out of fear that the books were banned under the law. Thus, the statute would been susceptible to a challenge of constitutional vagueness because it failed to require that the victim's expectation of privacy was reasonable, did not give adequate notice of what type of nonconsensual images were exempted and, therefore, chilled constitutionally protected expression.

Under the 2016 revision, a speaker is culpable when he discloses with "the intent to harm, harass, intimidate, threaten or coerce" the person depicted in a revenge porn image, and that person must have a reasonable expectation of privacy concerning the image.[112] The ACLU stamped its approval on the revised law. "Under the previous iteration the statute criminalized anyone who published or distributed a nude image without the consent of the person," said Will Gaona, ACLU policy director. "The most recent version narrows its application and gets behind the behavior it was intended to address."[113]

Vermont, Obscenity and Strict Scrutiny

The impact of the second challenge to a revenge porn law was definitive, although prosecutors in Vermont quickly sought to overturn the ruling.[114] In late June 2016, a county trial judge dismissed a case against Rebekah Van Buren, and struck down the state's "Disclosure of Sexually Explicit Images without Consent" statute (13 V.S.A. §2606(b)(1)) as unconstitutional under strict scrutiny analysis. The statute banned knowing disclosure without consent with "the intent to harm, harass, intimidate, threaten, or coerce the person depicted, and the disclosure would cause a reasonable person to suffer harm."[115]

The judge, however, focused on obscenity. Sexually explicit photos, or pornography, are not necessarily obscene, he said, which is a fundamental precept of the obscenity doctrine. Yet, the statute treated pornography and obscenity synonymously.

> The court must agree with Defendant that merely "nude" photographs cannot be considered obscene and thus subject to the lower standard of review and protection. Nude photographs may not involve any depiction of a sexual act or be prurient. A person might send such photographs with no intent to appeal to such interests. Although § 2606(a)(3) attempts to define nude to only include specific depictions, they could still fit those categories and not be obscene under the constitutional definition. What would have been clearer would have been to prohibit the disclosure of "obscene" photographs and depictions and then define that term in line with constitutional definitions. While there is argument that such revenge pornography should be considered obscene simply because of the intent it is used, there is no present authoritative law that would allow this court to take such a step in enlarging the area of unprotected speech under the First Amendment.[116]

The judge characterized the statute as content restrictive and presumptively unconstitutional. Therefore, the judge applied strict scrutiny analysis to test the statute's constitutionality. He ruled that the statute failed under the second prong of the test—it was not narrowly tailored—because Vermont provided alternatives to achieve its goal such as civil actions for injunctive relief and the right to bring a lawsuit against a defendant who knowingly disclosed nonconsensual sexually explicit images.[117]

Rhode Island

The vetoed Rhode Island statute identified the criminal mental state as "intentional," which is considered synonymous to purposeful. Under the bill, a person would have been guilty of "unauthorized dissemination of indecent material" when he "intentionally" disclosed or did so without affirmative consent of the depicted person and with no legitimate purpose.[118] (After the New York Court of Appeals ruling in *Marquan*,[119] the "no legitimate purpose" clause would have raised concerns, but a criminal culpability standard of intentionally would have been constitutionally acceptable.) But there was no requirement that the defendant intended harm. Its public interest exception provisions included the reporting and publishing ones identified in the first Arizona law and a catchall phrase of "when the dissemination constitutes a matter of public concern."[120]

The ACLU condemned the proposed law, saying "that the legislation would criminalize the retweeting or reposting online of nude images—including newsworthy images like those disseminated from Abu Ghraib without the direct consent of the person in the image. The prohibition applied even if the picture was initially taken and shared consensually. In addition, the legislation contained no requirement that sharing the images actually caused harm or emotional distress to anybody. As a result, the legislation made a criminal out of any person who shared online even newsworthy images."[121] Nevertheless, the Rhode Island House of Representatives passed its second revenge porn ban in March 2017 with no substantial revisions.[122]

The Proposed Federal Intimate Privacy Protection Act (IPPA)

When Congresswoman Jackie Speier introduced the IPPA in July 2016, 34 states had revenge porn laws on their books.[123] Speier's proposal would bring uniformity to revenge porn laws because states had taken differing approaches in their mens rea requirements, definitions of the unlawful speech and degrees of criminality. The Cyberbullying Research Center noted that,

> Most outlaw the "dissemination of intimate images" because of the lack of consent from the affected party, while some states recognize the behavior as an act of cyberharassment and stalking, and prohibit it in that respect. Generally speaking, each state's statute is different in classifying exactly what is unlawful. Using Florida law as an example (passed in November 2015, which makes the act a 1st degree misdemeanor and 3rd degree felony for repeat offenders), the state defines *sexual cyberharassment* as publishing a sexually explicit image of a person that conveys the personal identification information of the depicted person without the person's consent and for the purpose of causing substantial emotional distress. New Jersey, the first state to pass a law against nonconsensual porn, considers it a 3rd degree invasion of privacy if someone discloses any image in which intimate parts of another are exposed, and defines "disclosure" as selling, manufacturing, giving, providing, mailing, delivering, or advertising an image. The state of Virginia categorizes their law under *crimes involving morals and decency*, and considers it *the unlawful dissemination or sale of images of another*.[124]

The proposal may bring uniformity, but will it create victims because of its unconstitutional overreach and vagueness? It contains the standard exemptions for public interests images, voluntary public nudity and for online intermediaries already protected under Section 230 of the Communications Decency Act. But its culpability requirement raises concerns among some civil libertarians.

> Whoever knowingly uses the mail, any interactive computer service or electronic communication service or electronic communication system of interstate commerce,

> or any other facility of interstate or foreign commerce to distribute a visual depiction of a person who is identifiable from the image itself or information displayed in connection with the image and who is engaging in sexually explicit conduct, or of the naked genitals or post-pubescent female nipple of a person, with reckless disregard for the person's lack of consent to the distribution, shall be fined under this title or imprisoned not more than 5 years, or both.[125]

Under the bill, the culpable mental state is recklessness. "Recklessness" is an acceptable level of criminal blameworthiness. "If Ben had closed his eyes and fired a pistol repeatedly in different directions, knowing that several people were nearby and stood a significant chance of being killed, then Ben would have acted recklessly," Professor Colb explains.[126] Is a person who downloads a posted image and emails a nude reckless if he or she did not get consent from the individual depicted? If the answer is yes, a substantial number of online users, possessing no intent to harm, would be culpable under the proposed law.

Though Speier's office cited Neil Richards, privacy law expert at Washington University Law School in St. Louis, as backing the bill, his support cannot be accurately described as unequivocal. "I think this law does a good job of regulating nonconsensual pornography and protecting free expression by excluding information in the 'bona fide public interest' and limiting its scope to reckless disclosures," Richards said. "I'd prefer that the law limited itself to intentional disclosures, which would trade off some protection against revenge porn for a greater protection for free expression online. If passed, I think the bill may be challenged under the First Amendment."[127] Eugene Volokh, of UCLA School of Law, however, said, "this law seems quite narrow, and pretty clearly defined."[128]

But *Vocativ.com* also reported that three groups that gave consultation to Speier about the proposal, the Center for Democracy & Technology (CDT), the Electronic Frontier Foundation and the ACLU, said the bill was overly broad.[129] Not surprisingly given previous critiques of state revenge porn laws, the three civil liberties groups said the bill needed to include intent-to-harm and reasonable expectation of privacy requirements because anyone who shares an image once it has been disclosed would not necessarily know that the photo is nonconsensual, and the drafters needed to add specificity to the public interest exemption.[130]

Mike Masnick, editor of *Techdirt Blog*, offered an assessment of the bill and a prediction: "In the end, two and a half years of effort means that the bill isn't as horrible as some of the earliest suggestions, but it's still not clear that it's constitutional. It seems likely that the ACLU, and possibly others, will likely challenge this law should it pass and then I guess we'll find out what the courts actually think of it."[131]

Conclusion

If one were to draft a revenge porn statute that stood the best chance of surviving constitutional scrutiny, it would include an intent to cause serious emotional distress or harm requirement, link disclosure to a breach of reasonable expectation of privacy, provide a public interest and newsworthy exemption, explicitly shield third parties like websites unless they extort victims for financial gain and ban only images that would be considered obscene under the three-prong *Miller v. California* (1973) test.[132] Yet, no state has adopted such an approach, and the federal proposal is not a step in that free-speech protective direction. Thus, the flaws in existing statutes substantially increase the likelihood that a defendant will be deprived of his constitutional rights until, as defense attorney Bennett predicts, high level appeals courts step in.

Likewise, with the way states approach criminalizing consensual teen sexting. New Mexico has taken a bold step toward decriminalizing teen sexting, but, as this book went to press, there was little indication that other states were prepared to follow, much less go further and extend criminal immunity to third party teens who consensually share nude or sexually explicit photos. Until then, the likelihood that other teens will endure mockeries of justice experienced by North Carolina's Cormega Copening and Brianna Denson remains high.

Notes

1. Seth F. Kreimer, "Pervasive Image Capture and the First Amendment: Memory, Discourse, and the Right to Record," *University of Pennsylvania Law Review* (2011): 339, http://scholarship.law.upenn.edu/faculty_scholarship/302, p. 339 (accessed August 22, 2016).
2. Press Release, "Governor Susana Martinez Signs Legislation Increasing Sentences for Child Pornography Possession, Distribution, and Manufacturing," *State of New Mexico*, February 25, 2016, http://www.governor.state.nm.us/uploads/PressRelease/191a4150146 34aa89604e0b4790e4768/Governor_Susana_Martinez_Signs_Legislation_Increasing_Sentences_for_Child_Pornography_Possession__Distribution__and_Manufacturing.pdf (accessed July 28, 2016).
3. Joseph O. Oluwole and Preston C. Green III, *SextEd: Obscentity versus Free Speech in Our Schools* (Santa Barbara: Praeger, 2013), 195; Neb. Revised Statutes §28—1463 (Supp. 2009) (accessed July 28, 2016).

4. Oluwole and Green, *SextEd: Obscentity versus Free Speech in Our Schools*, 136–37; Fla. Stat. Ann § 847.0141, https://www.flsenate.gov/Laws/Statutes/2012/847.0141 (accessed July 28, 2016).
5. Adam Walsh Child Protection and Safety Act (2006), Pub. L 109-248, https://www.gpo.gov/fdsys/pkg/PLAW-109publ248/html/PLAW-109publ248.htm (accessed July 28, 2016).
6. Sameer Hinduja and Justin W. Patchin, "State Sexting Laws: A Brief Review of State Sexting and Revenge Porn Laws and Policies," Cyberbullying Research Center, July 2015, http://www.cyberbullying.org/state-sexting-laws.pdf (accessed July 20, 2016).
7. C. A. Goldberg, "State Revenge Porn Laws (last updated May 24, 2016)," http://www.cagoldberglaw.com/states-with-revenge-porn-laws/ (accessed July 19, 2016).
8. Steven Nelson, "Lawmakers Unveil Proposal to Take Nip Out of Revenge Porn," *U.S. News & World Report*, July 14, 2016, 2:07 PM, http://www.usnews.com/news/articles/2016-07-14/lawmakers-lay-bare-proposal-to-take-nip-out-of-revenge-porn (accessed July 28, 2016).
9. Katherine Gregg, "Raimondo Vetoes 'Revenge Porn' Bill, Saying it Could Chill Free Speech," *Providence Journal*, June 21, 2016, 10:59 AM, http://www.providencejournal.com/news/20160621/raimondo-vetoes-revenge-porn-bill-saying-it-could-chill-free-speech (accessed July 28, 2016).
10. "R. I. Gov. Raimondo First to Veto Revenge Porn Bill," *Lexis-Nexis State Net*, 2016, https://www.lexisnexis.com/communities/state-net/b/capitol-journal/archive/2016/07/01/ri-gov-raimondo-first-to-veto-revenge-porn-bill.aspx (accessed July 21, 2016)
11. Justin W. Patchin, "Summary of State Sexting Laws," Cyberbullying Research Center, July 9, 2013, http://cyberbullying.org/summary-of-state-sexting-laws (accessed August 10, 2016).
12. Miller v. Skumanick, 605 F. Supp. 2d 636 (M.D. Pa. 2008) aff'd Miller v. Mitchell, 598 F. 3d (3d Cir. 2010).
13. Hanna Rosin, "Why Kids Sext," *The Atlantic*, November 2014, http://www.theatlantic.com/magazine/archive/2014/11/why-kids-sext/380798/ (accessed August 10, 2016).
14. Kathy Martinez-Prather and Donna M. Vandiver, "Sexting Among Teenagers in the United States: A Retrospective Analysis of Identifying Motivating Factors, Potential Targets and the Role of a Capable Guardian," *International Journal of Cyber Criminology* 8 (January–June 2014): 21–35, 24, 26, http://www.cybercrimejournal.com/pratherVandiverijcc2014vol8issue1.pdf (accessed August 17, 2016).
15. *Emerging Patterns and Trends #1: Youth Produced Sexual Content* (Cambridge, UK: Internet Watch Foundation March 10, 2015), 3, 11, https://www.iwf.org.uk/assets/media/resources/Emerging%20Patterns%20and%20Trends%20Report%201%20-%20Youth-Produced%20Sexual%20Content.pdf (accessed August 17, 2016).
16. Randi Kaye, "How a Cellphone Picture Led to A Girl's Suicide," *CNN.com*, October 7, 2010, 3:51 PM EDT, http://www.cnn.com/2010/LIVING/10/07/hope.witsells.story/ (accessed August 17, 2016).
17. See Nick Wolf, "San Diego Jury Convicts Revenge-Porn Website Operator Kevin Bollaert," *The Guardian*, February 3, 2015, 7:58 EST, https://www.theguardian.com/culture/2015/feb/03/revenge-porn-website-operator-convicted-san-diego-kevin-bollaert (accessed August 17, 2016).

18. Kaplan v. California, 413 U.S. 115, 119–20 (1973).
19. Texas v. Johnson, 491 U.S. 397, 404 (1989).
20. Miller v. California, 413 U.S. 15 (1973).
21. U.S. v. Stevens, 130 S. Ct. 1577, 1586 (2010).
22. U.S. v. Stevens, 533 F. 3d 218, 235, n. 16 (2008).
23. Erznoznik v. Jacksonville, 422 U.S. 205, 212–13 (1975).
24. Clark v. Roccanova, 772 F. Supp. 2d 844 (2011).
25. Henry Campbell Black, *Black's Law Dictionary* (St. Paul: West Publishing, 1979), 889.
26. Elonis v. U.S., 135 S. Ct. 2001, 2009 (2015).
27. Danielle Citron, "How to Make Revenge Porn a Crime," *Slate.com*, November 7, 2013, http://www.slate.com/articles/news_and_politics/jurisprudence/2013/11/making_revenge_porn_a_crime_without_trampling_free_speech.html (accessed August 17, 2016).
28. People v. Marquan, 24 N.Y.3d 1 (2014).
29. State v. Bishop, COA14-1227 (N.C. Ct. App. June 16, 2015), http://caselaw.findlaw.com/nc-court-of-appeals/1705020.html (accessed August 17, 2016).
30. "R. I. Gov. Raimondo First to Veto Revenge Porn Bill."
31. David Kravets, "MPPA Opposes Proposed Minnesota Revenge Porn Law, Says it Limits Speech," April 1, 1016, 9 AM, http://arstechnica.com/tech-policy/2016/04/mpaa-opposes-proposed-minnesota-revenge-porn-law-says-it-limits-speech/ (accessed July 28, 2016).
32. Arechigo Stokka, "Minnesota Passes New Revenge Porn Law," Attorneys at Law (blog), 2016, http://www.arechigo-stokka.com/minnesota-passes-new-revenge-porn-law/ (accessed July 28, 2016).
33. Mary Ann Franks, "It's Time for Congress to Protect Intimate Privacy," *Huffington Post*, July 18, 2016, http://www.huffingtonpost.com/mary-anne-franks/revenge-porn-intimate-privacy-protection-act_b_11034998.html (accessed July 28, 2016).
34. "The Supreme Court 2014 Term: Leading Case: Federal Statutes and Regulations: Federal Threats Statute—Mens Rea and the First Amendment—Elonis v. United States," *Harvard Law Review* 129 (November 10, 2015): 331, 335, http://harvardlawreview.org/2015/11/elonis-v-united-states/ (accessed July 28, 2016).
35. J. H. Beale Jr., "Consent in Criminal Law," *Harvard Law Review* 8 (1895): 317, 323.
36. Stephen J. Schulhofer, "Consent: What it Means and Why It's Time to Require It," *McGeorge Law Review* 47 (2016): 665, 667, http://www.mcgeorge.edu/Documents/Publications/schulhoferTUOPLR474.pdf (accessed July 28, 2016).
37. Seth F. Kreimer, "Sex, Laws and Videophones: The Problem of Juvenile Sexting Prosecutions," in *Children, Sexuality and the Law*, ed. Sacha M. Coupet and Ellen Marrus (New York: New York University Press, 2015), 149.
38. Schulhofer, "Consent: What it Means and Why It's Time to Require It," 665, n. 35.
39. Jessica Roy, "Could Affirmative Consent Help Stop Revenge Porn," *New York Magazine*, July 6, 2015, 3:06 PM, http://nymag.com/thecut/2015/06/could-affirmative-consent-stop-revenge-porn.html (accessed July 28, 2016).
40. Kendra Alleyne, "Apex Woman is the Charged under North Carolina's New 'Revenge Porn' Law," *Campbell Law Observer*, April 12, 2016, http://campbelllawobserver.com/apex-woman-is-the-first-charged-under-north-carolinas-new-revenge-porn-law/ (accessed July 28, 2016).

41. Edwin H. Byrd III, "Reflections on Willful, Wanton, Reckless, and Gross Negligence," *Louisiana Law Review* 48 (1988): 1383–84, http://digitalcommons.law.lsu.edu/lalrev/vol48/iss6/3)(accessed July 28, 2016).
42. See 18 U.S.C. § 1460; 18 U.S.C. § 1461; 18 U.S.C. § 1462; 18 U.S.C. § 1463.
43. Clark v. Roccanova, 772 F. Supp. 2d 844, 846–47, 49.
44. Kreimer, "Sex, Laws and Videophones: The Problem of Juvenile Sexting Prosecutions," 150.
45. Miller v. Skumanick, 605 F. Supp. 2d 636 (M.D. Pa. 2008) aff'd Miller v. Mitchell, 598 F. 3d (3d Cir. 2010).
46. Kreimer, "Sex, Laws and Videophones: The Problem of Juvenile Sexting Prosecutions," 150.
47. Eugene Volokh, "Statutory Rape Laws and Ages of Consent," *The Washington Post* (blog), May 1, 2015, https://www.washingtonpost.com/news/volokh-conspiracy/wp/2015/05/01/statutory-rape-laws-in-the-u-s/ (accessed July 25, 2016).
48. Indiana Annotated Code § 35-42-4-4 (2014), http://iga.in.gov/static-documents/9/a/6/7/9a6777b4/TITLE35_AR42_ch4.pdf (accessed July 25, 2016).
49. A.H. v. Florida, 949 So. 2d 234 (Fla. Dist. Ct. App. 2007).
50. U.S. v. Annunziato, 293 F. 3d 373, 379 (2d Cir. 1961).
51. Paul Woolverton, "Lawmaker: Child Porn Law Misused Against Sexting Teens, But Tools Needed to Fight Predators," *Fayetteville Observer*, September 12, 2015, http://www.fayobserver.com/news/local/lawmaker-child-porn-law-misused-against-sexting-teens-but-tools/article_bff69e1f-de50-5bbb-b4a6-e003ff4efdd1.html (accessed July 25, 2016).
52. Kelly McLaughlin, "High School Quarterback and his Girlfriend both Charged by Cops for Privately Sharing Nude Photos of Themselves," *DailyMail.com*, September 5, 2015, 16:35 EST, http://www.dailymail.co.uk/news/article-3223533/North-Carolina-hgh-school-quarterback-girlfriend-charged-adults-exchanging-nude-photos.html (July 25, 2016).
53. Paul Woolverton, "Fayetteville Teen Facing Felony Charges in Sexting Case Agrees to Plea Bargain," *Fayetteville Observer*, September 11, 2015, http://www.fayobserver.com/news/local/fayetteville-teen-facing-felony-charges-in-sexting-case-agrees-to/article_f8c8e156-9660-57b4-a2b8-b65a6bd8bbb2.html (accessed July 25, 2016).
54. Ibid.
55. Ibid.
56. Nancy McClearly, "Suspended Jack Britt Quarterback Accused of Texting Sexual Graphic Pictures," *Fayetteville Observer*, August 31, 2015, http://www.fayobserver.com/news/local/suspended-jack-britt-quarterback-accused-of-texting-sexually-graphic-pictures/article_66414597-5155-5a84-a19d-e7bb3111a3af.html?mode=jqm (accessed July 26, 2016).
57. Woolverton, "Fayetteville Teen Facing Felony Charges in Sexting Case Agrees to Plea Bargain."
58. Ibid.
59. Paul Woolverton, "Sexting Charges Dismissed for Fayetteville Teenager," *Fayetteville Observer*, July 7, 2016, http://www.fayobserver.com/news/crime_courts/sexting-charges-dismissed-for-fayetteville-teenager/article_bae7b802-8b76-542b-9cd5-f0671cee3d47.html (accessed July 26, 2016).

60. "Student-Porn Case Shows a Law that Needs Fixing," *Fayetteville Observer*, July 10, 2016, http://www.fayobserver.com/opinion/editorials/our-view-student-porn-case-shows-a-law-that-needs/article_65c2cb40-2f05-5f50-a0c1-4b7792ad7400.html (accessed July 26, 2016).
61. Salter v. State, 906 NE 2d 212 (Ind. Ct. App. 2009).
62. Ibid., 213.
63. Ibid., 215.
64. Ibid., 223.
65. See Melissa R. Lorang, Dale E. McNiel, and Renee Binder, "Minors and Sexting: Legal Implications," *Journal of the American Academy of Psychiatric and the Law Online* 44 (March 2016): 73–81, http://www.jaapl.org/content/44/1/73.full#xref-ref-24-1.
66. In Re JP, 2012 Ohio 1451, http://scholar.google.com/scholar_case?q=sexting+consent+vagueness&hl=en&as_sdt=ffffffffffffe04&case=1822132883904602280 0&scilh=0 (accessed July 26, 2016).
67. Ibid., 2.
68. Ibid., 24.
69. Ibid.
70. Ibid., 34.
71. Joanna R. Lampe, "A Victimless Sex Crime: The Case for Decriminalizing Consensual Teen Sexting," *University of Michigan Journal of Law Reform* 46 (2013): 703, 711.
72. Shaun King, "King: 17-Year-Old Black Boy Sexting with 16-year-old White Girl and Guess Who's Charged with Child Pornography," *Daily News*, April 28, 2016, 1:45 PM, http://www.nydailynews.com/news/national/king-black-boy-sexting-white-girl-ends-child-porn-charge-article-1.2617742 (accessed July 28, 2016).
73. "Drop Levar Allen's Charges and Change Outrageous Laws," Change.org, 2016, https://www.change.org/p/drop-levar-allen-s-charges-and-change-outrageous-laws (accessed July 28, 2016).
74. Travis M. Andrews, "How Some National Media Called a Louisiana Sheriff Racist Over Incomplete Information," *Washington Post*, May 6, 2016, https://www.washingtonpost.com/news/morning-mix/wp/2016/05/06/how-some-national-media-called-a-louisiana-sheriff-racist-over-incomplete-information/ (accessed July 28, 2016).
75. "Louisiana Age of Consent and Statutory Rape Laws, 2016," http://age-of-consent.findthedata.com/l/19/Louisiana (accessed July 28, 2016).
76. "Sexting," LA Rev Stat § 14:81.1.1, http://law.justia.com/codes/louisiana/2011/rs/title14/rs14-81-1-1 (accessed July 28, 2016).
77. Robby Soave, "White Teen Girl Sends Nude Photos to Black Male. Police Arrest Minor for Child Porn," *Reason.com*, May 2, 2016, 3:50 PM, http://reason.com/blog/2016/05/02/white-teen-girl-sends-nude-photos-to-bla (accessed July 28, 2016).
78. Amy Adele Hasinoff, *Sexting Panic: Rethinking Criminalization, Privacy, and Consent* (Champaign: University of Illinois Press, 2015), 39.
79. Ibid., 41.
80. Mary Anne Franks, "Drafting an Effective 'Revenge Porn' Law: A Guide for Legislators," August 17, 2015, doi:10.2139/ssrn.2468823 (accessed August 1, 2016).
81. Ibid., 7.

82. Ibid., 6.
83. Danielle Citron, *Hate Crimes in Cyberspace* (Cambridge, MA: Harvard University Press, 2014), 152
84. Ibid., 150.
85. Ibid., 152.
86. Franks, "Drafting an Effective 'Revenge Porn' Law: A Guide for Legislators," 9, n. 44.
87. Danielle Keats Citron and Mary Anne Franks, "Criminalizing Revenge Porn," *Wake Forest Law Review* 49 (2014): 101, 133–34, http://isp.yale.edu/sites/default/files/page-attachments/Danielle%20Citron%20-%20Criminalizing%20Revenge%20Porn%20-%20FESC.pdf (accessed August 1, 2016).
88. Mark Bennett, "2015.41: Citron and Richards on Revenge Porn," *Defending People* (blog), February 26, 2015, http://blog.bennettandbennett.com/2015/02/2015-41-citron-and-richards-on-revenge-porn/ (accessed August 2, 2016).
89. Erwin Chemerinsky, "Op-Ed: Privacy vs. Speech in the Hulk Hogan Sex Tape Trial," *Los Angeles Times*, March 12, 2016, 5:00 AM, http://www.latimes.com/opinion/op-ed/la-oe-0314-chemerinsky-hulk-hogan-gawker-20160314-story.html (accessed August 2, 2016).
90. State v. Vanburen, No. 1144-12-15Bncr (Vermont Sup. Ct., June 30, 2016), https://www.documentcloud.org/documents/2998410-State-v-VanBuren-1144-12-15-Bncr.html (accessed August 3, 2016).
91. Mark Bennett, "Are States Criminalizing Revenge Porn Constitutional?," *Defending People* (blog), October 14, 2013, http://blog.bennettandbennett.com/2013/10/are-statutes-criminalizing-revenge-porn-constitutional/#obscenity (accessed August 3, 2016).
92. U.S. v. Stevens, 130 S. Ct. 1577.
93. U.S. v. Alvarez, 132 S. Ct. 2537 (2012).
94. Mark Bennett, "2015.4: Another Proposed Revenge-Porn Statute," *Defending People* (blog), January 2, 2015, http://blog.bennettandbennett.com/2015/01/2015-4-another-proposed-revenge-porn-statute/ (accessed August 3, 2016).
95. Ibid.
96. Ibid.
97. Brandenburg v. Ohio, 395 U.S. 444 (1969).
98. New York Times Co. v. United States, 403 U.S. 713, 726–27 (1971).
99. City of Billings v. Nelson, 322 P. 3d 1039, 1042–45 (2014).
100. Larry Alexander, "Free Speech and the Speaker's Intent: A Replay to Kendrick," *Columbia Law Review Sidebar* 115 (2015): 1, http://ssrn.com/abstract=2576384 (accessed August 2, 2016).
101. Leslie Kendrick, "Free Speech and Guilty Minds," *Columbia Law Review* 115 (2014): 1255, 1295, http://ssrn.com/abstract=2460950 (accessed August 2, 2016).
102. American Civil Liberties Union (Press release), "Bookstores, Publishers, News Media, Librarians, and Photographers Charge Law Violates Freedom of Speech," September 23, 2014, https://www.aclu.org/news/first-amendment-lawsuit-challenges-arizona-criminal-law-banning-nude-images (accessed August 1, 2016).
103. Antigone Books v Mark Brnovich, 2:14-cv-02100-PHX-SRB (July 10, 2015), http://mediacoalition.org/files/litigation/antigone-books-brnovich-final-decree.pdf (accessed August 1, 2016).

104. Arizona State Legislature § 13-1425, http://www.azleg.gov/FormatDocument.asp?inDoc=/ars/13/01425.htm&Title=13&DocType=ARS html (accessed August 2, 2016).
105. Vernellia R. Randall, Model Penal Code § 2.02. General Requirements of Culpability, University of Dayton Law School, http://academic.udayton.edu/legaled/crimlaw/02-Elements/04MPC2-02.htm (accessed August 1, 2016).
106. Sherry F. Colb, "Why Can't Jurors Distinguish 'Knowing' from 'Reckless Misconduct?,'" *Verdict*, January 11, 2012, https://verdict.justia.com/2012/01/11/why-cant-jurors-distinguish-knowing-from-reckless-misconduct (accessed August 1, 2016).
107. Ibid.
108. Mary Anne Franks, "Frequently Asked Questions," Cyber Civil Rights Initiative, 2016, http://www.cybercivilrights.org/faqs/ (accessed August 1, 2016).
109. Illinois Public Act 098-1142 (2014), http://www.ilga.gov/legislation/publicacts/fulltext.asp?Name=098-1142, (accessed August 1, 2016).
110. Clay Calvert, "Revenge Porn and Freedom of Expression: Legislative Pushback to an Online Weapon of Emotional and Reputational Destruction," *Fordham Intellectual Property, Media & Entertainment Law Journal* 24 (Spring 2014): 673–99.
111. Arizona State Legislature §13-1425 (B)1, 2, 3.
112. Arizona House Bill, AZ-2016-HB 2001 (March 11, 2016), https://legiscan.com/AZ/text/HB2001/2016 (accessed August 10, 2016).
113. Ryan Van Velzer, "Senate Passes Bill Revising 2014 'Revenge Porn' Law," *Arizona Capitol Times*, March 7, 2016, 4:30 PM, http://azcapitoltimes.com/news/2016/03/07/senate-passes-bill-revising-2014-revenge-porn-law/ (accessed August 3, 2016).
114. Mark Davis, "Vermont's First Revenge Porn Law Under First Amendment Challenge," *Seven Days*, August 2, 2016, 9:33 AM, http://www.sevendaysvt.com/OffMessage/archives/2016/08/02/vermonts-revenge-porn-law-under-first-amendment-challenge (accessed August 3, 2016).
115. Vermont Statutes Annotated §2606(b)(1), The Vermont Statutes Online, Vermont General Assembly, 2016, http://legislature.vermont.gov/statutes/section/13/059/02606 (accessed August 3, 2016).
116. Vanburen, No. 1144-12-15Bncr at 3.
117. Ibid., 4.
118. 2016—H7537, "An Act Related to Criminal Devices-Electronic Image Devices," amended 11-64-3. Unauthorized dissemination of indecent material. Rhode Island General Assembly, January Session A.D. 2016, http://webserver.rilin.state.ri.us/BillText/BillText16/HouseText16/H7537.pdf (accessed August 1, 2016).
119. People v. Marquan, 24 N.Y.3d 1 (2014).
120. 2016—H7537, "An Act Related to Criminal Devices-Electronic Image Devices."
121. American Civil Liberties Union of Rhode Island, "2016 Legislation," http://www.riaclu.org/legislation (accessed August 1, 2016).
122. Associated Press, "Rhode Island House Again Votes to Ban 'Revenge Porn,'" March 21, 2017, 5:51 PM, U.S. News & World Report, https://www.usnews.com/news/best-states/rhode-island/articles/2017-03-21/rhode-island-house-again-votes-to-ban-revenge-porn (accessed May 6, 2017).
123. Congresswoman Jackie Speier (Press Release), "Congresswoman Speier, Fellow Members of Congress Take on Nonconsensual Pornography, AKA Revenge Porn," July 14, 2016,

http://speier.house.gov/index.php?option=com_content&view=article&id=1866:-congresswoman-speier-fellow-members-of-congress-take-on-nonconsensual-pornography-aka-revenge-porn&catid=20&Itemid=7 (accessed August 2, 2016).

124. Sameer Hinduja, "Revenge Porn Research, Laws, and Help for Victims," Cyberbullying Research Center, July 14, 2016, http://cyberbullying.org/revenge-porn-research-laws-help-victims (accessed August 2, 2016).
125. Discussion Draft H.R. II, June 9, 2016, 4:02 PM, Congresswoman Jackie Speier, http://speier.house.gov/images/pdf/IPPA_Final.pdf (accessed August 2, 2016).
126. Colb, "Why Can't Jurors Distinguish 'Knowing' from 'Reckless Misconduct?"
127. Neil Schoenherr, "WashU Expert: Proposed 'Revenge Porn' Bill Balances Regulation with Protecting Free Expression," *The Source*, July 14, 2016, https://source.wustl.edu/2016/07/washu-expert/ (accessed August 2, 2016).
128. Tracy Clark-Flory, "Bill that Would Make Revenge Porn Federal Crime to be Introduced," *Vocativ*, July 14, 2016, 10:25 ET, http://www.vocativ.com/339362/federal-revenge-porn-bill/ (accessed August 2, 2016).
129. Ibid.
130. Ibid.
131. Mike Masnick, "Federal Revenge Porn Bill Not as Bad as It Could have Been, Still Probably Unconstitutional," *Techdirt.com*, July 15, 2016, 10:39 AM, https://www.techdirt.com/articles/20160714/17282334978/federal-revenge-porn-bill-not-as-bad-as-it-could-have-been-still-probably-unconstitutional.shtmlhttp://www.cybercivilrights.org/ccri-blog/ (accessed August 3, 2016)
132. Miller v. California, 413 U.S. 15 (1973).

· 7 ·

THE SHORT LIFE AND QUICK DEATH OF THE FIRST CYBERBULLYING LAW IN CANADA (AUGUST 6, 2013–DECEMBER 10, 2015)

The death of Nova Scotia's first cyberbullying law in December 2015 started with a tweet from a waggish teen and the foolish decision by an actress-turned-elected official to invoke the statute in retaliation.

Just about anyone in the world can go online and access a full-frontal nude image of Lenore Zann from her performance in the 2008 Showtime cable television series *The L-Word*.[1] More to the point, voters living in Truro-Bible Hill-Millbrook-Salmon River, Nova Scotia, Canada, can download the photo and other nude photographs of Zann from her movies any time they want.

Why are voters relevant? They elected Zann to Canada's Nova Scotia House of Assembly in 2009. She represented Truro-Bible Hill-Millbrook-Salmon River electoral district. During her first election campaign in 2009, operatives for the opposing Nova Scotia Liberal Party leaked the nude image to the news media in an effort to sabotage her campaign, and a digitally blurred version of it appear on television.[2] It didn't work. Zann won, and again in 2013.

The naked images of the Member of the Legislative Assembly (MLA) would not disappear from public scrutiny. In December 2013, a few months after her re-election, two of her constituents, teenager Nick Scissons and Ray McLennan, a citizen political commentator, tweeted a copy of that *L-Word* image. Scissons was the first to tweet. "What happened to the old Lenore?" he asked rhetorically.[3]

Scissons and Zann traded tweets.[4] She demanded that the high school student remove the image from his twitter account.[5] In a thinly veiled threat, she alluded to the province's soon-to-be enacted Cyber-safety Act, which she voted for. "ThankYouNS distribution of images of this nature fall under new Cyberbullying laws & is an indictable offence."[6]

McLennan joined the online squabble. His tweet, linked to a similar image, chastised Zann: "could Lenore Zann be harassing a HS student for tweeting these pornographic images of her [sic] *The L Word?*"[7] In another tweet, McLennan said, "you realize that haranguing on a (high school) student makes you look like a fool, not leadership material."[8] Zann reported Scissons and McLennan to the police and Nova Scotia's newly created CyberScan Unit.[9]

Nova Scotia's Cyber-safety Act (2013), "the first legislation of its kind in Canada that protects the victims of cyberbullying,"[10] authorized the Unit to investigate and judge accusations of cyberbullying. The Cyber-safety Act (CSA) defined cyberbullying as,

> any electronic communication through the use of technology including, without limiting the generality of the foregoing, computers, other electronic devices, social networks, text messaging, instant messaging, websites and electronic mail, typically repeated or with continuing effect, that is intended or ought reasonably be expected to cause fear, intimidation, humiliation, distress or other damage or harm to another person's health, emotional wellbeing, self-esteem or reputation, and includes assisting or encouraging such communication in any way.[11]

The Unit ordered Scissons and McLennan to stop cyberbullying.[12] Failure to comply, the Unit investigators told them, could result in a one-year court order limiting their use, or confiscation, of their computers, cellphones or other Internet service.[13] The Unit might also report them to the police who could charge them with criminal harassment, sexual harassment or defamatory libel, they were told.[14] The police, however, said there was no crime to investigate. Zann dropped her complaint.[15]

Zann miscalculated. Inadvertently, her heavy-handedness publicized the flaws of the new statute. "The recent case of Nova Scotia MLA Lenore Zann illustrates the act's breadth and problems around enforcement," said Canadian Civil Liberties Union's Cara Faith Zwibel in a newspaper opinion piece, urging that the law be amended to protect free speech rights. "Politicians deserve to be protected from true harassment and bullying just like anyone else, but we need to distinguish between true bullying and fair criticisms and comments, particularly when it comes to public officials. The fact that Ms. Zann has subsequently withdrawn her complaint is of no comfort—the involvement of the CyberSCAN unit and their threats worked, so there is no need for her to take things further."[16]

If any one individual can be credited for the demise of the Cyber-safety Act, it is David Fraser, author of Canadian Privacy Law Blog, partner at McInnes Cooper in Halifax, Nova Scotia, and outspoken critic of the Act since it was first proposed in April 2013 in response to the death of Rehtaeh Parsons, a target of alleged sexual assault, malicious sexting and months of slut-shaming.[17] Early on, Fraser said legislators rushed the bill through in response to the public outcry over Parsons's death without thoughtfully considering its impact on free expression. "The legislature has actually done a disservice to those they desperately want to help by hastily passing a law that will likely be struck down when the first victims go to the courts seeking assistance," wrote Fraser in an April 27, 2013 blog post.[18]

The scenario did not unfold as quickly as Fraser predicted, but soon enough. By December 2015, Fraser's arguments on behalf of Robert Snell, a businessman, charged under the act after posting comments on social media about his former partner Giles Crouch, persuaded the Nova Scotia Supreme Court to strike the Cyber-safety Act down.[19]

Global Phenomenon

Since the Internet and human nature are borderless, it should come as no surprise that cyberbullying is a global phenomenon. The United Kingdom, for example, relies mostly on analog-era laws to pursue cyberbullies, with the glaring exception of its "Disclosing private sexual photographs and films with intent to cause distress," or revenge porn, statute.[20] But no liberal democratic nation has moved as quickly as state legislatures in the U.S., and the Nova Scotia and the Canadian national governments to enact laws specifically to tackle offensive and abusive online expression. The Parliament of Canada passed Bill C-13, the Protecting Canadians from Online Crime Act, in December 2014.[21] The statute, effective March 10, 2015, criminalized the use of intimate images without consent and authorities may order online intermediaries and phone companies to track, preserve and hand over personal data and phone calls.[22] By coincidence, one of the first cases brought under Bill C-13 involved six male high school students in Nova Scotia, charged in July 2016 with distributing intimate images without consent and possession and distribution of child pornography following a year-long investigation.[23] Like the Cyber-safety Act, Bill C-13, was passed in response to the death of Rehtaeh Parsons.[24] Though Bill C-13 was widely criticized,[25] no one had challenged its constitutionality in court when this work went to press. (In March 2017, the students pled guilty to the charges, providing no clarity about the statute's constitutionality.)[26]

The failure of the Cyber-safety Act to survive constitutional review did not have a direct bearing on the fate of Bill C-13. Its demise, however, is further evidence that cyberbullying legislation passed in the frenzy of a moral panic is likely to trample over free expression rights and victimize law abiding individuals similar to the experiences of defendants in New York, North Carolina and Missouri. Are accused criminal cyberbullies really victims? A number of Nova Scotians, individuals investigated or prosecuted under the failed law, believed they were victimized and talked about suing for compensation by bringing a class action lawsuit.[27]

Free Expression in Canada

Canada and the U.S. share a free expression tradition dating back to John Milton's Areopagitica (1644) and William Blackstone's Commentaries on the Laws of England (1753)[28] Unlike the U.K., Canada and the U.S. have single documents that serve as written constitutions, the key difference being that unlike statutory and common law rights, constitutional rights "cannot be diminished or eliminated by ordinary legislative action, but only through a specified amendment process."[29] Canada created a new constitution in 1982, which incorporated its older Charter of Rights and Freedoms in 1982.[30] "Canada's legal system is quite open to using case precedents from both England and the United States when there are insufficient ones in the realm of Canadian law."[31]

The U.S. and Canada also share many core free expression values such as "individual self-fulfillment, truth attainment, and political discourse."[32] Yet, the Canadian Supreme Court is far more likely to uphold laws limiting free expression than its U.S. counterpart. That tendency stems largely from a two-step analysis imposed on it by Canada's constitution, Sections 1 and 2 of Canadian Charter of Rights and Freedoms.

Section 2(b) Fundamental Rights

Under the Canadian Charter, section 2(b), "Everyone" has the "fundamental freedom of thought, belief, opinion and expression, including freedom of the press and other media of communication."[33] In the landmark ruling, *Attorney General (Quebec) v. Irwin Toy Ltd.*, Chief Justice Dickson defined expression broadly, encompassing threats of violence, provided the meaning is conveyed in a physically violent manner.

> Activity which (1) does not convey or attempt to convey a meaning, and thus has no content of expression, or (2) which conveys a meaning but through a violent form of expression, is not within the protected sphere of conduct … it is clear, for example, that a murderer or rapist cannot invoke freedom of expression in justification of the form of expression he has chosen.[34]

In *Irwin Toy*, Dickson also identified three social values free expression protections promote. Plaintiffs must demonstrate that their speech promotes at least one of the three values, Dickson said, (1) seeking and attaining the truth is an inherently good activity; (2) participation in social and political decision-making is to be fostered and encouraged; (3) the diversity in forms of individual self-fulfillment and human flourishing ought to be cultivated in an essentially tolerant, indeed welcoming environment not only for the sake of those who convey a meaning, but also for the sake of those to whom it is conveyed.[35]

Section 1, Fundamental Rights

Section 1 of the Charter, however, checks the apparent expansiveness of free expression protections. "The *Canadian Charter of Rights and Freedoms* guarantees the rights and freedoms set out in it subject only to such reasonable limits prescribed by law as can be demonstrably justified in a free and democratic society."[36] In other words, courts may rule that expression is protected under Section 1, which frequently occurs. Yet, almost as frequently, the Supreme Court of Canada concludes that the statute limiting free expression is a reasonable limit on the defendant's right of free expression because the law protects another important societal interest. As Anglo-American constitutional law expert Grant Huscroft has noted,

> The real scope of the freedom of expression emerges only following consideration of section 1 of the *Charter* … Section 1 establishes a broad standard against which limits

> are to be judged, with the onus being on the government to demonstrate justification. At this stage of the analysis, the content of expression is not only relevant to the protection it will receive, it may be practically determinative. It is easier to limit expression the Court considers "low value" in nature.[37]

In the landmark criminal due process case, *R v. Oakes* (1986), the Supreme Court of Canada said the party invoking section 1, the government, must show by "a preponderance of evidence that the limitation is demonstrably justified in a free and democratic society" and that the "evidence offered to meet this standard 'should be cogent and persuasive and make clear to the Court the consequences of imposing or imposing the limit.'"[38] Next, government must meet a balancing test, showing that, "At a minimum, an objective must relate to societal concerns which are pressing and substantial in a free and democratic society before it can be characterized as sufficiently important. Second, the party invoking s. 1 must show the means to be reasonable and demonstratively justified."[39]

Fairness, Rationally Connected, Overbreadth, Vagueness and Proportionality

Part two of the balancing test is a proportionality test involving three components, the Court in *Oakes* explained: (1) "fair" and "rationally connected to the objective;" (2) the means of achieving the objective should "impair the right in question as little as possible [overbreadth and vagueness];" and (3) "Lastly, there must be proportionality between the effects of the limiting measure and the objective—the more severe the deleterious effects of a measure, the more important the objective must be."[40]

The Supreme Court of Canada applied Section 2 analysis of *reasonableness, overbreadth, vagueness* and *proportionality* in the landmark free expression case, *R v. Keegstra* (1990), in which the defendant, a teacher was charged under Section 319 (2) of the Criminal Code with "promoting hatred by communicating anti-semitic statements to his students."[41] Based on the Section 2 analysis, the Court concluded that Keegstra's statements were protected speech.

> Communications which are intended to promote hatred against identifiable groups do not fall within the ambit of a possible *s*. 2(b) exception concerning expression manifested in a violent form. This exception refers only to expression communicated directly through physical harm. Hate propaganda is not analogous to violence. It conveys a message that is repugnant, but the repugnance stems from the content of the message and not its form. As for threats of violence, they are not excluded from the definition of expression envisioned by *s*.2(b).[42]

The Court applied the balancing test. It noted that there was an "obviously rational connection" between the statute and its objective.[43] The Section 319(2) of the Criminal Code did not "unduly impair" freedom of expression, the Court said. "This Section does not suffer from overbreadth or vagueness; rather the terms of the offence indicate that S. 319 (2) possesses definitional limits which act as safeguards to ensure that it will capture only expressive activity which is openly hostile to Parliament's objective, and will thus attack only the harm at which the prohibition is targeted."[44]

The Court upheld the law criminalizing hate speech under a Section 1 analysis because it met the proportionality test—it had (1) "rational connection to the purpose of preventing the harm caused by hate propaganda" (2) it represented a "minimal impairment of the presumption of innocence" … (3) "the importance of preventing the harm caused by hate propaganda is not outweighed by Parliament's infringement."[45]

Writing for the majority, Chief Justice Brian Dickson characterized the Court's analysis as "contextual" and not "inflexible levels of scrutiny," categorization of expressive activity.[46] Columbia University Law Professor Kent Greenawalt argues that the Chief Justice Dickson, "inflexible levels of scrutiny" allusion was "undoubtedly a reference to American constitutional approaches."[47] In other words, the majority of the Court rejected having to select strict, intermediate, exacting scrutiny, or the rational basis tests to determine a statute's the constitutionality. Had the Supreme Court of Canada taken the U.S. approach, it would have had to apply strict scrutiny analysis.

Because hate speech restrictions imposed limits on a certain type of expression, they are content-restrictive. Therefore, under U.S. constitutional law, strict scrutiny applies to most content-based regulations of protected political and artistic free speech, certainly a hate-speech restriction.[48] Under strict scrutiny, the Canadian Court would have had to determine whether the hate speech provision of the Criminal Code of Canada advanced a compelling government interest and whether the law was the least restrictive means of achieving that interest.[49] For example, applying strict scrutiny in *R.A.V v. St Paul*, the U.S. Supreme Court ruled that a hate speech ordinance was "plainly not" "reasonably necessary to achieve" the "compelling interest" of St. Paul, Minnesota, because a content-neutral ordinance "would have precisely the same beneficial effect … The politicians of St. Paul are entitled to express [hostility toward racist speech]—but not through the means of imposing unique limitations upon speakers who (however benightedly) disagree."[50]

Canadian proportionality review does not reject U.S. forms of scrutiny, Thurgood Marshall Professor of Constitutional Law Harvard Law School Vicki C. Jackson, argues. Instead. Jackson contends, rationality, minimal impairment and proportionality tests "correspond with elements in U.S. 'strict,' 'intermediate,' or 'rational basis' scrutiny: the need for a sufficiently important or 'compelling' government purpose; the rational connection required between the means chosen and the end; and the 'minimal impairment' inquiry into whether there are less restrictive means towards the same goal."[51]

Nevertheless, as a general matter, Canadian free expression law is not as protective of free speech as First Amendment-free speech law. "For the most part, the Supreme Court of Canada defers to legislative judgments about both the need for speech restrictions and the reasonableness of the fit between the burden placed on the expressive activity and the advancement of the government's interest," notes comparative and free speech law professor Robert J. Krotoszynski.[52]

Vagueness, Overbreadth and "Reading Down"

Constitutional scrutiny under Canadian law includes vagueness, overbreadth and, as possible remedies, "reading down," or "reading in." Reading down, or in, are closely related to "severance,"[53] a judicial practice exercised by courts in the U.S. [54] "Reading down refers to a process in which courts adopt an interpretation of a statute so as to avoid constitutional problems that might lead to its complete invalidation. Courts used this remedy before the Charter by, for example, reading down municipal by-laws against lawn signs so that they did not apply to federal election signs."[55]

Vagueness and overbreadth challenges are rooted in principles codified in Section 7 of the Charter: "Everyone has the right to life, liberty and security of the person and the right not to be deprived thereof except in accordance with the principles of fundamental justice."[56]

Petitioners, however, must meet a two-part test to show that a statute infringes upon fundamental liberties—"show that the law interferes with, or deprives them of, their life, liberty or security of the person. Once they have established that s. 7 is engaged, they must then show that the deprivation in question is not in accordance with the principles of fundamental justice."[57]

Section 7 does not identify the principles, but "[o]ver the course of 32 years of Charter adjudication, [The Supreme Court of Canada] has worked to define the minimum constitutional requirements that a law that trenches on life, liberty or security of the person must meet … laws that impinge on life, liberty or security of the person must not be arbitrary, overbroad, or have consequences that are grossly disproportionate to their object."[58]

Arbitrariness

That constitutional sound statutes not impose arbitrary requirements and classifications is a precept of due process in liberal democracies.[59] In *Chaoulli v. Quebec* (2005), the Supreme Court of Canada said,

> A law is arbitrary where 'it bears no relation to, or is inconsistent with, the objective that lies behind [it].' To determine whether this is the case, it is necessary to consider the state interest and societal concerns that the provision is meant to reflect: In order not to be arbitrary, the limit on life, liberty and security requires not only a theoretical connection between the limit and the legislative goal, but a real connection on the facts. The onus of showing lack of connection in this sense rests with the claimant. The question in every case is whether the measure is arbitrary in the sense of bearing no real relation to the goal and hence being manifestly unfair. The more serious the impingement on the person's liberty and security, the more clear must be the connection.[60]

Vagueness, Overbroad and Reading Down

Canada and the U.S.'s doctrines of vagueness and overbreadth are essentially the same. Section 7 of the Charter provides protections from vague and overbroad laws. "It is a principle of fundamental justice that vague laws are invalid. Generally, if (1) a law is vague, and (2) deprives one of life, liberty, or security of the person, the law is void. This principle is called the 'void for vagueness' doctrine."[61]

The Court in *R. v. Nova Scotia Pharmaceutical Society* (1992) said, "A vague provision does not provide an adequate basis for legal debate, that is for reaching a conclusion as to its meaning by reasoned analysis applying legal criteria. It does not sufficiently delineate any area of risk, and thus can provide neither fair notice to the citizen nor a limitation of enforcement discretion."[62] In *Canadian Foundation for Children, Youth and the Law v. Attorney General of Canada* (2004), the Supreme Court of Canada offered a more straightforward definition, one that is typically used to describe the U.S. void-for-vagueness doctrine. "A vague law prevents the citizen from realizing when he or she is entering an area of risk for criminal sanction."[63]

Under Section 7 of the Charter, "[a]n overbroad law differs from a vague law in that an overbroad law may be perfectly clear, but go too far in impairing an individual's liberty."[64] In *R v. Heywood* (1994), the court explained,

> Overbreadth analysis looks at the means chosen by the state in relation to its purpose. In considering whether a legislative provision is overbroad, a court must ask the question: are those means necessary to achieve the State objective? If the State, in pursuing a legitimate objective, uses means which are broader than is necessary to accomplish that objective, the principles of fundamental justice will be violated because the individual's rights will have been limited for no reason. The effect of overbreadth is that in some applications the law is arbitrary or disproportionate.[65]

Canadian courts may "read down" or "read in" to save a statute. Courts, however, do not have a free hand to save a statute. The Court in *Heywood* noted,

> reading in or reading down will only be warranted where: (i) the legislative objective is obvious, and reading in or reading down would constitute a lesser intrusion on that objective than striking down the legislation; (ii) the choice of means used by the legislature is not so unequivocal that reading in or reading down would unacceptably intrude into the legislative sphere; and (iii) reading in or reading down would not impact on budgetary decisions to such an extent that it would change the nature of the legislation at issue.[66]

Canadian law professors David Schneiderman and Kent Roach say the Court has resorted to reading down or in to save overbroad laws that infringed on speech in *Keegstra*, *R v. Sharpe*, *R. v. Butler*, *Little Sisters* and *Khawaja*.[67] Keegstra, as discussed above, involved a statute banning hate speech.[68] In *Sharpe*, the Court upheld a criminal code prohibiting the possession of child pornography.[69] In *Butler* (1992), the Court upheld the validity of a law making it illegal to possess and sell obscene materials.[70] In *Little Sisters*, the Court ruled that the Customs Act, which allowed inspectors to select materials they believed to be obscene, was a violation of free expression but justified the procedure under Section 1.[71] In *Khawaja*, the Court rejected an argument that Canada's anti-terrorism act infringed upon free expression.[72] Consequently, Schneiderman and Roach are of the opinion that

> Canada's unstable freedom of expression tradition, as well as perhaps an unwarranted deference to the state and its officials and an overly optimistic view about the benefits achieved by restricting speech, can also be seen in the willingness of courts to salvage vague and overbroad laws by reading them down. Such remedies give front-line officials considerable discretion and may result in a chill on legitimate, albeit unpopular and unconventional, forms of expression. Despite its claim to being a fundamental

> freedom which has eclipsed other Charter rights, much more work remains to be done in securing the central place that freedom of expression should occupy in the evolving Canadian constitutional landscape.[73]

Crouch v. Snell

In *Crouch v. Snell*, the Supreme Court of Nova Scotia declined to read in or down to save the Cyber-safety Act, a testament to the statute's feverish conception and deeply flawed construction. The case involved two former business partners whose relationship had become acrimonious. Giles W. Crouch said that after he resigned from the company, Mediabadger, in late 2013,[74] Robert Snell, represented by Fraser, engaged in a "'smear campaign' against him on social media that continued until December 11, 2014 when a Justice of the Peace granted the Protection Order against Mr. Snell," which prohibited him from communicating directly or indirectly with him or about him, or to remove such comments from social media sites.[75]

In arguments before the court in August 2015, the Nova Scotia Attorney General's office defended the ex parte proceeding as necessary to protect the bullied victim from retaliation and that a public petition with 300,000 names called for new laws to tackle the speed and pervasiveness of online communications. "The definition [of cyberbullying], while broad, is not overly broad," Crown attorney Debbie Brown argued.[76]

About three months earlier, A. Wayne MacKay, a law professor at Dalhousie University's Schulich School of Law and chair of Nova Scotia's Task Force on Bullying and Cyberbullying,[77] defended the Act, though the Task Force had never recommended criminal prosecution as a remedy to cyberbullying.[78] He said legislators should revise the Act's ex parte proceedings to allow accused cyberbullies to defend them selves in court before restrictions are imposed. But in the final analysis, MacKay said, "the act is a necessary and positive addition to giving victims some remedies they didn't have before."[79]

In December 2015, the court struck down the entire Act, finding that several provisions of the statute, particularly those permitting ex parte proceedings and additional punishment without trial, were irrational, arbitrary, vague, overbroad and an infringement on fundamental rights under the Canadian Charter. Under a Section 2(b) analysis, the court determined that in general cyberbullying, as defined by the statute, is protected speech because it "conveys or attempts to convey meaning" and to "the extend that" it "falls short of violence or threats of violence."[80] Citing *Irwin v. Toy*, in its second step of the

2(b) analysis, the court found that the statute's purpose was speech restrictive. "Prevention of cyberbullying is a purpose that aims to restrict the content of expression by singling out particular meanings that are not to be conveyed, i.e. communication that is intended or ought reasonably be expected to cause fear, intimidation, humiliation, distress or other damage or harm to another person's health, emotional well-being, self-esteem or reputation."[81]

Applying the *Oakes* analysis of reasonableness, the court found that the infringement of expression could not be justified under Section 2 (b), even though the "Cyber-safety Act is social legislation that requires ... a greater degree of deference to the Legislature."[82] The Act, the court noted, failed to provide an "intelligible" guidance to help judicial administrative officials considering applications for protective orders from making arbitrary decisions. "It does not provide sufficiently clear standards to avoid arbitrary and discriminatory applications. The Legislature has given a plenary discretion to do whatever seems best in a wide set of circumstances."[83]

The Court found that the means—the exparte application process for a protection order—that legislators chose to achieve the objectives of creating "efficient and cost effective administrative and court processes to address cyberbullying, in order to protect Nova Scotians from undue harm to their reputation and their mental well-being"[84] were not rationally linked. Thus, the statute failed the *Oakes* rational-connection standard.[85]

The Act was a "colossal failure" in meeting the *MacDonald* minimal impairment test, the court said, because its definition ("any electronic communication ... intended or ought reasonably be expected to cause fear, intimidation, humiliation, distress or other damage or harm to another person's health, emotional well-being, self-esteem or reputation, and includes assisting or encouraging such communication in any way")[86] "unnecessarily catches material that has little or nothing to do with the prevention of cyberbullying."[87]

> The Attorney General submits that the *Act* does not pertain to private communication between individuals, but rather, deals with "cyber messages or public communications." With respect, I find that the *Act* restricts both public and private communications. Furthermore, the *Act* provides no defences, and proof of harm is not required. These factors all culminate in a legislative scheme that infringes on s. 2(b) of the *Charter* much more than is necessary to meet the legislative objectives.[88]

Because non-compliance could result in imprisonment, the court ruled, that the statute posed a threat to fundamental principles of the right to life, liberty and security under Section 7 of the *Charter*.[89] The irrationality of the ex parte proceedings was another reason for finding the Act to be arbitrary.[90]

The court found the Act to be overbroad, too. "By casting the net too broadly, and failing to require proof of intent or harm, or to delineate any defences, the Act limits the right to liberty in a way that has no connection with the mischief it seeks to address."[91]

As for vagueness, the court said, "The prohibition against cyberbullying is not overly vague. But … the added requirement that the respondent be deemed likely to engage in cyberbullying in the future is incredibly vague and not in accordance with the principles of fundamental justice."[92]

Ultimately, the court rejected severance, or reading in or down and struck down the Act it its entirety, noting that because "the *Act* was enacted to fill a 'gap' in the legislation does not mean that victims of cyberbullying will be completely without redress in the time it takes to enact new cyberbullying legislation. They will have the usual—albeit imperfect—civil and criminal avenues available to them."[93]

"The law showed all the hallmarks of legislation crafted in the heat of the moment, intended to address a political objective as much as a social one," Fraser wrote in an op-ed piece. "[Legislators] did not convene the experts and never consulted with Professor Wayne MacKay, who led the province's task force on this important issue. The law was doomed from Day 1: it was overbroad and ripe for abuse. Any new law needs to clearly articulate what is cyberbullying and what it is not. It needs to take into account the inherent vulnerability of young people and also consider the value we place on free expression."[94]

Conclusion

Eight months after, the Nova Scotia Justice Department had not launched an appeal or introduced a revision. The CyberScan Unit's web site notified readers that, "The CyberSCAN investigative unit will continue to operate but will shift focus to education and public awareness. Victims of online bullying can still call us for advice and help redirect their cases to the appropriate authority or agency for help."[95]

Meanwhile, Nova Scotian Rob Romard sought to become a plaintiff in a possible individual or class action against the provincial government for unfairly labeling him a cyberbully.[96] In March 2015, the CyberScan unit issued a warning to Romard, saying his Internet postings about Cape Breton Hyundai, a former employer, constituted cyberbullying.[97] Romard said, "he lost wages and his reputation has suffered as a result of being labeled a cyberbully.

'It's kind of like a wrongful conviction. There's no way for me to appeal this or anything.'"[98]

Fraser, who said others claiming victimization by the Act had contacted him, did not dismiss the possibility of bringing an individual or class action against the government. "There is a precedent for the courts saying 'You made a mistake, you abused people's charter rights, and you need to compensate people for that.' But there's not a lot of law out there and this statute was so unique in a lot of ways, there's no case law out there about an analogous sort of thing, which in a way is a good thing."[99]

Even if nothing comes of the talk to sue, it can be reasonable asserted that the Cyber-safety Act, forged in the heat of a moral panic, unfairly stigmatized Nova Scotians who engaged in constitutionally protected speech.

Notes

1. Neetan Zimmerman, "Here's The Naked 'Photo' This Politician Really Doesn't Want You to See," *Gawker.com*, December 16, 2013, 8:04 PM, http://gawker.com/heres-the-naked-photo-this-politician-really-doesnt-wan-1484524367 (accessed August 1, 2016).
2. Andrew Douglas, "I Liked Lenore Zann Better as a B-Movie Actress," *Frank Magazine*, http://www.frankmagazine.ca/node/2184 (accessed August 17, 2016).
3. Tristen Hopper, "Lenore Zann, Actress Turned Nova Scotia MLA, Launches Cyberbullying Investigation after Teen Tweets Nude Image of her from The L Word," *The National Post*, December 13, January 25, 2013, 6:53 AM ET, http://news.nationalpost.com/news/canada/lenore-zann-actress-turned-nova-scotia-mla-launches-cyberbullying-investigation-after-teen-tweets-nude-image-of-her-from-the-l-word (accessed August 1, 2016).
4. Ibid.
5. Ibid.
6. Ibid.
7. CBC, "Lenore Zann's Cyberbullying Report Catches another Tweeter," *CBC News*, December 14, 2013, 11:40 AM AT, http://www.cbc.ca/news/canada/nova-scotia/lenore-zann-s-cyberbullying-report-catches-another-tweeter-1.2464225 (accessed August 17, 2016).
8. Douglas, "I Liked Lenore Zann Better as a B-Movie Actress."
9. Ibid.
10. CyberScan, "Nova Scotia Cyber Safety," http://cyberscan.novascotia.ca/ (accessed August 1, 2016)
11. *Cyber-safety Act*, S.N.S. 2013, c. 2, s. 3(1), http://www.canlii.org/en/ns/laws/stat/sns-2013-c-2/latest/sns-2013-c-2.html (accessed August 17, 2016).
12. CBC News, "Lenore Zann's Cyberbullying Report Catches Another Tweeter," *National Post*, December 14, 2013, 11:40 AM AT, http://www.cbc.ca/news/canada/nova-scotia/lenore-zann-s-cyberbullying-report-catches-another-tweeter-1.2464225 (accessed August 1, 2016).

13. Douglas, "I Liked Lenore Zann Better as a B-Movie Actress."
14. Ibid.
15. Daily Mail Reporter, "Canadian Politician Condemns 'Cyber-bullying' by Teenager Who Put Her Lesbian Topless Shower Scene Online," *Daily Mail*, December 14, 2013, 16:51 EST, http://www.dailymail.co.uk/news/article-2523733/Nova-Scotia-politician-Lenore-Zann-cyberbullied-topless-shower-scene-photo.html (accessed August 1, 2016).
16. Faith Zwibel, "Zann Case Perfect Illustration of Cyber-Safety Law's Overreach," *Chronicle Herald*, January 2, 2014, 2:10 AM, http://thechronicleherald.ca/opinion/1176803-zann-case-perfect-illustration-of-cyber-safety-law%E2%80%99s-overreach (accessed August 9, 2016).
17. Emily Bazelon, "Sex Scourge," *Slate*, April 10, 2013, 6:43 PM, http://www.slate.com/articles/double_x/doublex/2013/04/rehtaeh_parsons_rape_case_why_do_these_keep_happening.single.html (accessed August 9, 2016).
18. David Fraser, "Analysis of the Nova Scotia Anti-Bullying Legislation," *Canadian Privacy Law Blog* (blog), April 27, 2013, http://blog.privacylawyer.ca/search?q=cyberbullying (accessed August 9, 2016).
19. Crouch v. Snell [2015] NSCC 340, http://www.courts.ns.ca/decisions_of_courts/documents/2015nssc340.pdf
20. Section 33 of the Criminal Justice and Courts Act 2015, United Kingdom National Archives, http://www.legislation.gov.uk/ukpga/2015/2/section/33/enacted (accessed August 17, 2016).
21. Statutes of Canada, Second Session, Forty-first Parliament, 62–63 Elizabeth II, 2013–2014, Parliament of Canada, http://www.parl.gc.ca/HousePublications/Publication.aspx?DocId=6830553 (accessed July 19, 2016).
22. APA NewsLaw, "On March 10, 2015, Bill 13 Came Into Effect. The Bill is Known as the Protection Canadians from Online Crime Act," March 11, 2015, https://apanewslaw.wordpress.com/2015/03/11/on-march-9-2015-bill-c%E2%80%9013-came-into-effect-the-bill-is-known-as-the-protecting-canadians-from-online-crime-act/ (accessed July 19, 2016.)
23. Michael McDonald, "Bridgewater High School Students Charged after Sharing Intimate Photos of 20 Girls Without Consent," *The Huffington Post*, July 9, 2016, 11:59 AM EDT, http://www.huffingtonpost.ca/2016/07/09/bridgewater-ns-cyberbullying_n_10904856.html (accessed July 19, 2016).
24. Bazelon, "Sex Scourge."
25. Evan Dyer, "Cyberbullying Bill Draws Fire from Diverse Mix of Critics," *CBCNews*, October 20, 2014, 6:48 AM ET, http://www.cbc.ca/news/politics/cyberbullying-bill-draws-fire-from-diverse-mix-of-critics-1.2803637 (accessed July 19, 2016).
26. Michael MacDonald and Alison Auld, "Nova Scotia Intimate-Photo Case Results in Guilty Pleas from All Six Accused, *The Daily Courier*, March 22, 2017, 2:54 PM, http://www.kelownadailycourier.ca/news/national_news/article_d59ac5b1-66ee-5646-9c1b-91daf571d880.html (accessed May 6, 2017).
27. Tom Ayers, "'Victims' of Defunct Nova Scotia Cyberbullying Law Consider Class Action," *LocalExpress.Ca*, June 13, 2016, 3:40 PM, https://www.localxpress.ca/local-news/victims-of-defunct-nova-scotia-cyberbullying-law-considering-class-action-suit-315209 (accessed July 19, 2016).
28. William Blackstone, "Commentaries on the Laws of England in Four Books," *Online Library of Liberty* 1 (2004–2016), http://oll.libertyfund.org/titles/2140 (accessed July 15, 2016).

29. Paul Bender, "The Canadian Charter of Rights and Freedoms and the United States Bill of Rights: A Comparison," *McGill Law Journal* 28 (1983): 811, 813, n. 1, http://papers.ssrn.com/sol3/papers.cfm?abstract_id=1425213 (accessed August 17, 2016).
30. Constitution Act, "Canadian Charter of Rights and Freedoms," *Minister of Justice and the Attorney of Canada* (1982), § 2(b), http://laws-lois.justice.gc.ca/eng/const/page-15.html (accessed August 17, 2016).
31. Selinar Koonar, "Justice Systems in Canada and the U.S," American Bar Association Business Law Section *Young Lawyer Forum Newsletter* (February, 2009), http://apps.americanbar.org/buslaw/committees/CL983500pub/newsletter/200906/koonar.pdf (accessed July 16, 2016).
32. Crouch v. Snell, at para 104.
33. Constitution Act, "Canadian Charter of Rights and Freedoms."
34. Attorney General (Quebec) v. Irwin Toy Ltd., [1989] 1 S.C.R. 927 at 931, 970, http://scc-csc.lexum.com/scc-csc/scc-csc/en/443/1/document.do (accessed July 19, 2016).
35. Ibid., 976.
36. Constitution Act, "Canadian Charter of Rights and Freedoms."
37. Grant Huscroft, "The Constitutional and Cultural Underpinnings of Freedom of Expression: Lessons from the United States and Canada," *Queensland Law Journal* 3 (2006): 186, http://ssrn.com/abstract=1357496 (accessed August 9, 2016).
38. Robert J. Krotoszynski Jr., *The First Amendment in Cross-Cultural Perspective: A Comparative Legal Analysis of the Freedom of Speech* (New York: New York University Press, 2006), 42.
39. R. v. Oakes, [1986] 1 SCR 103 at para. 9, https://scc-csc.lexum.com/scc-csc/scc-csc/en/item/117/index.do (accessed July 29, 2016).
40. R. v. Oakes, at para.70.
41. R v. Keegstra, [1990] 3 S.C.R. 697, https://www.canlii.org/en/ca/scc/doc/1990/1990canlii24/1990canlii24.pdf (accessed May 12, 2017).
42. Keegstra, at 698.
43. Keegstra, at 699.
44. Keegstra, at 700.
45. Keegstra, at 705
46. Keegstra, at 767.
47. Kent Greenawalt, "Free Speech in the United States and Canada," *Law and Contemporary Problems*, 55, 5 (Winter 1992): 22, http://scholarship.law.duke.edu/lcp/vol55/iss1/2 (accessed July 29, 2016).
48. United States v. Eichman, 110 S. Ct. 2404, 2409 (1990); Texas v. Johnson, 491 U.S. 397 (1989); Boos v. Barry, 485 U.S. 312 (1988); Carey v. Brown, 447 U.S. 455 (1980)
49. Reed v. Town of Gilbert, 135 S. Ct. 2218, 2222 (2015).
50. R.A.V. v. St. Paul, Minnesota, 505 U.S. 377, 396 (1992).
51. Vicki C. Jackson, "Constitutional Law in the Age of Proportionality," *The Yale Law Journal* 8 (June, 2015), http://www.yalelawjournal.org/feature/constitutional-law-in-an-age-of-proportionality (accessed August 17, 2016).
52. Robert J. Krotoszynski Jr., *The First Amendment in Cross-Cultural Perspective: A Comparative Legal Analysis of the Freedom of Speech* (New York: New York University Press, 2006), 43.
53. Crouch v. Snell, 2015, at paras. 212–14.
54. People v. Marquan, 24 NY 3d 1, 11 (2014).

55. Kent Roach, "Enforcement of the Charter—Subsections 24(1) and 52(1)," *Supreme Court Law Review* 62 (2013): 494, http://www.law.utoronto.ca/utfl_file/count/documents/Roach/Chapter%209%20Roach.pdf (accessed August 9, 2016).
56. Constitution Act, 1982, Canadian Charter of Rights and Freedoms, *Minister of Justice and the Attorney of Canada*, Section 7.
57. Carter v. Canada (Attorney General), 2015 SCC 5, at para 55, Judgments of the Supreme Court of Canada, https://scc-csc.lexum.com/scc-csc/scc-csc/en/item/14637/index.do (accessed July 29, 2016).
58. Carter v. Canada (Attorney General), 2015 SCC 5, at para 72.
59. Ohio Bell Telephone Co. v Public Utilities Commission, 301 U.S. 292, 302 (1937).
60. Chaoulli v. Quebec (Attorney General), 2005 SCC 35, at paras. 130–31, Judgments of the Supreme Court of Canada, https://scc-csc.lexum.com/scc-csc/scc-csc/en/item/2237/index.do (accessed July 18, 2016)
61. Centre for Constitutional Studies, University of Alberta, "Interpreting Section 7 of the Charter: Clarity, Vagueness and Overbreadth," Legal Rights Sections 7–14, September 1, 2008, http://ualawccsprod.srv.ualberta.ca/index.php/constitutional-issues/the-charter/legal-rights-sections-7-14/54-interpreting-section-7-of-the-charter-clarity-vagueness-and-overbreadth#_ftnref4 (accessed July 18, 2016).
62. R. v. Nova Scotia Pharmaceutical Society, [1992] 2 S.C.R. 606 at 639, Judgments of the Supreme Court of Canada, http://scc-csc.lexum.com/scc-csc/scc-csc/en/901/1/document.do (accessed July 8, 2016).
63. *Canadian Foundation for Children, Youth and the Law v. Attorney General of Canada*, [2004] 1 S.C.R. 76 at para. 16, Judgments of the Supreme Court of Canada, https://scc-csc.lexum.com/scc-csc/scc-csc/en/item/2115/index.do (accessed July 8, 2016).
64. Centre for Constitutional Studies, University of Alberta, "Interpreting Section 7 of the Charter: Clarity, Vagueness and Overbreadth."
65. R. v. Heywood [1994] 3 S.C.R. 764, at 792–93.
66. R v. Heywood, at 803–04.
67. Kent Roach "Enforcement of the Charter—Subsections 24(1) and 52(1) 494.
68. R v. Keegstra.
69. R. *v*. Sharpe, [2001] 1 S.C.R. 45, Judgments of the Supreme Court of Canada, http://scc-csc.lexum.com/scc-csc/scc-csc/en/item/1837/index.do
70. R. v. Butler, [1992]1 S.C.R. 452, Judgments of the Supreme Court of Canada http://scc-csc.lexum.com/scc-csc/scc-csc/en/844/1/document.do
71. Little Sisters Book and Art Emporium *v*. Canada (Minister of Justice), [2000] 2 S.C.R. 1120, Judgments of the Supreme Court of Canada https://scc-csc.lexum.com/scc-csc/scc-csc/en/1835/1/document.do
72. R. *v*. Khawaja, 2012 SCC 69, Judgments of the Supreme Court of Canada, https://scc-csc.lexum.com/scc-csc/scc-csc/en/item/12768/index.do
73. David Schneiderman and Kent Roach, "Freedom of Expression in Canada," *Supreme Court Law Review* 61 (2013): 522, http://www.law.utoronto.ca/utfl_file/count/documents/Roach/Chapter%2010%20Roach%20Schneiderman.pdf (accessed August 17, 2016).
74. Crouch v. Snell, at para. 17.
75. Crouch v. Snell, at paras. 22, 23.

76. CBC News, "Nova Scotia Anti-Cyberbulling Law Challenged in Court," August 25, 2015, 7:02 PM AT, http://www.cbc.ca/news/canada/nova-scotia/nova-scotia-anti-cyber-bullying-law-challenged-in-supreme-court-1.3202681 (accessed August 17, 2016).
77. A. Wayne MacKay, "Respectful and Responsible Relationships: There's No App for That – The Report of the Nova Scotia Task Force on Bullying and Cyberbullying," *Nova Scotia Task Force on Bullying and Cyberbullying*, February 2012, http://antec.ca/ProfessorWayneMacKay.pdf (accessed August 17, 2016).
78. Cara Sabatini, "Cyber Safety Law Bullied into Submission," *Now Toronto*, March 2, 2016, 7:09 PM, https://nowtoronto.com/news/cyber-safety-laws-bullied-into-submission (accessed August 17, 2016).
79. Leah Collins Lipsett, "Nova Scotia Cyber-Bullying Law Continues to Spur Debate," *The Star*, May 1, 2015, https://www.thestar.com/news/privacy-blog/2015/05/nova-scotia-cyber-bullying-law-continues-to-spur-debate.html (accessed August 17, 2016)
80. Crouch v. Snell, at para 106.
81. Crouch v. Snell, at para 112.
82. Crouch v. Snell, at para 121.
83. Crouch v. Snell, at para 137.
84. Crouch v. Snell, at para 147.
85. Crouch, at para 158.
86. *Cyber-safety Act*, S.N.S. 2013, c. 2, s. 3(1).
87. Crouch, at para 165.
88. Ibid.
89. Crouch, at para 181.
90. Crouch, at para 184.
91. Crouch, at para 187.
92. Crouch, at para 197.
93. Crouch, at para 220.
94. D. S. Fraser, "Reflect and Regroup: Cyber-safety Act was a Rush Job," *Chronicle Herald*, http://thechronicleherald.ca/opinion/1327807-reflect-and-regroup-cyber-safety-act-was-a-rush-job (accessed August 9, 2016).
95. "Important Notice," CyberScan.
96. Tom Ayers, "Victims of Defunct Nova Scotia Cyberbullying Law Consider Class Action," *LocalExpress.Ca*, June 13, 2016, 3:40 PM, https://www.localxpress.ca/local-news/victims-of-defunct-nova-scotia-cyberbullying-law-considering-class-action-suit-315209 (accessed August 9, 2016).
97. Chronicle Herald of Cape Breton Bureau, "Cyberbullying Notice Angers Sydney Man," March 5, 2015, 10:33 PM, http://thechronicleherald.ca/novascotia/1272948-cyberbullying-notice-angers-sydney-man (accessed August 9, 2016).
98. Ibid.; Tom Ayers, "Victims of Defunct Nova Scotia Cyberbullying Law Consider Class Action."
99. Ibid.

CASES INDEX

A

B

C

D

E

G

H

I

J

K

L

M

N

P

R

S

T

U

V

W

SUBJECT INDEX

A

B

C

D

E

F

G

H

I

J

K

L

M

N

O

P

R

S

T

U

V

W

Z

COMMUNICATION LAW

SUSAN DRUCKER
Series Editor

Acknowledging the variety of ways in which the disciplines of communication and law converge, the aim of this series is to publish books at the nexus of these two areas with particular attention paid to communication in law in the changing media landscape.

Utilizing both qualitative and quantitative methodologies, volumes in this series provide analysis of issues at the interdisciplinary and international level such as free and responsible speech, media law, regulation and policy, press freedoms and governance of new media.

For additional information about this series or for the submission of manuscripts, please contact Dr. Drucker at susan.j.drucker@hofstra.edu.

To order other books in this series, please contact our Customer Service Department:

(800) 770-LANG (within the U.S.)
(212) 647-7706 (outside the U.S.)
(212) 647-7707 FAX

Or browse online by series at www.peterlang.com.

Lightning Source UK Ltd.
Milton Keynes UK
UKHW021342180321
380579UK00017B/262

9 781433 132117